MEDIASPACE

MediaSpace explores the importance of ideas of space and place to understanding how we experience media in our everyday lives. Essays from leading international scholars address the kinds of spaces created by media and the effects that spatial arrangements have on media and cultural forms. Case studies focus on a wide variety of subjects and locales, from in-flight entertainment to the personal stereo and mobile phone, from the electronic spaces of the Internet to the shopping mall and 'smart car', and from the work culture of the dot.com boom to the performance rituals of reality TV.

MediaSpace contains both theoretical overviews and a geographically diverse selection of current research. Of primary interest within media and cultural studies, it will also prove necessary reading for geographers, sociologists and anthropologists concerned with issues of space and media.

Editors: **Nick Couldry** is Senior Lecturer in Media and Communications at the London School of Economics and Political Science. He is the author of *Media Rituals: A Critical Approach*, *Inside Culture* and *The Place of Media Power: Pilgrims and Witnesses of the Media Age*. **Anna McCarthy** is Associate Professor of Cinema Studies at New York University. She is the author of *Ambient Television: Visual Culture and Public Space*.

COMEDIA
Series Editor: David Morley

A GAME OF TWO HALVES
Football, Television and Globalisation
Cornel Sandvoss

HIDING IN THE LIGHT
On Images and Things
Dick Hebdige

HOME TERRITORIES
Media, Mobility and Identity
David Morley

IMPOSSIBLE BODIES
Femininity and Masculinity at the Movies
Chris Holmlund

THE KNOWN WORLD OF BROADCAST NEWS
Stanley Baran and Roger Wallis

MEDIASPACE
Place, Scale and Culture in a Media Age
Nick Couldry and Anna McCarthy

MIGRANCY, CULTURE, IDENTITY
Iain Chambers

THE PHOTOGRAPHIC IMAGE IN DIGITAL CULTURE
Edited by Martin Lister

THE PLACE OF MEDIA POWER
Pilgrims and Witnesses of the Media Age
Nick Couldry

SPECTACULAR BODIES
Gender, Genre and the Action Cinema
Yvonne Tasker

STUART HALL
Critical Dialogues in Cultural Studies
Edited by Kuan-Hsing Chen and David Morley

TEACHING THE MEDIA
Len Masterman

MEDIASPACE

Place, scale and culture in a media age

Edited by
Nick Couldry and Anna McCarthy

Routledge
Taylor & Francis Group

LONDON AND NEW YORK

First published 2004
by Routledge
2 Park Square, Milton Park, Abingdon, Oxon, OX14 4RN

Simultaneously published in the USA and Canada
by Routledge
270 Madison Ave, New York NY 10016

Routledge is an imprint of the Taylor & Francis Group

Transferred to Digital Printing 2006

Typeset in Goudy by Taylor & Francis Books Ltd

British Library Cataloguing in Publication Data
A catalogue record for this book is available from the British Library

Library of Congress Cataloging in Publication Data
MediaSpace : place, scale, and culture in a media age /
[edited by] Nick Couldry and Anna McCarthy.
p. cm. – (Comedia)
Includes bibliographical references and index.
1. Mass media–Social aspects. 2. Space and time–Social aspects.
3. Civilization, Modern–21st century. I. Couldry, Nick.
II. McCarthy, Anna, 1967– III. Series.
HM1206 .M433 2004
302.23–dc22   2003017056

ISBN 0–415–29174–7 (hbk)
ISBN 0–415–29175–5 (pbk)

Printed and bound by CPI Antony Rowe, Eastbourne

CONTENTS

vii

CONTENTS

CONTENTS

ILLUSTRATIONS

Cover photograph: *Remote Connection* by Andy Kropa, 2001

CONTRIBUTORS

Fiona Allon is Postdoctoral Research Fellow at the Centre for Cultural Research, University of Western Sydney, Australia. Her doctoral thesis, 'Altitude Anxiety: Being-at-home in a Globalised World', is currently being considered for publication. She has taught media theory and cultural studies at the University of Technology, Sydney; the University of Western Sydney; Goldsmiths College, University of London; and the Georg-August University, Göttingen, Germany. She has published widely in media studies and cultural studies books and journals.

Mark Andrejevic is Assistant Professor in the Department of Communication Studies at Iowa University, USA. He recently completed his doctoral thesis at the University of Colorado, Boulder, on the role of surveillance in reality-based television programming, and his research interests include the productive role of surveillance in the digital economy, the cultural geography of new media, and the critical analysis of popular culture. His article, 'The Kinder, Gentler Face of Big Brother: Reality TV in the Era of Digital Capitalism', is forthcoming in the journal *New Media and Society*.

Clive Barnett is Lecturer in Human Geography at the University of Bristol, UK. His current research includes work on cultural policy in the European Union and South Africa, on social movements, media and mobilization in South Africa, and on discourses of African post-colonialism. Forthcoming publications include *Spaces of Representation: Geographies of Media, Communication and Democracy* (Edinburgh University Press) and *Geographies of Democracy*, edited with Murray Low (Sage).

Göran Bolin is Assistant Professor and Head of Department of Media and Cultural Studies at Sodertorns Hogskola (University College), Sweden. He has headed several research projects since the 1990s, and current work includes projects on Swedish entertainment television and global media landscapes. His books include *Moves in Modernity* (Almqvist and Wiksell, 1992) and *Youth Culture in Late Modernity* (Sage, 1995), both edited with Johan Fornas.

xi

Michael Bull is Lecturer in Media Studies at the University of Sussex. He is the author of *Sounding Out the City: Personal Stereos and the Management of Everyday Life* (Berg, 2000) as well as numerous articles on audio media and social space.

John T. Caldwell is Chair of the Department of Film, Television and Digital Media at the University of California, Los Angeles. He is the author of *Televisuality: Style Crisis and Authority in American Television* (Rutgers University Press, 1995) and the editor of *Electronic Media and Technoculture* (Rutgers University Press, 2000), and has written articles in many leading journals. He is also a prolific television and video producer, and has won a number of awards for his productions, which include *Freak Street to Goa: Immigration on the Rajpath* (1989) and *Amor Vegetal: Our Harvest* (1998).

Nick Couldry is Senior Lecturer in Media and Communications at the London School of Economics and Political Science. He is the author of *The Place of Media Power: Pilgrims and Witnesses of the Media Age* (Routledge, 2000), *Inside Culture: Reimagining the Method of Cultural Studies* (Sage, 2000) and *Media Rituals: A Critical Approach* (Routledge, 2003). He has also written numerous articles on media, space and symbolic power. He has been interested in the theoretical interconnections between media and space since the beginning of his research.

Arlene Dávila is Associate Professor of Anthropology and American Studies at New York University. She is the author of *Latinos Inc.: Marketing and the Making of a People* (University of California Press, 2001) and *Sponsored Identities: Cultural Politics in Puerto Rico* (Temple University Press, 1997). She is also co-editor, with Agustin Lao, of *Mambo Montage: The Latinization of New York* (Columbia University Press, 2000).

Nitin Govil is Assistant Professor of Media Studies at the University of Virginia. He is the co-author of *Global Hollywood*, where he wrote on the history of international film copyright and contemporary cultural policy, and is currently co-authoring a study of the contemporary Indian film industry. He has also written on the globalization of Asian multimedia labor, race and US television, broadband television technology, and science fiction and the city.

James Hay is Associate Professor in the Department of Speech Communication, the Graduate Program in Cultural Studies, the Unit for Criticism and Interpretative Theory and the Unit for Cinema Studies at the University of Illinois–Champaign–Urbana. He is the author of *Popular Film Culture in Fascist Italy* (Indiana University Press, 1987) and editor of *The Audience and its Landscape* (Westview Press, 1996), as well as the author of numerous essays about media and social space.

Anna McCarthy teaches in the department of Cinema Studies at New York University's Tisch School of the Arts. She is the author of *Ambient Television:*

Visual Culture and Public Space (Duke University Press, 2001) as well as numerous articles on television and media. Her current research examines corporate activism and other forms of social advocacy in early television sponsorship.

Shaun Moores is Reader at the Centre for Research in Media and Cultural Studies, University of Sunderland, and Visiting Professor of Communication at La Sapienza, University of Rome. He is the author of *Interpreting Audiences: The Ethnography of Media Consumption* (Sage, 1993) and *Media and Everyday Life in Modern Society* (Edinburgh University Press, 2000). His next book, provisionally entitled *Media/Theory: A Thematic Introduction*, will be published by Routledge.

Susan Ossman is Visiting Professor of Anthropology at the Center for Contemporary Arab Studies, Georgetown University. She trained as an anthropologist at the University of California, Berkeley. She is the author of *Picturing Casablanca* (University of California Press, 1993) and *Three Faces of Beauty: Casablanca, Paris, Cairo* (Duke University Press, 2002), and the editor of *Miroirs Maghrébins* (CNRS, 1998).

Jeremy Packer is Assistant Professor of Media and Film Studies at Pennsylvania State University. He is co-editor of *Governing the Present: Foucault and Cultural Studies* (forthcoming, SUNY Press) and has published articles on safety, mobility and communications.

Lisa Parks is Assistant Professor of Film Studies at the University of California, Santa Barbara. She is the author of *Cultures in Orbit* (Duke University Press, forthcoming) and co-editor of *Planet TV: A Global Television Studies Reader* (NYU Press, forthcoming).

Andrew Ross is Director of the American Studies Program and Professor of Comparative Literature at New York University. His most recent book is *No-Collar: The Humane Workplace and Its Hidden Costs* (Basic Books, 2002). His other books as editor and author include *The Celebration Chronicles: Life, Liberty, and the Pursuit of Property Value in Disney's New Town* (Ballantine, 1999); *Real Love: In Pursuit of Cultural Justice* (New York University Press, 1998); *No Sweat: Fashion, Free Trade and the Rights of Garment Workers* (1997, Verso); *Science Wars* (Duke University Press, 1996); *Microphone Fiends: Youth Music and Youth Culture* (Routledge, 1994); *The Chicago Gangster Theory of Life: Nature's Debt to Society* (Verso, 1994); *Strange Weather: Culture, Science and Technology in the Age of Limits* (Verso, 1991); *Technoculture* (Minnesota, 1991); *No Respect: Intellectuals and Popular Culture* (Routledge, 1989); and *Universal Abandon? The Politics of Postmodernism* (University of Minnesota Press, 1988).

Mimi White is Professor of Radio–TV–Film at Northwestern University. She is the author of *Tele-Advising: Therapeutic Discourse in American Network Television* (University of North Carolina Press, 1992) and co-author, with James Schwoch and Susan Reilly, of *Media Knowledge: Readings in Popular Culture, Pedagogy, and Critical Citizenship* (SUNY Press, 1992).

INTRODUCTION

Orientations: mapping MediaSpace

Nick Couldry and Anna McCarthy

> Through every human being, unique space, intimate space, opens up to the world.
>> (Rilke, quoted in Bachelard, *The Poetics of Space*, 1969: 202)

> We live inside a set of relations that delineates sites which are irreducible to one another.
>> (Foucault, 'Of Heterotopias', 1986: 23)

This book is an interdisciplinary project that brings together work in media and cultural studies, drawing on geographical theories and spatially articulated methodologies. Linking the chapters is the proposition that media, particularly electronic media, and the social processes that shape our perception and use of space are allied phenomena. In these links, we can read the complexity of contemporary social life. One could almost call media and space the *obverse* of each other, necessarily connected but, as Foucault says, 'irreducible to one another'. Hence the term 'MediaSpace'. As electronic media increasingly saturate our everyday spaces with images of other places and other (imagined or real) orders of space, it is ever more difficult to tell a story of social space without also telling a story of media, and vice versa.

There are, however, no easy symmetries. The spatial orders that media systems construct and enforce are highly complicated, unevenly developed and multi-scaled. In this respect, the development of electronic media is a spatial process intertwined with the development of regimes of accumulation in capitalism. 'Rather than creating a homogeneous space of operation,' notes television historian Michael Curtin, 'communication technologies have made capital more mobile and hence even more sensitive to the differences between places' (2000: 52). This flexible and fractured spatial order, in turn, through its silent regulation of media flows, affects the terms on which media narratives can matter, where, and to whom, even if the implicit spatiality of media is hard to recognize in the 'space' of the media text.

Together, the chapters in this volume fill out, both in theory and in case studies, a conceptual realm we call MediaSpace. MediaSpace is a dialectical concept, encompassing both the kinds of spaces created by media, and the effects that existing spatial arrangements have on media forms as they materialize in everyday life. Like cyberspace, the kind of space defined by this concept is a curious, multidimensional one. It is on the one hand resolutely material, that is, composed of objects (receivers, screens, cables, servers, transmitters) embedded in particular geographical power structures (Ross, Dávila) and reflective of particular economic sectors in capitalism (Govil, Caldwell). On the other hand, as is evident in the commonplace antinomy that makes the image the opposite of 'reality', media – especially electronic media – take on spectral, evanescent characteristics that seem to remove them from the material plane of existence (Sconce 2000). The concept of virtuality belongs to this anti-concrete sense of spatiality, as it is premised on the idea that electronic media create an experience unmoored from the physicality of the body, of work and leisure spaces, of the environment (Miller and Slater 2000; McCarthy 2002). Virtuality and its cognate ideologies embody fantasies of escape from the material world and its messy realities, but of course this escape is premised on the ever-increasing consumption of material resources.[1] MediaSpace, then, at once defines the artefactual existence of media forms within social space, the links that media objects forge *between* spaces, and the (no less real) cultural visions of a physical space transcended by technology and emergent virtual pathways of communication. It is also expanding too. We can no longer ignore what Thrift and French (2002) call the 'automatic production of space' through software, a condition of spatialized governance in which media and space quite literally merge in architectural infrastructure. As they note, information relay and coding systems on which media technologies rely are increasingly incorporated into everyday places, from elevators to locks to generators, shaping the movements and behavioural options of the citizenry in social space (Thrift and French 2002: 314, 317).

In focusing our attention on the ways that media forms shape and are shaped by the experience of social space, the chapters in this volume make clear that the politics of media images and economies are not separate from the politics of space. If the latter can encompass a range of issues from racism in city planning to environmental disasters to the oil-fuelled violent crises that destabilize regions, then a spatially aware model of media studies necessarily finds itself taking issues like these into account. Tracking the mobility of media forms in social space leads us to numerous political realities. Some of these are covered by the chapters contained here: the environmental hazards of junked hardware in the Third World (Parks); the intertwining of entertainment dollars with modes of transportation dependent on the geopolitical order that supports US oil interests (Hay and Packer, Govil); the Taylorization of domestic labour through technologies of control (Allon). Academic labour, and the communications tools on which it depends, are not isolated from these realities. The microprocessors in laptop computers, on which so many of us depend, rely on Coltan, a rare ore that is mined in central Africa. As a widely circulated news story from

2001 vividly communicated, Coltan mining has helped fund civil wars and regional terror, as well as the destruction of the natural environment in the Republic of Congo and bordering nations (Harden 2001). This example is only one of many cases in which the West's experience of mediated instantaneity, convenience and mobility is dependent on a hidden spatial order. Virtuality, despite its connotations of diminished dependence on materiality and space, is itself the product of uneven development: the transformations it has wrought in the lives of the middle class in the West are mirrored by material transformations of the basic conditions of existence elsewhere in the world.

As this example suggests, the full recognition of the materiality of space, and spatial relations, does violence to certain visions, themselves perhaps quite comforting, of what media are and what understanding media is. If you doubt this, think for a moment about the difference between the two reflections which head this Introduction: the first is by one of the early twentieth century's greatest poets, the second is by one of the late twentieth century's greatest social thinkers. This difference condenses the historical tension through which modernity comes to terms with the material conditions of its own possibility. It marks out a shift from a vision of interior space as an unbounded, unconditional expanse to a redrawing of the self as a spatial field of multiple, heterogeneous forces and relations of power, of which the 'inner voice' is but one component.

But this shift is never complete. Space, particularly in the traditional concept of place, contains both the possibility of interiority, of wholeness, boundedness and plenitude, and the possibility of remoteness, alienation. When we say that we 'need our space', we are saying simultaneously that we want to retreat to a place that is all our own and that we want to put some distance between another and ourselves. Similarly, as material social relations, media forms encompass the possibility of joining and belonging in the present (this is Benedict Anderson's imagined community) as well as enabling contact with the past, through the circulation of place-based nostalgia and memory. Yet they also create distance (a friend's two-minute mobile phone call during lunch, for example) and anxieties about social control that may distract us from the historical present, in all its dimensions, including the political.

This dialectical sense of belonging and alienation, self and system, is integral to the experience of MediaSpace. Much research on the spatial processes of media is bound up with what Anthony Giddens called 'the fundamental question of social theory – the "problem of order"'. This is the problem of explaining 'how the limitations of individual "presence" are transcended by the "stretching" of social relations across time and space.'[2] Modern media are among the principal means through which a certain type of order has been introduced into large territories (Mattelart 1994). Yet the problem of order is also the problem of disorder. MediaSpace may be dominated by ideologies of control and individualized power (Allon, Bull), but, like any complex system, it is constantly under stress through forces of flux, transience and unmanageability (Latour 1993; Govil, White, Moores).

3

MediaSpace is a thoroughly interdisciplinary concept. A glance at the cita-
tions in this volume will communicate the influence of geographical theory on
media studies. If nearly two decades ago it rang true for geographers to claim that
'the media have been on the periphery of geographical enquiry for too long'
(Burgess and Gold 1985: 1), it still makes sense today for media researchers to
return the compliment. Other sites of disciplinary cross-pollination include
ethnographic research (both in its original, anthropological, form and as it has
migrated to other disciplines in the past ten to fifteen years); urban studies and
urban sociology; and cultural studies (by this we mean the type of cultural studies
that has been interested in social power and cultural politics outside of their
textual manifestations, rather than the type concerned primarily with literary or
philosophical questions). This collection brings together media theorists and
spatial theorists, sociologists and anthropologists, screen studies and urban
studies, political economy perspectives and cultural perspectives. This undisciplined range communicates the fact that the project of defining MediaSpace is
far larger than any single discipline.

As our contributors make clear, a geographically informed and spatially
sensitive analysis of media artefacts, discourses, and practices reveals forms of
inequality and dominance, knowledge and practice that are hidden from other
analytical techniques. Understanding media systems and institutions as spatial
processes undercuts the infinite space of narrative that media appear to promise;
it insists that our object of analysis is never just a collection of texts, but a
specific and material organization of space. Media, like all social processes, are
inherently stretched out in space in particular ways, and not others. A classic, if
now neglected, insight into MediaSpace is Debord's *Society of the Spectacle*, itself
inspired by the great social and spatial theorist Henri Lefebvre.[3] Leaving aside
Debord's analysis of consumerism, his book makes a fundamental point about
the spatial properties of the media that are essential to societies of mass
consumption:

> The spectacle presents itself simultaneously as all of society, as part of
> society, and as instrument of unification. As a part of society, it is
> specifically the sector which concentrates all gazing and all conscious-
> ness. Due to the very fact that this sector is *separate*, it is the common
> ground of the deceived ... and the unification it achieves is nothing
> but an official language of generalised separation.
>
> (Debord 1983, paras 2–3, emphasis in the original)

However we might want to inflect the details of Debord's argument four
decades later, he grasped the contradiction between the (limited) spatial
origins of media and the (general, indeed totalizing) claims made by, through
and on behalf of media. This gap between media rhetoric and actual spatial
organization is but one example of what Lefebvre called 'spatial violence'
(1991: 289). Like symbolic violence in Bourdieu's work (Bourdieu 1991), spatial

4

violence is a gap between representation and material organization that is natu-ralized out of everyday awareness. It is something we would rather, and generally do, forget. Yet not forgetting this spatial violence inherent to media is the first step in grasping the dynamics of MediaSpace and its territoriality (Sack 1986). Focusing on the levels of spatial structuring and restructuring that media systems produce reveals them as a historically particular organization of the scarce resources to make effective representations of social life (cf. Carey 1989). Media, then, emerge as one of the most important *dis*-placements at work in the relatively centralized 'order' of contemporary societies.

To help us grasp the processes through which MediaSpace is constructed we can diagram the various ways in which *it* has been or might be analysed in media and communications studies.

MediaSpace: five levels

Seemingly the most straightforward stage in the process of connecting media and space, geography and media analysis, is:

Level 1: *studying media representations*

This topic has generated much writing in geography[4] and media studies,[5] on media images of local, national and global space (Anderson 1983; Jameson 1984; Harvey 1990; Bruno 1993). But it is *only the first* stage of analysing MediaSpace, because it is limited in what it can say about the spatial dimen-sions of the media process itself. True, broadcast media (relatively speaking) give us 'de-spatialized' access to other places (Thompson 1993: 187). Media images and narratives are so liberally scattered across space that the spatially differentiated process that scatters them matters little for some purposes. Nonetheless, the past twenty years of audience studies, as well as our increasing sense of the global variations of media flows, make it increasingly clear that de-spatialized analysis of spatial images and texts alone can only go so far.

It would be quite wrong, however, to give the impression that all the stories at Level 1 have already been told. New stories are constantly calling to be told about the representations of national space in the Internet, the representations of social space through mobile communications, and so on; new stories, too, about how the contradictions between representations of space and place in different media are played out and reworked. Thus, as we show in this book, Level 1 continues to be highly relevant to the analysis of MediaSpace, even if the media in question extend far beyond the familiar panoply of television, radio and the press.

Increasingly, we have wanted to know more about the various places where media images are received, the very specific places where those images are produced, and the differentiated grids along which those images are distributed. This takes us to the next two levels of thinking about MediaSpace:

5

Level 2: the study of how media images, texts and data flow across space and, in so doing, reconfigure social space

This kind of work is concerned with the overall spatial and social configuration that results from a particular medium. A good example is the much-analysed situation of television linking certain types of places to certain other types of place, and leaving other places outside the network in the process. However, work on this level does not necessarily specify one singular set of processes or spatial effects. Rather, it is site-specific in its attention to local determinations. It is a kind of analysis with which anthropologists have been particularly concerned (see, for example, Wilk 1994; Abu-Lughod 1997; the essays in Abu-Lughod et al. 2002). In bringing the local into contact with various elsewheres, media are often seen as destroying regional specificity. This may sometimes be the case; however, ethnographic work on this mediation of contact suggests that a wider range of syncretic outcomes is possible.

Level 3: the study of the specific spaces at either end of the media process, the space of consumption and the space of production

If Level 1 addresses the question of spatial representation, Level 2 indicates the impossibility of treating media 'texts' as a-spatial forms. Level 3 intensifies this move away from textual interpretation, focusing on media as social processes as well as technologies and 'content'. These processes *extend beyond* the text and into the worlds of media institutions and organization. They encompass everything from the market research that precedes the image, to the production studio, to the editing suite to the broadcasting mast to the television set to the living room, bar or airport lounge where the image is received.

Implicit, however, in our insistence on complicating Level 1 (media representations of space) with Levels 2 and 3 (reconfigurations of space through media and the detailed spaces of media production and consumption) is an issue that cannot be addressed at any of those three levels: the question of scale. Scale is a difficult concept to define. The word *scale* is a complex and highly abstract noun that expresses a number of different kinds of proportional relations, from the comparative size of physical phenomena to the mathematically calculable relationship between an object and its representation. Scale shapes the kinds of decisions we make in analysing the empirical world, and it is a concept around which a number of ready-made critiques have emerged. Micro-level analyses, for example, are always open to the charge that they fail, in the words of one historian, 'to link the microsocial and the macrosocial, experiences with structures, face to face relationships with the social system or the local with the global'. Without these links, the argument goes, micro-analysis leads to 'an acceptance of a fragmented world view rather than an attempt to make sense of it' (Burke 2001: 116–17). By contrast, some sociologists have insisted on the absolute primacy of microscopic interactions, even over the macro-operations that other sociologists see at work (for example, Shotter 1993; see also Garfinkel 1967). A similarly axiomatic understanding of the priority of one scale of analysis over another can be found in the entrenched, conceptually exhausted clash between 'cultural studies' and 'political economy' (Garnham 1996; Grossberg 1996).

In media studies, the methodological issues raised by scale lead researchers to link specific questions of the geographical dimensions of media technologies, images and institutions to larger questions about processes of change (and explaining change), or patterns of meaning (and interpreting meaning). Ideally, the site-specific operations of media are in a dialogue with macro-level theories. When we try to analyse the way in which media have causal impacts, we cannot ignore the content of the representations which media as spatial process (Levels 2 and 3) put into circulation. But since those representations include representations of space (Level 1), we need at some point to try to integrate all three levels in order to grasp the scale on which media are involved in the changing dynamics of social life. We are unlikely, of course, to arrive at simple answers.

We can therefore define the next level on which MediaSpace can be analysed as:

Level 4: the study of the scale-effects, or complex entanglements of scale, which result from the operation of media in space

To illustrate what we mean by this, we can draw an analogy from Deirdre Boden and Roger Friedlander's (1994) account of 'the compulsion of proximity' in modern, complex, dispersed social worlds. In their schema, communication at a distance enables countless forms of co-ordination without people being physically present with each other. The result, they argue, is not to make co-presence less important for all purposes, since certain forms of co-presence (for example, with those at principal nodes of the stretched-out networks in which our lives are caught up) acquire particularly intense meaning. On the one hand, executives fly across the world to meet each other, fans gather from large distances to be in the presence of a celebrity. On the other hand, those who live far from the 'nodes' (Janelle 1991) of the global capitalist economy experience ever more intense forms of disconnection. Instead of space and place being simply reduced by modern forms of co-ordination at-a-distance, they are made more complex. In other words, we are caught in increasingly complex entanglements of scale, acting out through the patterns of our lives what Doreen Massey (1994: 149) memorably calls 'the power-geometry of time-space compression'.[6]

This suggests a final, fifth level of analysing MediaSpace. For, if the fourth level is concerned with the actual entanglements of scale engendered by mediated forms of social co-ordination, the fifth level is concerned with how we experience these entanglements, and, in short, live them:

7

Level 5: studying how media-caused entanglements of scale are variously experienced and understood in particular places

Many things may happen at this level. We may disguise entanglements of scale, pretending they do not exist; or we may integrate them so intensely into our everyday lives, that in certain respects they become taken-for-granted, or naturalized. We may give reasons for this or that organization of space;[7] or we may translate our awareness of them into more formal patterns of ritual or play or transgression. Clearly, Levels 4 and 5 closely overlap.

Elsewhere, we have both argued in more detail that whatever the (political, economic, rhetorical) forces that encourage us to think about media in more totalizing ways, it is more productive to think of media, as with all spatial processes,[8] as complex co-ordinations of presences and *absences* (see Couldry 2000; McCarthy 2001). The chapters in this book produce and build on flexible conceptual schemes that attend to both, and their interrelation. Part One of the book explores the theoretical implications of this point in various contexts.

Shaun Moores' chapter draws sympathetically, yet critically, on Joshua Meyrowitz's thesis that television leaves us with 'no sense of place' (Meyrowitz 1985). While accepting that Meyrowitz's question is a good one – how do media affect our sense of what interactional situation we are 'in'? – Moores insists that any simple narrative of the collapse of place falls far short of understanding how we actually use and live with media. Instead of the reduction of place and space, it is more plausible to think of what Scannell (1996) has called the 'doubling of place'. Media as we use them, Moores argues, multiply the situational interconnections that are possible between places, and this process is as relevant to the whole range of electronic media (from the telephone to the Internet) as to broadcasting. As in his previous work,[9] Moores is concerned to develop more subtle accounts of how the resulting spatial complexities are understood and negotiated by us as social agents. Moores illustrates the complexity of what is at stake through three contrasting vignettes. First, the interruptions to normal social and spatial routine effected by media events (Dayan and Katz 1992), such as the television coverage of the funeral of Princess Diana in 1997. Second, the non-eventful, indeed taken-for-granted, interweaving of online and offline situations in which Internet users routinely engage. Third, and finally, the competing definitions of 'situation' that arise when mobile phone users prioritize the multilocal private 'space' of their phone conversation over the unilocal 'public' space of the train carriage. The emerging picture is not, then, the collapse of place – indeed, our reasons for travelling to distant places to which media connect us have increased, not diminished – but instead the more subtle integration of our interactions with other places and agents into the flow of our everyday practice and experience.

Lisa Parks' chapter, 'Kinetic Screens', examines the question of mobility within a materialist analysis of the interface in the World Wide Web. Considering the interface as a kind of place and as a metaphoric vehicle, she complicates attempts to describe web navigation simply as electronic nomadism or space–time annihilation. Parks analyses how a variety of web applications and websites place the user in multiple senses. Software that allows users to trace the virtual pathways through which their data travel makes the abstraction of the Internet into a set of technologically linked physical sites, allowing users to make sense of electronic communication in visual, concrete and geographically specific terms. The result is a sense of 'trajective movement' that resonates with the intricate social pathways mapped by geographers like Torsten Hägerstrand. Importantly, Parks points out that attempts to visualize web use in spatial, concrete terms are forms of *literacy* education in the new medium of cyberspace, encouraging a reading practice based on a broader view of the spatial language of the web which contrasts with the ideas about virtual mobility and language that are put into circulation through various translation programs. Although they promise a sense of 'linguistic liquidity', such programs also suggest that knowing more than one language is unnecessary in the electronic world of interfaced communication. A host of managerial imperatives are contained within this universalist dream, and Parks points out the various ways that difference is both affirmed and negated in the linguistic projection of a global culture. Her chapter concludes by looking at how activism around uneven development, technology-driven global capitalism and environmental disaster are aided through the web's promise of mobility. Websites devoted to tracking the movement of obsolete computers from the West to the Global South reveal the commodity status of the computer and its place in international circuits of exchange and exploitation. These interfaces provide users with a 'way of accessing the political economy of the web in visual and geographic terms as it brings the material relations between computers, bodies, movements and territories into bold relief'.

The materiality of media objects and the physicality of electronically mediated communication raise the question of how media theory looks from the perspective of contemporary *spatial* theory. From the viewpoint of a geographer and spatial theorist, Clive Barnett explores this question through the specific lens of competing assessments of modernity's media-enabled political spaces. Barnett's aim is to move beyond accounts of the spatiality of 'mediated public culture' that conceptualize space merely as *a gap* bridged by media. For all their different insights, the critiques by Dewey, Innis and Williams of the mediated spatiality of modern democracies all fall prey, Barnett argues, to this problem. Instead, he suggests that we need both a more subtle account of how new spaces of sociality are being opened up by media-in-use *and* to pay closer attention to the simultaneous production of new material infrastructures which underlie media developments. For this Barnett turns to David Harvey and Doreen Massey's accounts of the spatial landscapes of contemporary capitalism, and the spatiality of commodity exchange of which the flows of media commodities are just one part. The result, Barnett argues, drawing on his research into the politics of post-apartheid South Africa, is to force us to rethink the *scale* (or the set of interconnected scales) on which such central normative concepts as the public sphere should be applied. In post-apartheid South Africa, for example, we cannot understand the scale and content of local and national politics without grasping the transnational networks on which many South African campaigners draw for resources and the context of their actions. The result is a more complex appreciation of the 'communicative spaces' that contemporary media 'produce'.

However, it would be a mistake, as we argued earlier, to believe that the pressing issues for the analysis of MediaSpace relate only to scale and how it is lived (Levels 2–5). At the same time it is necessary to rethink what is happening on Level 1, media's representations of space. Mimi White's chapter makes this point powerfully by inviting television theorists to rethink the standard ways they have understood (or rather, neglected) how television represents space and its own relation to space. White offers a radical re-reading of the traditional notion that television is above all a process of 'liveness'. She argues that this prioritization of *time* not only distorts many of the complexities and unevennesses of televisual 'live' time, but also neglects those many (probably more frequent) occasions when television offers itself to us primarily as connection *across space*. Indeed, even in those cases where others have thought the discourse of liveness predominant (for example, when CNN claimed to offer 'live' reporting from the Gulf War in 1991), what mattered more was space: the claim to link viewers through the reporter right to the place where (or near where!) the war was taking place. Less important than the temporal status of such televisual moments (quickly transmuted from 'live' present to 'history') is the claim of television to connect us to distant places. This feature of television's discourse is as important, White argues, in banal forms of television as in moments of crisis and media events. Shopping channels that show things to buy, or programmes which show the weather or traffic in other places, efface a detailed sense of temporal connection in favour of a spatial sense of being somewhere else. From this perspective, television needs to be reconnected to the history of what Tom Gunning (1986) calls the 'cinema of attractions', that is, the *trans-spatial* or *inter-spatial* spectacle which modern electronic media make possible.

These theoretically oriented articulations of the problems of mobility, temporality and modernity that find expression in various media forms raise the question of how the lived experience of space is organized through media. The chapters in Part Two take up this question in a range of locations and technological configurations. In 'The Marketable Neighborhood', anthropologist Arlene Dávila examines the competing efforts of artists, activists and marketers to brand the neighbourhood of East Harlem, New York, with images that seek to define the historically Latino identity of the neighbourhood in particular ways. As the forces of gentrification encroach upon East Harlem, murals depicting Latino culture, history and politics increasingly coexist alongside advertising images that harness commodity messages and projections of consumer identity to the idea of community and neighbourhood. What is at stake here is control over commodification of the intangible and evanescent forms of everyday experience – waiting, shopping, moving between work and leisure. The marketers' increasing interest in addressing Latino consumers takes into account community values in their visual interpellation of the gentrified 'other', aggressively privatizing outdoor space in East Harlem by cutting deals with property-owners and shopkeepers. Dávila shows how conflicts over who succeeds in defining the space of East Harlem are made visible in the ways that residents, shopkeepers, muralists and marketers approach outdoor surfaces. Her thoughtful and complicated approach to urban space as a location where commerce and community mingle, and where the contradictions within capitalist networks of commodification become visible, illustrates the value of an eye-level, visual account.

If our appreciation of media representations of specific spatial communities needs to be both more wide-ranging and more fine-grained, as Dávila argues, we must also, as the anthropologist Susan Ossman shows in her chapter, be prepared to think about the lived relations of MediaSpace in places that media research has not explored. Drawing on her pioneering ethnographies of beauty salons in France and North Africa,[10] Ossman demonstrates the complexities of how transnational circulations of images of the 'beautiful woman' flow through, yet are also renegotiated, in a diverse range of places. This diversity can be understood, she argues, through a three-way contrast. First, there are the 'proximate salons' where it is social links to the surrounding neighbourhood that are prioritized as media images of fashionable styles are taken up in discussion by members of a small, face-to-face community. In a second type of 'elite salon', imported discourses about beauty are negotiated in a very different way through private discussions between the styling artist and the rich individual client. In the middle is a third type of 'fast salon', where the individual's relationship to wider discourses of beauty is mediated through branded representations (of the salon, its products and styles), which short-circuit detailed individual negotiation in favour of a pre-legitimated menu of style choices, captured in media images. The result is to increase our appreciation of the diverse ways in which an apparently homogeneous media flow (behind which lies a powerful global beauty products industry) is reworked into very different spatial 'situations' in particular locations, differentiated by the variables of class, wealth and ethnicity.

Andrew Ross examines the media dynamics of gentrification from a different perspective, tracing how the 'dot.com bubble' of the 1990s created crises in urban land, property and labour markets as the urban terrain of artists, and the artists themselves, as cultural labourers, were recruited by the new media economy. New 'no-collar' workers found themselves included in a monied movement to occupy and gentrify urban space, underwritten by venture capitalists and large corporations. Ross situates this development within the broader history of gentrification struggles, focusing on the city of San Francisco and the varieties of bohemia that emerged and were discovered on its streets. In examining how lease laws and rental customs aided the displacement of the underclass in favour of artists who would eventually find themselves struggling for footing, Ross demonstrates that media industries are far from placeless. Rather, in his account of the rise of Silicon Alley in New York, he shows the value of metropolitan studies as a framework for approaching media organizations. The rise and fall of the media sector as a 'humane workplace' is interwoven with old stories of urbanism and new stories of reckless finance and speculation. The artists who served as worker-residents in the now downsized cyber-bohemias of American cities are not as mobile as the capital that produced them, nor as flexible. New media capitalism encourages the collapse of borders between work and play, between financial districts and so-called slums. As this chapter demonstrates, the utopian ideal of borderlessness and hybridized professional identity is a fantasy that media workers remaining in the no-collar sector can no longer afford.

Göran Bolin addresses another dimension of the managerial structuring of work and leisure in his architectural exploration of the role of television screens in Solna Centrum, a shopping mall outside Stockholm, Sweden. Drawing on long-term ethnographic and observational research, he examines the functions of television as a device for managing vision and bodies in space, situating the shopping mall television set within broader histories of consumer architecture. Bolin examines how cinematic ideals of spectatorship are thematically and structurally encoded in the space of the mall, and demonstrates how consumption creates continuities between televisual image regimes and earlier ones within the space of the mall. Bolin's detailed typography of screen functions and their implications for consumer culture studies opens out into a theoretical understanding of the general meaning of moving images and media use in consumer settings. Promoting consumption and policing theft, television screens are part of a broader system of administrative rationality, defined in Frankfurt School terms as capitalism's penetration of the life spheres of individuals. His account emphasizes the contingency and fragility of such systems, however, as ' "instrumental space" ... [which confronts] the social and expressive logic of the lifeworld, with its insistence on needs that lie outside of the economic rationality'.

John Caldwell's analysis of the explosion of spatial metaphors and structures in contemporary media production illustrates the value of combining close observational analysis with the study of media organizations. His analyses of the *mise en scène* within which production work takes shape as a professional culture examines how unspoken relations of power and economic status are encoded in work environments across a variety of industrial spheres. Caldwell argues that spatial languages and practices in the industry minimize the competitive nature of the business and its labour exploitation, constructing locations for work and professional networking that emphasize utopian ideals of collaboration, collectivity and creative autonomy. Discourses of new technology underwrite this promise by making the spatial mobility of such activities as editing and sound design seem effortless and endless. The ritual spaces of trade conventions work to create a sense of community between antagonistic sectors of the industry, translating relations between customers into images of rational enterprise even as open conflict demonstrates the inadequacy of such images. Spatialized accounts of industrial relations allow media producers a sense of control over the rapidly changing and uncertain economic environment of media work, Caldwell argues, maintaining boundaries between ranks, sectors and firms as the changeable logic of the industry threatens to render such boundaries irrelevant. Caldwell's analysis illustrates how, at the same time as our appreciation of both the multilayeredness of MediaSpace relations and their local variety is deepening, we are confronted time and again by the need to grasp *new configurations* of MediaSpace. Technological and industrial changes continue to put media into and in between spaces from which they were previously absent. The chapters in Part Three each analyse a different aspect of this process.

Mark Andrejevic analyses the way in which private space is increasingly being transformed into potential 'public space' – indeed, '*publicity* space' – through the spread of webcam technology into private homes. Drawing on a detailed study of the discourses of the so-called webcam 'movement' – people who 'expose their lives part-time' for pleasure, status and/or financial gain – Andrejevic points to an unholy triangle of power relations that connects reality television, Bill Gates' vision of the 'fully documented life' (cf. Allon's chapter), and the emerging surveillance-based rationalization of the online economy. Audience analysis has no purchase on webcam broadcasting practice, which is more 'many-to-few' than 'one-to-many'. What matters instead are the new parameters of amateur media production which are, however, poorly understood through popular myths of an interactive, democratic 'revolution'. Instead, through a detailed discussion of the discourses of webcam users themselves, Andrejevic shows that what is at stake here is not the expansion of participation in mediated public space, but the incorporation of once private space ever more effectively into *workspace*: a 'digital enclosure' in which surveillance is not only the universal precondition, but increasingly rethought as an opportunity for self-promotion. Far from being a crude imposition of power, this new incarnation of MediaSpace is reflected in how the individual now understands and enacts her/himself as a responsible and willing agent in an ever-expanding space of spectacularized commodification.

James Hay and Jeremy Packer's chapter extends this dialectic between (private) leisure space and the (public) spaces of work and governmentality – between 'democratization' and surveillance – through a meticulous analysis of the long-standing history of incorporating 'media' into regimes of mobility. They connect the rhetorical landscape of the United States post-9/11 (the marketing of the Segway Human Transporter in winter 2001, extensive use of cars as carriers of political messages, and the current Bush administration's FreedomCAR project) with the history, prehistory and genealogy of the 'smart' car in modernity. Their subtle and historically rich analysis shows how the notion of 'auto-mobility' has always spliced together discourses of mobility with those of the 'free' but governable self. The 'intelligence' of the media-enhanced automobile is inseparable from a whole communication infrastructure (linking radio, cameras and other media) of which the vehicle is only one relay-point. At the same time, amplifying the argument of Andrejevic, Hay and Packer show how this communication (and surveillance) infrastructure is translated into new forms of driving practice and drivers' self-understanding, particularly discourses of technologically enabled 'safety' and 'responsibility'. From this perspective, 'auto-mobility' (and its cognate 'mobile self') emerge as both central to modernity's strategies of centralization and distance-management and as requiring a rethinking of the very notion of 'mediation' (if conceived simply as the way media link autonomous points of the media process). Instead (cf. Barnett's chapter), Hay and Packer insist on the need for a more integrated account of how new (essentially mediated) technologies of the (mobile, responsible, regulable) self have emerged.

Fiona Allon's chapter, 'Smart Living in the Absolute Present', traces the production of a particular kind of mediated spatiality – the networked space of the 'smart house', as imagined particularly by Microsoft's Bill Gates – to consider the wider implications of mediation for the spatial organization of social life. Against the hyperbolic claims about the 'time-space compression' of the Information Age, she argues that a more nuanced and detailed spatial logic is actually at work: not the loss of annihilation of space or the end of a sense of place, but new kinds of places, spatialities and temporalities. The 'smart house' is presented as a mode of living characterized by simultaneous connectedness and separation, heightened privacy and public engagement, mobility and inertia. A significant locus of both production and consumption, the networked house is a strategic arena in the emerging system of media and information capitalism. Allon locates the history of the smart house within a *genealogy* of technologized domesticity in which media technologies enable a 'friction-free' subjectivity. The archetypal friction-free subject, Bill Gates, replaces the housewife of the post-war modern kitchen with the technocratic figure of the (masculine) knowledge class. This new domestic subject is the ideal consumer and producer of 'the promise of technologies to enable individual empowerment and connectivity, while simultaneously enhancing surveillance, isolation and control'.

Nitin Govil's chapter, 'Something Spatial in the Air', examines another televisualized space, one in which media functions include, but are not limited to, surveillance, isolation and control. Govil's original and wide-ranging analysis of the industrial, regulatory and textual practices that comprise the in-flight entertainment industry traces the role of media in the constitution of *Airspace*, both as a regulatory and geopolitical phenomenon and as an experiential arena marked by the confluence of consumer-oriented practices (branding), leisure and work itineraries, and the security and immigration initiatives of individual states. Govil notes that: 'Abstracted from the geopolitics of locality, but dependent upon their reproduction, blunting at every moment the very corporeal tactility of movement, but embracing its representation in the globalized logic of consumer mobility, the in-flight experience articulates the drama of travel in a space that can hardly be considered "neutral".' In examining the production of the space of in-flight entertainment, Govil locates media systems for tracking flight and for alleviating boredom within modern histories of geography, histories in which aviation has played crucial political and epistemological roles. The paradoxes of air travel – its contradictory imbrication of stillness and extreme velocity, its intertwining of leisure and national security, its costs and its industrial uncertainties – find their way into the media texts and systems that are built into the chairs on which we sit.

Michael Bull's concluding chapter explores how two other mobile media technologies (the personal stereo and the mobile phone) have quickly and radically transformed our experience of the boundaries between private and public space in the contemporary city. Bull's account starts from Simmel's (1950) fundamental insights in the early twentieth century into individuals' strategies of privacy through stylistic self-differentiation. There is an essential continuity between Simmel's classic insights and the way that mobile media (which allow us to carry our preferred music and private conversations as we move) facilitate the individualization of the city's soundscape. Drawing on both his book-length study of the personal stereo[11] and more recent interviews with mobile phone users (including users of car phones: cf. Hay and Packer's chapter), Bull develops a rich account of how urban space is being aestheticized and privatized, extending Richard Sennett's (1994) earlier insights into the erosion, or at least transformation, of public space. As Bull makes clear, we cannot understand such processes through simple condemnation. For there is a dialectic between, on the one hand, the new spaces of personal intimacy which media enable in the midst of overcrowded public spaces and, on the other hand, the larger-scale impacts of such spatial diffraction on the character of public space as a whole. Your nonplace[12] is my intimate space, and vice versa. The wider consequences of this process of individualization are, Bull concludes, inherently ambiguous and unstable.

Collectively, the chapters in this volume argue that once we think media and space, communications theory and spatial theory, *together*, we cannot avoid addressing complex interrelations of scale and ambiguities of consequence. While the study of historical dynamics is essential (as many of the following chapters show), it must be articulated with close studies of the spatial specificities of culture and infrastructure. Further, while 'new media' are an essential part of what we research, no simple narrative of sudden transformation or imminent liberation can capture the historical depth and spatial reach of the 'mediascapes' (Appadurai 1990) which we inhabit and on which we ceaselessly reflect. On the contrary, as Henri Lefebvre, a theorist of both space and representation, noted, it is precisely the *ambiguities* of place, scale and culture onto which we must retain our hold.

Acknowledgement

Both editors would like to acknowledge the invaluable help of Torey Liepa in finalizing the manuscript.

Notes

1 See Robins (1997), for a thorough deconstruction.
2 Giddens (1984), p. 35.
3 For analysis of the tense relationship between Lefebvre and the Situationists (including Debord), see Highmore (2002), pp. 137–42.
4 Jackson (1985); Anderson and Gale (1992); Carter (1987); Daniels (1993); Duncan and Ley (1993); Kobayashi and Mackenzie (1989).
5 Higson (1994); Morley and Robins (1995).
6 See also Zukin (1992); Smith (1993).
7 On the importance of people's 'reason-giving accounts' of space and place, see Agnew (1987), p. 231.
8 Hagerstrand (1975), p. 7; Pred (1986), p. 25.
9 Moores (1996).
10 Ossman (2002).
11 Bull (2001).
12 Auge (1994).

Bibliography

Abu-Lughod, L. (1997) 'The Interpretation of Culture(s) after Television', *Representations* 59 (Summer): 109–34.

Abu-Lughod, L., Ginsburg, F. and Larkin, B. (eds) (2002) *Media Worlds: Anthropology on New Terrain*, Berkeley: University of California Press.

Agnew, J. (1987) *Place and Politics: The Geographical Mediation of State and Society*, Winchester, MA: Allen & Unwin.

Anderson, B. (1983) *Imagined Communities*, London: Verso.

Anderson, K. and Gale, F. (eds) (1992) *Inventing Cultures: Studies in Cultural Geography*, Melbourne: Longman Cheshire.

Appadurai, A. (1990) 'Disjuncture and Difference in the Global Cultural Economy', in M. Featherstone (ed.), *Global Culture*, London: Sage.

Auge, M. (1994) *Nonplaces: Towards an Anthropology of Supermodernity*, London: Verso.

Bachelard, Gaston (1969) *The Poetics of Space*, Boston, MA: Beacon Press.

Boden, D. and Molotch, H. (1994) 'The Compulsion of Proximity', in D. Boden and R. Friedland (eds), *NowHere: Space, Time and Modernity*, Berkeley: University of California Press.

Bourdieu, P. (1991) *Language and Symbolic Power*, Cambridge: Polity Press.

Bruno, G. (1993) *Streetwalking on a Ruined Map: Cultural Theory and the City Films of Elvira Notari*, Princeton, NJ: Princeton University Press.

Bull, M. (2000) *Sounding Out the City*, Oxford: Berg.

Burgess, J. and Gold, J. (eds) (1985) *Geography, the Media and Popular Culture*, Beckenham: Croom Helm.

Burke, P. (ed.) (2001) *New Perspectives on Historical Writing*, University Park, PA: Pennsylvania State University Press.

Carey, J. (1989) *Culture as Communication*, Boston, MA: Unwin Hyman.

Carter, P. (1987) *The Road to Botany Bay: An Essay in Spatial History*, London: Faber and Faber.

Couldry, N. (2000) *The Place of Media Power: Pilgrims and Witnesses of the Media Age*, London: Routledge.

Cresswell, T. (1996) *In Place/Out of Place*, Minneapolis: University of Minnesota Press.

Daniels, S. (1993) *Fields of Vision: Landscape, Imagery and National Identity in England and the United States*, Cambridge: Polity Press.

Dayan, D. and Katz, E. (1992) *Media Events*, Cambridge, MA: Harvard University Press.

Debord, G. (1983) *Society of the Spectacle*, Detroit: Black and Red.

Duncan, J. and Ley, D. (eds) (1993) *Place/Culture/Representation*, London: Routledge.

Foucault, M. (1986) 'Of Other Spaces', *Diacritics*, 16(1): 22–7.

Garnham, N. (1995) 'Political Economy and Cultural Studies: Reconciliation or Divorce?', *Critical Studies in Mass Communication*, 12(1): 62–71.

Giddens, A. (1984) *The Constitution of Society*, Cambridge: Polity Press.

Grossberg, L. (1995) 'Cultural Studies vs. Political Economy: Is Anybody Else Bored with this Debate?', *Critical Studies in Mass Communication*, 12: 72–81.

Gunning, T. (1986) 'The Cinema of Attractions: Early Film, its Spectators and the Avant-Garde', *Wide Angle*, 8(3–4): 63–70.

Hägerstrand, T. (1975) 'Space, Time and Human Conditions', in A. Karlqvist, L. Lundqvist and F. Snickars (eds), *Dynamic Allocation of Urban Space*, Farnborough: Saxon House.

Harden, B. (2001) 'The Dirt in the New Machine', *New York Times*, 12 August, Section 6: 35.

Harvey, D. (1990) *The Condition of Postmodernity*, Oxford: Blackwell.

Highmore, B. (2002) *Everyday Life and Cultural Theory: An Introduction*, London: Routledge.

Higson, A. (1994) *Waving the Flag: Constructing a National Cinema in Britain*, New York: Oxford University Press.

Jackson, P. (1985) *Maps of Meaning: An Introduction to Cultural Geography*, London: Unwin Hyman.

Jameson, F. (1984) 'Postmodernism, or the Cultural Logic of Late Capitalism', *New Left Review*, 146.

Janelle, D. (1991) 'Global Interdependence and its Consequences', in S. Brunn and T. Leinbach (eds), *Colllapsing Space and Time: Geographical Aspects of Communication and Information*, London: HarperCollins.

Kobayashi, A. and Mackenzie, S. (eds) (1989) *Remaking Human Geography*, London: Unwin Hyman.

Latour, B. (1993) *We Have Never Been Modern*, trans. Catherine Porter, Cambridge, MA: Harvard University Press.

Lefebvre, H. (1991) *The Production of Space*, Oxford : Blackwell.

Massey, D. (1984) *Space, Place and Gender*, Cambridge: Polity Press.

Mattelart, A. (1994) *The Invention of Communication*, Minneapolis: University of Minnesota Press.

McCarthy, A. (2001) *Ambient Television*, Durham, NC: Duke University Press.

—— (2002) 'Cyberculture or Material Culture? Computers and the Social Space of Work', in 'Screens', special issue of *Etnofoor* (Antropologisch-Sociologisch Centrum, Amsterdam, The Netherlands).

Meyrowitz, J. (1985) *No Sense of Place*, Oxford: Oxford University Press.

Miller, D. and Slater, D. (2000) *The Internet: An Ethnographic Approach*, Oxford: Berg.

Moores, S. (1996) *Satellite Television and Everyday Life*, London: John Libbey.

Morley, D. and Robins, K. (1995) *Spaces of Identity*, London: Routledge.

Ossman, S. (2002) *Three Faces of Beauty: Casablanca, Cairo, Paris*, Durham, NC: Duke University Press.

Pred, A. (1986) *Place, Practice and Structure: Social and Spatial Transformation in Southern Sweden 1750–1950*, Cambridge: Polity Press.

Robins, K. (1997) 'Cyberspace and the World We Live In', in R. Burrows and M. Featherstone (eds), *Cyberspace/Cyberbodies/Cyberpunk*, London: Sage.

Sack, R. (1986) *Human Territoriality*, Cambridge: Cambridge University Press.

Scannell, P. (1996) *Radio, Television and Modern Life*, Oxford : Blackwell.

Sconce, J. (2002) *Haunted Media: Electronic Presence from Telegraphy to the Internet*, Durham, NC: Duke University Press.

Sennett, R. (1994) *The Conscience of the Eye*, London: Faber.

Shotter, J. (1993) *Conversational Realities*, Thousand Oaks, CA: Sage.

Sibley, D. (1995) *Geographies of Exclusion*, London: Routledge.

Simmel, G. (1950) 'The Metropolis and Mental Life', in K. Wolff (ed.), *The Sociology of Georg Simmel*, New York: Free Press.

Smith, N. (1993) 'Homeless/Global', in J. Bird et al. (eds), *Mapping the Futures*, London: Routledge.

Thompson, J. (1993) 'The Theory of the Public Sphere', *Theory, Culture and Society*, 10(3): 173–89.

Thrift, N. and French, S. (2002) 'The Automatic Production of Space', *Transactions of the Institute of British Geographers*, 27(3): 309–35.

Wilk, R. (1994) 'Colonial Time and TV Time: Television and Temporality in Belize', *Visual Anthropology Review* 10 (1): 94–102.

Zukin, S. (1991) *Landscapes of Power: From Detroit to Disney World*, Berkeley: University of California Press.

Part I

MEDIA THEORY/
SPATIAL THEORY

1

THE DOUBLING OF PLACE

Electronic media, time-space arrangements and
social relationships

Shaun Moores

Introduction: place pluralized, not marginalized

The title of this chapter is a phrase borrowed from the work of a theorist and
historian of broadcasting, Paddy Scannell (1996).[1] For Scannell (1996: 172),
one of the remarkable ('magical') yet now largely taken-for-granted consequences of radio and television use is what he calls the 'doubling of place'. His
idea that these media serve to '"double" reality' is developed in an analysis of
the distinctive character of public events (and of 'being-in-public') in late
modern life: 'Public events now occur, simultaneously, in two different places:
the place of the event itself and that in which it is watched and heard.
Broadcasting mediates *between* these two sites' (Scannell 1996: 76). In
proposing a 'phenomenological approach' to the study of radio and television
(see also Scannell 1995), which is concerned in part with the 'ways of being
in the world' (Scannell 1996: 173) that have been created for viewers and
listeners, he goes on to argue that, for audience members in their multiple,
dispersed, local settings, there are transformed 'possibilities of being: of being
in two places at once' (ibid.: 91). Of course, it is only ever possible for any
individual to be in one place at a time physically, but broadcasting nevertheless permits a 'live' witnessing of remote happenings that can bring these
happenings experientially 'close' or 'within range', thereby removing the
'farness' (ibid.: 167).[2]

I want to suggest in this chapter that Scannell's concept of the doubling of
place and his reflections on the altered 'possibilities of being' for media users,
while they appear in a book devoted to the study of broadcasting, might also be
applied more generally in the analysis of those electronic media, such as the
Internet and telephone, which share with radio and television a capacity for the
virtually instantaneous transmission of information across sometimes vast
spatial distances. Broadcasting, as Scannell has shown, has its own characteristic communicative features, which serve to distinguish it in various ways from
computer-mediated or telephone communication (allowing for the fact that

presenters of programmes are increasingly encouraging their viewers and listeners to email or phone-in). However, radio and television can be considered alongside the Internet and telephone precisely because of the common potential that all these media have for constructing experiences of simultaneity, liveness and 'immediacy' in what have been termed 'non-localized' (Thompson 1995: 246) (I prefer the term 'trans-localized') spaces and encounters.[3]

In my view, there are a number of advantages to be gained from grouping these electronic media together in a single field of investigation. Such a field could be a valuable site of connection between studies of so-called 'new media', always 'a historically relative term' (Marvin 1988: 3), and of more established modes of electronically mediated communication, including the use of an 'old technology' like the (static) telephone. Additionally, it could help to bridge a problematic gap between the existing academic areas of 'mass' and 'interpersonal' communications, and to raise questions about the limits of a 'circuit' model of culture that relies on distinguishing institutional moments of production and consumption. While this model has been employed in the analysis of broadcasting (for example, see Moores 1997), it turns out to be far less helpful when attempting to understand what is going on between the participants in Internet 'chat' or in telephone conversations, where the positions of 'performers' and 'audiences' may be constantly shifting as they typically do in local face-to-face interactions.[4]

The work of Joshua Meyrowitz (1985) would have to be a foundational text in the field of investigation I am outlining here. His pioneering book on electronic media makes a seemingly improbable link between Erving Goffman's sociology, which was concerned among other things with the 'definition of the situation' in instances of social interaction (see especially Goffman 1959), and the 'medium theory' of Marshall McLuhan (see especially McLuhan 1964), which related the development of media technologies to time-space transformations. Bringing together their rather different perspectives, Meyrowitz (1985: 6) asserts that: 'Electronic media affect us ... not primarily through their content, but by changing the "situational geography" of social life.' He advances a theory of 'situations as information-systems' (see also Meyrowitz 1994), in which the emphasis is on how 'patterns of information flow' serve to define the situation. This argument does not invalidate the work done by Goffman and others on co-present interaction in physical settings; rather it 'extends the study of situations' to include a range of encounters in and with 'media "settings"' (Meyrowitz 1985: 37–8).

Clearly, Meyrowitz's reflections on the altered 'situational geography' of social life correspond in some respects with what Scannell has to say about the time-space arrangements of broadcasting, but whereas Scannell points to the doubling of place, Meyrowitz suggests that cultures in our 'electronic society' are 'relatively placeless' in comparison with those of previous social orders (the phrase in the title of his book is 'no sense of place'). As he explains, this title is intended as a 'serious pun' in which place can be understood to mean 'both social position and physical location' (Meyrowitz 1985: 308). His main thesis is that social roles and hierarchies, through which people have traditionally come to 'know their place', are being transformed as electronically mediated communication transcends the boundaries of physical settings, making these boundaries more 'permeable'. To take a dramatic example used to illustrate the general thesis, he states that: 'A telephone or computer in a ghetto tenement or in a suburban teenager's bedroom is potentially as effective as a telephone or computer in a corporate suite' (ibid.: 169–70).

Whether or not we accept Meyrowitz's perspective on the transformation of place as 'social position' (quite frankly, I feel this particular aspect of his theory tends to overestimate the degree of change; see also Leyshon 1995: 33–4), there is still a problem with the suggestion that place as 'physical location' is of little or no consequence today, and that it is therefore necessary for us to move 'beyond place' in theorizing communication and culture. The boundaries of place, in the second sense of the word here, are certainly more permeable or 'open' (Massey 1995) than they were in the past, and it is also the case that, as Anthony Giddens (1990: 17–21) explains, the social organization of time and space has been abstracted or 'pulled away' from locales in conditions of modernity, yet this does not necessarily lead to the loss of a sense of place. Indeed, Scannell (1996: 141) accuses Meyrowitz of not putting enough emphasis on the locales of broadcasting, 'above all the studio', from which distant viewers and listeners in numerous other places are addressed. Furthermore, via the Internet, there is the creation of what have been called 'virtual places' in 'cyberspace' (for example, Mitchell 1995: 21–2) or 'text-based virtual realities' (Turkle 1996a: 15), media settings for social interaction that might best be seen as 'overlaying' the physical locations of those computer users who access them.

My preference, then, is for a conception of place as pluralized (not marginalized, as Meyrowitz would have it) by electronic media use. As Nick Couldry (2000: 30) asks, 'Why not argue that media coverage massively *multiplies* the interconnections between places, rather than weakening our sense of place?' In turn, once we recognize the 'hitherto impossible possibility of being in two places ... at once' (Scannell 1996: 172), it is necessary for us to recognize that social relationships can be pluralized too. There are opportunities in late modern life, at least for those with the economic and cultural resources to access relevant technologies of electronically mediated communication, for relating instantaneously to a wide range of spatially remote others, as well as to any proximate others in the physical settings of media use. Both these sorts of 'relating to others' (Duck 1999) merit serious consideration, as does the complex interplay between them. This potential pluralizing of relationships also raises some further issues to do with the 'presentation of self' (Goffman 1959) or with 'performing identity' (Cameron 1997) in and across multiple social realities (see Schutz 1973).

With a view to illustrating and extending the introductory comments made here, concerning electronic media, time-space arrangements and social relationships, I want to devote the rest of this chapter to a discussion of three brief accounts of media use (drawn from recently published research). Each of the selected accounts features a different electronic medium, but all offer examples of what, following Scannell, could be termed a doubling of place.

Public events and the interruption of routine

The first of these accounts is a quotation found in Robert Turnock's study of British television viewers' responses to news of the death and coverage of the funeral of Diana, Princess of Wales, in 1997:

> My family and I watched the entire funeral. My husband has his own business, but he was shut for the day as a mark of respect ... we just felt it was the appropriate thing to do. At times it was difficult because we have a thirteen-month-old baby and sometimes he got bored, so we took it in turns to entertain him. We watched BBC1 until she reached her final resting place around 2.15 p.m. We stayed at home in our breakfast room, drinking tea and crying. It did not feel right to go out on such a sad day.
>
> (Turnock 2000: 99)

Perhaps the main theme in this written account is the suspension or interruption of routine. Its author tells of her husband's business being 'shut for the day as a mark of respect', of watching one television channel for hours on end, of remaining in their 'breakfast room' until the afternoon and of staying indoors because it 'did not feel right to go out on such a sad day'. I will come shortly to a discussion of why she and her family (with the exception of the 13-month-old baby) might have felt that way about the death of a public figure they had never met face-to-face, 'in person', but to begin with it is necessary to say something about how the 'eventfulness' of public events is intimately bound up with the 'dailiness' that it disturbs, if only temporarily.

Scannell (1996: 149) asserts that dailiness is the key 'organizing principle' of broadcasting, and that the principal challenge for broadcasters is to provide 'a daily service that fills each day, that runs right through the day, that appears as a continuous ... never-ending flow – through all the hours of the day, today, tomorrow and tomorrow and tomorrow', in such a way that viewers and listeners can come to feel 'entitled' to expect it as a reliable, familiar and predictable aspect of their days (as 'ready-to-hand' and 'available', in phenomenological terms). In contrast, eventful happenings like the death of Diana, who was a relatively young member of the British royal family, or to take a more recent example, the September 11 attacks on New York's World Trade Centre in 2001, are unexpected, 'occasional things' that 'show up' as eventful 'against a background of uneventful everyday existence'. (Having said that, some eventful occasions are planned and anticipated well in advance, forming part of a national or global calendar of events, and it is precisely the role of news to try to 'routinize eventfulness' as an 'everyday phenomenon' [Scannell 1996: 160].) Daniel Dayan and Elihu Katz (1992: 5), introducing a study of what they refer to as 'media events', one case of which was Diana's wedding ceremony years before, make an argument that is similar to Scannell's: 'The most obvious difference between media events and other … genres of broadcasting is that they are, by definition, not routine. In fact, they are *interruptions* of routine; they intervene in the normal flow of broadcasting and our lives.'

The 'normal flow' of broadcasting, as Dayan and Katz refer to it, has its source in the seriality of programming (soap opera is perhaps the best example of this serial form), and in the cyclical or recursive organization of the schedules (Scannell 1995: 7). In turn, television scheduling is typically designed to match a channel's 'mixed' programme output with the projected flow of day-to-day lives, the routinized 'time-space paths' (see Giddens 1984: 113) along which potential viewers in different social positions are assumed to be moving.[5] Television viewing is usually, though not exclusively (see McCarthy 2001), carried out in household contexts, where attention to particular programmes has often been divided and contested (a classic qualitative study of television's uses in the home is Morley 1986). It is in such a setting that the family in the first account is watching television, and the problem of having to 'entertain' a bored baby is typical of the kind of mundane distractions that viewers face in their routine domestic circumstances. Indeed, some television programmes, especially those shown at times of the day, like breakfast time, when people's physical presence in front of the screen is unpredictable, assume a distracted viewer who will drop in and out of the highly fragmented broadcast.

Let me return now to a question raised earlier, which is asked by Turnock (2000: 35) himself: 'How is it possible to grieve over someone that you have never met?'[6] I should make it clear at this point that many of the respondents featured in Turnock's research data did not report feelings of grief, but others (including the author of this account) do seem to have experienced great upset over Diana's death. Answering Turnock's question requires an understanding of the role of electronic media, and broadcasting in particular, in the construction of 'celebrity'. It also invites reflection on the ways in which relations of familiarity and estrangement today are 'mapped' onto the changing situational geography of social life. For instance, Giddens (1999: 11–12), commenting on the significance of Nelson Mandela as a 'global celebrity', notes that when Mandela's image 'may be more familiar to us than the face of our next-door neighbour, something has changed in the nature of our everyday experience'. Similarly, although she was a member (by marriage) of the British royal family rather than a political leader, Diana was 'known' to millions around the world through her frequent media appearances. Her 'performance of "ordinariness"' (Couldry 2001: 231) in media settings, despite

25

the fact that she occupied a quite extraordinary social position, may help, in part, to explain the sense of loss felt by some people following her death (see also Kear and Steinberg 1999).

Writing several years ago, John Langer (1981: 355) remarked that most television personalities have a ' "will to ordinariness", to be accepted, normalized, experienced as *familiar*'. This includes not just show hosts, news readers and soap opera actors, but also politicians and other public figures who (often on the advice of 'public relations' consultants) present themselves on screen in ways that are intended to project 'intimacy' and immediacy, despite their positions of power and status. Although Diana was undoubtedly a sign of 'glamour', which might be thought to place her in the same bracket as a film 'star', she clearly possessed the 'will to ordinariness' described by Langer, and her performed sincerity in the famous *Panorama* interview broadcast on BBC1 was probably the classic example of that will at work. Not all viewers will have interpreted her self-presentation on that occasion as 'a case of the real thing' (Scannell 1996: 74), yet she offered audiences the possibility of what John B. Thompson (1995: 219) terms 'non-reciprocal intimacy at a distance' in a 'mediated quasi-interaction'. As Meyrowitz (1985: 120) puts it, if audience members take up such offers, then mediated relationships of this type can, over time, 'lead to a "new genre of human grief" ' when familiar media figures die, and on a personal note he reveals that the murder of John Lennon in 1980 'was strangely painful to me and my university colleagues who had "known" him and grown up "with" him'.

Before moving on to a discussion of the next account, I want to conclude this section by making it explicit how the first account serves as an illustration of the doubling of place. On the one hand, then, television seems to have constructed for these viewers, who were 'drinking tea and crying' in their private domestic setting, something of the experience of being at 'the event itself'. 'The *liveness* of broadcast coverage', writes Scannell (1996: 84), 'offers the real sense of access ... This *presencing* ... of a present occasion to an absent audience ... can powerfully produce the effect of being-there, of being involved (caught up) in ... the occasion.' Diana's funeral service and its associated rituals, with the exception of the burial to which public access was denied, were made available to them (in a re-presented form) by broadcasting, but on the other hand, as Scannell has noted, such a televised public event might also be said to 'occur' in the place of viewing (since its occurrence is 'doubled' by broadcasting). Dayan and Katz (1992) ask whether it is still appropriate to speak of a 'public' event when it 'takes place' and is ritually performed, at least partly, 'at home' and 'in private'. They believe that it is, justifying their assertion by employing the concept of the 'diasporic ceremony': 'Attendance takes place in small groups congregated around the television set, concentrating on the symbolic center, keenly aware that myriad other groups are doing likewise ... a ceremony is created to encapsulate the experience of "not being there" ' (Dayan and Katz 1992: 146).[7]

The Internet as part of everyday life

The second account is a personal reflection by Lori Kendall (2002: 7), an ethnographer who has investigated participation in an Internet forum or 'mud' (a 'multi-user domain') that she names *BlueSky*:

> Online interactions can at times become intensely engrossing … However, … when mudding for long periods of time, I frequently leave the computer to get food, go to the bathroom, or respond to someone in the physical room in which I'm sitting. If the text appearing on my screen slows to a crawl or the conversation ceases to interest me, I may cast about for something else offline to engage me, picking up the day's mail or flipping through a magazine.

If the previous account was about an 'eventful' interruption of routine, then this one is of interest to me precisely because it places Internet use in the context of ordinary, day-to-day life. Kendall's description of her own mundane domestic practices (combining 'online interactions' with various 'offline' activities such as eating, chatting to somebody in the same 'physical room' and 'flipping through a magazine') could easily be an account of routine, distracted television viewing in the home, if we were to substitute her references to 'mudding' on the computer with ones to glancing at a television screen. As she acknowledges, being online 'can at times become intensely engrossing', just as the television viewers in the previous account were engrossed by the unfolding occasion that they witnessed from their private domain, but at other times, when the text on her computer screen 'slows to a crawl' or when she ceases to be interested in the ongoing 'conversation' between participants (in what are known to their users as 'rooms') in the mud, part of her engagement is with people and objects in the immediate physical environment.[8]

So this second account is, once again, about a pluralizing of place and relationships. Indeed, Kendall (2002: 7–8) notes that 'although the mud provides for me a feeling of being in a place, that place in some sense overlays the physical place in which my body resides'. While 'hanging out' with regulars in the 'virtual pub' (that is, with fellow participants in *BlueSky*), she is, like each of them, simultaneously located in a physical setting. This is a simple yet crucial point for us to take on board when studying the Internet, because as Daniel Miller and Don Slater (2000: 4–7) argue, much of the early academic literature on computer-mediated communication (for a valuable review of that body of literature, see Kitchin 1998) has tended to focus on the constitution of 'places *apart from* the rest of social life', rather than seeing the Internet 'as continuous with … other social spaces' and 'as *part of* everyday life'.[9] As in the analysis of television cultures, our attention needs to be given both to the 'presencing' of places on the screen and to those places in which the screen is viewed and interacted with, including public locales such as Internet cafés (see Wakeford 1999).[10]

27

The work of Sherry Turkle (1996a) is in certain respects an instance of that 'earlier generation of Internet writing' which Miller and Slater are so critical of, since its emphasis is on the 'apartness' of cyberspace, a parallel 'life on the screen' in which it is possible for participants to break free of the limitations of their physical existence to create alternative and experimental 'modes of being' (see also Turkle and Salamensky 2001). In her account of social relationships and self-presentations in muds, then, she interprets these 'real-time' interactive domains as virtual stages on which to 'play' collaboratively with identity, or rather with multiple identities. She recognizes, much as Goffman (1959) did when he employed various dramaturgical metaphors in his analysis of social behaviour, that the self in (offline) everyday life routinely plays 'different roles in different settings at different times ... when, for example, she wakes up as a lover, makes breakfast as a mother, and drives to work as a lawyer' (Turkle 1996a: 14). However, according to Turkle, there are two main distinguishing features of online identity construction. First, her work stresses the fact that most participants in muds are known to one another only through their own 'textual descriptions', and so 'the obese can be slender, the beautiful plain, the "nerdy" sophisticated' (Turkle 1996a: 12). Caroline Bassett (1997), among others, makes a similar case for muds as places in which to experiment with performing or 'doing' gender, including acts of 'gender-switching'. Second, citing the frequent use of multiple 'windows' on the same computer screen, Turkle (1996a: 14) proposes that selves may now exist in 'many roles' and 'many worlds' at the 'same time'.

Turkle's observations about online interactions and performances are interesting, but what saves them from being merely another account of the 'utopian' possibilities of virtual cultures is the link that she makes with participants' offline lives. As well as mudding herself, in the role of participant observer, she conducted face-to-face conversational interviews with some fellow 'mudders' in an effort to make sense of the connections (or disconnections) between those identities they construct on the screen and their presentations of self in what one of her interviewees called the 'RL window' (RL stands for 'real life'). This kind of approach to researching the Internet attempts to hang on to two related contexts, namely 'the social spaces that emerge through its use (online)' and 'the circumstances in which the Internet is used (offline)' (Hine 2000: 39). For example, she presents detailed case studies of two students, Stewart and Robert, both of whom had spent many hours mudding on a regular basis (see also Turkle 1996b: 165–73). Whereas Stewart is seen by Turkle to have been 'acting out' his emotional problems through a fantasy alias in the setting of a mud, without ever satisfactorily resolving them, Robert is understood to have been 'working through' the difficulties that he brought with him from RL. Although I am a little uncomfortable with Turkle's analytical judgement as to what constitutes the good or bad psychological consequences of mudding, these two cases do, nevertheless, demonstrate the value of combining data that is drawn both from electronically mediated and physically co-present communication.

Returning to Kendall (2002: 225), it is important to note the conclusion of her ethnographic study, which involved not just virtual contacts with anonymous others but also attendance at occasional (and therefore eventful) face-to-face group meetings of several of the *BlueSky* participants: 'Online relations do not occur in a cultural vacuum. However much people may desire to leave behind the constraints of their offline cultural backgrounds ... their social interactions online remain grounded in understandings and contexts that intersect with offline realities.' In the case of the virtual pub that she investigated, the majority of regulars were American, male, white and middle class, working as computer programmers or in similar computer-related employment. Indeed, most were routinely 'logging on' from a workplace setting, with the main periods of heavy usage being lunchtime and late afternoon, Pacific standard time. The mud that is described in her book is a collectively performed 'masculine space' in which 'patterns of speech, persistent topics, and a particular style of references to women and sex create a gendered environment' (Kendall 2002: 72). There is a blurring of the spheres of work and leisure here, since much of the chat actually revolves around the uses of computer technology. For these reasons, she insists that it is important to understand *BlueSky* as one site, among many, both in online and offline social realities, where a version of 'hegemonic masculinity' is reproduced on a daily basis.

Two 'theres' there in mobile phone use

The third account is a story told by sociologist Emanuel A. Schegloff (2002: 285–6), which is set in a train carriage in New York:

> A young woman is talking on the cell phone, apparently to her boyfriend, with whom she is in something of a crisis. Her voice projects in far-from-dulcet tones. Most of the passengers take up a physical and postural stance of busying themselves with other foci of attention (their reading matter, the scene passing by the train's windows, etc.), busy doing 'not overhearing this conversation' ... Except for one passenger. And when the protagonist of this tale has her eyes intersect this fellow-passenger's gaze, she calls out in outraged protest, 'Do you mind?! This is a private conversation!'

A further echo of Scannell's concept of the doubling of place is to be found in Schegloff's own commentary on that story of mobile phone (or 'cell phone') use. This young woman at the centre of the tale is, in his words, 'in two places at the same time – and the railroad car is only one of them. The other place that she is is "on the telephone" ... there are two "theres" there' (Schegloff 2002: 286–7). We are not accustomed to thinking of speaking on the telephone as an instance of 'being-in-place' (see Casey 1993: xv), and yet the participants in telephone conversations, whose bodies reside in separate physical locations, are constructing what Schegloff (2002: 287) terms 'occasions of talk-in-interaction', in which there is a shared virtual co-presence, rather like that created by 'synchronous' Internet chat.

Although Schegloff does not state it explicitly, the story that he recounts is, in my view, one in which plural and competing definitions of 'the situation' become apparent. The protagonist, who is physically on a train journey and in the public setting of 'the railroad car', is, she protests, having a 'private conversation' (for further discussion of mobile phones as 'devices for private talk in the company of strangers', see Sussex Technology Group 2001). While her assertion is in some ways surprising, given that she is speaking 'in far-from-dulcet tones' and so her voice is clearly audible to other passengers in the same carriage, and while this assertion is also a possible source of humour in the narrative, there are still signs that could support such an indignant expression of personal experience: '*this* young woman is talking to her *boyfriend*, about intimate matters, in the usual conversational manner – except for the argumentative mode, and this also, perhaps *especially*, makes it a private conversation' (Schegloff 2002: 286). Interestingly, almost all of the fellow passengers collaborate to support this woman's defining of the situation. In ethnomethodological terms, they are 'doing "not overhearing this conversation"'. They cannot help but overhear the argument (or at least one side of it) but pretend not to hear, busily looking down at their 'reading matter' or else out of the carriage windows, thereby avoiding eye contact with the mobile phone user so as not to intrude openly on another's intimate business. Of course, there is a single passenger who, as Schegloff's tale implies, refuses to accept the performed pretence, perhaps as a result of being irritated by the intrusion of private talk into a public setting. What I am suggesting is that, at the point where eye contact is made, the two 'theres' there end up colliding with one another.

By way of conclusion, I want to discuss two further sets of issues that are raised by this story of mobile phone use, because each is important for the way in which we understand electronic media, time-space arrangements and social relationships today. The first has to do with the complex links between communications, mobility and proximity in late modern life. Earlier, we looked at examples of simulated co-presence in electronically mediated communication, where 'the character and experience of "co-presence"' is transformed 'since people can feel proximate while still distant' (Urry 2002: 267). Given such a capacity for presencing at a distance (see also Meyrowitz 1986 on the 'paraproxemics' of television), or for multiple (imaginative and virtual) 'mobilities' via electronic media, why is it, then, that people continue to feel the need for corporeal travel in order to be with others in physical places (what has been called 'the compulsion of proximity'; see Boden and Molotch 1994)? As John Urry (2002: 256) asks, quite simply, 'Why do people physically travel?'

Schegloff's account is, after all, about an event occurring on a train journey. He tells us that this train is taking commuters home from Manhattan to Long Island at the end of a working day, and the context is therefore one of physical mobility, or a 'moving-between-places' (Casey 1993: 280). Passengers in the carriage evidently have an investment in travelling home physically, just as they would have had an investment in travelling to work that morning. 'Getting-there' and being-there, in embodied ways, are presumably significant acts for them (although, of course, 'telework' involving the use of information and communication technologies has helped to shift the relations between home and work for some people; see Haddon and Silverstone 1995). Indeed, the compulsion of proximity is not only evident in the day-to-day routines of commuters like these. Following the death of Diana, there were embodied acts of 'pilgrimage and witnessing' (see Couldry 2000: 37–8) to sign condolence books and lay flowers with other mourners in public places, or even to be in attendance in central London near the event of the funeral itself (where the service could be viewed on large, outdoor television screens). Similarly, as was reported in my discussion of Kendall's work at the end of the previous section, several of the mudders who participated in BlueSky from time to time felt the need to meet face-to-face in a physical location.[11]

The second set of further (closely related) issues arising out of Schegloff's story, and one which I touched on briefly in my discussion of the first account, has to do with what Giddens (1990: 140), in his wide-ranging study of the consequences of modernity, sees as the intersection of estrangement and familiarity with changing arrangements of proximity and distance. In marked contrast to pre-modern cultures, in which an encounter with a stranger would have been a relatively rare occurrence, contemporary urban places may be the site of fleeting contacts with hundreds, or perhaps even thousands, of unknown others every day. Goffman's concept of 'civil inattention' is the name he gave to a form of 'unfocused interaction' that is routinely played out in public places, such as city streets where passers-by acknowledge each other's physical presence with a swift glance before 'casting the eyes down as the other passes – a kind of dimming of lights' (Goffman 1963: 84). While train carriages are not quite the same sort of public places as city streets, partly because the passengers are in one another's company for a longer period than are passing pedestrians, what seems to have upset the protagonist in Schegloff's narrative is her fellow passenger's refusal to perform 'polite estrangement' (Giddens 1990: 81), the conventional 'courtesy' of averting the gaze.

Conversely, if known others in pre-modern cultures typically inhabited a shared physical location (as they still do in certain circumstances), then social relationships of familiarity in the late modern age can be 'stretched' across distances. Telephones, static as well as mobile, are technologies that have clearly helped to facilitate this stretching or extension of relationships (which has been thought by some to involve a simultaneous 'shrinking' or compression of the world; see Moores 2002). Historically, according to Claude S. Fischer (1991), the telephone industry's 'discovery' of sociability was not immediate, and yet a significant proportion of the medium's information flows is now made up of 'intrinsic' calls for friendship and 'kinkeeping' purposes (see Moyal 1992) or, more colloquially, 'calling just to keep in touch' (Drew and Chilton 2000).[12]

Paul Drew and Kathy Chilton (2000) offer a fascinating conversation analysis of the transcripts of telephone calls made by family members living some distance apart. They point out that the regular timing of such calls is usually based on knowledge about the daily or weekly routines of the known others being contacted: 'so, for example, a daughter might telephone her mother on Sunday evenings, at a time when she knows that her mother will have finished her evening meal, but before she settles down to watch some favourite television programme' (Drew and Chilton 2000: 137). Among the types of 'small talk' found in their data is what they term an 'oh-prefaced environmental noticing'. These noticings were occasionally spontaneous references to happenings in the local physical environments of the telephone users, but in addition they often included 'aural noticings' concerned with 'voice quality, background noise, etc.', which indicates that 'if shared local resources are prime targets for the making of small talk, then perhaps shared resources from the aural environment are ... likely to trigger comment in telephone conversation in the absence of mutually accessible physical resources' (Drew and Chilton 2000: 151). This brings us back, ultimately, to where the chapter (and also the final section of the chapter) began. By drawing our attention once again to the media settings (in this case, for talk-in-interaction) that overlay the physical locations of electronic media users, Drew and Chilton are returning to the pivotal idea that place, and experiences of being-in-place, can be pluralized in and by electronically mediated communication.

Notes

1 I am grateful to Annette Hill, Joanne Hollows and Nick Couldry for inviting me to speak about the material in this chapter to research seminars at the University of Westminster (Centre for Communication and Information Studies), Nottingham Trent University (Media and Cultural Studies Research Group), and the London School of Economics and Political Science (Interdepartmental Programme in Media and Communications). I am also grateful to the students on my 'Electronic Media' MA module at the University of Sunderland, where some of the arguments made here were first rehearsed.

2 A key point of reference there, for Scannell, is the concept of 'de-severance', employed by Martin Heidegger (1962: 138) in his discussion of the 'spatiality' of 'Being-in-the-world'. Indeed, Heidegger (1962: 140) briefly mentioned the medium of radio himself, pointing to its potential role in 'the conquest of remoteness' and a 'de-severance of the "world"'.

3 It should be remembered that there are instances of 'asynchronous' electronically mediated communication, for example when a programme is broadcast weeks after it was recorded (although it may still have the feeling of a live transmission), when an email is opened the day after it was sent, or when a message left on a telephone answering service is played back hours later. It should also be remembered that other media, including film and print media, might be seen to offer a doubling of place for their users, yet these media do not have the potential for instantaneous communication across large distances (and therefore cannot create the same sense of simultaneity and immediacy available from radio, television, the Internet and telephone).

4 As will become clear later in the chapter, it is even possible to conceive of broadcasting as involving 'para-social interaction' (Horton and Wohl 1956) (more precisely, 'social para-interaction', see Jensen 1999: 182) or else 'mediated quasi-interaction' (Thompson 1995: 84–5), in which co-presence is simulated. Whilst I find these concepts helpful, there is a danger that the 'para-' or 'quasi-' prefix might be taken to indicate that the type of communication found here is somehow less 'authentic' than communication in local face-to-face interactions.

5 Exceptions to this general rule are the 'themed' channels now available from cable, satellite and digital broadcasters, such as the 24-hour 'rolling news' stations that foreground 'hourly cycles of repetition' in offering a sort of continuous 'news-on-demand' (Richardson and Meinhof 1999: 8–9).

6 Interestingly, his explanation of how this is possible revolves around a reading of Diana as a soap opera heroine, whose 'character' went through emotional 'ups and downs', making available 'melodramatic identifications' to audience members (see also Ang 1990).

7 So the promise and possibility of 'being-there' electronically (in the words of BBC Radio Five Live's soccer World Cup trailer, 'We'll take you there') are combined with the 'not being there', or 'being-here', that is equally fundamental to audience participation in mediated state or sports events, but is not necessarily detrimental to a sense of public occasion. Speaking from personal experience, as I watched live television coverage of my own national soccer team playing in the 2002 World Cup finals on the other side of the globe ('interpellated', no doubt, by the ideology of patriotism), I was 'keenly aware' that others were simultaneously 'doing likewise', either in private households or in public bars. Indeed, coverage of the matches was interspersed with the images and sounds of public gatherings 'back home', while commentators made frequent reference to the 'local' times and places of viewing, since the global division of 'time zones' meant that afternoon or evening games in Japan were broadcast at breakfast or lunchtime in England, disturbing the daily routines of many viewers.

8 It is interesting that a virtual place is often referred to as a 'room'. Similarly, people speak of 'visiting sites' on the World Wide Web. So in circumstances of 'digital sociality' or 'virtual travel' (Urry 2000: 70), some of the vocabulary associated with local physical settings or with 'corporeal travel' is being employed in an effort to contextualize, or to 're-embed', 'disembedded' social relations (see Giddens 1990: 79–80).

9 See also Kevin Robins (1996: 25), who offers what is in some ways a similar critique of the idea that cyberspace can be treated as a separate and alternative reality.

10 When attending to the presencing of places on the computer screen, it should be noted that, although the focus of my discussion here is on participation in muds, many other places (and people) are 'accessible' via the Internet. For example, see Miller and Slater (2000) on 'chat room' and 'ICQ' (stands for 'I seek you') interactions, Donald Snyder (2000) on live 'personal webcam sites', and Nancy K. Baym (2000) on a 'Usenet newsgroup community'. When attending to the uses of televisions, computers and other electronic media in household settings, it is also worth noting an argument made by Sonia Livingstone (2002: 158–9), who contends that family members today are often 'living together separately' in multi-screen domestic cultures.

11 Urry (2002: 269) talks about the ways in which communications conducted via mobile phones and 'text-messaging' services are 'enabling the flexibilization of people's paths through time-space', so that the precise times and places of face-to-face meetings may now be negotiated 'on the road' (and see Ling and Yttri 2002, for illustrations of the use of 'mobile communication' to co-ordinate physical mobilities).

12 Of course, a significant proportion is also made up of talk between strangers. For example, see Gary Gumpert (1990) on the practices of 'phone sex', in which participation with an unknown other (or others) facilitates the construction of fantasy narratives and personae, or else Deborah Cameron (2000) on 'call centre' workers who must routinely engage in 'standardized interactions' with members of the public.

Bibliography

Ang, I. (1990) 'Melodramatic Identifications: Television Fiction and Women's Fantasy', in M.E. Brown (ed.) *Television and Women's Culture: The Politics of the Popular*, London: Sage.

Bassett, C. (1997) 'Virtually Gendered: Life in an On-line World', in K. Gelder and S. Thornton (eds) *The Subcultures Reader*, London: Routledge.

Baym, N.K. (2000) *Tune In, Log On: Soaps, Fandom, and Online Community*, Thousand Oaks: Sage.

Boden, D. and Molotch, H.L. (1994) 'The Compulsion of Proximity', in R. Friedland and D. Boden (eds) *NowHere: Space, Time and Modernity*, Berkeley and Los Angeles: University of California Press.

Cameron, D. (1997) 'Performing Gender Identity: Young Men's Talk and the Construction of Heterosexual Masculinity', in S. Johnson and U.H. Meinhof (eds) *Language and Masculinity*, Oxford: Blackwell.

—— (2000) *Good to Talk? Living and Working in a Communication Culture*, London: Sage.

Casey, E.S. (1993) *Getting Back into Place: Toward a Renewed Understanding of the Place-World*, Bloomington and Indianapolis: Indiana University Press.

Couldry, N. (2000) *The Place of Media Power: Pilgrims and Witnesses of the Media Age*, London: Routledge.

—— (2001) 'Everyday Royal Celebrity', in D. Morley and K. Robins (eds) *British Cultural Studies: Geography, Nationality and Identity*, Oxford: Oxford University Press.

Dayan, D. and Katz, E. (1992) *Media Events: The Live Broadcasting of History*, Cambridge, MA: Harvard University Press.

Drew, P. and Chilton, K. (2000) 'Calling Just to Keep in Touch: Regular and Habitualised Telephone Calls as an Environment for Small Talk', in J. Coupland (ed.) *Small Talk*, Harlow: Longman.

Duck, S. (1999) *Relating to Others*, 2nd edn, Buckingham: Open University Press.

Fischer, C.S. (1991) '"Touch Someone": The Telephone Industry Discovers Sociability', in M.C. Lafolette and J.K. Stine (eds) *Technology and Choice: Readings from 'Technology and Culture'*, Chicago: University of Chicago Press.

Giddens, A. (1984) *The Constitution of Society: Outline of the Theory of Structuration*, Cambridge: Polity Press.

—— (1990) *The Consequences of Modernity*, Cambridge: Polity Press.

—— (1999) *Runaway World: How Globalisation is Reshaping our Lives*, London: Profile Books.

Goffman, E. (1959) *The Presentation of Self in Everyday Life*, New York: Anchor Books.

—— (1963) *Behavior in Public Places: Notes on the Social Organization of Gatherings*, New York: Free Press.

Gumpert, G. (1990) 'Remote Sex in the Information Age', in G. Gumpert and S.L. Fish (eds) *Talking to Strangers: Mediated Therapeutic Communication*, Norwood: Ablex.

Haddon, L. and Silverstone, R. (1995) 'Telework and the Changing Relationship of Home and Work', in N. Heap, R. Thomas, G. Einon, R. Mason and H. Mackay (eds) *Information Technology and Society: A Reader*, London: Sage/Open University.

Heidegger, M. (1962) *Being and Time*, Oxford: Blackwell.

Hine, C. (2000) *Virtual Ethnography*, London: Sage.

Horton, D. and Wohl, R.R. (1956) 'Mass Communication and Para-social Interaction: Observations on Intimacy at a Distance', *Psychiatry*, 19: 215–29.

Jensen, J.F. (1999) '"Interactivity": Tracking a New Concept in Media and Communication Studies', in P.A. Mayer (ed.) *Computer Media and Communication: A Reader*, Oxford: Oxford University Press.

Kear, A. and Steinberg, D.L. (eds) (1999) *Mourning Diana: Nation, Culture and the Performance of Grief*, London: Routledge.

Kendall, L. (2002) *Hanging Out in the Virtual Pub: Masculinities and Relationships Online*, Berkeley and Los Angeles: University of California Press.

Kitchin, R. (1998) *Cyberspace: The World in the Wires*, Chichester: Wiley.

Langer, J. (1981) 'Television's "Personality System"', *Media, Culture and Society*, 4: 351–65.

Leyshon, A. (1995) 'Annihilating Space? The Speed-up of Communications', in J. Allen and C. Hamnett (eds) *A Shrinking World? Global Unevenness and Inequality*, Oxford: Oxford University Press/Open University.

Ling, R. and Yttri, B. (2002) 'Hyper-coordination via Mobile Phones in Norway', in J.E. Katz and M. Aakhus (eds) *Perpetual Contact: Mobile Communication, Private Talk, Public Performance*, Cambridge: Cambridge University Press.

Livingstone, S. (2002) *Young People and New Media: Childhood and the Changing Media Environment*, London: Sage.

Marvin, C. (1988) *When Old Technologies Were New: Thinking about Electric Communication in the Late Nineteenth Century*, New York: Oxford University Press.

Massey, D. (1995) 'The Conceptualization of Place', in D. Massey and P. Jess (eds) *A Place in the World? Places, Cultures and Globalization*, Oxford: Oxford University Press/Open University.

McCarthy, A. (2001) *Ambient Television: Visual Culture and Public Space*, Durham, NC: Duke University Press.

McLuhan, M. (1964) *Understanding Media: The Extensions of Man*, London: Routledge and Kegan Paul.

Meyrowitz, J. (1985) *No Sense of Place: The Impact of Electronic Media on Social Behavior*, New York: Oxford University Press.

—— (1986) 'Television and Interpersonal Behavior: Codes of Perception and Response', in G. Gumpert and R. Cathcart (eds) *Inter/Media: Interpersonal Communication in a Media World*, 3rd edn, New York: Oxford University Press.

—— (1994) 'Medium Theory', in D. Crowley and D. Mitchell (eds) *Communication Theory Today*, Cambridge: Polity Press.

Miller, D. and Slater, D. (2000) *The Internet: An Ethnographic Approach*, Oxford: Berg.

Mitchell, W.J. (1995) *City of Bits: Space, Place, and the Infobahn*, Cambridge, MA: MIT Press.

Moores, S. (1997) 'Broadcasting and its Audiences', in H. Mackay (ed.) *Consumption and Everyday Life*, London: Sage/Open University.

—— (2002) 'Thinking Metaphorically about the Media and Globalization', Paper presented at a conference on the future and implications of global media, Center for Global Media Studies, Washington State University, July 2002.

Morley, D. (1986) *Family Television: Cultural Power and Domestic Leisure*, London: Comedia.

Moyal, A. (1992) 'The Gendered Use of the Telephone: An Australian Case Study', *Media, Culture and Society*, 14: 51–72.

Richardson, K. and Meinhof, U.H. (1999) *Worlds in Common? Television Discourse in a Changing Europe*, London: Routledge.

Robins, K. (1996) 'Cyberspace and the World We Live In', in J. Dovey (ed.) *Fractal Dreams: New Media in Social Context*, London: Lawrence and Wishart.

Scannell, P. (1995) 'For a Phenomenology of Radio and Television', *Journal of Communication*, 45(3): 4–19.

—— (1996) *Radio, Television and Modern Life: A Phenomenological Approach*, Oxford: Blackwell.

Schegloff, E.A. (2002) 'Beginnings in the Telephone', in J.E. Katz and M. Aakhus (eds) *Perpetual Contact: Mobile Communication, Private Talk, Public Performance*, Cambridge: Cambridge University Press.

Schutz, A. (1973) 'On Multiple Realities', in *Collected Papers*, vol. 1, The Hague: Martinus Nijhoff.

Snyder, D. (2000) 'Webcam Women: Life on Your Screen', in D. Gauntlett (ed.) *Web.Studies: Rewiring Media Studies for the Digital Age*, London: Arnold.

Sussex Technology Group (2001) 'In the Company of Strangers: Mobile Phones and the Conception of Space', in S.R. Munt (ed.) *Technospaces: Inside the New Media*, London: Continuum.

Thompson, J.B. (1995) *The Media and Modernity: A Social Theory of the Media*, Cambridge: Polity Press.

Turkle, S. (1996a) *Life on the Screen: Identity in the Age of the Internet*, London: Weidenfeld and Nicolson.

—— (1996b) 'Parallel Lives: Working on Identity in Virtual Space', in D. Grodin and T.R. Lindlof (eds) *Constructing the Self in a Mediated World*, Thousand Oaks: Sage.

Turkle, S. and Salamensky, S.I. (2001) 'Technotalk: E-mail, the Internet, and Other "Compversations"', in S.I. Salamensky (ed.) *Talk, Talk, Talk: The Cultural Life of Everyday Conversation*, New York: Routledge.

Turnock, R. (2000) *Interpreting Diana: Television Audiences and the Death of a Princess*, London: BFI Publishing.

Urry, J. (2000) *Sociology Beyond Societies: Mobilities for the Twenty-first Century*, London: Routledge.

—— (2002) 'Mobility and Proximity', *Sociology*, 36: 255–74.

Wakeford, N. (1999) 'Gender and the Landscapes of Computing in an Internet Café', in M. Crang, P. Crang and J. May (eds) *Virtual Geographies: Bodies, Space and Relations*, London: Routledge.

2

KINETIC SCREENS

Epistemologies of movement at the interface

Lisa Parks

In a recent essay, entitled 'Transporting the Subject', Caren Kaplan suggests that 'The value placed on mobility in representations of subjectivity in cyberspace or new technologies is not new ... but can be seen to be the full articulation of something old: travel' (Kaplan 2002: 35–6).[1] Rather than consider web navigation as a form of travel, I am interested in exploring how it is that we have come to imagine or know ourselves to be moving – whether navigating or surfing – while sitting (or with the advent of wireless, while walking, driving, riding, flying) at an interface.[2] I use the term 'epistemologies of movement' to suggest that there are different ways of signifying and interpreting (or seeing and knowing) movement at a web interface. I do not mean to suggest that all web-users experience movement in the same way; rather, I want to develop a way to understand the meanings of online navigation in more material and semiotic terms. Each of the interfaces I discuss structures opportunities to supplement the somewhat amorphous term 'cyberspace' with a consideration of 'the place of the interface', which I delineate in this chapter through discussion of data visualization, web art, translation portals and documentary photography. By considering the place of the interface, I hope to complicate critical and popular discourses that promulgate fantasies of digital nomadism as unfettered flow or networking, bodily transcendence, or instant connectivity, and expose the prevailing tendency to understand web navigation as yet another example of the 'annihilation of time/space'.[3]

This 'annihilation of time/space' discourse emerged over the past several decades, underpinned by the work of such scholars as Marshall McLuhan, Stephen Kern, Harold Innis and Joshua Meyrowitz, all of whom offered (sometimes technologically determinist) accounts of the cultural changes wrought by communications technologies in the nineteenth and twentieth centuries.[4] While this work provided crucial observations about changes in the social, economic and political order, it tended to sidestep the fact that time/space shifts have been experienced unevenly and in different ways in different parts of the world. As a result, its assimilation into the mainstream has spawned widespread acceptance of the idea that new technologies of communication inevitably generate a placeless globalism and enable individuals to move through time/space much faster and more extensively. What is troubling is the extent to which such ideas have gone unquestioned in the context of digitization. That the annihilation of time/space discourse holds powerful sway in the computer age is evident in the very selection of the term 'navigator' to describe the web-user or in the celebratory naming of the World Wide Web as an 'Information Superhighway'.

What is perhaps most unfortunate about the idle embrace of the 'annihilation of time/space discourse' is that it has deferred research into how the meanings, knowledges and experiences of time/space and movement have themselves shifted with different technologies, geographies, users and sociohistorical conditions. Instead, the annihilation of time/space logic has served a fantasy of digital nomadism that imagines the web navigator is able to move freely, change identities at will, and travel the world without restriction. Such a fantasy is also an extension of what I have called the fantasy of global presence that emerged with the first live international satellite television broadcasts in the 1960s.[5] Both negate the material specificities and limits of network infrastructures in order to privilege and centralize a transcendent Western subject that is imagined as existing above and beyond technology rather than in relation to it.

In this chapter, I attempt to complicate such logic by discussing movement in relation to specific web interfaces and by demonstrating how epistemologies of movement are derived through a combination of geographic, artistic, linguistic and photographic systems of signification. First, I consider how we can understand the place of the interface with a traceroute application called VisualRoute and a web mapping art project called *1:1*. While these interfaces target different users they articulate movement with technological literacy rather than transparency, exposing aspects of the web infrastructure that are often buried beneath the veneer of 'cool' design. Second, I explore how machine translation interfaces organize epistemologies of movement based on the recognition of linguistic differences. While there is a tendency for translation interfaces to structure linguistic traps by making English the lingua franca, projects such as the Translation Map emphasize crucial relations between movement, language and difference. Finally, I discuss an interface that documents a terminal form of movement – the global distribution of obsolete computers. Focusing on the Basel Action Network's images of e-waste processing centers in Guiyu, China, I argue that we need a multivalent model for understanding movement at the interface that considers the mobility of Chinese computer salvage workers in relation to the web navigators who may access such images on the BAN website. Each of these sites of analysis is offered to make discussion of web navigation more material, to complicate discourses of digital nomadism, and to encourage technological literacy, aesthetic experimentation, processes of differentiation, and exposure of global inequalities at the interface.

The place of the interface

While scholars have begun to analyze the spatial conditions of computer use whether in the home, the office or in transit, few have considered the ways in which users make sense of their own navigational process. That is, few have studied the visual signifiers or mechanisms that enable web-users to imagine themselves as 'navigating' while sitting at an interface. When most computer users 'navigate' the World Wide Web, they have little understanding of the infrastructure through which they are connected and are able to 'move' to different parts of the world. This is in part because so few websites actually visualize or display the infrastructure, which Manuel Castells calls the 'technical geography', through which the user's data move (Castells 2001). The visualization of the user's movement through the World Wide Web, his/her process of navigation, is effaced at the interface. What we see, instead, is the economic mobility of digital corporations such as Microsoft and Netscape whose browsers feature animated logos which signal the movement of data from servers to the monitor and reinforce the corporation's status as data portal, carrier or delivery system. In some cases, windows pop open either indicating a buffering process is taking place (when streaming media) or there is a connectivity problem, but otherwise we expect data to 'move' seamlessly and speedily from one place to another on the web. The issue in which I am interested here, however, is the idea that web-users are encouraged to imagine themselves as 'navigating', and yet most users have little or no understanding of the material conditions and infrastructure through which such navigation occurs. What is at stake here are issues of technological literacy. By effacing the infrastructure through which data moves, web interfaces tend to keep users naïve about the apparatus that organizes and facilitates online navigation and how its processes occur in time and extend across space.

This leads me to VisualRoute.com, which is a traceroute application designed as a diagnostic device for network administrators who need to locate connectivity problems and server slowdowns on the web.[6] VisualRoute provides a display of the trajectory through which data 'moves' when a user navigates from one point to another on the World Wide Web. In addition, it specifies the number of hops (jumps from one Internet Protocol [IP] address to another), IP addresses, node names, city locations, time zones and network ownership. It also indicates the round-trip travel time. For instance, Figure 2.1 demonstrates that a trajectory from Santa Barbara, California to Lusaka, Zambia occurs in 656 milliseconds, takes 18 hops, traverses nodes in San Diego, Atlanta, Middletown, NJ, and Lusaka, Zambia through networks owned by Cox Communication, AT&T, UUNET Technologies, and ZamNet Communication Systems.

By presenting a near real-time visualization of the user's path from his/her computer to a specific IP, along with a listing of all of the nodes and geographic locations through which the data moves, VisualRoute helps to define the place of the web interface. VisualRoute's website addresses network administrators explaining that the utility will allow them to ask: 'why can't I get there from here?', but I would suggest that such an application should be optionally displayed on all websites: for in displaying the user's path the interface conveys knowledge about the technical geography of the World Wide Web, enabling the user to understand navigation or online movement in terms of hops, round-trip duration, network ownership and location.

Since most interfaces are designed for either maximum efficiency or an aesthetic that Alan Liu calls 'information cool', they tend not to circulate technical knowledge about their own operation, and thus as they circulate data they perpetuate 'knowledge gaps' between experts and amateurs and information rich and poor communities (Liu, forthcoming). In so doing, they also negate an understanding of the situatedness or place-based discourses of web use. The fact that such traceroute data is readily available but is not well known implies it would almost be too horrifying to see one's own online trajectories because it might involve a recognition of the self as data moving at unrecognizably high speeds. Such a perspective issues an interesting challenge to theories of media spectatorship predicated upon identificatory processes involving photographic realism and anthropomorphic representation.

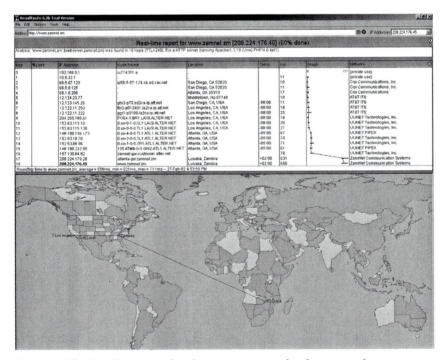

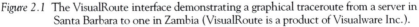

Figure 2.1 The VisualRoute interface demonstrating a graphical traceroute from a server in Santa Barbara to one in Zambia (VisualRoute is a product of Visualware Inc.).

Source: Visualware Inc.

VisualRoute's maps are especially useful since, as of yet, there is no realistic mode of visual representation for online movement. (There is, of course, the sound of the modem, and there have been attempts in action and science fiction films [such as *Swordfish*, *The Net* and *Enemy of the State*] to represent online movement with digital effects that reveal wormhole-like structures.) The perspective of online movement defies realist conventions and can only really be described in Paul Virilio's terms – that is, as an 'aesthetic of disappearance', a 'logistics of perception' or a 'kinematic optics' – terms that engage questions of speed, vision and telecommunication (see Virilio 1986; 1991; 1997a; 1997b). Using traceroute applications, however, may be one way to foreground online distribution routes and speeds that are often kept invisible, and to encourage users to better understand the specificities of the time/space or place of the interface. By visualizing the user's online movement, the traceroute display also implies the need to conceptualize how an individual might identify with or imagine becoming data or a trajectory. These displays seem to concretize what Virilio calls the 'trajective' – a space between the subjective and objective, a 'being of movement from here to there, from one to the other' (Virilio 1997a: 24). VisualRoute maps the trajective by setting categories of web duration and extension such as the 'hop' and the 'network' against the backdrop of conventional global cartography, inviting the user to recognize him//herself as a being of movement, or 'trajective', rather than an anthropomorphic body.

Trajective movement at the interface can be understood as a set of highly specified paths or routes as opposed to a practice of navigation that is presumed to occur at all times, through all spaces, at the will of any user. This notion of the trajective coincides with the work of time geographers such as Torsten Hägerstrand, Nigel Thrift and Don Parkes who, beginning in the 1970s, attempted to map the everyday trajectories and itineraries of individuals differently placed within stratified socio-economic systems.[7] In effect, their work gave the spatial field of geography a temporal dimension. Time geographers used their diagrams to foreground the constraints placed on different individuals who moved through the same socio-economic system within a given duration. Both time geography and VisualRoute map individuals' movements through large infrastructures, whether socio-economic systems or digital networks, but since time geographers are structuralists they emphasize the fact that these infrastructures are themselves constituted by and reproduced through such movements. As Torsten Hägerstrand states, 'people are not paths, but they cannot avoid drawing them in time-space'.[8] What is interesting is how Hägerstrand's comment changes in the context of digitization as interfaces such as VisualRoute now provide a way of conceiving of people as paths drawn in the time-space of the web, especially since users can be directed through any number of routes to get to the same web address.

The work of Swedish digital artist Lisa Jevbratt presents another way to conceptualize the place of the interface. Several of her projects attempt to map the web, but I will discuss one in particular, *1:1*, which was developed in phases in 1999 and 2001.[9] The project, which has been exhibited at the Walker Art Center, the Whitney Museum, and the Transmediale Festival in Berlin, is also available online.[10] Jevbratt's *1:1* attempted to create a database that would contain IP addresses to all websites. To generate the database Jevbratt programmed a webcrawler to, as she puts it, 'knock on the doors' of all potential IP addresses, which range between 0.0.0.0 and 255.255.255.255. The crawler determined whether or not a website existed at each numerical address and stored information about whether it was accessible to the public or not in the database. Because of the massive scale of the web, the crawler only reached approximately 2 per cent of the spectrum, and placed 186,000 sites in the database. Jevbratt began another search in 2001 in order to try to understand how the contours of the web had changed in two years. The webcrawler visited those same IP addresses two years later to determine whether the websites still existed or if they had moved.

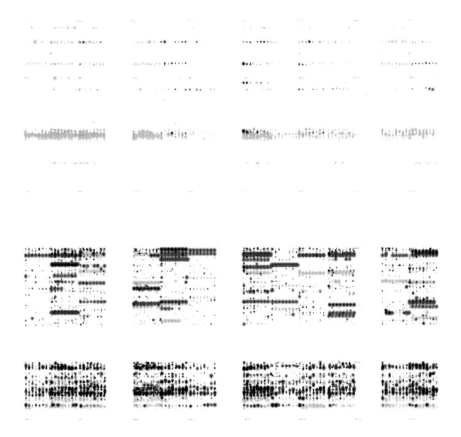

Figure 2.2 Screen capture of Jevbratt's *1:1* Migration interface.
Source: Lisa Jevbratt.

In addition to generating this database, Jevbratt designed a series of interfaces that would enable users to navigate this slice of the web contained in the database (that is, all the IP addresses gathered by her crawler). Jevbratt's five interfaces, entitled 'Migration', 'Hierarchical', 'Every Access', 'Random' and 'Excursion', not only function as web browsers, but also as visual analyses or pictorial interpretations of the web, since they composite and compare data gathered by the crawler in 1999 and 2001. The Migration interface, for instance, is made of blotches of bright red and green pixels set against a white background that correspond with IP addresses gathered in 1999 and 2001 respectively (see Figure 2.2). The interface looks like a homage to abstract expressionism, but Jevbratt calls it a 'landscape painting', insisting that database visualizations such as this can 'generate a new topography of the web'. By clicking where there is a blotch of color, the user can try to access a website, discovering that some of the websites function, that some have moved, and that others require passwords for access. Most significant is the way the interface illustrates that *the web itself moved* during this two-year period: some blotches of green and red overlap, suggesting those IPs remain the same while others spread into different areas. Jevbratt's 1:1 encourages the user to recognize the web itself as a highly dynamic and constantly moving infrastructure, and to see and imagine his/her practices of navigation as part of a massive network architecture that is material and changing.

Another of the 1:1 interfaces, Every Access, represents all of the websites found in 1999 and 2001 by the crawler. Each pixel in the interface frame is color-coded and corresponds with a website. If the crawler received access the color is green; if it could not access the site it is red; and those sites where the crawler was redirected are blue. By clicking anywhere in this colorful frame of green, red and blue densities, the user will encounter an accessible, inaccessible or redirected website. While Migration illustrates the web's movement, Every Access exposes the fact that there are significant sections of bandwidth that are completely blocked off to most web-users, restricted to those with military and/or corporate passwords. In this sense, 1:1 makes clear that online navigation is not free and unfettered, but rather it involves digital barriers that result from the way the web has been apportioned to and used by certain institutions which often have a stake in prohibiting access to information.

While VisualRoute illustrates the user's trajectory and brings the technical geography of the web into bold relief, Jevbratt's 1:1 offers a series of interfaces that generate technological literacy by visualizing data about the web and allowing the user to access it in various ways. Using these five interfaces, Jevbratt explains, 'one experiences a very different Web than when navigating it with the "road maps" provided by search engines and portals. Instead of advertisements, pornography, and pictures of people's pets, this Web is an abundance of inaccessible information, undeveloped sites and cryptic messages intended for someone else.'[11] By visualizing only a very small portion of the web, 1:1 manages to reveal some very significant patterns about its content. For instance, many of the websites in the database are military or government sites that require special codes for access and thus remain off-limits to most users. Some websites, which are unfinished and unvisited, do not provide information so much as they take up space, causing us to rethink assumptions that web navigation is unrestricted and always informative. Finally, 1:1 demonstrates powerfully that the web is not static, but is itself a moving infrastructure. By comparing data from 1999 and 2001, Jevbratt's multiple interfaces track and illustrate macro-level changes occurring on the web that are simply too massive, dispersed and fast to perceive through a visual discourse of realism.

Both VisualRoute and 1:1 produce epistemologies of movement by fostering literacy about the web's infrastructure and the material practices that work to constitute it. While VisualRoute is a diagnostic device for network administrators trying to solve connectivity problems, 1:1 is a web art project which experiments with database formation, graphic-user interface design and web browsing. While VisualRoute uses conventional cartography to illustrate the user's online trajectory, 1:1 employs abstract data visualization techniques to expose the invisible architectures and concentrations of power that shape the web's topography. Both projects foreground the randomness of the web. VisualRoute shows that a user could traverse a different path each time he/she tried to access the same website. Project 1:1 illustrates the eclectic and unpredictable range of websites that a user could access (or be barred from) on the web. Finally, both of these interfaces attempt to render the web's totality while inscribing the singularity of the user's navigation within it.

Combined, then, VisualRoute and 1:1 offer unique ways of visualizing web navigation and understanding movement at the interface. What is fundamental to both is the assumption that the user should and could understand the technical geography of the web. Extending epistemologies of movement at the interface thus involves extending technological literacy and challenging the notion that such knowledge is unnecessary and uninteresting to most users. It involves recognition and discussion of the new categories and parameters of time/space rather than a presumed annihilation of them. The place of the interface can be understood as the specific path(s) through which data move at a certain rate at a certain time. This place generates the potential for a trajective experience predicated upon a recognition or knowledge of the self as an abstraction of movement (rather than an anthropomorphic form), an array of multiple paths and uneven byways that may transfer, redirect or expire rather than fundamentally inform or transform.[12]

Translation at the interface

A further issue I would like to explore in relation to interfaces and movement is that of machine translation – the automatic translation of one language into another by a computer. One of the ways in which we infer we are moving at the web interface is by encountering foreign languages we cannot read or speak –

that is, when we hit thresholds of cultural intelligibility. Translation always involves at least a metaphoric if not a geographic leap as one language is turned into another. An online encounter with words in a foreign language may index a geographic region, but there is not necessarily a correlation between language and geography in cyberspace. Still, the material play of languages can become a way of interpreting movement at the interface. For it is ultimately through systems of signification and differentiation that movement can be understood as occurring at an interface that is perceived as still.

There is a long history of subtitling and dubbing at screen interfaces, and these forms of translation, which have driven the global film and television industries, are readily apparent and sometimes even jarring. Machine translation is designed to be much more transparent, however, so that the user simply clicks an icon and suddenly a web interface is translated into his/her native tongue (though sometimes full of mistakes). Machine translation is being widely implemented on the web and was first launched publicly at the Alta Vista portal in 1997, with the introduction of Babelfish (after the translating fish in *The Hitch Hiker's Guide to the Galaxy* by Douglas Adams). Babelfish supports translations between English and Chinese, French, German, Italian, Japanese, Korean, Portuguese and Russian, putting English at the center of the services it offers. In other words, translation exists primarily (though not exclusively) between English and a host of other languages. By 2001, Babelfish was handling 30 million translation requests per month (McKinsey 2001). Portals such as Yahoo and Google also now offer translation options, allowing the user to click a website into English or other languages that the browser supports.

The major players in the global market for machine translation are Systran (based in Paris), IBM, Lernout & Hauspie (Belgium) and the Japanese companies NEC, NTT and Fujitsu. These companies are all working to integrate machine translation into web interfaces and to power online translators. As IBM's Brian Garr remarks, 'The World Wide Web allows for the creation of global communities, but that can't happen with language barriers' (McKinsey 2001). The global community that Garr imagines is one constituted though a technologized erasure of linguistic difference, which may extend what Rita Raley refers to as 'global English'. As Raley explains, 'global English is a discursive feature of a late-capitalist episteme, and one with decidedly material effects;…it has also to do with a kind of myopia that is at once linguistic, cultural, and critical. It is, in other words, what lies behind the notion that "everyone now speaks English"' (Raley 1999: 53). While 'language barriers' may be obstacles to the operations of global digital capitalism, they are crucial to the production of *difference* within and across transnational cultures. The fact that machine translation is motored by US corporations such as IBM suggests that efforts to establish a 'global community' are likely tagged to the goal of making the web a smoother place for big business, which likely hinges on global use of English. This is especially problematic, since the prediction is that there will be 560 million non-English speaking users of the web by 2003 (McKinsey 2001).

Because of this some machine translation initiatives are attempting to diffract this myopia. A project entitled Native-Languages Interpretation & Communication Environment (NICE), based at the Carnegie Mellon's Language Technologies Institute, involves machine translation of native languages, such as Mapudungun in Chile and Inupiaq in Alaska. This project sets out to 'reinstate indigenous languages in official uses outside the home' and 'prevent the disenfranchisement of speakers of indigenous languages' since the web continues to be coded in a handful of 'major' languages (such as English, Spanish and Japanese).[13] The project allows linguistic minorities to establish online mobility since material related to education, health, agriculture and local government is translated into indigenous languages. Translation in this case facilitates the capacity for linguistic minorities to navigate the web in their own language, and in the process to have the potential to form new technological literacies and online communities. Despite such initiatives, English-reading web-users arguably have greater online mobility because their language is not only supported but it is positioned at the center of most major online translation portals. I would argue that this is ultimately a false mobility, however, since English-centric machine translation discourages English-reading web-users from learning new languages and from being able to recognize and experience *difference* at the interface. Without difference at the interface there is very little room to move. Difference shapes and reproduces both the potential for and perception of movement. If, as Rainer Schulte suggests, translation achieves a 'reorientation in the interaction with foreign cultures', then the online transparency of linguistic difference threatens to sustain an illusion in which English-reading web navigators remain convinced that they are 'moving' through the 'global community' of the World Wide Web, but may in fact be more trapped than ever in the dominance of their native tongue.[14]

The relationship between global mobility and language is further reinforced by various wireless machine translation prototypes that are being developed. The Tongues project, for instance, is a joint initiative between Lockheed Martin and the US Army to create a portable speech-to-speech language translator to support army chaplains in Croatia. Tongues provides real-time translation of conversation between English and Croatian. Another project, called Ling Wear, is being developed by the Interactive Systems Labs of Carnegie Mellon and the University of Karlsruhe (Germany). It is a wearable translation device designed to 'assist tourists, visitors, humanitarian and military personnel that are moving in foreign language environments'.[15] These projects enable military officials and tourists to navigate geographic territories more seamlessly using real-time portable translation devices. But what does it mean exactly *to move through a foreign-language environment* if a machine instantly translates it into your native tongue?

Ian Chambers' (2002) recent work on language, history and mobility is useful here. He suggests that language should be understood as a historically situated medium that actively transforms and sets the parameters for new forms of global transit and transition. He writes: 'The texture of language – of translation and the transit it provides and provokes – acquires an unsuspected complexity and thickness; its poetics supplement and subvert sociological and political transparency' (2002: 30). The idea of *language* as a medium is particularly relevant in an era of global digitization when the materiality of the world becomes code. If language is one of the rubrics through which we know and understand technologized movement, then what are the implications of having the capacity to translate foreign languages at web interfaces into one's native tongue? Put another way, does the user really 'move' if machine translation in effect effaces the foreign language environment and the challenge of navigation through it?

What interests me is the way that machine translation, both at desktop and wireless platforms, may alter our understandings of movement at the interface. On the one hand, it may generate a sense of linguistic liquidity, allowing users to seamlessly permeate language barriers and access forms of cultural consciousness that were previously inaccessible. And, on the other hand, it may create a linguistic trap by encouraging users to assume they can move across borders, through the world, knowing only one language. While considering such possibilities it is worth noting that most of the institutions funding machine translation projects are not driven by an impulse toward cross-cultural engagement, equitable exchange or mutual understanding. Rather, they are motivated by the twin goals of efficiency and transparency, and are primarily supporting transnational business operations, technical documentation efforts, military campaigns (especially in the former Yugoslavia, and probably now in Afghanistan) and global tourism. Some multinational corporations even describe themselves as 'geocentric' companies, which means that they try to develop products and advertising campaigns that 'transcend geographic frontiers and cultural specificities by creating messages intended to be universal from the outset' (Guidere 2001: 10). Such companies as World Lingo target business clients, indicating 'Site stickiness is double when a website is translated. Visitors stay for twice as long.'[16] The company insists that translation 'makes good business sense' because 'users are four times as likely to buy if addressed in their native tongue'.[17] World Lingo claims it supports the world's '10 most popular online languages', and its Instant Website Translator converts any English website into French, German, Italian, Spanish, Portuguese, Dutch, Greek, Korean, Chinese or Japanese. Like Babelfish, World Lingo not only puts English at the center of its online translation services, but the list of languages it supports, while international, reads like a relic of colonial empire.

Although machine translation may make the world more manageable for the elite – that is, corporate executives (IBM, SRI, ATT, NTT), technical experts, military officials and world travelers – it may also, in the process of selecting, combining and arranging multiple languages, teach us something about the structure and poetics of language that we ourselves have not yet recognized or understood. And if machine translation can alter what we know about language itself, it would in turn impact the way we imagine and interpret our own mediated movements. As Chaimbers reminds us, translating a foreign language or culture does not leave one's own language and culture unaffected. Translation is fundamentally about being moved. Digital artists Warren Sack and Sawad Brooks grasp this clearly and are in the process of developing an interface called 'The Translation Map' that will visualize online translation processes in a spatial context. As Sack and Brooks explain, the project is motivated by the fact that 'discussion on the net is dominated by the English language', and that the web is not engaging and involving people across cultures and languages as much as it could. The Translation Map supports 'an understanding of translation as movement across and between networks and territories'.[18] Rather than offer instant bilingual translations, like Babelfish or World Lingo, it will 'facilitate multi-lingual communication between online environments'. The software and interface will provide opportunities for users to work collaboratively online to translate a message and enable them to track it visually as it moves from addressee to addressee and from language to language. The Translation Map will generate a visualization of the translation process as it takes place in language and time, and a geographic visualization of its movement with 'an understanding that its linguistic translation will not necessarily be consistent with the boundaries of nations'.[19] Sack and Brooks are using this project to emphasize language translation 'as a problem of border crossing, movement and spatialization', which they insist is 'an alternative to the technocratic idea that translation-is-decryption'.[20]

If translation can be conceptualized as a movement between languages that involves recognition of differences, then most machine translation, by automating this process into one that occurs at an almost incomprehensible speed, re-moves the user from it. By enabling users in dispersed online environments to engage in and see translation as collaborative and situated work, The Translation Map preserves the moment of recognizing difference. As Irit Rogoff suggests, 'It is in the movement between cultures, their intertextual weavings and constant readings of one another, that the presumed experience of the other comes about' (Rogoff 2000: 49). The worst scenario, then, is if machine translation worked so seamlessly, transparently and efficiently that it erased altogether the movement between languages and their differences. The Translation Map promises to encourage 'readings of one another' so that *difference* is not lost. Instead, it is shared, witnessed, de-territorialized and constantly recurring. The way this project unfolds and is used will determine the extent to which web navigators are able to interpret different languages as spaces for movement rather than information barriers.

Terminality at the interface

Thus far I have considered how movement can be considered in relation to VisualRoute and 1:1, both of which provide information about the technical geography of the web and help users understand in more material terms the layout of the infrastructure through which they 'move'. I have also suggested that online translation interfaces can activate knowledges of movement by facilitating users' recognition of different languages. While many of these services run the risk of negating difference, such projects as The Translation Map and NICE may offer ways of preserving it and extending epistemologies of movement at the interface. In each of these instances, I have tried to complicate the idea of digital nomadism with a more materialist approach to the interface, illustrating that web navigation has limited duration and routes, must fulfill requests for access codes, or prohibits communication across languages not at the center of translation services.

In this section, I suggest a final way to conceptualize movement at the interface by considering the geophysical movement of the very computer beneath one's fingertips. In other words, I discuss the global distribution of obsolete computers that once enabled users to navigate the web. Since computers are manufactured with limited lifespans – that is, as machines that have structured obsolescence – it is important to consider where they end up. One might imagine the computer as analogous to the automobile whose use value has expired and ends up in a salvage yard because it is no longer fast enough or can no longer effectively transport people from place to place. Because computers are being produced, consumed and discarded around the world at an increasingly rapid rate, they too have their own salvage yards, which I suggest serve as the metaphoric endpoints of movement at the interface.

Rather than provide statistics and charts about the global manufacturing and distribution of computers, I discuss an activist website that has exposed where the West's old computers go when they are determined no longer useful. We can learn something about the multiple meanings of movement by considering the concept of computer terminality. In *Terminal Identity*, Scott Bukatman defines terminality as a form of subjectivity that emerges in science fiction and cyberpunk discourse. He writes that: 'Terminal identity is a form of speech ... and a potentially subversive reconception of the subject that situates the human and the technological as coextensive, codependent, and mutually defining' (Bukatman 1993: 22). For Paul Virilio, terminality involves the slow erosion of citizenship. In giving up movement for statis, the terminal citizen, he claims, 'abandons himself, for want of something better, to the capabilities of captors, sensors and other remote control scanners', and loses the power to move through and intervene in the world (Virilio 1997a: 20). While Bukatman and Virilio use the concept of terminality to explore how time spent (or imagined) at the interface reconfigures subjectivity, I use it to refer to the endpoint of the computer's use value, which, in this context, involves its movement or relocation from post-industrial to developing countries where it is disaggregated into parts and recycled into raw materials.

The Basel Action Network (BAN) is an international activist consortium that investigates hazardous waste conditions worldwide. It emerged in 1992 after adoption of the Basel Convention on the Control of Transboundary Movements of Hazardous Wastes and their Disposal, and one of the organization's most recent and high profile projects has been the investigation of the e-waste crisis in Asia.[21] Referred to as the 'dirty little secret of the high tech revolution', e-waste involves the exportation of obsolete computers and electronics from information rich countries to developing countries in Asia.[22] Communities in China, India and Pakistan have become processing centers where computers, television sets and other electronic machines are disassembled, separated and melted into raw materials. In the process, a huge number of workers are regularly exposed to toxic elements such as lead, beryllium, mercury and cadmium, which are released into the earth and water supplies of these communities. The BAN web interface is a way of accessing the political economy of the web in visual and geographic terms as it brings the material relations between computers, bodies, movements and territories into bold relief.

In December 2001, representatives of BAN and Greenpeace China visited Guiyu, in China, to investigate the conditions of workers in the region's e-waste industry. They generated a preliminary report, 'Exporting Harm: The High-tech Trashing of Asia', took photographs, collected soil and water samples, and made a video based on the investigation. Some of this material is available on BAN's website. The report establishes the environmental devastation, legal complexities and political economy of e-waste, as well as the culpability of the United States. Of particular interest here is a series of photographs on the website that dramatically illustrate the concept of computer terminality. Consider one, for instance, entitled 'E-scrappers', which shows seven workers kneeling beneath a tall pile of casings for computers and other electronics (see Figure 2.3). The caption explains that '100,000 such migrant workers labor in Guiyu, breaking down imported computers in hundreds of small operations like this one in a four-village area surrounding the Lianjiang River.' As the workers sift through the ruins for reusable parts, their bodies half buried, another scrap heap as tall as the building next-door hovers above them, looking as if at any moment it could tumble. The landscape of their labor has become that of the computer undone. Another image, called 'Wire-burning village sorting' (see Figure 2.4), shows workers picking though wires torn out of old computers. The caption reads: 'The wires are sorted by day and burned by night in this village. The families live right in the burn-yards.' Here wire from the West's obsolete computers becomes the earth's ground floor, and again, as machines are disassembled, it is impossible to separate the village topography from the computer's insides. The workers not only sit in mounds of wire, they are surrounded by the invisible polycyclic aromatic hydrocarbons and dioxins generated from burning it, giving a more fatal spin to the digital euphemism of 'being wired'. Finally, an image entitled 'Child on Garbage' (see Figure 2.5) shows a small boy, about 3 years old, sitting atop a scrap heap from which long blades of green grass emerge. His blackened feet are a result of the traces of toner cartridges and powder strewn about. The caption reads: 'Migrant child from Hunan province sits atop one of the countless piles of un-recyclable computer waste imported from around the world.' The boy looks into the camera and the image asks the navigator to see this mound of electronic ruins as his playground.[23]

These image interfaces illustrate how the West's computer waste shapes the landscapes and lifeworlds of Chinese migrant workers. They lend new meaning to Allucquere Rosanne Stone's insistence that the virtual age 'happens not in some theoretical space' but to one's 'own flesh and blood' (Stone 1995: 21). Village space in Guiyu is organized and defined according to the materials that are separated, such as plastics, casings, toner cartridges, circuit boards and wire. Most of this material originates from North America but some of it is from Japan, Australia, South Korea and Europe. What is perhaps most powerful about the online circulation of these images is that they compel the navigator to imagine the obsolescence and endpoint of every computer with which he/she accesses this site, and thus to recognize the computer's terminality. Put another way, the interface positions the user subjunctively by indexing computer obsolescence and staging its disaggregation within the representational frame, forcing the user to confront the fatality of the computer and the interface, both of which are socially constructed as taking us *anywhere in the world but the end.* These interfaces map out a set of dynamic relations involving technology, labor,

Figure 2.3 A typical e-scrapping dismantling operation. Some 100,000 such migrant workers labor in Guiyu, breaking down imported computers in hundreds of small operations like this one in a four-village area surrounding the Lianjiang River, Guiyu, China. December 2001.

Source: Basel Action Network.

history and territory that prompts the user to confront questions about finality and death that are usually off-limits or irrelevant in cyberspace. They become the metaphoric endpoints of a seemingly endless and speedy digital network, confronting us with the debris accumulation, inertia and toxicity that make up the arduous underbelly of the World Wide Web.

It is impossible to contemplate movement at the interface, then, in isolation from the lives of workers, whose bodies are fused among the computer's disassembled parts. In the global digital economy not all workplaces are filled with new flat-screen monitors, ergonomic chairs and color laser printers. As these images illustrate, some are filled with cracked-open computers, separated scraps and scorched earth. Their place of work has become the inside of the machine – the part that is kept off-limits, locked up, closed off in Western consumer societies. These interfaces also serve as powerful metaphors for the unequal and exploitative relations between information rich and poor economies in the world. They dramatize the way extraction is rearticulated in a post-industrial economy as the commodification of obsolescence itself, as the West's old

Figure 2.4 Women picking through wires torn out of computers. The wires are sorted by day and burned by night in this village. The families live right in the burn-yards. Cancer causing polycyclic aromatic hydrocarbons and dioxins will result from burning wires made from PVC and brominated flame-retardants. Guiyu, China, December 2001.

Source: Basel Action Network.

computers are shipped across the Pacific and trucked to Chinese processing centers for recycling and a modicum of revenue. Instead of displaying the user's visual route or performing a translation, these images demand a conceptualization of the differential and hierarchical movements that occur through, and constitute, the interface in the first place.

What I am suggesting is that we need complex and multivalent models for understanding movement at the interface. How might we extend the discussion of movement at the interface to account for the distribution practices that generate toxic working conditions in Guiyu? How do the trajectories of web-users differ from those of workers who move from village to village to disassemble electronics? What is the difference between navigating Guiyu online and migrating there in the flesh? Is there a way to understand the interface as both a figurative gateway and a material object that is built and broken apart? Understanding movement at the interface involves acknowledging that we live in a world in which some people navigate the web for information while others navigate the inside of the computer for subsistence. Since most computer hardware is manufactured and assembled in such countries as Taiwan, China, Thailand, Korea, Singapore, Malaysia and the Philippines, these images also serve as a reminder that the computer itself, as a material object, has a life-cycle as a geographic movement that begins and ends in Asian developing countries.[24]

Figure 2.5 Migrant child from Hunan province sits atop one of the countless piles of un-recyclable computer waste imported from around the world. Guiyu, China, December 2001.

Source: Basel Action Network.

Like the traceroute map with which I began this chapter, these interfaces generate ways of understanding movement at the interface in more place-based terms. Irit Rogoff argues that we must turn to such images, and visual culture more generally, to better understand contemporary global conditions, because geography, she claims, is an epistemology in crisis. Its conventional cartographies are no longer adequate for representing the complexities of post-industrial and post-colonial conditions in the world (Rogoff 2001: Introduction). The BAN interface serves as a 'geography' in a very material way, telling us about the place-based conditions and movements of bodies and computers in China. Like VisualRoute trajectories, BAN's images expose the speed of the computer, especially processes of their production and consumption, as well as the specific locales or nodes in Guiyu that are traversed and linked. While VisualRoute encourages the user to recognize him/herself as an array of paths, the BAN interface daringly invites the user to see him/herself as part of the computer terminality that has resulted from more than a decade of global web navigation and computer use.[25]

Conclusion

This chapter has drawn on and combined material from software developers, digital artists, corporate translators and environmental activists in an effort to suggest the need for different epistemologies of movement at the interface. The goal of my larger project is to develop a model of media analysis that will explore (a) geophysical movements; (b) phenomenological motions; (c) political (im)migrations; and (d) socio-economic mobilities in relation to one another. To construct such a model, I am imagining the media interface as a 'kinetic screen' – as an aestheticized frame and technologized time/space constituted by and through various types and combinations of movements, motions, migrations and mobilities.

I have attempted here to sketch out some preliminary ways of conceptualizing movement at the interface across disciplinary borders and in relation to specific semiotic and material conditions articulated through and beyond the screen. Considering the interface in this way involves understanding the global distribution of computer hardware in relation to the global navigation structured by its software. It involves recognizing that languages and their translation underpin *difference* in the world, and that difference sustains movement epistemologies. Finally, it involves complicating the navigator metaphor with other complex positionings, such as the trajective, which encourages the exposure of the web's transparent infrastructures and transitional devices as the user maneuvers through it.

Notes

Author's note: Earlier versions of this chapter were presented as papers at the Gendering Cyberspace Conference, University of Southern Denmark, 2001; the Interfacing Knowledges Conference, UCSB, 2002; and the Society for Cinema and

Media Studies Conference, Denver, 2002. I would like to thank Anna McCarthy, Nick Couldry, Anil de Mello, Wolfgang Ernst, Lev Manovic, Lisa Jevbratt, Chris Newfield, Miha Vipotnik and the Missing Links partners for helpful feedback and encouraging words, and Melissa McCartney for research assistance.

1 Travel and mobility have become important tropes in recent cultural and social theory. See, for instance, Clifford (1992), pp. 96–116; Kaplan (1996); Urry (2000); Massumi (2002); and Morley (2000).

2 Cinema scholars have been interested in these questions for quite some time. See, for example, Kirby (1997); Friedburg (1994); and Deleuze (1986).

3 For a more detailed understanding of the discourse of digital nomadism, see Makimoto and Manners (1997). They explore how digital technologies make work-life more nomadic. Some cyberfeminist work exemplifies this fantasy of digital nomadism by assuming transformations in the gendered subject during online excursions without discussing the specific material or semiotic conditions that may either facilitate or prohibit such transformations.

4 For work that helped to structure this 'annihilation of time and space' discourse see McLuhan and Lapham (1994, reprinted edn); McLuhan and Powers (1992) (reprinted edn); Kern (1986); Innis (1991) (reprinted edn); Shivelbusch (1987); Meyrowitz (1986).

5 The impulse for transparency in digital navigation reinforces a Western fantasy of 'global presence' that emerges with the first live international television shows in the 1950s and 1960s. See my essays 'Our World, Satellite Televisuality and the Fantasy of Global Presence' (in Parks and Kumar 2002); 'As the Earth Spins: NBC's Wide Wide World and Early Live Global Television' (in Parks 2001a: 332–49); and 'Satellite and Cyber Visualities: Analyzing the Digital Earth Project' (in Mirzoeff 2003).

6 VisualRoute website, available at: http://www.visualware.com/visualroute/index.html

7 For discussions of time-geography see Hägerstrand (1970) 'Space, Time and Human Conditions' (in Karlqvist 1975). See also Pred (1977), pp. 207–21; Parkes and Thrift (1975), pp. 651–70; May and Thrift (2001).

8 Cited in Rose (1993), p. 30.

9 Lisa Jevbratt's digital art project 1:1 was exhibited in New Langton Arts Bay Area Award Show, San Francisco (1999); Transmediale, Berlin, Germany (2000); Art Entertainment Network, Walker Art Center, Minneapolis (2000); The Altoids Curiously Strong Collection (2000); Obsession, Rosenberg Gallery, Towson, Maryland (2000); The Whitney Museum Artport Biennial 2002, New York.

10 To access the 1:1 interfaces go to: http://cadre.sjsu.edu/jevbratt/c5/onetoone/2/index_ng.html

11 See Lisa Jevbratt's description of 1:1 available at: http://cadre.sjsu.edu/jevbratt/c5/onetoone/2/index_ng.html

12 For a discussion of the trajective and GPS interfaces see Parks (2001b), pp. 209–22. An expanded version has been translated into German for the Geography and the Politics of Mobility art exhibition and catalogue, Generali Foundation Gallery, Vienna, Austria, 2003.

13 See the Native Languages Interpretation & Communication Environment (NICE) Project website at: http://www-2.cs.cmu.edu/~sfarce/NICE/NICE_Intro.html

14 Rainer Schulte continues, 'It is the constant flow from the one to the other that heightens our awareness of otherness and activates a mental alertness to the fact that no two cultures perceive the same phenomenon in the same way – as no two people see the same thing in the same situation' (Schulte 1999: 44).

15 Ling Wear website, available at: www.is.cs.cmu.edu/mie/lingwear.html

16 World Lingo website, available at: http://www.worldlingo.com/products_services/
website_translation.html

17 Ibid.

18 Walter Sacks and Brooks Sawad, The Translation Map website, available at: http://
www.cs.unm.edu/~sawad/walker/proposal/test5.html

19 Ibid.

20 Ibid.

21 The Basel Action Network website provides information about hazardous waste
conditions and issues in different parts of the world. For a history of the organization
go to: http://www.ban.org

22 See the report 'Exporting Harm: The High-Tech Trashing of Asia' at www.ban.org.

23 Collectively, these interfaces also function as an important counterpoint to the
global digital utopias constructed in the advertising campaigns of multinational
conglomerates such as ATT, Microsoft and Worldcom. Many of these ads celebrate
global mobility, showing people around the world using new digital technologies or
navigating the web with great ease. For a critique of these ads, see Nakamura (2000).

24 I thank Anna McCarthy for helping me to make this point.

25 BAN reports that the life span of the computer recently reduced from four to five
years, to two years, even though many of the machines remain functional. This
means that the computer waste is multiplying at an unprecedented rate. See
'Exporting Harm: The High-Tech Trashing of Asia', available at www.ban.org.

Bibliography

Bukatman, S. (1993) *Terminal Identity: The Virtual Subject in Postmodern Science Fiction*,
Durham, NC: Duke University Press.

Castells, M. (2001) *Internet Galaxy: Reflections on the Internet, Business and Society*,
Oxford: Oxford University Press.

Chambers, I. (2002) 'Citizenship, Language, and Modernity', PMLA, 117:1.

Clifford, J. (1992) 'Traveling Cultures', in Grossberg et al. (eds), *Cultural Studies*, New
York and London: Routledge.

Deleuze, G. (1986) *Cinema 1: The Movement-Image*, Minneapolis: University of
Minnesota Press.

Friedburg, A. (1994) *Windowshopping*, Berkeley: University of California Press.

Guidere, M. (2001) 'Translation Practices in International Advertising', *Translation
Journal*, 5:1.

Hägerstrand, T. (1970) 'What about People in Regional Science?', *Papers of the Regional
Science Association*, 24: 7–21.

Innis, H. (1991) *The Bias of Communication*; reprinted edn, Toronto: University of
Toronto Press.

Kaplan, C. (1996) *Traveling Theory*, Durham, NC: Duke University Press.

—— (2002) 'Transporting the Subject', PMLA, 117:1.

Karlqvist, A., et al. (eds) (1975) 'Space, Time and Human Conditions', in *Dynamic Allocation of Urban Space*, Lexington: Saxon House.

Kern, S. (1986) *The Culture of Time and Space, 1880–1918*, Boston, MA: Harvard
University Press.

Kirby, L. (1997) *Parallel Tracks: The Railroad and Silent Cinema*, Durham, NC: Duke
University Press.

Liu, A. (forthcoming) *The Laws of Cool: The Culture of Information*, Palo Alto: Stanford
University Press.

Makimoto, T. and Manners, D. (1997) *Digital Nomad*, London: John Wiley & Sons Ltd.

Massumi, B. (2002) *Parables for the Virtual: Movement, Affect, Sensation*, Durham, NC: Duke University Press.

May, J. and Thrift, N. (eds) (2001) *Timespace: Geographies of Temporality*, London: Routledge.

McKinsey, K. (2001) 'The Mother of all Tongues', *Far Eastern Economic Review*, 19 April.

McLuhan, M. and Lapham, L.H. (1994) *Understanding Media: The Extensions of Man*, reprinted edn, Boston, MA: MIT Press.

—— and Powers, B.R. (1992) *The Global Village: Transformations in World Life and Media in the Twenty First Century*, reprinted edn, Oxford: Oxford University Press.

Meyrowitz, J. (1986) *No Sense of Place: The Impact of Electronic Media on Social Behavior*, Oxford: Oxford University Press.

Morley, D. (2000) *Home Territories: Media, Mobility and Identity*, London: Routledge.

Nakamura, L. (2000) '"Where Do You Want to Go Today?" Cybernetic Tourism, the Internet and Transnationality', in B.E. Kolko, L. Nakamura and G.B. Rodman (eds), *Race in Cyberspace*, New York: Routledge.

Parkes, D. and Thrift, N. (1975) 'Timing Space and Spacing Time', *Environment and Planning*, A.7: 651–70.

Parks, L. (2001a) 'As the Earth Spins: NBC's Wide Wide World and Early Live Global Television', *Screen*, 42.4: 332–49.

—— (2001b) 'Plotting the Personal: Global Positioning Satellites and Interactive Media', *Ecumene: A Journal of Cultural Geographies* (London, UK), 9.2: 209–22.

—— (2003) 'Satellite and Cyber Visualities: Analyzing the Digital Earth Project', in N. Mirzoeff (ed.), *The Visual Culture Reader 2.0*, London and New York: Routledge.

—— and Kumar, S. (eds) (2002) *Planet TV: A Global Television Reader*, New York: New York University Press.

Pred, A. (1977) 'The Choreography of Existence: Comments on Hägerstrand's Time Geography and its Usefulness', *Economic Geography*, 53: 207–21.

Raley, R. (1999) 'On Global English and the Transmutation of Postcolonial Studies into "Literature in English"', *Diaspora: A Journal of Transnational Studies*, 8.1: 51–80.

Rogoff, I. (2000) *Terra Infirma: Geography's Visual Culture*, London: Routledge.

Rose, G. (1993) *Feminism and Geography: The Limits of Geographical Knowledge*, Minneapolis: University of Minnesota Press.

Schulte, R. (1999) 'Translation Studies as Model for Revitalizing the Humanities', in K. Mueller-Vollmer and M. Irmscher (eds), *Translating Literatures, Translating Cultures*, Palo Alto: Stanford University Press.

Shivelbusch, W. (1987) *The Railway Journey: The Industrialization of Time and Space*, Berkeley: University of California Press.

Stone, A.R. (1995) 'Sex and Death Among the Disembodied: VR, Cyberspace, and the Nature of Academic Discourse', in S.L. Starr (ed.), *The Cultures of Computing*, Oxford: Blackwell.

Urry, J. (2000) *Sociology Beyond Societies: Mobilities for the Twenty First Century*, London: Routledge.

Virilio, P. (1986) *Speed and Politics*, New York: Semiotext(e).

—— (1991) *The Aesthetics of Disappearance*, New York: Semiotext(e).

—— (1997a) *Open Sky*, London: Verso.

—— (1997b) *War and Cinema: The Logistics of Perception*, London: Verso.

3

NEITHER POISON NOR CURE

Space, scale and public life in media theory

Clive Barnett

Media, scale and the elision of representation

Modern political theory connects the legitimacy of democratic rule to the capacities of citizens to exercise reasonable political judgement through the medium of public communication (Ferree et al. 2002). In assessing this relationship, a number of commentators identify the media as bearing primary responsibility for the decline of active citizenship and the decay of democratic trust. The media have encouraged cognitive dependence, narcosis and the attenuation of critical faculties (Zolo 1992); they have eroded the capacity of citizens to trust in public institutions and hold them accountable (O'Neill 2002); they have undermined the autonomy of science and a robust public culture of criticism (Bourdieu 1998); they have led to widespread civic disengagement and the withering of social capital (Putnam 1995). One variant of these melodramatic narratives of the decline of democracy is the argument that the acceleration of processes of mediated communication and information transfer overwhelms the capacity for reasoned debate and discussion. The speeding-up of communications leads to the rhythm of deliberate, deliberative judgement being replaced by spectacular display and appeals to emotion. There is a counter argument that holds that the acceleration of communication is the very essence of the democratizing potential of new media technologies. Electronic town halls, online democracy, and instant referenda are all seen as providing problem-free, value-neutral means for more participation and better, more direct political expression. In this argument, increasing speed is used to signify the overcoming of distance, both literally and metaphorically, in the sense of transcending social division and political delegation. Technology is presented as having the potential to alleviate socio-economic inequality and political divisions by virtue of its apparent ability to transcend the materialities of space and time. This rhetoric extends beyond corporate marketing strategies. It informs the communitarian left-liberalism of 'the third way' (Leadbetter 2000), which embraces a communicative idealization of globalization to present whole sets of political and policy positions as obsolete. And it also underwrites the millenarian ultra-leftist optimism of Hardt and Negri's best-selling *Empire* (2000), in which a planetary capitalist system with media and information at its heart is imagined to be prone to incessant destabilization by myriad local insurgencies that are immediately transmitted world-wide through its own networks of publicity.

Each of these political visions assumes that political issues can be reduced to problems of more or less efficient communication. The celebration of new technologies like the Internet as ideal for direct, plebiscitary democracy, or for the proliferation of subterranean resistance networks, assumes that democracy is primarily about the expression of personal preferences or group interests outside of any context of transformative, deliberative justification (Sunstein 1992). They combine an unquestioned ideal of individual autonomy with an unquestioned norm of singular will. It is essential to confront the persistent elision of the problem of representation that characterizes celebrations of the immediacies of new technologies. The stretching-out and speeding-up of communication does not do away with the normative issues of delegation, authorization, trust and accountability that define modern understandings of democratic rule (Barnett 2003). Moving beyond populist clichés requires us to rethink the plasticity of space and time. Time and space are not compressible forms moving towards a teleologically determined vanishing point. Communications technologies do not therefore obliterate time and space. They re-cast the organization of the spatial and temporal scenes of social life. This chapter sketches the outlines of an alternative conceptualization of the relations between the geographies of communication and democratic public life, one that rests on two related propositions: that space is produced, and that scale is networked.

Communications and spatial formations of public life

To approach the relationship between communications and the plasticity of space and time in a more productive way, it is useful to consider the work of three very different writers, John Dewey, Harold Innis and Raymond Williams. Taken together, these three sketch the basis for a nuanced understanding of the formative relationships between time, space, communications and public life. Dewey's progressive social liberalism understood democracy in a very broad sense, as a mode of associational living shaped by openness to new experience. He argued that the material transformations of communications laid down the possibility of an expanded public life. Dewey's definition of the public combines an emphasis upon self-transformation with a focus upon instrumental and purposive collective action. A public involves 'conjoint, combined, associated action' that addresses the problem of how to control certain phenomena: 'publics are constructed by recognition of extensive and enduring indirect consequences of acts' (Dewey 1927: 47). The emergence of publics is intimately tied to the material organization of space and time through networks of economic trade, migration and transport. A public only emerges through a degree of abstraction from social contexts of face-to-face interaction, when the extent of social life requires combined action to address issues that stretch beyond the scope of small communities. Dewey's diagnosis of the eclipse of the public turned on the contradictory relationship he discerned between the pluralization of publics necessary to address the complexity of modern life, and the imperative for some co-ordination and channelling of this plurality to enable effective public action. The creation of a democratic state at a continental scale during the nineteenth century was tied together socially and politically through 'railways, travel and transportation, commerce, the mails, telegraph and telephone, newspaper' (ibid.: 113). But continuing economic development meant that the scope of indirect consequences has become so intensified, complicated and extensive that the ability of citizens to perceive and know them, rather than simply feel and suffer them, has been undermined. There was now, Dewey argued, 'too much public, a public too diffused and scattered and too intricate in composition' (ibid.: 137).

For Dewey, the eclipse of the public is not merely a matter of functional diversification, spatial and temporal extension, and epistemological complexity. The proliferation and fragmentation of publics is associated with the increase in the amount of distracting amusements in the form of movies, radio and cheap transport. The main problem, for Dewey, with modern popular culture is that it encourages forms of identification that are shifting and unstable. In creating the conditions for an expanded public, capitalist industrialism has also facilitated excessive geographical mobility and encouraged a flourishing of cheap and accessible popular culture that together undermined the stable conditions required for a public to come into existence (ibid.: 140–1). This evaluation reveals an understanding of communication as a medium for the sharing of meanings, one that overcomes divisions and brings life to the deadened materiality of physical means of transmission (ibid.: 184). The ideal of communication stands as a norm of shared understanding and mutually beneficial self-activity that transcends the divided world of capital and labour. The transcendence of the social relations of capital and labour in Dewey's philosophy underwrites the image of a 'great society' being reconstituted as a self-governing public of shared interest through the medium of educative communication.

Like Dewey, the work of Canadian political economist Harold Innis was focused upon the formative relationships between the patterns and meanings of social life. The central theme in Innis' theory of communication is that of 'bias'. This refers to two elements, one related to experience, one related to knowledge. First, Innis proposed that particular technologies emphasize a certain aspect of experience, either time or space. Second, different communications technologies favour centralization or decentralization, hierarchical or egalitarian distributions of power, and open or closed systems of knowledge. The bias of communication is therefore determined by the extent to which a particular medium favours extension in space or duration over time (Innis 1951). Innis developed a political phenomenology of communications, in which certain dimensions of experience were associated with particular patterns of power relations. This argument rested on a strong evaluative opposition between the space-binding technologies of control and time-binding technologies of shared understanding. The former enable the spatial extension of interactions, but are associated with the pre-eminence of instrumental knowledge and bureaucratic rule. Innis sees in the history of modern communications a steady ascendancy of space-binding technologies, which enlarge the scales of social organization, and in so doing, enhance the potential for the monopolization and centralization of control (Innis 1950). The main thrust of Innis' critique is that modernity is overwhelmingly biased towards the spatial over the temporal. This spatial bias of modern communications in turn undermines the ritual, meaningful character of social life. The spatial or temporal bias of communications is also strongly culturally coded. Spatially biased media such as writing, printing, and more recently photography, emphasize visuality over orality, the eye over the ear, and space over time (Innis 1951: 130–1). New popular cultures based on mechanization are dominated by an ethos of ephemerality and superficiality, in order to appeal to the large numbers of people that spatially extensive markets demand (ibid.: 82–3).

In contrast to Innis, one might consider the spatial and temporal dimensions of social processes as being intimately related rather than diametrically opposed. One such revision is Anthony Giddens' account of time-space distanciation as a medium of modern power relations. This refers to the ways in which social life and social systems are stretched by different mediums (money, commodities and writing), which re-articulate relations of spatial and temporal presence and absence. Time and space are not understood as neutral mediums for social and system integration, but as plastic configurations whose forms are inherently related to the constitution and transformation of relations of power, exploitation and domination (Giddens 1984: 256–62). As a modality of time-space distanciation, print-writing is crucial to modern state-formation. It facilitated the centralization of national authority, through uniform codes of law and administration and a uniform vernacular language; and the decentralization of national administration, as a mobile and easily reproducible means of communication. The example of modern state-formation therefore revises Innis' one-dimensional analysis of power and knowledge. Far from simply extending the coercive capacities of centralized authorities, the spatial extension of modern power through communicatively mediated time-space distanciation depends upon the development of innovative forms of reciprocal social relations, expressed in the struggle for the extension of modern practices of representative citizenship.

Furthermore, the cultural dimension of Innis' account is also called into question by considering processes of state-formation. It is now a commonplace that the formation of modern nation-states needs to be understood as having a cultural dimension in addition to administrative and coercive elements. The most influential cultural theory of nation-state formation and nationalism is Benedict Anderson's *Imagined Communities* (1983). For Anderson, communities are distinguished not by their degree of authenticity, but according to 'the style in which they are imagined' (ibid.: 6). What defines modern nationalism, from this perspective, is that it is a mass mediated form of social interaction that combines distinctive forms of public culture with private practices. Anderson's theory cuts across the conceptual oppositions of ritual and information that underwrite Innis' analysis of the bias of communication. Newspapers are certainly a means of transmitting information, but they are also embedded in practices of ritual sharing, which enable the emergence of new sense of self based on imagining oneself to be engaged in the same activity as anonymous and absent others at the same time. By folding ritual and transmission together in the notion of communicative style, Anderson emphasizes that symbolic meaning and control are not opposed dimensions of communicative practice (see also Carey 1989: 13–36). The power-effects ascribed to space-binding communications by Innis are not alien to time-binding communications, nor are space-binding technologies necessarily as inimical to social reciprocity as he suggested.

Compared to Innis' somewhat mechanical materialism, Raymond Williams shared with Dewey a strong emphasis on the constitutive relationships between pattern and meaning that distinguish different configurations of communications. What is distinctive about Williams' approach to cultural analysis is that it focused upon the ways in which different social contexts are differentiated by the forms of connection and relation through which social life is made to hang together. His work is informed by a strong sense that experience is plastic, not shaped by the content of media, but determined by the variable forms of connections with others and the world. Williams' histories of cultural institutions are guided by a democratic ethos of inclusive communication. This communicative imagination is at one and the same time an empirical entry point for the analysis of cultural practices and an evaluative framework, using norms of communication to judge different practices according to their adherence to principles of equal participation in a multiple range of communicative practices.

An example of this focus upon the production of the forms and configurations that shape social experience is Williams' elusive notion of mobile privatization. This refers to the double movement of localization of social interactions into the regulated spaces of the domestic sphere, and an accompanying imperative for new kinds of contact, a movement that Williams diagnosed as being characteristic of the social changes wrought by new communications technologies in the twentieth century (1974: 26). There is in this idea the kernel of an essentially geographical conceptualization of radio and television, in so far as Williams approaches media as a set of institutionalized practices that organize and give meaning to the spatial and temporal dimensions of modern social life (see Moores 1993). The dominant sense of Williams' usage of mobile privatization is, however, of a movement away from engaged forms of public association, and an extension of a private attitude (Williams 1989: 171). But one can just as easily argue that the re-articulation of spaces and mobilities

might extend publicness into new areas, not least that of the home, so fundamentally transforming the meaning of what counts as public. Detached from a
melancholic analysis of modernity, the notion of mobile privatization directs
attention to the ways in which cultural technologies bring individuals and
groups into contact with people, places and events that are distant, enabling
identifications with dispersed communities of interest, affiliation and feeling.

Dewey, Innis and Williams belong to a broader line of modern thought that
understands time and space to be constructed through human practice. They
each develop understandings of media and communications in terms of the
variable formation of the dimensions of public life, combining an emphasis on
new forms of sociability with new forms of concerted action. However, in each
of these thinkers, new patterns of association are evaluated by reference to the
idealized being-in-common of a genuine community, so that the innovative idea
that modernity is shaped by the changing spatio-temporality of communications
is expressed in an idiom of loss. With this in mind, the next section considers
less melancholic considerations of the public-forming qualities of modern
communications.

Media publics and spaces of interaction

The dis-embedding and re-embedding of institutions and interactions over
extended times and spaces imply that there is a distinctive phenomenology of
mediated public culture. The building blocks of experience are shaped by
temporal and spatial configurations of communications media, understood in
the broadest sense. As already noted, there is a long tradition that points to the
ways in which media technologies enable new forms of integration over
expanded spatial scales. The paradigm of this understanding is the rise of print
capitalism and print culture. The combination of low cost, high durability and
high mobility accounts for the cultural impact of print in reshaping culture and
politics over extended scales, typically that of the territorial nation-state. The
capacity of print media to detach symbolic forms from local contexts and re-
inscribe them in new contexts depends on the physical transportation of
tangible objects over material infrastructures. Nationalism, as a cultural form, is
a product not just of newspapers and novels, but also of postal systems and railways. This doubled sense of communication and transport is captured in human
geographers' research on time-space convergence, understood as a function of
improving transport efficiency that progressively overcomes the friction of
distance (see Brunn and Leinbach 1991).

Telecommunications and broadcasting mark a decisive break with previous
communications media. They cannot be easily contained within the paradigms
developed around print culture precisely because of the distinctive relationship
between communication, infrastructure and transportation that distinguishes
them. Beginning with the advent of the telegraph, communication is detached
from the transportation of tangible objects over space (Carey 1989: 203–4).

Electronic communications technologies *uncouple time and space*, so that the transmission of information or symbolic forms over space can take place without the physical transportation of objects (Thompson 1995). Thus, spatial transportation is no longer dependent on temporal distanciation, giving rise to the sense of immediacy associated with the telephone, radio, television and now the Internet. And the flip side of the reduction of transmission time to close to zero is that the experience of simultaneity is detached from conditions of shared spatial locale with persons or events. This accounts for the distinctively modern experience of *despatialized simultaneity* (ibid.), referring to the way in which the experience of 'now' is detached from shared locales, and how the sense of 'distance' is detached from physical movement and travel. Both are now shaped by the available means of communication. This suggests that media forms re-articulate spaces of public and private action. They extend 'presence-availability' beyond contexts of physical proximity and the immediate corporeal limits of the body (Giddens 1984: 122). As such, electronic media and communications produce virtual spaces of 'para-social' interaction, characterized by more or less rudimentary forms of co-presence (see Samarajiva and Shields 1997). This leads beyond a consideration of communications networks solely in terms of conduits for the transmission of information, redirecting attention to the distinctive forms of communicative action and subjectivity that different mediums open up (Hillis 1998).

This conceptualization of the time-space constitution of public communication is particularly important in understanding the role of cultural technologies in constructing modern meanings of the home as both a public and private space. Radio and television are among a range of domestic technologies through which the process of mobile privatization has been sustained. Broadcasting in particular has been pivotal in reshaping relationships between public and private: 'broadcasting redefined the geography of public and private, relocating a new version of public sphere within the privacy of the domestic' (Donald 1992: 82–3). The scrambling of categorical divisions between private domesticity and public life accounts both for the centrality of gendered meanings in shaping the development of broadcasting and for the broader role of broadcasting as a technology for gendering public life in particular ways (Lacey 1996). The gendered inscription and re-inscription of public and private space through cultural technologies such as radio and television require a revision of highly abstract, rationalist understandings of the grounds through which proper public action and political mobilization should be conducted. Paddy Scannell presents broadcasting as a means by which modern life has been re-enchanted and made meaningful, acting as a medium for the 're-personalization' of public life (1996). The characteristic 'for-anyone-as-someone' structure of the communicative process of radio and television repersonalizes public life according to norms of sociability, sincerity and authenticity: '[b]roadcasting transposes the norms of everyday interpersonal existence into public life' (ibid.: 172). Private life and public events are now intermingled in new spatialities, and public life is

as much about pleasure and enjoyment as about reason, information and education. The saliency of public events must accord with the rhythms and norms of
everyday life: 'The world, in broadcasting, appears as ordinary, mundane, accessible, knowable, familiar, recognisable, intelligible, shareable and communicable
for whole populations. It is talkable about by everyone' (Scannell 1989: 152).
By rendering public life accessible to all, broadcasting cultivates a form of
reasonable subjectivity, characterized by a willingness to listen and openness to
other viewpoints that is essential to the maintenance of a shared public life. On
this account, popular media culture is embedded in wider social transformations
through which the virtues required to engage in public life are reordered around
a set of traditionally feminine-coded competencies (Hartley 1996).

The distinctive phenomenology of broadcasting culture suggests that the
'where' of public life needs to be rethought in terms of the spaces opened up by
spatially extensive networks of media communication. This implies a fundamental transformation in the norms of public action and conduct. Samuel
Weber notes that mediated communication is stretched out across three locations: the place where images and sounds are recorded and produced; the places
where they are received; and the spaces in between, through which images and
sounds are transmitted (Weber 1996: 117). This sense of the space in-between
through which any communication must pass points towards the fact that the
experience of 'despatialized simultaneity' depends on putting in place a complex
material infrastructure that enables the uncoupling of time and space.
Communications technologies do not overcome distance and separation, they
render them invisible. The experience provided by radio and television is
divided across multiple spaces and times, and extended beyond the immediate
emplacement of the sensuous body. This implies that the unity of place as the
site of experience is shattered, and 'with it the unity of everything that defines
its identity with respect to place: events, bodies, subjects' (ibid.: 125). The
geographies of modern media practices therefore require a reassessment of the
normative value ascribed to values of identity, authenticity and place in both
ethics and politics, suggesting instead a practical philosophy of dissemination
and displacement (Peters 1999).

The distanciated geographies of mediated public intimacy associated with
radio and television direct analysis to the ways in which different media allow
caring and moral action to be extended across time and space. As Bruce
Robbins (1999) observes, the main lesson Anderson's theory of imagined
communities discussed earlier is that the scale of human feeling is dependent on
the variable institutionalization of technologies and social organizations. The
forces that once stretched and embedded culture at the national scale might
well now be 'steering it beyond the scale of the nation' (ibid.: 21). Robbins
points out the crucial role of media institutions in mobilizing what he calls
'global feeling', and is keen to avoid the tendency to present mediated forms of
identification as modes of alienated, vacuous attachment by virtue of the inter-
cession of distance. There is a particular ethical and political stake in insisting

that proximity and distance should not be thought of in terms of an opposition between concrete presence and alienating absence. This opposition allows media technologies to be both chastised for fostering inauthentic forms of identification and celebrated for reconstituting a lost sense of community. In contrast to both of these judgements, the dependence of patterns of interaction, identification and subjectivity upon particular configurations of temporally and spatially mediated communication should be treated as the basis for a social theory of the flexible spatial and temporal formation of trust, interest, empathy, belonging and care which does without the consolations of idealized images of community and communication (Silverstone 1999).

The social-theoretic phenomenologies of media culture discussed in this section underscore the ways in which the dimensions and meanings of public life are shaped by the spatial and temporal relationships opened up by media practices. There is still, however, in the work reviewed here, a persistent tendency to conceptualize space as a gap or a distance bridged by different media, indicated by recourse to a 'grammar of interaction' (see Gregory 1994: 117–19). The focus upon the interactional potentials opened up by different media tends to underplay the significance of the production of the material infrastructures that enable communication. With this in mind, the next section reconnects the interactional dimensions of communications to the temporal and spatial dynamics which underwrite the production of communicative spaces under conditions of generalized commodification.

The production of communicative spaces

I want to suggest that it is necessary to supplement the grammar of interaction that underwrites mainstream media and communications studies with an analysis of the organizational, economic and politically determined production of the material infrastructures of space and time. This task might draw fruitfully on David Harvey's analysis of the production of capitalist spatiality. Harvey explicitly challenges conceptualizations of space understood in terms of the friction of distance, or as a gap to be overcome. Instead, the contradictory relationships between fixity and mobility are central to Harvey's geographical imagination. According to his argument, space and time are not progressively overcome, they are perpetually reconfigured.

Harvey conceptualizes how the production of space opens up new possibilities for interaction and circulation only by laying in place fixed material and organizational infrastructures that are characterized by their own forms of inertia. In Harvey's account, capitalism is driven by a contradiction between investments made at one point in time and the imperative to devalue these during crises of over-accumulation (Harvey 1982). In this narrative, a series of communications innovations (turnpikes, canals, railways, the telegraph, telecommunications) reduce the costs of circulating commodities, labour, money – value – through space and time. The more capitalism develops, the more it embeds tendencies to geographical and temporal inertia: it takes a specific organization of space to annihilate space; and it takes capital a long turnover time to facilitate the more rapid movement of the rest. The material and organizational mediums through which space and time are co-ordinated eventually come to serve as a brake on the further expansion and speed-up of accumulation, leading to a reorganization of spatial and temporal configurations. The recurring theme in this conceptualization is the contradictory process of creative destruction through which the material configurations of accumulation laid down in one period of development are transformed in a subsequent period of crisis.

Harvey's conceptualization of the crisis-dependent dynamics of the production of capitalist spatiality is linked to an analysis of socio-cultural change and political mobilization. Innovations in the means of communication not only enable new phases of capital accumulation, but they are also associated with new political forms, new forms of cultural expression, and new forms of social experience (Harvey 1990). There is an implicit phenomenology of modernity in this understanding of capitalist space, one most clearly expressed in the notion of 'time-space compression' (Harvey 1989). This should not too readily be assimilated to other, similar sounding formulae, such as time-space convergence or time-space distanciation, precisely because it is derived from a conceptual analysis that explicitly breaks with friction-of-distance understanding of time and space implied in both those other notions. Time-space compression refers to the idea that the expression of crisis in the periodic restructuring of the spatial and temporal configurations of everyday life disrupts stabilized patterns of meaningful social action. Crisis at one level of a social totality is mediated through the changing material dimensions of space and time, triggering changes in structures of cultural expression and consciousness that are also experienced in crisis mode.

Compared to the accounts of spatiality and temporality discussed earlier in this chapter, Harvey's conceptualization of the production of space is more sensitive to the ways in which the restructuring of communications involves both the convergence and divergence of differentially situated actors. This emphasis has been most fully developed in critical elaborations that have challenged Harvey's implication that material transformations in communications lead to a uniform shift in modes of consciousness. Doreen Massey (1994) argues that greater attention should be paid to the power-geometry of contemporary spatial and temporal restructuring. This refers to the ways in which groups and individuals are differently located in relation to flows, interconnections and mobilities. Processes of time-space compression are socially stratified by class, gender, race and ethnicity, and other unequal social relations. Placement within these relations will define crucial differences in degrees of movement and interaction, and differences in the forms and degrees of power deployed in relation to such networks (Bridge 1997; Kirsch 1995; Leyshon 1995).

Harvey's analysis of the contradictory imperatives of fixity and mobility in shaping the landscapes of capital accumulation is particularly appropriate to the case of media and communications, because of the extent to which the commodification of these sectors depends upon the putting in place of complex material and organizational infrastructures through which expanded circulation can take place (see Mosco 1996). The low incremental costs of media reproduction lead to an imperative to expand market share as the easiest avenue of expanding profitability and extending accumulation. However, this imperative to expand circulation is dogged by the problem of maintaining the economic scarcity of commodities that are durable and easy to reproduce. These contradictory tendencies, between the drive towards expanding market share and extending the spatial scope of markets on the one hand, and the difficulty of maintaining price-regulated scarcity on the other, mean that the development of media and communications is shaped by a double imperative of *circulation and containment* (Gaines 1991). The expansion and deepening of the spatial scope of media commodity production depends on containing the circulation of media commodities within formal boundaries of commodity exchange. Understanding media commodification in terms of the double movement of circulation and containment requires an acknowledgement of the extent to which the constitution of modern media publics has historically depended upon the political and cultural construction of private property rights in various media products (Lury 1993). The key point is that, historically, this process has embedded cultural technologies at particular scales, primarily those of the nation-state. But this contingent stabilization, while facilitating commodification and patterns of accumulation in one period, has gradually come to serve as a restriction on further accumulation. Thus, from the interpretation developed above, the development of new media such as satellite television, video, the Internet, the Walkman, and mobile telephony can all be understood as having been motivated by an explicit aim to reorder the stable national regimes of policy and regulation that have historically shaped broadcast radio and television cultures, in order to facilitate the deepening and widening of the scope of media commodification. But it is important to underscore the point that commodification is not something that befalls modern, democratic public culture from the outside. The spatial politics of media commodification is central to the construction and contestation of different understandings of publicness. What is more, it should not be supposed that genuine public life is best contained within one particular geographical scale. This means that predominant approaches to media citizenship need to be rethought.

Rethinking the spatiality of media citizenship

Media citizenship is defined according to overlapping rights to information, rights to receive and register opinions, and rights to fair and diverse representation. This raises a set of questions concerning the structuring of access to material resources (money, free time), symbolic resources (languages, idioms, meanings) and social resources (membership of social relationships, or social capital) necessary for participation in the cultural practices (Murdock 1994; Garnham 1999). The importance of the concept of media citizenship is that it moves beyond binaries between production and consumption, textual meaning and creative use, to focus upon the institutional dimensions through which cultural value is produced, reproduced, and contested. The theme of media citizenship was initially developed in relation to debates about the future of national media and cultural policies. Normatively, it is an idea that implicitly presumes that citizens' access to cultural resources is spatially congruent with the scale of formal political participation at the national scale. Over the last two decades, stabilized patterns of national regulation of media and communications have been transformed. As suggested in the last section, the restructuring of corporate ownership and market control, the development of new communications technologies, the increasing convergence of computing, telecommunications and media, and the reorganization of the scales at which regulatory and policy decisions are made can all be understood as being driven by the imperative to produce new material and institutional infrastructures for the extension of capital accumulation over larger spatial scales at an accelerated pace.

The most sustained consideration of the relationships between the changing scales of media economies and the possibilities of democratic citizenship is the work of Nicholas Garnham. His interpretation of globalization is premised on the assumption that the territorial scope of political and economic power must be matched by the territorial scope of a singular universal media public. The public sphere concept, he argues, necessarily implies a strong concept of universality, understood in a procedural sense as a minimum set of shared discursive rules necessary for democratic communication (see Garnham 2000). On these grounds, globalization is seen as leading to a disempowering fragmentation of the public sphere. From the assumption that democratic citizenship requires a singular and universal public sphere coterminous with the territorial scale at which effective political power is exercised, Garnham (1997: 70) deduces that 'the process of cultural globalization is increasingly de-linking cultural production and consumption from a concrete polity and thus a realizable politics'. Conceptually, Garnham's argument runs together an assumption about the spatial scope of power, which he considers to be universal on the grounds that capitalism is now a global system, with an argument for a universal set of norms embodied in a singular institutional structure of mass media (Garnham 1993).

Garnham's evaluative opposition between the ideal of a universal and singular public sphere versus pluralistic fragmentation depends upon an unquestioned assumption that political power is naturally territorialized. This presumes that the key issue in assessing globalization is determining the most appropriate territorial scale at which power should be subjected to democratic oversight. An alternative is to think of debates about globalization as the occasion for reassessing how we conceptualize the spatiality of geographical scale (see Low 1997). If the scales at which social integration and cultural engagement are modulated are no longer necessarily congruent with the scales of national political participation, then this might open up new possibilities for political action, not least at the national scale itself (Staeheli 1999). In contrast to the assumption that political power is always exercised within a territorialized power-container of one scale or another, John Keane argues that the conceptual relationships between media and democracy should be based on a networked conception of political power. The power of large-scale organizations, like states and corporations, depends on 'complex, molecular networks of everyday power relations' (Keane 1991: 146). This means that power is much less consolidated, centred and coherent than is often supposed by areal, territorial conceptions of scale. And it follows that the 'often uncoordinated and dispersed character of state power makes it more susceptible to the initiatives of social movements and citizen groups, backed by countervailing networks of communication, which change prevailing codes and practice the art of "divide and rule" from below' (ibid.: 144–45). In turn, Keane (1995: 8) suggests that the public sphere is better understood as 'a complex mosaic of differently sized, overlapping, and interconnected public spheres'. According to a networked model of space and scale, spatially extensive public networks might include large numbers or small numbers of people, and vice versa. The key variable is the durability of networks, the extent to which they are institutionally embedded, and the ways they exercise influence. From this capillary perspective on power, conceptualizations that idealize unified and territorially bounded media publics are ill suited to assessing the progressive potential of contemporary transformations in the spatial organization of media and communications. They underestimate the potential of a multiplicity of networked spaces of communicative practice to induce changes in organizations and political institutions. This suggests that Garnham's either/or formulation of the main questions facing theories of media and democracy needs to be rethought. The fundamental issue is not whether effective democratic media publics can be constituted at the same global level to match the jump of scale by capital and by administrative and regulatory authorities. The pressing question is, rather, whether and how actors embedded at different territorial scales are able to mobilize support and resources through spatially extensive networks of engagement (Cox 1998).

To illustrate this final point about the relationships between media, politics and the networked spatiality of scale, it is worth considering an example, taken from the process of contested media reform in post-apartheid South Africa. Formal democratization has been associated with an opening up of a previously tightly controlled media system to international investment, a diversification of radio and television outlets, increased levels of competition and commercialization, and the heightened commodification of audiences. At the same time, as part of a broader emergent culture of transparency and public accountability, an infrastructure of independent media regulation has been established. These structural and organizational shifts have opened up new opportunities for locally embedded social movements to mobilize media attention as a means of applying pressure on local, provincial and national political and business elites. In particular, they have enabled the development of an oppositional 'politics of shame', in which grassroots organizations are able to mobilize mainstream media attention as a lever for bringing pressure to bear on powerful actors (see Barnett 2003, chapter 7). It is not necessary to idealize the democratic potential of media in order to acknowledge this possibility that media attention can be mobilized to act upon the conduct of powerful political and economic actors, especially in a context such as post-apartheid South Africa, where both public and private organizations are publicly committed to constitutional government and to discourses of service delivery and institutional transformation. After an initial post-election lull in political mobilization after 1994, South Africa has witnessed an upsurge of grassroots oppositional activism. This process is associated with new forms of issue-based mobilization. These include environmental movements mobilizing against the impacts of industrial pollution, national mobilizations around government policy on HIV/AIDS issues, more localized campaigns around housing, infrastructure and service delivery, as well as the role of South African activist organizations in the broader politics of anti-globalization campaigns. What these all share are two characteristics. First, attracting and maintaining mainstream media attention has been crucial to these new forms of grassroots activism, for mobilization and validation purposes, but in particular as a means of exerting pressure on powerful institutional actors. But second, dense networks of connection between South Africa-based activists and organizations and wider international campaigns have shaped the forms of campaigns and protests used to achieve this objective. Routinized Internet-based communication between locally embedded activists and spatially dispersed campaigns is crucial as a means of sharing information, developing strategy, raising funds and borrowing discourse and repertories of protest.

The South African experience illustrates two related issues. First, the political significance of media and communications is not technologically determined, but in large part depends upon the capacity of social interests for mobilization, organization and self-representation. Second, the ability of activists to organize political action *through* media spaces and communications networks is dependent on the politics that has been going on *around* the media in South Africa in this period. The shaping of independent regulatory authorities has become a new site through which citizen participation can be channelled. In South Africa in the mid-1990s, the politics of independent regulation saw significant successes for progressive organizations in embedding procedures for accountability, transparency and public participation into national communications policy and law. This success has been pivotal in the pluralization of media cultures and the popularization of news agendas in this period. However, the ongoing internationalization of South African communications policy has more recently seen the degree of participation and accountability curtailed by a prioritization of investment-led regulatory principles. In turn, there is an emerging network of Southern African media activism, sharing information and expertise, and engaging in multiple policy contexts. This internationalization of media reform movements underscores the point that the success of campaigns for the continuing democratization of mass media *within* South Africa will be shaped by the capacity of nationally embedded actors to draw upon networks of support and resources that stretch beyond the confines of the nation-state. The point of this brief excursus on South Africa is not, then, to reiterate the cliché that new media and communications are rendering the nation-state irrelevant as an arena of progressive political action. Quite the contrary, it is to emphasize that the real significance of new practices and scales of communication is still most likely to be found at national levels. Re-scaling the networks through which social movement mobilization is organized enables the development of new forms of political action that are still most often articulated with the scale at which citizenship rights continue to carry most substantive weight, that of the nation-state.

Conclusion

This chapter has argued for a reorientation of the normative geographies of media theory around the dual theme that space is produced and scale is networked. The common rhetoric about the death of distance works to hide practices of inter-mediation from view, whether these are policies, regulatory systems, corporate structures or social practices. The idea of the 'production of communicative spaces' is meant to capture the double emphasis upon both the production of new spaces of communicative sociality through social practice and the institutional production of material infrastructures of communication. It underscores the sense that the social uses of modern communications technologies open up new spaces of sociability and interaction, which transform the ways in which ordinary people engage in a wider world of publicly significant processes and events, as well as transforming the nature and meanings of those processes and events themselves. But it also reminds us that the social production of the spaces of communicative action needs to be supplemented with an analysis of the dynamics of the production of the material infrastructures of communication, an analysis that requires an understanding of the politically contested process of commodification, regulation and policy-making. Thinking of the active production of communicative spaces therefore helps us keep in view the extent to which the politics that goes on in and around media is neither neatly contained within the space of a national polity, nor is it free-floating in a weightless global space. Rather, the politics of media citizenship involves the articulation of interests and subjectivities embedded at spatial scales that flow through, around and under the national scale.

Bibliography

Anderson, B. (1983) *Imagined Communities*, London: Verso.

Barnett, C. (2003) *Culture and Democracy: Media, Space, and Representation*, Edinburgh: Edinburgh University Press.

Bourdieu, P. (1998) *On Television and Journalism*, London: Pluto Press.

Bridge, G. (1997) 'Mapping the Terrain of Time–space Compression: Power Networks in Everyday Life', *Environment and Planning D: Society and Space*, 15, 611–26.

Brunn, S. and Leinbach, T. (1991) *Collapsing Space and Time: Geographic Aspects of Communication and Information*, London: HarperCollins.

Carey, J. (1989) *Communication as Culture*, London: Routledge.

Cox, K. (1998) 'Spaces of Dependence, Spaces of Engagement and the Politics of Scale', *Political Geography*, 17, 1–23.

Dewey, J. (1927) *The Public and its Problems*, Athens, OH: Ohio University Press.

Donald, J. (1992) *Sentimental Education*, London: Verso.

Ferree, M. et al. (2002) 'Four Models of the Public Sphere in Modern Democracies', *Theory and Society*, 31, 289–324.

Gaines, J. (1991) *Contested Culture: The Image, the Voice, and the Law*, London: BFI Publishing.

Garnham, N. (1993) 'The Mass Media, Cultural Identity, and the Public Sphere in the Modern World', *Public Culture*, 5, 251–65.

—— (1997) 'Political Economy and the Practice of Cultural Studies', in M. Ferguson and P. Golding (eds), *Cultural Studies in Question*, London: Sage, pp. 56–73.

—— (1999) 'Amartya Sen's "Capabilities" Approach to the Evaluation of Welfare: Its Application to Communications', in A. Calabrese and J-C.

Burgelman (eds), *Communication, Citizenship, and Social Policy*, Lanham, MD: Rowman and Littlefield, pp. 113–24.

—— (2000) *Emancipation, the Media, and Modernity*, Oxford: Oxford University Press.

Giddens, A. (1984) *The Constitution of Society*, Cambridge: Polity Press.

Gregory, D. (1994) *Geographical Imaginations*, Oxford: Blackwell.

Hartley, J. (1996) *Popular Reality*, London: Arnold.

Harvey, D.W. (1982) *Limits to Capital*, Oxford: Blackwell.

—— (1989) *The Condition of Postmodernity*, Oxford: Blackwell.

—— (1990) 'Between Space and Time: Reflections on the Geographical Imagination', *Annals of the Association of American Geographers*, 80, 418–34.

Hillis, K. (1998) 'On the Margins: The Invisibility of Communications in Geography', *Progress in Human Geography*, 22:4, 543–66.

Innis, H. (1950) *Empire and Communication*, Oxford: Oxford University Press.

—— (1951) *The Bias of Communication*, Toronto: University of Toronto Press.

Keane, J. (1991) *Media and Democracy*, Cambridge: Polity Press.

—— (1995) 'Structural Transformation of the Public Sphere', *Communication Review*, 1, 1–22.

Kirsch, S. (1995) 'The Incredible Shrinking World: Technology and the Production of Space', *Environment and Planning D: Society and Space*, 13, 529–55.

Lacey, K. (1996) *Feminine Frequencies: Gender, German Radio, and the Public Sphere, 1923–1945*, Ann Arbor: University of Michigan Press.

Leadbetter, C. (2000) *The Weightless Society*, London: Texere.

Leyshon, A. (1995) 'Annihilating Space? The Speed-up of Communications', in J. Allen and C. Hamnett (eds), *A Shrinking World*, Oxford: Oxford University Press.

Low, M. (1997) 'Representation Unbound', in K. Cox (ed.), *Spaces of Globalization*, New York: Guilford.

Lury, C. (1993) *Cultural Rights: Technology, Legality, Personality*, London: Routledge.

Massey, D. (1994) 'A Place Called Home?', in *Space, Place and Gender*, Cambridge: Polity Press, pp. 157–73.

Moores, S. (1993) 'Television, Geography and "Mobile Privatization"', *European Journal of Communication*, 8, 365–79.

Mosco, V. (1996) *The Political Economy of Communication*, London: Sage.

Murdock, G. (1994) 'New Times/Hard Times: Leisure, Participation and the Common Good', *Leisure Studies*, 13, 239–48.

O'Neill, O. (2002) *A Question of Trust*, Oxford: Oxford University Press.

Peters, J.D. (1999) *Speaking Into the Air: A History of the Idea of Communication*, Chicago: University of Chicago Press.

Putnam, R.D. (1995) 'Bowling Alone: America's Declining Social Capital', *Journal of Democracy*, 6:1, 65–78.

Robbins, B. (1999) *Feeling Global*, New York: New York University Press.

Samarajiva, R. and Shields, P. (1997) 'Telecommunication Networks as Social Space: Implications for Research and Policy and an Exemplar', *Media, Culture and Society*, 19, 535–55.

Scannell, P. (1989) 'Public Service Broadcasting and Modern Public Life', *Media, Culture and Society*, 11, 135–66.

—— (1996) *Radio, Television, and Modern Life*, Oxford: Blackwell.

Silverstone, R. (1999) *Why Study Media?*, London: Sage.

Staeheli, L. (1999) 'Globalization and the Scales of Citizenship', *Geography Research Forum*, 19, 60–77.

Thompson, J.B. (1995) *The Media and Modernity*, Cambridge: Polity Press.

Weber, S. (1996) *Mass Mediauras: Forms, Technics, Media*, Stanford: Stanford University Press.

Williams, R. (1974) *Television: Technology and Cultural Form*, London: Fontana.

—— (1989) *Resources of Hope*, London: Verso.

Zolo, D. (1992) *Democracy and Complexity*, Cambridge: Polity Press.

4

THE ATTRACTIONS OF TELEVISION

Reconsidering liveness

Mimi White

Vamping for time

The television coverage of the launch and explosion of the space shuttle *Challenger* on 28 January 1986 is considered an exemplary moment of television (Doane 1990; Mellencamp 1990; Penley 1997). The launch was televised live, with great fanfare, because it was the culmination of NASA's 'Teacher in Space' program. In the wake of the explosion, the major US news networks switched into 'disaster' mode, preempting regular programming and forgoing commercial breaks to examine an event that was immediately characterized as a national tragedy. The networks rushed to set in place the appropriate apparatus for this mode of reporting, contacting experts from across the country, establishing the necessary terrestrial and satellite links, and so on. In televisual terms, the response to the significant technological failure represented by the *Challenger* explosion was the activation of an equally impressive, if less immediately visible, technological apparatus.

The *Challenger* event and the mode of news coverage it instigated raise questions about the nature of liveness in contemporary television, particularly its status in television theory. Notably, the *Challenger* explosion, among other technological and natural disasters, is widely discussed in conjunction with catastrophe on television. Precisely in its atypicality – the interruption of regular programming, the absence of advertising, the endless rehearsal of the explosion, the direct address of anchors, live, on television – television reporting of catastrophes has been considered as the epitome of television, the condition in which the medium most fully expresses its specificity, offering the possibility, however illusory, of 'touching the real'. A sophisticated version of this approach is advanced by Doane.

> Television's greatest technological prowess is its ability to be there – both on the scene and in your living room (hence the most catastrophic of technological catastrophes is the loss of the signal). The death associated with catastrophe ensures that television is felt as an

immediate collision with the real in all its intractability – bodies in crisis, technology gone awry. Television catastrophe is thus character-ized by everything which it is said not to be – it is expected, predictable, its presence crucial to television's operation. In fact, catas-trophe could be said to be at one level a condensation of all the attributes and aspirations of 'normal' television (immediacy, urgency, presence, discontinuity, the instantaneous, and hence forgettable).

(Doane 1990: 238)

This understanding of catastrophe and television relies on foundational assumptions about liveness as a defining characteristic of the medium, detailed in the parenthetical aside enumerating the qualities generally subsumed by the concept of television liveness. In Doane's account, liveness aligns with catas-trophe as an ideal event for television transmission: immediacy, urgency, presence, instantaneity, etc. Catastrophe and liveness are thus posited as an ideal pair. Here, and elsewhere, liveness constitutes a key concept for television studies, variously proposed as television's ontology, exposed as the medium's underlying ideology, or deposed as television's alibi for truth and objectivity (Arnheim 1958/1969; Ellis 1982; Feuer 1983; Dayan and Katz 1992). It is considered one of the defining qualities of the medium, distinguishing it in its singularity and immediacy from cinema in particular. Catastrophe emerges as a theoretical paradigm because it so neatly fulfills the imperatives of liveness. Catastrophe coverage, then, plays itself out as a category of temporal transition, in the live reportage of events that typi-cally involve human danger and, often, fatality.

The stress on liveness in these terms has been overly determined by a variety of factors. Some of these include essentializing notions of television history, the privileging of institutional discourses on broadcast journalism, or focusing on a narrow range of programming. In other cases, liveness stands in for all of televi-sion through a metonymic fallacy; that is, because television can be live, liveness is then considered to be the defining characteristic of the medium. Finally, liveness rises to significance in efforts (explicit and tacit) to cast televi-sion theory in distinction to, but on the model of, cinema apparatus theory of the 1970s, as television and film are defined in terms of their distinctive discur-sive and ideological operations.

In this chapter, I propose the need to reassess liveness, and to re-examine how it functions in familiar contexts such as television news (both everyday and catas-trophic), but also in a wider range of live programming. In some cases, history, duration and memory emerge as central constituents of television's discursive operations. In other instances, liveness is invested in representations where spatial location supersedes temporal immediacy. There are many versions of live televi-sion that have much less to do with catastrophe than with banality, space, and what I formulate as a 'television of attractions'. This latter idea adapts work on early cinema as a way of emphasizing television's proclivities for spatial display. Often these varied tendencies are co-present. The rest of this chapter offers a wide-ranging discussion of some key perspectives on liveness. In the process, ideas previously mooted in discussions of television theory – history, banality and space – appear as crucial components of the medium's capacities for liveness.

This interrogation of television liveness can be initiated by returning to the case of the *Challenger*. On CBS, as Dan Rather sat at his anchor desk that morning, waiting for more information, he announced to his audience that what they were seeing was 'a newsman vamping for time'. With this assertion, he referenced the process of putting the story together while expressing his own, temporary, loss for words. Such an avowal, exposing the process of story production, is most likely to occur during live coverage of events, especially in moments of so-called catastrophe coverage. For delivering a news story takes time, not only gathering information and data, but also formulating a narrative structure and, in the case of electronic news, putting the necessary technology in place to allow information to flow. But in the immediacy of live coverage following a so-called catastrophe, something decisive rarely occurs.

Even as the *Challenger* rose into the sky and exploded, the reaction of onlookers near the launch pad was ambiguous, as if they were uncertain about what they were witnessing.[1] The assessment of catastrophe in this case required the passage of time. The event could be definitively designated a catastrophe retrospectively, not only after it occurred, but also after sufficient time elapsed to allow for expert analysis to certify it as such. In this sense at least, catastrophe and disaster are closely tied to historical narrative. Moreover, the temporality of 'live' catastrophe is often very different for participants/victims than it is for those who witness, study, or report it. This significantly complicates the nature of the live television event and its theoretical implications. The conflation of catastrophe and television liveness too often elides temporal and spatial distinctions between the perspectives of participant-victims, witness-reporters and television viewers. In the interval of these elisions, catastrophe too readily comes to be identified with the time when 'I' learn about the event, rather than with the event's own temporal dimensions.

For example, in Penley's (1997) analysis of the *Challenger* explosion, she notes that the astronauts did not die at the moment of the explosion, but when their capsule splashed down minutes later. This fatal event was not witnessed by cameras, reporters or television viewers, and was barely discussed in the 'live' reporting following the explosion. Indeed, Penley notes that the actual time of fatality for the astronauts was not widely reported. Based on her discussion, it would seem that catastrophe is not a singular event; nor is it necessarily apparent to those who witness, record, report or receive the story. The sense, for example, that the *explosion* was the moment of fatality is not borne out for the long term, though this was certainly one of the public meanings of its continual replaying on tape on television.

Meanwhile, during the CBS coverage immediately following the explosion, Dan Rather ran out of things to say, and announced it; and yet he kept on going. The particular term he used to describe his own activity – vamping – refers to both improvisation and seduction, with the anchor making up the show as he goes along in order to hold the audience until more information, a more detailed version of the story, becomes apparent. In this regard, the use of a term identified with female seducers (vamps) is interesting, as Rather's performance preempted daytime television programming, with its confessional and performative talk shows, serial melodramas and consumerist game shows, all genres primarily associated with female viewers, especially housewives. Here, the vampish nature of television liveness and catastrophe coverage fully emerge, including a tragic, even melodramatic, narrative and the improvisational virtuosity of the news anchor.

At the center of this was the once (and only once) live launch footage, repeated over and over again. Despite its explosive and apparently definitive closure, it required the assembly of experts to elaborate a story which the footage could then be used to illustrate, specialists who could make the event speak in its full historic and catastrophic dimensions. As if to confirm the insufficiency of the 'live' footage as visible evidence, Dan Rather even secured a tabletop model of the shuttle, with detachable rocket boosters, which he used to demonstrate the sequence of events as it was presumed to have happened. The 'vamp' here was restored to his proper gender as a male playing with a model rocketship.

The very process of clarifying the nature of the catastrophe (to the extent that it was indeed clarified) rendered the footage of the launch and explosion mute on its own terms. This involved the passage of time, placing events in the past, and the ongoing production of a retrospective narrative to explain the sequence of events leading up to the explosion in different terms than those used to narrate the original live launch. The initial live image of the launch was not *a priori* a disaster, but had in a crucial sense to be made catastrophic, a status achieved through the process of narrative elaboration of a past sequence of events – an historical narrative. The *Challenger* television coverage that was most immediate, and most 'live' was also the most indeterminate, spectacular and 'vampish'. At first, there was only an image of uncertain meaning – an attraction – and an anchor performing without a script.

This is similar to other live, unplanned television events, for example the assassination attempt on President Ronald Reagan. The footage in this case was shaky and partial, and hard to read in its own right. However, it was repeated on television over and over again, with news experts narrating and interpreting the event that could not be clearly discerned by viewers, despite the evidence offered by the footage from on-the-scene news cameras. The discursive elaboration and excessive repetition was readily apparent, so much so that the sketch comedy program *Saturday Night Live* quickly offered its own parodic version of this footage.[2] In other words, catastrophe on television is not always best understood in terms of the live moment. Instead, catastrophe more typically develops through ongoing co-articulations of liveness and historicity. In the process, normatively distinct temporal and spatial categories of language and experience – proximity and distance, past and present – are brought together in relationships of mutual implication.

This intertwining of conventionally distinct modes of time and space is not restricted to catastrophe coverage, but permeates all sorts of special event, 'live' programming. Consider, for example, the first broadcast of the final episode of the situation comedy *Cheers* in Spring 1993. The screening of this episode was heavily promoted by the NBC network and its local affiliates, including live coverage of a party at the Boston bar on which the show was based. Immediately following the program, the Chicago NBC affiliate carried a report from Boston, with anchor Ron Magers declaring, 'The last episode [of *Cheers*] is *now* TV history.' The intermingling of news and entertainment programming apparent here is sufficiently familiar as to be banal. More interesting is the condensation of temporalities, as the news anchor declares in the present tense that the episode is 'now history'.

Of course, the very success of the program, enabling this sort of ballyhoo, also assured that the episode could be widely seen in the near future in network reruns and syndication. The 'historical' nature of the episode had everything to do with the show's currency for attracting audiences at the moment it was aired and with its future marketability. In addition, the historicity of the episode had already been celebrated once, at the time of the final taping, prior to its broadcast, as reported in entertainment magazine shows on television. Liveness in this context – the live report from Boston, the news anchor's comment on the episode's status as history – draws on past, present and future in highly self-conscious terms, linking textual, programming and institutional aspects of television. In such circumstances, *histoire* as a linguistic case, as story and as history comes asymptotically closer to *discours* as present-tense liveness. As a product of television's discursive and ideological practices, liveness is blatantly reconfigured through highly mediated, self-reflective narrational strategies and historicizing temporal tourniquets.

Live television in theory

My unease with received ideas of television liveness, and the privileging of catastrophe and disaster as uniquely expressive of televisuality, stems from interpretive elisions. 'Liveness' – as presence, immediacy, actuality – becomes a conceptual filter to such an extent that other discursive registers are ignored. As a result, television's pervasive discourses of history, memory and preservation are too readily dismissed, relegated to secondary status, a veneer to be stripped away from a foundational liveness. Indeed, television is widely seen as a key apparatus of popular culture which contributes to the fundamental loss of historical consciousness. Similarly, the emphasis on the temporality of liveness on television (immediacy, interruption) distracts from consideration of the medium's spatial articulations. In this regard, it may be useful to review some of the prevailing ideas about 'liveness' and television, beyond the context of news coverage of catastrophic events.

79

Caldwell notes that Marshall McLuhan introduced the foundation for the academic myth of liveness, 'when he defined the medium as an "all-at-once-ness" created by global television's erasure of time and space' (Caldwell 1995: 28). Feuer (1983) offers an initial reconsideration of liveness, emphasizing its ideological, rather than ontological, aspects. Feuer characterizes the work of Zettl as exemplary of an ontological/aesthetic approach to questions of liveness; and in response she delineates the ways in which television, far from 'live' in most literal senses, is fully in fee to elaborate technological and institutional practices of mediation. 'Clearly television is best described as a collage of film, video, and "live," all interwoven into a complex and altered time scheme' (1983: 15). Feuer provides an important critique of traditional television aesthetics. Yet she maintains the centrality of liveness as the prevailing ideology of the medium, promoting an impression of immediacy to overcome the fragmentation that would otherwise expose contradictions. Thus while she initiates a critique of liveness as ontology, she ends up elevating it as an even more potent force, as the ideological and technological sleight of hand at the heart of the medium's strategies of address. 'In terms of mode of address,' she writes, 'I have argued that notions of "liveness" lend a sense of flow which overcomes extreme fragmentation of space' (1983: 19).

Here, and elsewhere, 'liveness' became especially important in the effort to define the specificity of the television apparatus. Liveness served to characterize fundamental differences (ontological and/or ideological) between film and television as distinctive media. Given film theory's emphasis on the ideological affects of the basic cinematographic apparatus, and disposition of cinema spectators in movie theaters (Baudry 1985; Metz 1985), television in some sense *had* to be different. From this perspective, if film was *histoire* (Metz 1985; Silverman 1983), then television was *discours*; if the cinema engaged the gaze, then television attracted the glance; if cinema was strongly based on images, television was rooted in sound.[3] 'Liveness' was a key term that subsumed these alleged differences, inscribed in everything from the electronic scanning that generates the video image to the modes of production, rhetoric and address prevalent on television.[4]

These perspectives on liveness have been widely reiterated in subsequent work on television. For example, Dayan and Katz (1992) developed an influential model of media events based specifically on the pre-planned live broadcast of relatively singular events that interrupt routine television programming. This includes such diverse events as Papal visits, the Olympics, royal weddings, the moon landing, and so forth. Media events carry considerable cultural and social meaning based on the unusually large viewership they attract and the dramas of celebration, social integration and loyalty to a larger society they perform. Dayan and Katz offer what is effectively a functional-ritual interpretation and taxonomy of media events. In the process they develop a perspective on live television that is the 'flip side' of treatments of catastrophe. The pre-planned nature of media events, as they use the term, differentiates them from live news reporting of unforeseen events.

Dayan and Katz cast their discussion in terms of genres, rather than in terms of theoretical perspectives on television in relation to liveness and catastrophe. In the process they suggest relationships between different forms of liveness. At the same time, catastrophe television theory is precisely interested in the ways in which liveness always threatens to spill over into catastrophe. Thus, while it may be possible to differentiate the President Kennedy assassination from the Kennedy funeral, Dayan and Katz overlook the fact that the Kennedy visit to Dallas was initially a media event that turned into the assassination. Similarly, the televised *Challenger* explosion began as a media event in the Dayan and Katz sense, but unexpectedly erupted into what they would call a news event, or a catastrophe. Crucially, from my perspective, the distinction they offer can only be ascertained once an event is complete. In other words, one can only be certain if something is a news event or a media event (or a catastrophe or a celebration) once the event is over, closed off in the past. As such, what they offer are actually categories of historical understanding, and not inherent qualities of events as they transpire on television.

Liveness as presence and immediacy is also considered by some critics to ground the phenomenological experience of all reception, even when it comes to a prerecorded fiction series. For example, Mumford (1994) asserts the importance of the impression of liveness in relation to fiction programming and syndication:

> One feature of the television apparatus that undoubtedly works to enhance the audience's tendency to turn habitually to a specific spot on the dial is the quality of 'liveness' that attaches to every telecast and that Jane Feuer has argued allows a particular program 'to insinuate itself into our lives.' The fact that television transmission *can* occur simultaneously with the event being depicted creates the impression that every TV transmission is in some sense 'live,' regardless of its actual temporal relationship to the real-world events it purports to present. ... Ideologically, 'liveness' encourages us to accept what we see on television as, among other things, accurate – 'real' because it is 'really' happening – rather than elaborately constructed and mediated ... the experience of viewing five-day-a-week telecasts of soaps and other series is inflected by television's overall sense of liveness, intensifying the degree of intimacy already created between the habitual viewer and her favorite program.
>
> (Mumford 1994: 174)

In all of these contexts, liveness is the master term or key word that subsumes a host of other qualities and characteristics. Liveness serves as the conceptual anchor for the properties considered essentially televisual – immediacy, presence, reality affects, intimacy, and so on. However, just because television *can* be live does not mean it is always seen through this lens.

Arguments along these lines ultimately offer technology, or one aspect thereof, as ontology. One might just as well say that because television *can* be taped, there is always a residual impression that all television transmission is previously recorded. Indeed, given the ratio between live and taped programming, the range of common practices that make this distinction clear to viewers, and the routine use of video recorders to time-shift program viewing (for live and prere-corded telecasts), this seems a wholly viable position, if one really wants to specify the experience of television in singular terms.

In all of these approaches, television's presumed essential liveness, albeit ideological, overwhelms the medium's ubiquitous self-reflexive and historio-graphical discourses, and its articulations of multiple registers of time and space, manifest at all levels and in a wide range of television formats and genres. This includes such practices as laugh-tracks, or transitions to commercials and station breaks that routinely signal the medium's artifice, its discursive labor. (And these are the very kind of conventions that viewers routinely notice and often disparage, especially because they assert themselves as artifacts of institu-tional intervention within discourses that otherwise might appear more seamless.) Moreover, with routine previews of upcoming programs, including the news, included in everyday telecasts, it is difficult to imagine that many viewers maintain 'liveness' as the singular, preeminent term that defines their viewing posture vis-à-vis television. Yet scholars persist in deploying the term, foreclosing the range of theoretical approaches to understanding the appeals – aesthetic and social – of the medium.

In television news, the very idea of liveness is strongly associated with partic-ular discursive strategies for recounting events – first person, present tense, direct address to camera, and so on (Feuer 1983; Morse 1986). This is combined with an insistence on a privileged spatial and temporal proximity to events thus recounted. Reporters are usually near the site where events have taken place; and the events have often occurred recently, and are sometimes even ongoing as the reporter speaks. The importance of spatial proximity – even at the expense of the video images that are supposedly sacrosanct in television news – is enacted when stations have reporters from distant locations file reports by phone in cases when a video-feed is not available. In these instances, a voice emanating from somewhere in the vicinity of the event, even prerecorded, is considered a better sign of liveness than the report of an anchor who may be reading the news at the very same time the reported event is transpiring, but from a greater distance.

This was demonstrated in an extreme form during the Persian Gulf War, when CNN had three reporters located in a hotel in the center of Baghdad when the allied forces launched the initial air attack on 16 January 1991. Through the course of the first night of the war, attention focused on the reports they filed relating what they were seeing and hearing as the bombing continued. On this basis CNN promoted itself as having authoritative command of the news flow as the war proceeded. However, what is so startling about the coverage was the nature of the information available to the reporters and the ways in which CNN promotion of their live reportage was cast in terms of history. Both of these aspects of the reporting were expressed in self-reflexive terms. As a result, the 'catastrophic' interruption (in the global political arena and on television) represented by the Gulf War became the occasion for quite literal meditations on the place of television news.

From the earliest coverage, reporting strategies were extremely self-conscious about the act of reporting, and emphasized the conditions of production and reception of the reporting as it was taking place. The CNN reporters discussed where they were located in the hotel, and described the night sky filled with tracers and explosions resembling fireworks and fireflies. Despite the constant reports about the apparently successful progress of the 'strategic' attack that they were witnessing, they also acknowledged that they could not say what the targets were, or assess the accuracy of the air strike. After all, it was dark, and they were miles from the actual targets. Yet their more persistent speculative, impressionistic and positive reports became the basis for a general sense of optimism regarding the success of the bombing as a surgical strike, a sentiment that was relayed through CNN reporting during the evening and into the first Pentagon press conference.[5]

The deployment of as much information as possible, no matter how indefinite, secured status for CNN as the 'one source' to which others were turning for information, and defined its commanding historical vantage on the war just as it was starting. At the same time, the fact that the CNN's rolling reports were being followed by important political figures around the world – from the White House and the Pentagon to the Middle East – was an integral part of the news stories. This was both a self-elevating and a self-congratulatory strategy, again linking liveness and history; and hinged on the felicitous spatial location of three CNN reporters.

When the bombing began, three CNN reporters in a Baghdad hotel were able to secure and maintain an open phone line, communicating about the war from the perspective of witnesses in the center of the action, behind enemy lines. The very fact that they occupied this geographical position was an essential element of their reporting, drawing attention to their unique situation. Through the course of their reports, in the context of ongoing discussion about the success of the air strike, the technologies of reporting and of waging war were closely affiliated. The unprecedented deployment of technology to wage war and the (alleged) resulting precision bombing came to be identified with CNN's feat of precision telephony. Both of these technological deployments were described as unprecedented historical achievements. Meanwhile, the actuality of live television journalism boiled down to nothing much to say, even if everything that was said was construed as having momentous impact by virtue of being near the events, live and of historic proportions. The war and its reporting mutually reconstructed and supported one another as significant events, a perspective reinforced by the US-based CNN anchors.

Yet for all this expertise and successful reporting, the live reportage also suggests the inadequacy of the vantage point on events from the inside of the Al-Rashid Hotel. While they were in the middle of the city under attack, the reporters had little access to information beyond what they could see and hear from their hotel room, which became the focus of their reports. At the same time, all the talk about where they were situated in the hotel, with its sheer weight of literal description, threatened to unravel the value of what they reported. At times it seemed like nearly all the reporters could do was to describe their own situation as the war proceeded elsewhere, around them. For example: 'To paint the picture for you where we are physically, of where we are right now: we are in the hall on the floor and we can look through open doors on either side.'

The case of the Gulf War, like the *Challenger* explosion, offers an exemplary moment of live television reporting in the disaster mode, interrupting routine prime-time television in favor of continuous coverage without commercial interruption (though commercials were added by the second day of the war). Ultimately, the meaning of the immediacy of the live, catastrophic news resided in the self-promotional value that CNN could assert on the basis of the live reporting from the midst of the air strike: 'we were there'. But this liveness was simultaneously present and past: a function of both spatio-temporal proximity (presence) and historical achievement (past). Moreover, the historical (significant and unprecedented) act of live reporting from the center of Baghdad resulted in substantial broadcasting of such details as where the reporters were crouching in the room, which direction they were facing, and even what they had had for dinner. The live events that received the most detailed reports found fullest expression in the banality of ordinary actions, and in the ongoing verbal details of spatial orientation.

Rethinking liveness: the attractions of space

The importance of spatial representation to ideas about liveness is inscribed in television history. An often recounted event from the first broadcast of the landmark television show *See it Now*, broadcast in 1951, involved Edward R. Murrow presenting views of the Atlantic and Pacific Oceans on screen at the same time. Here, space functions as spectacle, a visual attraction transmitted in the present tense of live television. The temporality of these images in terms of when they were shown was far less pertinent than the presentation of two discrete and distant places being shown simultaneously. This particular pair of images also displays the national space of North American network television coverage at the time. Crucially, this image also calls attention to itself as a technologically enabled, mediated representation, by showing something that no one person could 'really' see. The juxtaposition of the two oceans that border the United States (from sea to shining sea) demonstrates the technical and representational prowess of the apparatus – live or otherwise. The impressiveness of live transmission hinges – in this example historically, but also in much of contemporary live television – on the spatial pyrotechnics of images that function as visual spectacle.

Here, and in other contexts, television begins to define its appeal according to the logic of attractions theorized by Gunning (1986) in relation to early cinema. For Gunning, early cinema is characterized by an absence of diegesis, fundamental discontinuity and an emphasis on spectacle for its own sake. The cinema of attractions is exhibitionist, exemplified by the recurring direct looks into the camera by performers; it solicits the attention of spectators by displaying visibility for its own sake. Television's ability to *show* things, and its interest therein, has been unduly muted by theories of the glance, of the medium's reliance on sound over image to convey meaning and regulate spectatorship, and of liveness as a fundamentally temporal category.[6] Yet television has demonstrated an abiding interest in visual spectacle for its own sake, in the televisual attraction.

Rethinking the medium in these terms provides a framework for reconsidering some forms of liveness on television, though attractions are hardly restricted to live television or to non-fiction programming formats. It accounts, for example, for the insistent replaying of footage such as the *Challenger* explosion, the assassination attempt on Ronald Reagan, or the self-annihilating 'bomb's eye' views of attacks on Iraq during the first Gulf War. Crucially, these *recorded* images, as attractions, are historicized, rather than enlivened, by the processes of narrativization which are brought to bear on them. In addition, the concept of a television of attractions accounts for diverse forms of live television that are decidedly non-catastrophic, represented by such programming as votes in the US House of Representatives telecast on C-SPAN, Home Shopping Club, and weather channels that broadcast continuous live radar images without commentary.

In all of these cases, relatively static images are shown for a considerable duration, often with little or no variation. Consider, for example, the way C-SPAN often presents voting in the House of Representatives. For routine votes in Congress, C-SPAN displays a static shot of the House from a single camera position in extreme long shot. Typically, the room is all but empty, as representatives sporadically appear, almost indistinguishable in the depth of the frame, to cast their votes. A running tally of the vote is superimposed on the screen, along with information about the time remaining before the vote is final. A non-diegetic classical music track is played over the image, but there is no voice-over, no commentary, no debate and no expressed conflict (which is displaced to the ongoing but unpredictable change in numbers on the screen tallying the vote). Here the sparse image speaks for itself as sheer spectacle, however minimal, of the North American democratic process. What is important for present purposes is that this image is held on screen for television viewers to watch, even though there is apparently nothing much to be seen or heard.

C-SPAN is not alone in purveying live television in a minimalist visual style. The Home Shopping Club, especially in its first decade, provides another example of live television programming that diverges considerably from the catastrophe or disaster model, while exhibiting spare visual aesthetics. The Home Shopping Club, a television shopping channel, offers items for viewers to purchase directly 24 hours a day. Until the mid-1990s, items could only be purchased while they were shown on screen, displayed for consumer scrutiny, with the predominance of extreme close-ups (of, for example, a ring, a collectible figurine, a baseball trading card, or a computer being offered for sale). Each item was shown in a series of tight shots that went on for several minutes at a time. Products were accompanied by graphic titles that provided information for the viewers about the item, product code, number, price, the toll-free number to call for purchase, and so on.

For smaller items, especially jewelry, the program availed itself of specific, visible production equipment to show off the merchandise to best advantage. Early on, this included the use of a knitting needle protruding into the frame, jiggling pendants and gold chains, to create light reflections to enhance the visual appearance. Tabletop rotating platforms, mirrored stands, refraction and star filters, and the intrusion of a model's hand were also common techniques. When this equipment first appeared in the mid-1980s, program hosts would often comment on the beautiful effects it created. One by one, each product was presented to be viewed and, it was hoped, purchased, by viewers. Along with the host's continual patter about the singular qualities of each item, and testimonial phone calls from viewer-shoppers, the Home Shopping Club presented a succession of visual attractions in such a manner as to encourage viewers to buy what they saw (White 1992).

With these particular strategies of visual and temporal representation to sell its products, the Home Shopping Club established its own internal flow through the spectacle of commodity space-time. The prevailing shot scale was determined by the size of the items being sold, while temporal duration was influenced by a combination of inventory stock and the number of calls a particular item attracted. The time available to purchase an item was not only limited, but was also often represented by an on-screen timer counting down the minutes left to phone in and make a purchase. Products moved on and off the screen every four to fifteen minutes: now you see it, now you don't; now you can buy it, now you can't. Narrative comes in obliquely, in the voice-over phone calls that viewer-shoppers carry on with program hosts.

The Home Shopping Club is characterized by a fundamental discontinuity, absence of diegesis and an emphasis on spectacle. While these qualities have been specifically, if variously, associated with 'liveness' and 'catastrophe' in the context of television studies, they are also the strategies of the early cinema, a non-live medium, described by Gunning as a cinema of attractions. Along these lines, the Home Shopping Club deploys exhibitionism and visual display to aggressively solicit the attention of all viewers in line with the consumerist exhibitionism of television in general. The succession of attractions – live images of merchandise – however minimal the visual repertoire, is designed to solicit attention, to 'shock' viewers into buying what they see displayed on television.

C-SPAN and Home Shopping Club are only two examples of recent, live US television that contribute to an understanding of television attractions. The banality of these examples, the near absence of conventional narrative, and the frankly 'boring' formats are important to the overall conceptualization not only of the attraction, but also of liveness, which is too often explored in much more compelling dramatic and historical contexts. By contrast, Congressional votes and Home Shopping Club are predominantly live, but they are hardly catastrophic, and have little to do with fatality. On the whole, these programs produce much weaker diegetic effects and affective responses than network news coverage of catastrophes. But in the contemporary formation of television practice, C-SPAN and Home Shopping Club are, in real terms, equally significant examples of liveness. As a result, it is crucial to reconceptualize liveness not only in conjunction with history, but also in tandem with the concept of television attractions – including banality, spectacle, space and abstraction.

For Gunning, the fascination of the cinema of attractions is closely connected to the spectacle of modern life itself, including the very technology of cinema used to display images which would draw audiences in through the combination of illusionary power and exoticism. In other words, the appeal of the attraction is linked to modernity and new technologies of representation.

As a medium which quite immediately commodifies temporal and spatial flow, television transforms the nature of the attraction, tying it even more closely to contemporary consumer culture for some viewers. The space-time of the television attraction is produced in relation to the commodity space-time of television itself. This is literally played out in Home Shopping Club, when the time of product display is coequal with the time it is available for purchase, and the visual space is defined in proportion to the scale of the item. Thus, if a sweater is being sold, a host/model will fill the screen, while if a ring is up for sale, a model's hand will occupy the same framed space.

The television attraction also introduces the possibility of something on the order of a televisual 'accursed share' (Bataille 1988). Bataille's concept of the accursed share refers to the surplus of energy that any system, natural or cultural, generates, an excess beyond the needs of functional utility that must be expended. I am adapting this concept in relation to television to focus on instances where the television image offers an excessive visibility and visuality that does not conform to the commodity space-time of regular programming divisions, or directly serve the interests of narrative, live or historical. This excess of meaning can occur even when the visual attraction is characterized by formal minimalism – such as House votes on C-SPAN, for example – or through the excessive redundancy typical of catastrophe and disaster coverage. All of these images underscore television's preeminent ability to *show* things, live and historical, however banal. This capacity for excess is amplified with the expansion of contexts of distribution and reception enabled by satellite and cable television systems on a global scale. For what constitutes an image 'for use' in the logic of television space-time for viewers in one place may function very differently for viewers in other places who have ready access to the same images. Two examples from European television can help clarify this point. Both involve regular live telecasting of highly routinized and mechanized images in a fixed minimalist visual repertoire, obviously deployed for specific purposes. At the same time, both are daily programs available for viewing (at least in 1994) on cable systems throughout Europe. One was on a channel from Austria, the other from Spain.

Almost every weekday morning, an Austrian channel featured a one-hour program called *Wetterpanorama*. The program consists of a succession of shots each lasting about two minutes. The images are captured by remote, robotic cameras slowly panning back and forth (about 140 degrees) disclosing the landscapes of spa or ski resort villages in Austria. Graphic titles at the bottom of the screen provide information about current weather conditions, snowfall amounts and a phone number to call the resort; intermittently, a schematic map of a particular Austrian region appears on screen with the names and locations of the upcoming landscapes. The soundtrack accompaniment is Austrian/Alpine folk music. Depending on weather conditions, the camera enclosure might be fogged or wet from rain; in heavy snows, it is virtually impossible to see anything. But in every instance, the camera perspective on the landscape is identical.

The instrumental 'use value' of these images seems apparent. Someone in the immediate region, or with ample free time and money, could evaluate climatic conditions in different resorts to decide where he/she might want to go skiing that afternoon, or the upcoming weekend. *Wetterpanorama* in this sense functions as an extended commercial promotion for resorts in direct proportion to immediate weather conditions. At the same time, these 'live' images are distributed via satellite across a geographic area that far exceeds their instrumental or referential value (I was watching them in Helsinki, Finland). Further, they occupy telecast time equally for all viewers, whether or not they have any interest in going to any of the places on display. Moreover, the formal aesthetics of presentation are fully in line with the materialist aesthetics of 1970s avant-garde cinema – with the identical framing of various locales, the random cutting in and out of images conveyed by an ever-slow panning camera revealing an empty landscape, the similarities and differences between the multiple landscapes, the absence of human action within the frame, paucity of narrational material, and the materiality of the apparatus itself when raindrops or fog limit the scope of vision and call attention to the box containing the camera.

These images offer both nothing and everything to the viewer who is not planning a spa weekend. In all their stark, mechanized liveness they emphasize the spatial reach of the representational apparatus of television. In this sense

television is a medium about images and spaces, and not preeminently determined by temporality and 'liveness'. The images also offer a fantasy about travel
and mobility, whether or not it is actualized by a viewer. Finally, they enact an
abstracted aesthetics of vision and seeing enabled by, but by no means requiring,
live transmission. At the same time, as television programming goes, this is
quite simply *boring*; nothing happens, except weather in places remote from
most of the viewers. It comprises an excess of meaning for the program, beyond
its promotional value for the various resorts included.

At almost the exact same time, weekday mornings, a television station in
Spain airs a morning news program, including traffic information, for
commuters, *Trafico*. The traffic coverage is provided by live signals sent from
remote, stationary cameras located in a number of commuter arteries in several
major cities in Spain. The images were initially in black and white, but more
recently were changed to color. Throughout the news program, the station
offers traffic reporting in segments that involve cutting from camera to camera,
including graphic titles to indicate the time. Along the lines of *Wetterpanorama*,
the intended instrumental value of the images is relatively clear: if you are
about to leave your house and travel on commuter routes, you can see current
traffic conditions. For those already en route, the information is inaccessible.
For those staying home, or traveling in other areas, the information is of no
immediate use. At the same time, the mechanized, remote, live images underscore television's primacy as a spatial-representational apparatus, its ability to
show conditions, live and otherwise, from a variety of vantage points. In the
black and white version, and with stationary rather than moving images, *Trafico*
is even more visually spare than *Wetterpanorama*. This segment of the news is
also liable to instigate a slightly different range of fantasy. Especially for those at
home watching television, it is a fantasy that might confirm and reassure
viewers who do not have to navigate through or around current traffic jams – a
fantasy of domestic leisure. But it is also, in its stark minimalism, an image of
urban activity and mobility, in this case made literal by the pictures of drivers in
their cars.

Wetterpanorama and *Trafico* may seem rather far afield from the more central
concerns of catastrophe or history raised at the beginning of this chapter.
However, they are central to the larger reconsideration of the notion of 'liveness' on television and the ways in which the term has been too readily
disintricated from its historicity, spatiality and banality. The live images at the
center of both these programs – as well as in other examples mentioned above –
are striking in the ways in which they link routinization, mechanization, liveness
and space to mundane aesthetic and formal practices. However, in their very
banality these practices highlight television's singular ability to show things, its
involvement in attractions and spectacles of the everyday variety.[7] Beyond the
specific, meaningful images of the US democratic process at work, morning
drive conditions in Spanish urban centers, objects to purchase, or quaint resort
village landscapes in Austria, these attractions and spectacles of everyday life

are available to all viewers who have the particular channel on their broadcast or cable system. This is the case whether the particular viewers are targeted or not by the apparent intended purport of the program.

Liveness as an essentially discursive practice is thus a multiform phenomenon on television. Catastrophe and disaster can hardly be considered the paradigmatic manifestation of television's foundational ideological liveness. On the contrary, catastrophic liveness is routinely imbricated with the historical dimensions of events and their narrative production in these terms. Liveness-as-attraction displays television's exhibitionist propensities, its proclivity to materialist minimalism as visual aesthetic, the importance of spatial representation as a significant component of liveness, and the ordinariness of visual spectacle as part of everyday television culture.

Notes

1   I diverge here from the interpretation of this footage by Patricia Mellencamp (1990), who reads the reaction of McAullife's parents as knowing in a glance that their daughter (the teacher who joined the astronauts on the shuttle) was gone. I construe their initial response as one of anxious uncertainty.

2   In the case of *Saturday Night Live* (SNL), the character of 'Buckwheat' (originally from *The Little Rascals*, Buckwheat was one of the 'regular' characters portrayed by actor Eddie Murphy on *SNL*) was 'gunned down' on the program, an event depicted with pre-filmed video footage directly imitating the 'live' video of the Reagan assassination attempt. This parodic footage was replayed constantly during the course of one *SNL* episode.

3   Altman (1984), Ellis (1982) and Flitterman-Lewis (1987), among many others, exemplify these tendencies in the development of television theory.

4   Caldwell (1995) discusses and critiques many of these same issues in a slightly different context; see especially pp. 22–32 and 336–57.

5   A more detailed account of this reporting is offered in White (1994).

6   Again, in different terms, Caldwell (1995) has offered critiques of these positions. His theory of televisuality emphasizes the medium's interest in showing things visually.

7   The Internet has proliferated sites that offer views of weather or traffic, akin to the programs I discuss in this chapter. In these instances, webcams and the World Wide Web extend the phenomenon in question, also including tourist sites. There are some differences between how these function on television and the Internet, however. For example, on the computer, the viewer/user may be able to choose what to see from the available repertoire of webcam locations, and for how long he/she views the site, which may or may not involve a moving camera, views of varying temporal duration, and so on. In some cases, a viewer can to some degree even manipulate the camera perspective. Thus the websites that offer landscape views do not have the same sense of randomness of encounter with other spaces that television versions provide, nor do they have the same sense of regulated spatial-temporal access.

Bibliography

Altman, R. (1986) 'Television/Sound', in T. Modleski (ed.), *Studies in Entertainment: Critical Approaches to Mass Culture*, Bloomington: Indiana University Press, pp. 39–54.

Arnheim, R. (1958/1969) 'A Forecast of Television', in *Film Art*, London: Faber and Faber.

Bataille, G. (1988) *The Accursed Share*, vol. 1, R. Hurley (trans.), New York: Zone Books.

Baudry, J.-L. (1985) 'The Ideological Effects of the Basic Cinematic Apparatus', in B. Nichols (ed.), *Movies and Methods, Volume II*, Berkeley: University of California Press, pp. 531–42.

Caldwell, J. (1995) *Televisuality: Style, Crisis, and Authority in American Television*, New Brunswick, NJ: Rutgers University Press.

Dayan, D. and Katz, E. (1992) *Media Events: The Live Broadcasting of History*, Cambridge, Mass.: Harvard University Press.

Doane, M.A. (1990) 'Information, Crisis, Catastrophe', in P. Mellencamp (ed.), *Logics of Television: Essays in Cultural Criticism*, Bloomington: Indiana University Press, pp. 222–39.

Ellis, J. (1982) *Visible Fictions: Cinema, Television, Video*, London: Routledge.

Feuer, J. (1983) 'The Concept of Live Television: Ontology as Ideology', in E.A. Kaplan (ed.), *Regarding Television*, Frederick, Md.: University Publications of America/American Film Institute, pp. 12–22.

Flitterman-Lewis, S. (1987) 'Psychoanalysis, Film, and Television', in R. Allen (ed.), *Channels of Discourse*, Chapel Hill: University of North Carolina Press, pp. 172–210.

Gunning, T. (1986) 'The Cinema of Attractions: Early Film, its Spectator, and the Avant-garde', *Wide Angle*, 8:3–4, pp. 63–70.

Mellencamp, P. (1990) 'TV Time and Catastrophe, or *Beyond the Pleasure Principle* of Television', in *Logics of Television: Essays in Cultural Criticism*, Bloomington: Indiana University Press, pp. 240–66.

Metz, C. (1985) 'Story/Discourse: A Note on Two Kinds of Voyeurism', in B. Nichols (ed.), *Movies and Methods, Volume II*, Berkeley: University of California Press, pp. 543–9.

Morse, M. (1986) 'The Television News Personality and Credibility', in T. Modleski (ed.), *Studies in Entertainment: Critical Approaches to Mass Culture*, Bloomington: Indiana University Press, pp. 55–79.

Mumford, L. (1994) 'Stripping on the Girl Channel: Lifetime, *thirtysomething*, and Television Form', *Camera Obscura*, 33–34, pp. 167–90.

Penley, C. (1997) *Nasa/Trek: Popular Science and Sex in America*, New York: Verso.

Silverman, K. (1983) *The Subject of Semiotics*, New York: Oxford University Press.

White, M. (1992) *Tele-Advising: Therapeutic Discourse in American Television*, Chapel Hill: University of North Carolina Press.

—— (1994) 'Site Unseen: An Analysis of CNN's *War in the Gulf*', in S. Jeffords and L. Rabinovitz (eds), *Seeing Through the Media*, New Brunswick, NJ: Rutgers University Press, pp. 121–41.

Part II

WORK, LEISURE AND THE SPACES IN-BETWEEN

5

THE MARKETABLE
NEIGHBORHOOD
Commercial Latinidad in New York's East Harlem

Arlene Dávila

> The best way to reach Hispanic consumers is through the use of 8
> sheets (6' x 12' posters) right in their own communities. The
> Hispanic market is America's fastest growing consumer segment,
> expanding faster than the general population. ... It makes sense
> to be visible in their communities.
>
> (Vista Media, 'Hispanic American Marketing')

In recent years, New York's East Harlem, also known as 'El Barrio', an historically
important stronghold of Puerto Rican and Latino New York, has increasingly
been coveted by developers, and by old and new residents. Fueling this interest in
el Barrio are rising rents and an increasingly tight real estate market attracting
new residential and commercial tenants to predominantly black and Latino upper
Manhattan neighborhoods such as Harlem, the South Bronx and Washington
Heights. State Federal government policies, like the Upper Manhattan
Empowerment Zone, for their part have served as catalysts for outside development, putting pressure on local businesses and residents.[1] Even the politics of
multiculturalism has helped erode the borders that once maintained these
communities as ethnic enclaves, rendering their once despised differences into
potential ethnic or historical attractions. Consequently, throughout upper
Manhattan communities, Latinos are now placed at the center of numerous
struggles as they debate their future as Latino/a strongholds or as gentrified neighborhoods. At stake here is the meaning of the so-called Latinization of US cities,
when the dis-location and displacement of Latino populations is simultaneous
with and even expedited by these processes. Moreover, the present struggles are as
revealing of contemporary Latino cultural politics as they are of the place of
culture in the structuring of space.

Outdoor advertising is centrally relevant to current transformations. As El
Barrio's landscape becomes more uniform, these ubiquitous signs take on other
aspects, as registers which inscribe meaning onto space. The kind of products
being advertised, the different audiences alluded to, and the language and cultural

references contained in the ads, are all signs that communicate meaning alongside
that expressed by murals, flags, chain stores and other markings of space. They
indicate the kind of neighborhood we are entering, the people that inhabit it,
their potential likes, tastes and ethnic backgrounds. More poignantly, outdoor ads
are illustrative of the identities that the market invests in particular neighborhoods, summoning us to inquire how they may be affecting or becoming
intertwined with current transformations in El Barrio.

The high concentration of outdoor advertisements in El Barrio is neither a
new nor an uncontested development. Given the area's propensity to be
targeted by the alcohol and tobacco industries, these ads have in fact been a
bone of contention among both residents and critics alike. On the one hand,
they are shunned for commercializing ethnic neighborhoods, for commodifying
space, travel and movement in similar ways that other types of site-specific
advertising, such as ambient TV, now cannibalize activities like waiting or
lounging (McCarthy 2001). Conversely, because of their public nature, outdoor
ads are seen to constitute a relatively more open medium for interaction and
resistance by consumers than other media (Jackson and Thrift 1995). In
contrast to television or print ads, outdoor ads can be defaced, written over and
transformed in ways that are publicly visible beyond the confines of the viewing
moment. Obviously, then, advertising and commercialization have complex and
contradictory meanings and effects that evidently will be at play in El Barrio.
Yet it is not simply the commercialization of urban space in East Harlem that I
seek to problematize in this chapter. Rather, it is its effects and relationships
with other visual forms and modes of signification through which residents have
built community and inscribed meaning into their neighborhood. I am
concerned specifically with advertising in relation to street art, primarily murals
and writing or graffiti. These street art forms have long served as visual markers
of Latinidad, functioning as mediums of remembrance, protest, celebration, in
addition to providing an important income-generating activity for some local
residents. However, they are now increasingly affected by the commercial
competition over space.

Indeed, gentrification may be rendering El Barrio less distinct by the type of
shops, restaurants, street vendors and public architecture (such as *casitas* –
brightly colored little houses evoking Caribbean architecture) that signaled it as
Latino, but it has seemingly not reduced its commercial treatment as 'Latino'
space, providing another dimension to current cultural politics of space there.
Advertising, after all, operates more in the realm of images, symbols and ideas,
and of audiences constructed on the basis of the need for niche-market
consumers, and less on the particular characteristics of specific constituencies.
The placement of ads in El Barrio is also an outcome of the growing popularity
of targeted and segmented marketing as part of the advertisers' struggle for
eyeballs, which has taken them onto the streets and has led to the targeting of
more specific constituencies. These trends, combined with cheaper rates for
advertising in black and Latino neighborhoods, have led to the posting of

ethnic-specific ads throughout the area, from storefronts to any visible wall, thus publicly marking one's entrance to an ethnically marked urban space. The number of outdoor ads in Spanish, full of putatively Latino themes, is quickly noticeable along 96th Street and Lexington Avenue at the edge of East Harlem. They openly declare that one is entering El Barrio. This is in direct contrast to the new cafés and renovated buildings that may make it inadvertently pass for any other strip in the city.

In this chapter, I examine the marketing and commercialization of urban space in El Barrio, and suggest that these processes involve less a contest over the signification of outdoor surfaces or of East Harlem's public identity as a Latin neighborhood, and more one over who is involved in its definition, and for what ends. Put simply, I highlight a central aspect of contemporary processes of gentrification in urban cities: that is, when properly marketed, ethnicity is always a recourse for particular culture industries, such as ethnic-driven advertising. What concerns me here is the different ends to which it is deployed, the politics that are advanced, and the people and interests that are involved in the different economies that it sustains. Indeed, as Zukin (1995), Sassen (1998), Holston and Appadurai (1999) among others have shown, 'culture' in contemporary cities is increasingly an instrument in the entrepreneurial strategies of government and businesses, serving both as a means of selling, framing and structuring space and as a medium for contesting such practices to reclaim space and advance alternative meanings. Its variety of manifestations, however, are not always fully problematized and distinguished in the literature, where there is a great need for situated examinations of the uses of culture within the range of cultural entrepreneurial strategies and discourses that are promoted by corporations, residents and government policies. Instead, the trend is to conflate culture with such disparate domains as heritage, architecture, high art, advertising, malls and entertaining venues, in ways that do more to veil than to expose the different dynamics affecting the production, circulation and consumption of culture.

The concept of culture is obviously one of the most contested terms in the social sciences, and I do not claim to be able to document each and every one of this concept's reverberations or definitions that coexist in the plans for the future development of El Barrio.[2] I do, however, seek to call attention to the contest between marketable ethnicity and more politicized manifestations in El Barrio, both of which are constituted and deployed materially and discursively to frame and contest space, and are recurrent in debates over gentrification, as they are throughout US cities. The examination of these processes requires that we look at the different uses and meanings vested in outdoor surfaces by, among others, residents, shopkeepers, muralists and marketers in relation to larger struggles over the neighborhood's identity and meaning. In this chapter, I consider outdoor marketers and street artists, and in particular the work of James de la Vega, one of the area's most visible outdoor artists. I argue that despite their different approaches to the neighborhood, marketers, shopkeepers

and street artists share a similar interest in publicly asserting Latinos' perma-
nence and existence in the face of the ongoing forces of gentrification. Indeed,
sometimes they even work in tandem, blurring the line between street art and
commercial art, but always leading to the ethnicization and commercialization
of East Harlem, processes that run in parallel. The important difference
between these systems of signification, however, is the objects and treatment of
culture, with one promoting marketable ethnicity and commercial interests,
and the other seeking validation and participation, and the promotion of local
artists and voices. How these processes affect the neighborhood's identity and
the different ends to which such identity is being deployed are the issues to
which I now turn.

Space vendors: marketers, speculators and shopkeepers

Marketers have traditionally coveted ethnic neighborhoods for placement of
their outdoor advertising.[3] These neighborhoods have cheaper placement rates
for ads, as well as an aggregate of highly concentrated populations who,
presumed to be ethnically and linguistically homogeneous, provide a supposedly
large and accessible base of consumers. Today, however, ethnic neighborhoods
are even more desired by marketers due to their growing interest in highly
targeted outdoor advertising, helped in large part by the work of specialized
outdoor marketing companies such as TDI/Infinity and Vista. In recent years,
these companies have grown increasingly standardized along advertising
industry conventions, segmenting and measuring their markets, for instance in
ways that have afforded them greater visibility as a legitimate and effective
advertising alternative. According to the Outdoor Advertising Association of
America (OAAA), outdoor advertising expenditure reached $5.2 billion in
2001, with a growth rate of approximately 10 per cent a year during the last
decade – a faster pace of growth than other sectors of the industry
(www.OAAA.org, 2001). Outdoor advertisers now count with syndicated
measurements of their reach and with new means for tracking and mapping
neighborhoods for target marketing. More important, they have developed
innovative tactics to secure the exclusive right to sell outdoor space. This has
been achieved through the establishment of contracts with landlords, private
companies and the government, granting them the exclusive sale and commercial use of a variety of private and public venues in the city. In yet another
example of the ubiquity of 'privately owned public space' (Kayden et al. 2000),
advertisements can now cover entire subways and buses, and when there is
seemingly no space available, companies can readily adapt the urban landscape
to their benefit, installing the needed street furniture, such as telephone booths
and bus shelters, to put up their ads.[4]

Developments such as these have greatly facilitated outdoor marketers'
objectives and promise of providing maximum exposure to a large range of products, or in industry lingo, 'neighborhood penetration', at a fraction of the rate

charged by broadcast media.[5] The ensuing outcome is the increased commodification of travel and movement, as the placement of television monitors in public spaces commodifies the act of waiting (McCarthy 2001). Meanwhile, the promise of maximum coverage is evidenced in the slogan for TDI/Infinity, one of the largest outdoor companies to target Latinos. Presenting itself as the only medium able to overcome differences in language, style and taste among Latinos, it proclaims that 'no matter which radio stations they tune into, whether they watch Spanish or English-language television or what newspapers they read ... [an outdoor ad] meets 6 out of 10 Hispanics face-to-face in their neighborhoods each month'![6] This coverage is further expanded through the simultaneous sponsorship of public festivals and events. Indeed, one company advertising representative calculated that the TDI/Latino promotion during the 2000 Puerto Rican Day Parade had reached an excess of two million people, simply through ads strategically placed on subway exteriors, phone kiosks and street walls throughout El Barrio.

The largest beneficiaries here are, obviously, speculators and outdoor advertisers rather than many of the local shopkeepers on whose walls the ads are posted. A longstanding merchant, owner of one of the 'farmacias Latinas' (known for the numerous services they provide for their customers, from fax service, to copies, money orders, lottery tickets, phone cards, religious paraphernalia and medical advice), told me that he had been selling his walls to outdoor advertisers for ten years for only $50 every six months. When I alerted him to how much more money he could charge, the old man did not flinch or show surprise and quickly dismissed me by insisting that 'a wall is a wall, people want to make a penny for everything. I don't care.' It would not surprise me to learn that other vendors are equally underpaid for their building walls. Indeed, the launch of the TDI/Latino promotion responds to this kind of opportunity for profit. With this new unit, this global outdoor advertising company can stake a stronger claim to neighborhoods like East Harlem and other Latino bases in the city by acquiring 'Latino wall' through the establishment of exclusive contracts with the owners of the most visible and hence profitable neighborhood spaces.

Not surprisingly, the unit is spearheaded by two Latinos. A common trend in global marketing is to achieve immediate expertise in selling to culturally different constituencies by hiring expert personnel from the areas. It is headed by Joel, a Cuban-American from New Jersey, and Mike, a young Ecuadorian marketer from Queens, both of whom stated their determination to increase their company control and exclusive sale of Latino outdoor space. True to their role as representatives of 'their' Latino community, they described their work as one of representing Latino culture, through popular representations turned into ethnic knowledges, as well as through ethnic assertion. Indeed, as with other culturally targeted advertising, outdoor ads can also be seen as public statements, and a gauge to measure advertisers' recognition of minority consumers, long neglected as an advertising-unworthy population. In this tenor, covering Latino neighborhoods with 'the right kind of advertising' was a gauge of empowerment and recognition. They were especially concerned with placing ethnically sensitive ads, especially 'elegant' (more costly) ads that would supplant the stereotypical cigarette and beer advertising which has long dominated minority spaces.

These claims are at best tenuous if we consider that such measures of empowerment are first and foremost beneficial to corporations, not to Latinos, and that they are only sustained by dominant images of Latinos as poverty-stricken, crime-ridden and unworthy consumers. Indeed, Latinos have come a long way in the eyes of advertising executives, yet, as I note elsewhere, Latinos and Latino neighborhoods are coveted in so far as they promise them a contained and cheaper venue for their ads (Dávila 2001). In other words, their commercial treatment is concomitant with their consideration of Latinos and other minorities as second-class consumers, undeserving of the kind of advertising investments that other population segments receive.[7] Hence the dominance of cheaper outdoor ad formats for addressing this constituency. Latino outdoor marketers are well aware of these dynamics, knowing that it is not advertising density but *advertising quality* that provides a measurement for advertising spending parity.

The result of this targeted marketing effort is the Latinization of El Barrio's landscape through advertisements in Spanish and/or full of ethnic-sensitive maxims and images. Johnny Walker, for example, touts 'con el buen gusto se nace' and 'se ve que sabes', associating the taste for whisky with that for one's roots. Meanwhile, Tecate beer reminds Latinos that Spanish is better than English with 'Cerveza es mejor que beer', and milk advertisers appeal to Latinas' supposedly greater maternal instinct through grandmothers that prompt us with 'Y usted, les dio suficiente leche hoy?' or, 'Did you give your loved ones enough milk today?' And when Latinidad is not directly marketed through language, it is indexed through 'urban style' ads, synonymous with black and Latino urban culture: Air Jordans, Converse, Newport cigarettes and hip-hop. Indeed, East Harlem, along with the South Bronx and Sunset Park among other places, are marked as 'Latino' in outdoor advertising maps and routinely included in Hispanic marketing tours, where they are shown to and paraded for prospective outdoor marketing clients, and depending on their needs, sold as undifferentiated spaces whose value and commonality reside in their aggregates of Latino residents, or else as hubs for particular Latino sub-nationalities. Through arbitrary assignments, the same neighborhood may hence be described as a perfect target to reach Mexicans, Puerto Ricans or Dominicans in ways that have little to do with the ethnic make-up of particular neighborhoods, and more to do with the needs of particular advertisers. It was most likely in this spirit that the young Latino market tour leader, who led me through Brooklyn's Sunset Park in Summer 1999, stated confidently that he was able to distinguish between these neighborhoods by the colors displayed in their storefronts: green for Mexicans, blue for Dominicans and red for Puerto Ricans. This arbitrary assessment, most likely based on an incorrect assumption from which colors are most featured on the flags of these countries, evidences how in the hands of outdoor marketers the content and meaning of 'Latino' and 'Latinness' are constantly shifting according to the needs of particular advertisers. The effects of these strategies are amply evident in El Barrio, where it is common to see ads that either dramatize national distinctions or, alternatively, appeal to unity among different Latino groups. Ads for 'Pronto Envio' and Tecate beer are posted in the storefronts of *taquerias* on Lexington Avenue, instead of in Puerto Rican establishments. Indeed, local shopkeepers themselves are also engaged in these dynamics, since covering their storefronts with ads is an important medium for making strategic linkages to particular constituencies, by communicating that they specialize in this or that product or service, or that they are equipped to serve the tastes of particular groups. One local shopkeeper noted that: 'I have black, Mexican and Puerto Rican customers. The cigarette and beer ads work for all, but for the Mexicans I put up the ads from Siempre Envio and the phone cards.'

However, the principal boundary enacted by outdoor advertisements is that between El Barrio as a Latino/a neighborhood, its contiguous neighborhoods, and the rest of the city. This is communicated not solely through the language or ethnic specificity of a given ad, but also by the types of ads, the products they advertise, and most directly, by their location and ubiquity. A Latino neighbor-hood, according to two advertising representatives I spoke to, is one that has many Latinos and is therefore cheaper to cover with ads. 'To me it's all very clear,' as one rep stated. 'From 96 Street up there's no problem. It's Hispanic. All the way from First to Park, and from there on, they are all Afro-Americans. And from 135 upwards, they are all Dominicans.' Notwithstanding his confi-dence about these boundaries, these areas are in fact not as unproblematic as he describes. As noted earlier, the border of 96th and 100th Street is in fact one of El Barrio's most gentrified areas. One can even trace the process of gentrifica-tion by following the type of advertisements that are springing up and those that are fading. Some high-traffic areas like Lexington Avenue are filled with advertisements, but other avenues look like the mostly advertising-free, clean and demure Upper East Side to the south. In the upper 100s, however, ads are far more common. But the point that this rep makes about these neighborhoods giving 'free rein' to advertisers is still accurate. These much poorer communities are believed to be more passive and thus less likely to challenge the commercial swamping of their space. Thus, the number of advertisements functions as an index of poverty and marginality: the poorer you are, then the more likely it is that you will find yourself surrounded by advertising. Particularly apparent in these neighborhoods is the type of ad the industry calls 'eight-sheets' (5'H x 11'W), which for a long time have been the cheapest and most common format in ethnic neighborhoods, where they are sold in bulk packages for approxi-mately $150 a month, and placed primarily outside points of sale, for example on the walls of grocery and convenience stores. This type of advertisement is not seen in upmarket neighborhoods where, as Joel told me, residents would be bothered by their 'ubiquity' and 'ordinariness'.

Additional markers of El Barrio's physical and spatial boundaries are also provided by the type of products advertised and the placement of the ads. Above 96th Street, advertising suddenly begins to address a community of basic goods consumers, through ads for coffee, food, milk, beer and cigarettes, or money transfer companies, but it is rare to see luxury products advertised. The contrast could not be greater when compared with the demure ads placed in the residential areas of the Upper East Side, which closely adjoins El Barrio, or with the flashy ones on Time Square, where they are a central component reinstating the area's position as a stronghold of New York's symbolic economy in and beyond the city. In El Barrio, it is primarily basic consumer goods and cheap luxuries – beer, cigarettes, coffee, candy, milk – or social services that are advertised, a choice of products which forcefully inscribes the marginality of the neighborhood and its residents/consumers. This status is also communicated by the placement of eight-sheets in the less prestigious venues, such as corner walls, rather than in the expensive, glossy, illuminated and protected phone and transportation booths, which are common advertising venues in midtown and upmarket neighborhoods in the city. More susceptible to damage because of the venue position, eight-sheets are also more likely to be deemed cheapening and debasing to an area. As Joel stated: 'There are a lot of problems with eight-sheets. They are exposed and can be easily damaged, they are not illuminated, and they are associated with cigarettes. They have a bad rep[utation].'

Indeed, many eight-sheet advertisements in East Harlem are likely to be damaged, faded and/or covered with writing. Unlike ads placed in phone booths and bus stops, which are protected by glass, eight-sheet ads require the constant supervision of a concerned seller in order to prevent them and, by association, the products' images from being damaged or vandalized. But El Barrio is not Time Square. Once installed, many ads are often forgotten, sometimes long after the advertising contract has expired. Many are left hanging until the space is sold to another advertiser. The faded ads are a stark reminder that advertisements may be commonplace in ethnic neighborhoods, but they are not there on the belief of the profitability or advertising value of the community. Advertisers may be attracted to El Barrio by cheaper rates, or by the possibility of reaching a supposedly homogenous and easy target; alternatively they may be offered the space for free, or at below market rates as an add-on to a larger ad campaign in mid-Manhattan or trendy SoHo. But ethnic neighborhoods are never the advertisers' top priority. Although not an eight-sheet, the faded giant mural advertisement for Channel 47 across 106th Street, which was up for almost two years, until the space was sold to HBO Latino in Spring 2001, is an example of one of many forgotten ads in East Harlem. Such ads invest the neighborhood with a sense of decay while the advertiser is provided with free and continuous, even if faded, exposure.

In this way, outdoor advertisements constantly communicate for and on behalf of El Barrio to the outside world, and always at multiple levels. In their content, they assert Latino/a culture through their language and by drawing on themes stereotypically recognized as 'Latino', or that showcase differences among various Latino subgroups. Additionally, through the use of medium, location or even advertisers' care of their ads, ads can also reinscribe and thus mark the neighborhood's marginal identity *vis-à-vis* the rest of the city. After all, El Barrio is no advertising hub. Notwithstanding signs of affluent consumers entering the area, it still remains an advertising-unworthy neighborhood where advertisers have to be lured and attracted. If and when they leave – whether their ads need replacing or upkeep, while in the meantime they mark decay and marginality – is another matter altogether.

Conversations and engagements

Once posted, street ads become part of larger webs of street communication where there is seldom a public sign, be it an ad, a mural or a street painting, that remains untouched and does not serve as a gauge of public opinion. Assessing the spatial and communicative impact of outdoor ads thus requires examining them in relation to the various other signs, images and messages which may subdue, challenge or transform their commercial meaning, even when the intention of these more grassroots types of expression may be difficult or impossible to establish. For instance, the vandalization of the first murals of Mexican icons in East Harlem – that of singer Alejandro Fernandez, painted by local artist James de la Vega as a welcome to the Mexican community – is an unequivocal statement of ethnic tensions between Puerto Rican 'long-timers' and the Mexican 'newcomers' (Tirado and Cardalda 2001). But how do we interpret the graffiti/writing painted over an outdoor ad, or the mural harmoniously painted next to another? Is the first instance an oppositional statement to the commercial message *per se*, or perhaps a more general claim to space chosen for its value and visibility? Is the second evidence of accommodation between street art and advertisements? Moreover, how are street art and its messages affected by the commercial sale of, and competition over space?

Before considering these questions, it is important to draw some distinctions between graffiti/writing and murals, and to examine how they may mediate the relation of these different forms of street art to outdoor ads. An obvious difference is that murals are generally considered to be more time-consuming than graffiti, which by definition are always quick and spontaneous, and often done covertly and illegally, even if the designs may have been equally or more carefully planned than a mural. Because of this, graffiti are principally defined by their illegality, which is the very quality that makes them conducive to public and unrestrained communication (Philips 1999). Hence the affirmation by Lady Pink, a famed graffiti artist and one of the first women to paint in El Barrio's Wall/Hall of Fame – an internationally famed graffiti wall within the graffiti and hip-hop world – that 'we're art pirates'. This is in contrast to the artist James de la Vega, to whose work I will soon turn, who calls himself 'a street artist' and is annoyed when people describe him as 'a graffiti artist'. De la Vega stresses that he always gets a permit for his work on wall spaces, and that the intention of his art is to uplift rather than 'debase' the neighborhood (this is in contrast to the general belief that graffiti are a bad thing for an area). This is not how graffiti/writing artists see themselves, or define their work, and this dominant association should not be interpreted as evidence of strict boundaries between graffiti and mural artists, or their work. The point here is the greater status awarded to murals and mural painting by the Latino artistic and cultural establishment as an uncontested sign of assertion and identity, in contrast to graffiti, whose political identity is more contested.

The politicized identity of murals stems from their history in Latino grassroots politics, particularly the social movements of Chicanos and Puerto Ricans in the late 1960s and 1970s, where they were pivotal visual expressions of social demands and activism. This role, to a lesser degree also evident today, has afforded murals wide public recognition as important places of memory and vested their authors with the role of 'cultural workers' and community artists (Pitman Weber et al. 1998).[8] This aspect of the art form was most recently represented by the murals of the Puerto Rican Collective, a group that has since disbanded but whose members are still cultural activists in El Barrio. The Collective was formed in 1996 as a committee of the National Congress for Puerto Rican Rights, in preparation for the 100th anniversary of the US occupation and colonization of Puerto Rico. Murals, such as that of Puerto Rican revolutionary Lolita Lebron which declares, 'If men don't work for our independence, we women will do it', are part of this initiative.

Figure 5.1 Murals transform walls into a mass medium for political communication in El Barrio, New York.

Source: Arlene Dávila.

By contrast, graffiti has been a consistently derided and misunderstood expressive art form. In particular, although a multi-ethnic and multi-racial phenomenon from the start, it has generally been associated with 'black cultural products' of hip-hop culture (as are break-dancing and rap) as opposed to rightful expressions of Puerto Rican and Latino culture where it is Hispanocentric definitions that dominate (Rivera 2003). It is also tied to more overtly commercialized urban expressions, though in fact graffiti and mural art increasingly share more similarities than differences. For one, graffiti/writing artists have undoubtedly as many artistic aspirations as do mural artists, who in turn are hardly the grassroots artists who have traditionally been romantically associated with the genre. Mural and graffiti artists are actively commissioned by government and private entities in similar ways, rendering both groups likely candidates for co-optation and engagements with different interests. Such engagements can arguably transform the content and imagery of these works as well as the public identity of these artists, be it as artists, art pirates, political or cultural workers. But conversely, they can also feed into it, in so far as it presupposes and helps encourage the vision that motivated the sponsorship in the first place. For example, most murals, whether done independently or under commission, display mostly Puerto Rican flags, salsa heroes and cultural nationalist messages, thus actively asserting Puerto Rican culture, heroes and memory, similar to the themes historically employed by Latino muralists. This stance is even evident in

Figure 5.2 Memorial murals, often featuring flag imagery, are sites of personal memory and community affirmation in El Barrio.

Source: Arlene Dávila.

memorial murals, commissioned in memory of the deceased (many of whom are youth victims of violence) who are frequently shown next to flags or other forms of nationalist iconography.

Similar nationalist iconography is also evident in the murals of Mexican artists. Consider the work of Ricardo Franco, the author of the 'Viva Zapata' mural painted outside a local *taqueria*, which he described as a statement of solidarity with the indigenous people of Mexico and the suffering of Mexicans everywhere. In it, the Mexican flag, the Virgen de Guadalupe and Aztec symbolism adorn the face of Comandante Marcos, as do the words: 'un mundo donde quepan muchos mundos' ('a world where many worlds can coexist') – a message of tolerance and coexistence that, as the artist explained, is needed by indigenous peoples in Chiapas as much as it is by Mexican immigrants in the US.

For their part, graffiti artists are hired by record companies to make advertisements for rap artists, for Coca-Cola and other consumer products, and whenever there is a need for urban packaging to provide 'street credibility'. In other words, they are as intent as muralists on forging and maintaining a particularly Latin/urban imagery. The Hall of Fame is a good example. This was the outcome of the illegal appropriation of a schoolyard wall, which developed into a local attraction and an important forum for graffiti artists to gain wide recognition and exposure, including postings on graffiti websites and dissemination by tourists and graffiti enthusiasts. The wall displays the characteristic complex visual interplay of language deconstruction and imagery identified with this urban art form, along with nationalist images. Ezo, who organized the painting of the wall four times in the late 1990s and in 2000, explained: 'There's always a Puerto Rican icon in there. There were artists from all over, but mostly Puerto Ricans, and there was always a Taino, or a Puerto Rican flag, because it's part of my consciousness.'

Arguably, then, murals and graffiti provide alternative or oppositional statements to the purely commercial dominion of space provided by ads, whether through spontaneous commentary or sabotage, as in the case of graffiti painted over ads, or through the display of Latino heroes and the commemoration of historical events that do not revolve around objectified images of commercial Latinidad. Additionally, both genres provide artists with a way to gain exposure that may lead to income-producing commissions, as well as room for self-expression, communication and enjoyment. However, this is dependent on accessing walls and space, with or without consent, calling us to consider the ongoing negotiations and interests invested in the contest over wall space. These struggles are not just over turf, identity and meanings, they are also over money. Artists may work without permits, but in order for their work to be visible they need to negotiate with merchants and landlords who, in turn, decide if they will sell their wall space to advertisers or sell, or commission, it to a muralist in the hope of establishing or maintaining good community relations.

A vivid example of these negotiations can be seen in the story of one of the area's most memorable outdoor works, the 'Salsa Heroes' mural, originally painted in 1996 at the corner of 104th Street and Third Avenue. As I noted elsewhere, this is one of the most contested spaces in East Harlem due to its proximity to the proposed cultural crossroads and attraction to rent-seekers because of its closeness to the 103 Street and Lexington Avenue subway station. The mural, featuring past and present New York-based Puerto Rican salsa heroes such as Ismael Rivera, Hector Lavoe, Tito Puente and Marc Anthony, was authored by James de la Vega, the area's most renowned street artist, whose career provides additional evidence of the changing value of public walls and open space.

De la Vega is the son of Puerto Ricans who left the island before the 1950s to work on farms in the eastern United States, and settled permanently in New York. His family has close ties in East Harlem's Puerto Rican community and is well known in the area, and locals are always hanging out or greeting him on the street and in his shop. Since the early 1990s, de la Vega has painted some of the most famous murals in the area, including the first Mexican theme mural, the Salsa Heroes mural, as well as others which show Puerto Rican heroes alongside nationally recognized heroes of liberation struggles (from Marcos to Malcolm X to José Marti) and self-help, spiritual and nationalist messages. Today, from his storefront art shop, de la Vega functions as a public intellectual and community spokesperson. He receives requests for tours of his murals from students and visitors, as well as commissions from the Hope Foundation, Banco Popular, Old Navy Stores and others. His fame has made him perhaps the most controversial artist in the area.

After earning a BA from Cornell in 1996 and returning to El Barrio, noto-riety came relatively fast for de la Vega. As in other university campuses, Latino students at Cornell were then enmeshed in struggles to establish Latino studies programs. This fueled a great deal of cultural activism, which doubtless contributed to de la Vega's artistic inspirations. As he noted, it was time away from El Barrio that confronted him with the area's deterioration and inspired him to paint areas – primarily empty walls and abandoned build-ings – that needed 'beautifying' and uplifting through murals of assertion and cultural renewal. The Salsa Heroes mural, celebrating Puerto Rican musi-cians, was one of these works. It was painted for free outside a store, which later became a pawnshop, after de la Vega secured permission of the store-owner, an old family friend. Not surprisingly, it was quickly recognized as an expression of Puerto Ricans' connection to the area by institutional entities and the public alike, as evidenced by its lengthy existence without deface-ment by graffiti, a common way for people and passers-by to engage with the messages of murals. Extending the mural's notoriety was its depiction of beloved Puerto Rican musicians, some of whom, like Tito Puente, were recently deceased.

I was therefore surprised to discover that the mural had been painted over sometime in early 2001. The musical heroes were still there, but the mural had obviously been repainted. This time, flanking the musicians were pictures of chains, bracelets, watches, wedding rings, electric pianos, guitars, DVD-players and other products sold in the pawnshop, along with an oversize sign proclaiming, 'We buy'. When I asked what had happened to the mural, I learned that the store-owner had wanted de la Vega to retouch or repaint it (it had faded from exposure to the elements), but was unable to pay the artist's fee. The owner turned instead to a local painter who agreed to do the job for under $500. Unlike de la Vega, this new artist, author of other commercial murals in the area, was willing to accommodate the store-owner who wanted both the acclaimed landmark and the advertising for his store.

This accommodation of advertisements and murals is not uncommon. Not only do local merchants advertise through murals, but non-commercial murals necessarily share the same spaces with 8 by 10 sheet advertisements, and vice versa, in ways that make it difficult to determine who it was that first discovered and covered a bare wall: a graffiti artist, a mural artist, a business owner or a marketer? Sometimes, the ads appear to cover a mural, while at other times the graffiti or murals seem to be painted around ads. In most instances, however, street artists and outdoor marketers seem to respect each other's spatial rules and boundaries, an accommodation that is most often mediated by whoever is in charge of the surface in contention. In the case above, for instance, the merchant was fully aware that murals have community relations value. He had wanted to keep the mural along with his advertisement, even if he had been

Figure 5.3 A pawnshop owner's commercial imagery incorporates pieces of a mural celebrating Puerto Rican musicians, painted several years ago by renowned muralist James de la Vega.

Source: Arlene Dávila.

unable, or unwilling, to pay de la Vega. Additionally, murals have the added value of having a greater longevity than ads. Ads come and go, but murals can survive years of exposure, providing decoration and community relations.

For local artists, commercial murals provide an opportunity to show their artistry and earn money, underscoring the point that it is not solely large corporations who have a stake in the commercialization of urban space. Yet this connection is not always evident. Artistic claims are, after all, often established on the disavowal of commercial interests. De la Vega, for instance, insisted that he would never have complied with the store's wishes, or sold his art for commercial purposes. He maintains his 'non-commercial' identity by drawing a stark distinction between 'artists who fight against the machine and those that paint for the sake of money'. Yet this is not to say that he is averse to commercialism; a goal sought by all street artists. The primary distinction he makes is thus not necessarily one's engagement in commercial and promotional work or having commercial interests fund or become associated with your message, but rather whether a message remains autonomous or is tainted and compromised by the commercial involvement. As de la Vega himself notes, whether sponsored by the Hope Foundation or Old Navy Stores, he is the one to decide the content and nature of his message and the images that he paints. Granted, de la Vega has come a long way since the time when he painted free murals, and unlike other street artists he can afford a degree of autonomy over his work. Most often, muralists are commissioned by merchants, and the messages and artistic images that they paint are always in conversation with commercial messages of services rendered and products sold. The distinctions he makes, however, underscore the active struggles over artistic legitimacy, and for representation, that are always waged around wall space in El Barrio, and are even constitutive of the medium of street art. These struggles revolve around multiple axes, but are always at odds with outdoor advertising's largely arbitrary treatment of urban space.

Murals, advertising and the gentrified neighborhood

Though murals were the catalyst of de la Vega's success and public image, he has moved to other forms of public art, particularly conceptual, didactic or moralizing. This 'New Age-y art', in the words of one commentator, has attracted criticism. De la Vega explains that his decision to change was made solely on the basis of his individual artistic trajectory, though, most significant for our purposes, his motivations were also tied to shifts in the neighborhood itself. De la Vega first turned to murals to address the decay and abandonment of East Harlem, which he found run down, full of empty walls and abandoned buildings which he believed could be improved by a mural with strong symbolic messages, an image or a flag. But in his view, new construction and renovations have rendered this task largely irrelevant. To make his point, he referred to the site of one of his early murals, 'In Memory of Sammy', on 102nd Street, which was erased after the building was bought and renovated by Mount Sinai Hospital. Many of his earlier murals have suffered a similar fate, and are now only seen on postcards and other paraphernalia for sale in his studio. De la Vega still paints commissioned murals, but his primary work revolves around painting and writing inspirational messages of uplift and self-help. Most significantly, de la Vega's art and messages have dramatically shifted. His street work no longer features Puerto Rican flags or other nationalistic symbols and imagery, as if to stress its universal reach. It is no longer directed solely at the Puerto Rican community, nor does it touch on political and social issues. Instead, it embraces philosophical or welcoming messages of harmonious integration, which are more approving and appeasing than critical or questioning of the rapid changes in the area. Moreover, he is no longer limited to the neighborhood of El Barrio: such messages as 'Become your dream' or 'You are your own best investment', all signed 'de la Vega', are now as easily found painted in white chalk along 14th Street as they are in the photographs of his street work and T-shirts for sale in his El Barrio storefront studio/gallery ninety blocks to the north. De la Vega's move is arguably guided by his artistic aspirations – 'art' is principally defined by its universal appeal and applicability over and above its ever present ethnic, cultural and social content and significance. What I found noteworthy were the connections between his shift in imagery and style and the processes of gentrification and change undergone by the community. These are processes that his work, albeit indirectly, is simultaneously fueling and representing.

Indeed, artists are recognized agents of gentrification, many times to their own regret, and the coming of artists to El Barrio has raised poignant questions about their effects on gentrification. But no one has been as aggressive as de la Vega in seeking new audiences by advertising throughout the city (mostly through chalk messages on sidewalks), by hosting open workshops, by selling 'I Love Spanish Harlem' T-shirts, and holding neighborhood tours for high school and college students, and in the event attracting much attention and criticism to his work. Some people hold him up as an example, while others resent him for turning their neighborhood into a ghetto 'show and tell'. Some feel that he has distanced himself from his roots, embracing and expediting the area's gentrification. De la Vega is aware of these criticisms, but he insists that this move was a necessary one to ease racial tension. As he noted:

> I've been accused of promoting gentrification, but my interest lies with whoever moves here. I can't do anything about who moves here, that's beyond my control, except to foster respect and make people get along. … What are we going to do, scream to people that they should get out of Spanish Harlem?

The fact is that de la Vega may have left overt Latino imagery behind, but he has neither lost nor stopped cultivating an urban style that is also an expression of Latinidad. This style may be regarded as less 'Puerto Rican' or 'Latino' by some area residents, since it does not include flags or nationalistic murals, but it is unequivocally seen and consumed as such by many locals and outsiders alike. After all, it is de la Vega's renowned El Barrio origins and persona that attracts locals and outsiders to his shop, and which sustain his legitimacy as an 'urban' public artist. His messages and street art are very much informed and fed by his involvement in El Barrio. Discussion and criticism of de la Vega's work are hence more suggestive of the ongoing conversations about the interplay between street art, marketing and the gentrification of El Barrio. Thus, when his murals were inexplicably vandalized in Summer 2002 – defaced with black paint – a rumor spread that it was not only about personal jealousy, but also a statement of frustration toward his overt marketing practices. Some people believed he had crossed the line with his promotion of his work and of El Barrio, indicating residents' awareness of the precariousness of marketing as a political strategy of assertion. For others, this scandalous act gave them more reason to support de la Vega. An anonymous letter in the local newspaper *Siempre* claimed that his murals belonged to the community, they were no longer de la Vega's, that it was not he but the community that had been damaged by this act.[9] This incident vividly indicates the range of responses and sentiments triggered by the ongoing attempts at marketing culture in El Barrio, so demanded according to many as a medium to mark Latinidad into space in ways that may potentially hinder gentrification, but not surprisingly, also so feared. Most of all, these responses represent a warning about how to market the area, and for what aims.

Altogether, though with different objectives, de la Vega and other artists are not unlike outdoor marketers, centrally involved in promoting and maintaining a distinct Latino feel in the area, whether this is done through overt nationalistic messages or abstract messages of self-motivation and uplift, or even by fostering conversations about the gains and perils of marketing El Barrio. As seen, in so far as ethnic marketing requires the existence of a culturally specific niche, which can be marketed as such, outdoor marketing will likely continue to reinstate El Barrio's public identity as a Latinized neighborhood. What the work and outlook of de la Vega and other street artists suggest, relative to advertising, however, is that for them the area's Latinness is not easily reducible to particular images or icons; rather, it is directly tied to transformations and specific developments in the community. Moreover, their work is unavoidably tied to local tensions and contents, in this case to tensions triggered by processes of gentrification. Their work thus becomes a conduit of protest, expression, competition and wider dynamics in the community at large, sensitive barometers of local tensions and changing demographics of their area. They belong to the moment, not solely to corporate capital's need for ethnic niche-markets and images. As we saw, for marketers, walls in El Barrio are interchangeable with those of any other Latino neighborhood in the city – the same ad can be placed here as in other Latino identified areas. The goal, then, is to anchor El Barrio's walls for future profit, and this has particular consequences for who is involved, for what reason and who has a right to the space. Ultimately, in the contest over space, it is not necessarily the promotion or negation of a Latino content, but rather on what bases and who and what is involved in its promotion, and can participate culturally and economically from this activity. That is, the public conversation between advertising and street art should be gauged on the artists that now make a name, a profit and a claim to these walls, as well as on the types of economies and different artistic forms that are fostered in them. Most important, they need to be gauged on the messages, exchanges and critiques that are facilitated by these analogous, yet starkly different, expressive forms.

Notes

1 East Harlem is part of New York's designated empowerment zone, one of the first six urban empowerment zones introduced after the law came into effect in 1994. Additional zones are located in Chicago, Detroit, Baltimore and the Philadelphia-Camden (New Jersey) metropolitan area, places undergoing similar dynamics to those documented in this chapter. Recently, other zones have been added in cities as varied as Pulaski County, Arkansas; Syracuse, New York; Fresno, California; and San Antonio, Texas.

2 See, for instance, Abu-Lughood (1991), Brumann (1999) and Ortner (1999) among others. Briefly, scholars have critically exposed the assumptions of homogeneity and harmony, consensus and authenticity and other misleading meanings that are continually associated with the term. Also problematic is the use of 'culture' to veil social inequalities, as when used as a synonym for 'ethnicity' and difference. Here I find useful Appadurai's discussion of culture as articulation and 'boundary of difference' (1996) and other descriptions of culture that treat it not as a given but as socially constituted, objectified and mobilized for a variety of political ends.

3 In this chapter, I define outdoor media as billboards, bulletins, street furniture media and transit media (in buses, subways, etc.). They do not include 'out of home' media, which the outdoor marketing industry uses to define any type of medium that reaches consumers out of their homes, such as radio or speaker phone announcements.

4 Though different and smaller in scale, the concessions outdoor advertisers receive are comparable to those given to developers by the New York City's 1961 zoning resolution, which gave private ownership of public spaces to developers in exchange for their development into plazas and parks for the public. These publicly accessible spaces, however, are seldom as accessible to the public as was intended by the legislation (Kayden et al. 2000). While street furniture, which depends on its accessibility to the public, is exempted from these criticisms, similar questions can be raised about the private–public juncture they represent in regard to control of public space.

5 For instance, the most expensive outdoor media (rotary bulletins) cost $3.90 for ten GRP (or, Gross Rating Point equal to the number of impressions as a percentage of total population). In contrast, thirty seconds of a prime-time television spot may cost $20.54 per thousand viewers.

6 See TDI/Infinity Outdoor Latino marketing brochure, 'Impacting the Latino Market', TDI, New York.

7 I discuss these issues in greater detail in Dávila (2001).

8 See Pitman Weber et al. (1998) for a discussion of the community-based mural movement among Chicanos, and Vélez-Ibañez (1996) for the contemporary repercussions of the US Mexican mural movement. A discussion of the political content and message of murals in New York City is provided by Cardalda and Amilcar (2001) and Taylor (1999).

10 Anonimo, 'Perdio la Comunidad', Siempre, 16 July–5 August 2002, p. 15.

Bibliography

Abu-Lughod, L. (1991) 'Writing against Culture', in R. Fox (ed.), *Recapturing Anthropology: Working in the Present*, Santa Fe: School of American Research Press.

Anonimo (2002) 'Perdio la Comunidad', *Siempre*, 16 July–5 August 2002: 15.

Appadurai, A. (1996) *Modernity at Large: Cultural Dimensions of Globalization*, Minneapolis and London: University of Minnesota Press.

Brumann, C. (1999) '"Writing for Culture": Why a Successful Concept Should not be Discarded', *Current Anthropology*, 40: S1–S27.

Cardalda, E. and Amilcar, T. (2001) 'Ambiguous Identities: The Affirmation of Puertorriquenidad in the Community Murals of New York City', in A. La-Montes and A. Dávila (eds), *Mambo Montage: The Latinization of New York*, New York: Columbia University Press, pp. 263–90.

Dávila, A. (2001) *Latinos Inc: Marketing and the Making of a People*, Berkeley, CA: University of California Press.

Holston, J. and Appadurai, A. (1999) 'Introduction', in J. Holston (ed.), *Cities and Citizenship*, Durham, NC: Duke University Press.

Jackson, P. and Thrift, N. (1995) 'Geographies of Consumption', in D. Miller (ed.), *Acknowledging Consumption: A Review of New Studies*, London: Routledge, pp. 204–37.

Kayden, J. with The New York City Department of City Planning, The Municipal Art Society of New York (2000) *Privately Owned Public Space: The New York Experience*, New York: John Wiley and Sons, Inc.

McCarthy, A. (2001) *Ambient Television: Visual Culture and Public Space*, Durham, NC: Duke University Press.

Outdoor Advertising Association of America (2000) 'Outdoor Advertising Today: The Positive Role of Outdoor Advertising in the United States', http://www.OAAA.org.

Phillips, S. (1999) *Wallbangin': Graffiti and Gangs in Los Angeles*, Chicago: University of Chicago Press.

Pitman Weber, J., Cockcroft, J., Cockcroft, E.S. and Keppel, B. (1998) *Towards a People's Art: The Contemporary Mural Movement*, New Mexico: University of New Mexico Press.

Rivera, Raquel (2003) *Nuyoricans in the Hip Hop Zone*, New York: Praeger.

Vélez-Ibañez, C. (1996) 'Making Pictures: U.S. Mexican Place and Space in Mural Art', in *Border Visions: Mexican Cultures of the Southwest United States*, Tucson: University of Arizona Press, 244–64.

Vista Media, 'Hispanic American Marketing', http //www.vistamediagroup.com/hisp_am.html

Zukin, S. (1995) *The Cultures of Cities'*, Oxford: Blackwell.

6

MEDIA, BODIES AND SPACES OF ETHNOGRAPHY

Beauty salons in Casablanca, Cairo and Paris

Susan Ossman

It might seem easy to determine the spaces where one might conduct research on the media. Even more so, perhaps, for anthropologists, who tend to favor methods of research based on face-to-face interactions. If most of us continue to do ethnography even when questioning the ways our predecessors have thought about *ethnos*, it is because we continue to believe that some kind of special knowledge can result from ongoing involvement in particular spaces with people we get to know. It is by living where the people or practices we hope to understand reside that ethnographers might acquire the kinds of context-laden experience fundamental to anthropological knowledge. One would think, therefore, that the ethnographer's contribution to a better understanding of the mass media would be derived mainly from studies of the institutions that produce the media, day-to-day accounts of film crews shooting, or the protocol offices that take care to present national leaders for television and the like. Alternatively, one might imagine ethnographers working diligently to observe how the media are consumed: families in front of television sets, kids at the movies or teenagers in cyber cafés. Indeed, studies of both types have contributed to our understanding of how the media are made and how they shape everyday life. The work of the ethnographer as presented in such studies of production and consumption involves moving into the place of media-making or consumption. This moving in is determined by the time and space of an event; for instance, the making of a film. Or it is set according to a space of consumption – the living room or cyber café – usually mapped in terms of the attributes of those involved in the interaction (for example, Chinese villagers, immigrant youths in Paris, retirees in an English country town).[1]

Anthropologists are often very astute in carefully moving from the spaces of their observation toward these more general frames of reference such as cultures or states, classes or ethnic groups. As the anthropological literature has shown, an increased sensitivity to how culture is not uniform but creative of varieties of expression, positioning or practice, many of us increasingly play off these contextualizing generalities in ways that draw attention to shades of expression and experience. But a problem remains – the kinds of events or cultures that set the background to our observations cannot be simply assumed. This is a problem that has been much debated in anthropology of late, in part because of the realization that the media are reshaping the landscapes we thought we had mapped once and for all. In the context of a critical reappraisal of the meaning of culture, a substantial body of writing on how we ought to study 'global' or 'transnational' currents of exchange has been published. These critical writings have questioned our assumptions about how nations and cultures are consti- tuted and the role played by the mass media in this process. They have challenged us to develop new manners of conceiving of locality and of cultural cohesion. How can we chart how media, migrations and travel are related to the opening up of novel imaginations of space, time and togetherness? From where might we be able to observe such apparently all-encompassing phenomena? Often, the local is the place from which we expect to be able to 'see' global process. Sometimes one might even observe it on an individual body. But the 'there' of the global, which seems to be both creative of and different from these sites of research, often remains nebulous and abstract, described by some writers as typified by 'non-spaces' (Augé 1992). James Ferguson and Akhil Gupta, among others, suggest that what is needed to think beyond globalization as a kind of generalized emptiness or sameness is a re-evaluation of how we conceive of the process of localization (Bhabha 1995; Gupta and Ferguson 1997). If there seems to be an interdisciplinary consensus on the need to redefine our objects of study to grasp the elusive processes engendered by intensified exchanges among and amidst world areas, concrete research in this area is more often envisioned than carried out. A renewed, empirical approach to such questions requires the development of new compar- ative approaches and a better understanding not simply of media texts but of how the media construct the spaces of our world (Marcus 1999: 89; Couldry 2000). This in turn has implications for how we conceive of spaces in general, and spaces where one might engage in ethnography in particular.

These issues are heightened in relation to studies of mediated processes, so crucial to developing methods of study that help us to grasp the intricacies of emerging forms of global exchange and social organization. Often, the *mise-en-scène* adopted by ethnographers in the course of describing the workings of media consumption contrast the face-to-face, grounded world of physical expe- rience to some other world of television, Internet exchange or globalized texts. This tends to lead to developing stories of how subjects use the media to achieve various kinds of out-of-body dreams. Such bodiless worlds are presented as offering alternatives to the grounded world of the apparently set cultures in which we live – alternatives some associate with processes of power, influence and globalization. The many individual stories of media ethnography are thus set against a two-toned backdrop. No matter how fine-tuned and sensitive the portrayal of individual variations, the global and local, here and there or reality and image remain clearly distinguished. However, as Gupta and Ferguson

suggest, 'if one begins with the premise that spaces have always been hierarchi-
cally interconnected, instead of naturally disconnected, then cultural and social
change becomes not a matter of cultural contact and articulation but one of
rethinking difference *through* connections' (Gupta and Ferguson 1997b: 35).
The question remains – how do we begin to draw these connections? From
where might one observe the making of difference? Might there not be different
ways of moving through and mapping any given space (Silverstone 1998)?

In what follows, I will describe how media ethnography might draw on
observable connections while moving out of a notion of globalization as a
process that works in terms of local cultures being disrupted by interventions
from afar. I will do so in typically ethnographic fashion, by describing how I
designed and carried out an ethnographic experiment between 1991 and 2000.
The space of this work began in Casablanca, it then stretched out in several
steps and a variety of manners toward Paris and Cairo, then back again to
Casablanca. The aim of this project was to understand how different kinds of
beauty are made in a world that claims to homogenize our faces and figures. It
focused on how feminine beauties are produced not only in the made-up world
of fashion magazines, TV soaps or symbolic imaginations, but also on the streets
and in the homes of three cities linked by partially shared languages, histories
and ways of judging such beauties. My assumption was that we cannot understand processes of embodiment by which we draw images into ourselves simply
by observing how certain models are mimicked by women of certain social
classes or ethnic groups. At least in complex urban areas like Casablanca, it is
almost impossible to work according to any assumption of some single, underlying cultural ground. In Casablanca one must reach out toward other places to
see the way the city itself has emerged as Morocco's major business center
during the twentieth century. French colonial policies, Italian architects and
Egyptian films have played distinct roles in forming the image of the modern
city (Ossman 1994). Their roles have been just as crucial to imagining the
variety of bodies and looks that inhabit this urban space.

Moving out of Casablanca

In the early 1990s I lived in Casablanca, a port city where Arabic, three Berber
dialects and French are liberally mixed; the business capital of a kingdom variously known for its unique architectural styles, the spectacular extravagance of
its royal ceremonies and, at least at the time, for its repressive political practices
(Ossman 1994). Against the dizzy background of the city, I set eyes on the
figure that would help me to shape the spaces where my research might require
me to go: the woman in search of embodying ideals of beauty. I followed this
lady as her magazines and face creams led me to the places they came from:
French perfumeries or Cairene writer's pens. Out from Casablanca, the space of
beauty expanded to include Egyptian singers and French advice columnists,
presenting me with a space of symbolic, commercial and populational exchange

that, at the very least, proved the error of too readily associating any form of expansive regional trade or influence with North American or any other strictly national power.

Thus, an initial space for studying media and bodies in Casablanca can be seen as located where the images produced by the major media centers of Paris and Cairo meet. By drawing out the very different lines of exchange between this major North African port, the former colonial 'metropole' and the major center of media production in Arabic, it became possible to focus on the processes by which Casablancans are made in the context of a space that is neither generalized, abstract nor 'global', nor characterized by some kind of local knowledge about bodies and space that one might simply observe by engaging in day-to-day interactions in the city. While a rhetoric of the 'modern' body is disseminated by advertisements on television, fashion magazines or medical practices in Casablanca, just like everywhere else, the accents in which this tale is told bear the discursive patterns of Paris and Cairo. Modern manners of carefully measuring bodies and faces are akin to those used to plan new avenues or draw up plans for homes (Rabinow 1988). But for all of their claims to universality, these forms are not just from anywhere. The ways in which they are used play on ideas of tradition and influence and culture in a manner that seeks to develop originals in a world set in a paradoxical quest for engendering innovation out of sameness. We can comment on these processes by studying spaces that are not defined as global, or modern, or Western or Arab, but determined by the intensity of exchanges and processes that we can chart.

The space of beauty I explored could only be created by beginning in Casablanca – starting in Paris, for instance, would not have rendered the same map and the same kinds of research problems. One might see this space as following Arjun Appadurai's (1989) suggestions of following people and places and things in their movements as guides to how we set out the contours of our study. And indeed, the space I was working with did follow patterns of exchange, language and people. However, unlike Appadurai's more recent suggestion that one should follow these moves in terms of specific 'scapes' – of media, finance or whatever – my concept of the space I was exploring could not be reduced to that of a 'beauty-scape' (Appadurai 1996). The point of the exercise was not simply to show that the flows of things or ideas differ according to various spheres of value or kinds of activities, but to select a topic that offered a critical perspective on society.

In Casablanca, language, politics or the arts, even economic theory, pulls people back and forth between North and South, East and West each day. To select a topic that interrogated links amidst the East and West of the Arab world at the same time as Europe seemed to me to open up the possibility of presenting realities that dualistic approaches usually missed or deliberately sought to hide. This space, once spread out in this way, revealed historical depths one might not have expected. These are not those of Braudel's *longue durée*; they fail to propose a central historical actor of the stature of his

Mediterranean. The cloth of the history I weave is not whole, not only because much more work on the history of this region's salons, styles and beauties remains to be done, but due to the fact that I focused on exchanges between places that I determined according to patterns of exchange I identified in the contemporary world. This approach did lead to some exquisite finds. I read, for instance, in an Egyptian feminist magazine of how Egyptian 'sittat' or 'hawanim' (ladies) claimed that by the 1930s that no Egyptian women wore the veil any more – and how it was suggested that it was time for Cairene feminists to encourage the French colonial powers to help to liberate their Arab sisters in North Africa (Ossman 2002: 39)!

Amidst the exchanges in my triangle of investigation, a single modern body could be identified. The 'new woman' of the 1920s could be located in Egyptian magazines of the period, and traced to how she appears today on television or in the latest fashion spreads throughout the region. Everywhere, her figure is light – in contrast to the heavy body of tradition. (This was the case even if the actual measurable proportions of what people in each city today consider heavy or thin differ, with Cairo leaning toward a broader interpretation of slimness, Parisian thinness quite down to the bone, and Casablanca somewhere in-between.) This model lady is similar to her sisters in America or China or Japan, but does this make her global (Ferrié 1998)? Is it only by identifying her with a specific nation or giving her a cultural affiliation that one might learn what meaning to give the manner in which she is adorned?

If the initial setting up of a space crisscrossed by Egyptian songs, French newspapers and Moroccan radio shows allowed me to trace the historical spread of the modern woman, noting how her lines are measured according to the grids of the modern city, it also led me to notice how distinct products and places and conversations went into the making of what was ostensibly a single modern girl. Why was it, I wondered, that such a diversity of looks was consciously adopted by different sets of Casablancan *belles*? The homogenized body of the new woman might explain something about a common flight from the countryside, and the perceived heaviness of tradition. But it did not explain how people now work with the modern body to create new looks and new differences. Beyond the moves between tradition and modernity some truly important differences between women, and people in general, are in the making. These cannot be observed simply in terms of flows of people or things or as a process by which an individual inscribes his or her adhesion to a set of values or identities by adopting specific styles. There are also social institutions and exchanges that play an essential role in the manner that styles and the social differences they symbolize are embodied.

The first movement of my work had me dancing from city to city in a space that was not set to the rhythm of the global/local two-step. It showed me how plays on another couple, that of tradition and modernity, became a shared story over the twentieth century and how certain women in each city read their personal and family histories into this generalized story of evolution. Following my butterfly-like beauties flitting from city to city was essential to the progress of my understanding of the continuities and disjunctures in the initial space of my research. As indeed was noticing how cities themselves are places the butterflies of fashion flocked to, symbols of the kinds of modern ladies the media presented. But my sources reminded me that the city itself was not enough to transform an awkward girl from the provinces into a stylish *Parisienne* (Steele 1998: 75). They showed that being a part of a national culture, for instance, was not sufficient to belonging to the world of the new woman, even if one was from a colonizing, fashionable country like France (Ossman 1998; Zdatny 1999). Some other space of research had to be found to explore the processes by which certain beauties were well nourished in some well-stocked fashion cocoon while others were left to forage for what ideas they could gather in open fields. Specific places have always played a role in working out how to embody some beautiful image observed in a magazine – specific techniques have to be learned or practiced by people who have mastered the craft of making others picture-perfect.

Beauty salons are not the only places where fashion is embodied, but they became the central ones of my study. For a female ethnographer, beauty salons offer ample opportunity for both observation and debate. All salons engage with images from fashion or women's magazines, television and radio broadcasts. But their mirrors also reflect vastly different skills and ways of measuring them on the part of the beauticians. They show us diverse ways of using media to shape clients' hair or massage their bodies. They show the writer her own face among others, subjecting her to the same kinds of advice on her looks as those given to other clients by hairdressers and aestheticians. The aim and nature of this advice varies in terms of the kind of establishment in which one finds oneself – which kind of salon one goes to has a lot to do with who one is: money, education or a husband's eyes differ. Just as the ethnographer has several kinds of theoretical frameworks to choose between, often playing one against the other in mirrored reflections, so some women move from one kind of salon to another in an effort to play on the kinds of looks they produce for themselves in the very different worlds each kind of salon represents. Salons are thus an ideal location to see how mediation links in complex ways with the experience of place and difference.

Three cities/three salons

One of the things that drew me into salons in Casablanca was the fact that they have become places were nearly any woman of any socio-economic group can easily go. In Morocco, the idea of going out to the salon has been assimilated to the same kind of excursion as going to the *hammam*, the collective steam bath, often referred to in English as a 'Turkish bath'. Even husbands who would be unhappy should their wives take a bus downtown or take a stroll, view it as a kind of necessary evil that they go to neighborhood beauty salons or the *hammam* simply to chat, even when they do not need to have their hair done. Salons followed the French to Casablanca, initially serving their belles, then extending their services to local Jewish women and members of the urban elite from such cities as Fez or Meknes. According to my research, it was during the 1970s that girls in 'ordinary' families began to wear popular French-style hairdos, and by 2000 every neighborhood had a salon. But rather than showing a simple homogenization of beauty practices, the spread of the new institution introduced and molded new kinds of social differences, even if it did offer its clients choices of self-presentation derived from similar forms. In the course of following women and pictures and beauty recipes from salon to salon and observing who went where, when, and for what reason, I began to be able to develop a typology of salons in terms of the kinds of spaces that offered them context.

The first kind of salon I thought of as the proximate salon – its context being usually referred to as a 'hay' or 'derb', both of which translate as 'neighborhood'. Women's movements toward these salons were frequent, but inscribed in a relatively small radius; typically their homes were within walking distance. This salon, while known to all, tended to be most visually closed off from the street. Rarely does a man enter such a salon in Casablanca (the same is often true in Paris, although in Cairo male hairdressers can be found). This enclosure recalls the world of the *hammam*. Inside, the salon is often cramped with furniture, whether it is large or small. People stop by to just sit and chat, so it is important to have a couch, magazines and sometimes a television. The space of the media might seem important – for even the walls are often decorated with images taken from magazines and discussions often revolve around articles in magazines like *nis' al maghrib* ('Moroccan Woman') or *sayeddati* ('Miss'). But in the process of working on people's looks, direct reference to the media is usually confined to citing the hair color of a well-known singer or the cut of a famous actress. Although photographs from magazines might be offered as models to follow, the palette of possible styles is limited in several ways. Beauticians in these salons are not always able to faithfully reproduce what is presented in a magazine. This can be due to the fact that they do not have the opportunity to receive ongoing professional training, as do many of their colleagues who work. Indeed, some hairdressers or aestheticians who work in proximate salons have never attended a beauty school. In Cairo, for instance, many male hairdressers explained that they had been apprentices to their fathers. Even when the beauticians are skilled enough to produce their clients as copies of media images, they might not have access to the kinds of products and machines required to produce certain styles. This is perhaps most pronounced in the area of aesthetic treatments that require expensive machinery for weight-loss or anti-wrinkle treatments. Even if the salon owner has the means to invest in such equipment or to purchase the most fashionable brands of beauty products, it is not always expected that he or she do so. For the single most important thing to notice about proximate salons is that looks there are debated by anyone present.

Conversations in this kind of salon limit the kinds of looks one expects to see produced there because they introduce imagined reactions of the neighbors one might meet in the street as well at that of the would-be fiancé and his relatives. The idea of media-as-model that is often invoked to suggest that the aesthetic choices of women and men are increasingly subordinated to very specific images of fashion and beauty projected by the media does not quite work here. Yes, there are changes in the looks produced in proximate salons. These are related to how various fashions are developed on television, in magazines or on billboards. But the process of embodying fashion is subordinated here to the comments of people in flesh and blood – the eyes of the imagined comments of a community imagined less as a nation than as a neighborhood.

This kind of salon can be contrasted to a second type: that of the elite, making-you-special salon, where a man, often assumed to be gay, teases your hair into a style he claims is designed 'just for you'. While the proximate salon is a place of face-to-face sociability – real and imagined –, the elite salon plays on ideas of specialness, be it of 'Andre' who is an artist of the hair, or of the client as artist of her own life. In such salons, people usually come from all over the city, or even other places or countries, to have their bodies massaged and hair styled. The imaginary space is not one of warm, cozy, controlled exchanges, but of a world lit up by the bright lights of fame. The space of the 'just for you' coiffeur extends to include the names of the famous institutes the beautician has attended, and those of the famous people the client might be getting prepared to meet. Photographs on the wall often include signed photos of actresses or princesses the hairdresser has 'done'. Discussions between the hairdresser and the client often fix on important people or upcoming occasions. Similarly, this space of beauty spreads out to be included in conversations at inaugural balls or the weddings of the daughters of well-known families. Such questions as, 'Did Andre do it, darling?' often set up discussion about the beauticians who help women to become, not like pictures, but to 'be pictured as they are – to develop in outward form their inner self', as one hairdresser put it, while 'being more beautiful than the wife of X, according to the gossip of Mrs Y'.

In proximate salons, one finds oneself encircled by people, talk and opinions about one's looks, but also one's behavior. In elite salons, too, one might debate the choice of a school for the kids with the beautician, or ask his advice on where to buy a certain brand of lipstick. But these discussions tend to be strictly personal, they do not include a group of people who are actually present. Opinions, like the kinds of images that make beauty in media, are expressed as distant but all-important others. Their 'opinion' is articulated by the beautician as artist whose role is to prepare his client in the same manner as a fashion designer sews a couture dress: made to order but with the requirements of this year's fashion clearly in mind. This fashion is not usually reproduced from a given model but liberally interpreted in terms of the specific client. Beauticians and aestheticians in these salons emphasize the unique qualities of each client, emphasizing that every woman can be beautiful. Although most elite salons do have the latest machines and access to products of all kinds, and those who work there are highly trained, their way of working women into fashion's dictates is not based on getting them to conform to any given image. Although certain kinds of bodies might be considered easier to involve in fashion because they are sleeker and smoother, and certain treatments are aimed at achieving the body as a 'canvas' of sorts, giving color and form to hair and bodies is perceived not as merely imitating some image, but expressing the distinctive self of the client. The hairdresser or make-up artist is thus represented as a form of portrait painter instead of a slave-master for this year's fashion.

One thing that elite and proximate salons share is the way that some kind of social judgment intervenes through the hairdresser or the other clients in shaping the looks of the client. If this did not happen, it would be considered that he or she had not quite done his or her job. In a third type of salon, one the other hand, it is the image and the client's personal opinion that is considered to be the measure of the hairdresser's art. In what I call 'fast salons', the dyad of the client and hairdresser is distinct, even if a line of clients are often placed side to side along a large mirror. A fast salon draws people from almost anywhere into it, but its claim to space is more about being anywhere than having a specific name or place. A Jacques Déssange salon in Paris or Casablanca should, ideally, offer the same quality and type of service. In either place, salons such as these tend to attract clients who work or live near them – not because they cannot go elsewhere due to family expectations, but rather, because they are often at a loss for time and desirous of knowing in advance what they will resemble when they leave the salon. Fast salons, like fast food restaurants, offer clients menus of style. The various faces of women and men are sometimes numbered, but more often given names like 'Alexandra' or 'Sophia' or 'Bruce' that are expected to personalize them, or perhaps give them a particular national or international flavor ('Natasha' might be portrayed in a way reminiscent of a Soviet-era spy, for example). Increasingly, videos of styles produced in a given salon bring some of these styles out of the world of the single frame. Certain haircuts are high-lighted in videos in order to show how they can be arranged for specific occasions, adapting to beach holidays, office meetings or jogging. In fast salons, beauticians are expected to deliver what is represented in these pictures. This might involve discussions on all manner of things between the hairdresser and the client, but the professional here represents neither the neighbors nor the world of high fashion. Instead, he or she appears as a specialized professional whose competence is expressed in the cleanliness and quickness of this kind of salon. The beautician must be able to faithfully repro-duce the models selected by the client, and these are often discussed in terms of social categories related to profession, age or marital status, or described as 'sporty', 'refined' or 'boyish'. The relationship of such categories to the eyes and evaluation of particular individuals is rarely discussed beyond references to 'significant others', a centrality of couple that is again reflected in the client/beautician engagement. Otherwise, it is 'society' that seems to argue that a short 'cute' cut with blue streaks can be appropriate for a woman in her twenties and 'society' or 'how things are done' that argue against garish hair color for a middle-aged man. In a fast salon, it is not uncommon for a client to simply describe a new hairstyle to the beautician. But often, I have observed, the beautician will ask his client to examine the salon menu and give him a clearer idea of what she wants. He wants to be as accurate as possible in his work, for he knows that he will be judged according to his ability to interpret the client's words. Providing a visual model helps him not only to get a sense of how to relate words to the desired result, it also sets a standard against which his work can be judged.

Working through the apparent sameness of the salon in terms of diverse kinds of salon spaces I found that what seems to be a similar institution, proposing roughly similar routines, ideals of beauty and fashion, in fact ascribes to three distinctly different modes of evaluating beauty. Attending to these allows us to escape the alternative spaces of locality and globality, imprisonment versus liberty, to find several manners of moving amidst three diverse manners of evaluating the self, one's relationship with other people and to media images of beauty. Noticing who feels able or comfortable engaging these under what circumstances may indeed be a better gauge of someone's economic potential and personal well-being than standard measures of economic success or social status. Although many individuals tend to patronize one or another of these types, we must keep in mind that some women move from salon type to salon type according to what they want to have done, for what price and how quickly. It is also important to note that not everyone has the possibility of making such moves. The reasons for this should not be reduced to contrasts of traditional women to modern ones, or to set notions of social class (Grewal and Kaplan 1997). In many cases, wealthy women never go to salons – indeed, the richest and most famous have their hairdressers come to their homes. Many young working women of modest means especially spend a significant part of their income on going to salons, buying clothes or otherwise working on their looks.

The three types of salon spaces I identified are not exclusive – women cross from one salon to the next, and move between distinct manners of judging and presenting themselves and others with ease as well. It is in the play between these different worlds that the character of an individual, the unique feeling of a city or the particular style of a beauty salon is created. By taking into account the mix not only of lived spaces associated with proximate salons in neighborhoods, fast salons one goes to in a lunch hour, or elite salons one lingers in all afternoon, it becomes possible to explore how the use of media differ in each kind of social space. It also becomes possible to theorize about how adopting certain ways of judging media images, and the images of other people or given style, can act as arguments for the primacy of one or another mode of judgment and the social arrangements associated with it.

Conclusion

Linked comparisons thus begin by stretching out a space inscribed by the flow of media, people and things. The directions of this stretching rely not on some general 'flow' of media, but on ethnographic study in a place where media narratives and pictures are present, where they are debated and embodied. It is the media and conversations present in salons that led me to draw out the lines of my space of study, which ended up linking cities that are not usually connected in educational institutions or research agendas. In their manner of confounding spaces like those of Europe, the Arab world or the Mediterranean as they are formed and re-formed by daily discourse in the media, as well as in conversations and academic institutions, salons in Casablanca are not alone. I found them to be of special interest because they shape looks as examples and arguments – not necessarily in terms of copies of models, as some would have it. By noticing from where and when clients go to particular salons, then analyzing these comings and goings with respect to the relationships we observe in the ever-present mirror, we thicken not just our ethnographic descriptions, but the way we conceive of modern or global spaces. This gives new critical momentum to our work. It helps us to observe patterns of differentiation. These differences are in turn related to the worlds of judgment that we cannot lay a finger on, but that help to shape looks, ideas about oneself and relationships to the pictures and stories of the media.

Note

1   An overview of anthropological contributions to the study of the media is offered in Abu-Lughod, Ginsburg and Larkin (2002).

Bibliography

Abu-Lughod, L., Ginsburg, F. and Larkin, B. (2002) *Media Worlds: Anthropology on New Terrain*, Berkeley: University of California Press.

Appadurai, A. (1996) *Modernity at Large: Cultural Dimensions of Globalization*, Minneapolis: University of Minnesota Press.

Augé, M. (1995) *Non-Places: Introduction to an Anthropology of Supermodernity*, London: Verso.

Bhabha, H. (1996) *The Location of Culture*, London: Routledge.

Couldry, N. (2000) *The Place of Media Power*, London: Routledge.

Ferrié, J.-N. (1998) 'La petite robe ou le dépassement des limites dans un régime de civilité', *Mimesis: imiter, représenter, circuler, Hermes*, no. 22, Paris: CNRS Editions.

Grewal, I. and Kaplan, C. (eds) (1997) *Scattered Hegemonies, Postmodernity and Transnational Feminist Practices*, Minneapolis: University of Minnesota Press.

Gupta, A. and Ferguson, J. (eds) (1997a) *Culture, Power, Place: Explorations in Critical Anthropology*, Durham, NC: Duke University Press.

—— (1997b) *Anthropological Locations: Boundaries and Grounds of a Field Science*, Berkeley: University of California Press.

Marcus, G. (1999) *Ethnography Through Thick and Thin*, Princeton: Princeton University Press.

Ossman, S. (1994) *Picturing Casablanca: Portraits of Power in a Modern City*, Berkeley: University of California Press.

—— (1998) 'Savoir se montrer modèles, modes et salons de coiffure à Casablanca', in S. Ossman (ed.), *Miroirs maghrébins: itinéraires de soi et paysages de rencontre*, Paris: CNRS Editions.

—— (2002) *Three Faces of Beauty: Casablanca, Paris, Cairo*, Durham, NC: Duke University Press.

Rabinow, P. (1989) *French Modern: Norms and Forms of the Social Environment*, Cambridge, MA: MIT Press.

Silverstone, R. (1998) 'Les espaces de la performance: musées, sciences et rhetoriques de l'objet', *Mimesis: imiter, représenter, circuler, Hermes*, no. 22, Paris: CNRS Editions.

Steele, V. (1998) *French Fashion: A Cultural History*, London: Berg.

Zdatny, S. (1993) 'Fashion and the Class Struggle: The Case of Coiffure', *Social History*, 18:1.

7

SPACES OF TELEVISION

The structuring of consumers in a Swedish shopping mall

Göran Bolin

Consumption is a prominent feature of everyday social life, and a task that most people undertake on a daily basis. The banal activity of buying such things as food, clothes and other consumer goods for ourselves and our families is a routine task on which we seldom reflect, and especially not while we are in the midst of our shopping rounds, making specific choices among the consumer goods on offer. The routine of shopping, however, is an extremely important ingredient in late capitalist economies, without which the industrial wheels of the Western (post-)industrialized world would come to an immediate halt. As Karl Marx noted in his discussion of the commodity in the first chapter of volume one of *Capital* (Marx 1867/1974), production and consumption are intimately linked in an indissoluble relationship. In the production process commodities are formed, and their value becomes realized first with the consumption of the commodity. Without consumption there would thus be no production.

Marx, however, concentrated more on the moment of production than on the moment of consumption, as have many of his followers. However, the last couple of decades have witnessed an increased awareness of the weight of consumption among cultural theorists, with French sociologist Jean Baudrillard (1970/1988 and 1973/1975) among the first to acknowledge its importance for the general economy of capitalist societies. In his writing, Baudrillard points to the fact that consumers constitute a productive force who work at consuming things in order to uphold the capitalist system. In this way, the ethic of consumption has replaced the work ethic (Bauman 1998), and consumption has become a duty rather than a pleasure or a right (Baudrillard 1970/1988: 80). In the wake of this increased emphasis on the moment of consumption and on consumer practices, some commentators have even polemically appointed 'the consumer as global dictator' in today's market economy, where consumption has become the 'vanguard of history' (Miller 1995: 1).

The increased focus on consumption has sometimes led to the conclusion that consumers have become more powerful in relation to producers, and that they have tactics to counter the strategies of producers and market agents in order to overcome their subordinate position, claims most often inspired by Michel de Certeau (1984/1988). However, while it is true that consumers cannot be individually controlled in minute detail, it does not follow from this that individuals' freedom to choose automatically leads to *power over* producers or distributors within the market. It is probably more accurate to regard this new form of 'power' as a *support to* the capitalist market system, and a way in which the late modern market economy has been refined and developed. As the capitalist economy aims to produce surplus value in the form of profit, a refinement of this system means to smooth the process wherein commodities travel from their production sites, via networks of distribution, to possible customers, and ultimately to the consumption of goods by consumers. One way in which this system could be refined is to make the process faster, and the work invested in commodities to become more rapidly realized in the consumption of goods, and thus turned into profit. This profit can then be reinvested in new commodity production, distribution and new purchases, and so on.

Another way to realize this rationalization of the process is to make the places of consumption, the sites where consumers meet with commodities, make their choices, buy and then leave, as functional as possible. The shopping mall can be seen as a place that is built and designed for this very purpose. Shopping malls are most often constructed as passageways with many entrances and exits, so that people can enter from several directions and move through the consumption site in a variety of ways and patterns. In this sense, they become 'machines' for selling, in the words of Émile Zola (1883/1927, e.g.: 32, 46, 78; cf. Friedberg 1993: 80), constructed in the economic rationality that strives for maximum profit. The physical shape of these sites is of course important, and stairs, escalators and aisles are designed for the purpose of keeping the flow of customers steady. The physical character of the site is not the only thing that determines the way people move about, however. The 'placeness' of the site, the physical surroundings, has also a *symbolic dimension* that is equally important in the structuring of the site for consumption purposes.

The architectonics of the site determine in a 'hard' way the possible means for moving about in a mall. One cannot walk through walls, for example, and one has to move between floors by using the stairs, the lift or the escalator. These physical characteristics of the place decide which ways are possible to move about and, in this regard, they set the limits for one's actions. The semiotic surroundings, however, make up the 'soft' determining premises for moving about. Through signs, advertisements, display windows, television sets, information monitors, as well as through music, sounds and odours, one is directed in ways that are functional for the purpose of the mall. If the 'hard' structuring architectonics talk to our tactile senses, the semiotic structuring devices talk to our visual and aural senses.[1]

In this chapter, I discuss these structuring devices, taking as my example a fairly ordinary shopping mall in a suburb on the outskirts of Stockholm in Sweden. I approach the subject from a functionalist perspective, analysing the

127

relation between physical place and symbolic space, and how these factors contribute to the task of executing one of the fundamental features in capitalist economy: dispersing goods to consumers.

In the first section, I give an introductory overview of the consumer setting of Solna Centrum, in the suburb Solna, north of Stockholm city, both historically and as a physical place and symbolic space.[2] I especially focus on the architectonics and symbolic surroundings and their ability to structure bodies in space for the purpose of closing the circle involving production and consumption. In the second section, I expand on the history of moving images in consumer settings, placing Solna Centrum and the ways that symbolic space is handled there in relation to this history. I especially focus on television and moving images in the mall, although I draw on a range of material, including the soundscape in the mall. My discussion on functions takes as its starting point some reflections on the position of the television set in the mall (i.e. *where* in the shopping mall specific sets are placed, and in what context), as well as their content (i.e. *what* specific genres or programmes are displayed). Following on from the argument on functions, I discuss the possible implications of the placement of television screens and the content they carry, especially in relation to discourses of consumption. The third section examines the strategies of the mall management to administer bodies in consumer settings. I particularly focus on the rationales that lie behind such strategies. Finally, I discuss the administrative practices from a lifeworld/systems approach. I do this in a discussion of the relation between the economic system and forms of publicness that have their roots in the specific Swedish historical context, where, among other things, the struggle over the category of 'home' has been a significant feature.

Solna Centrum as consumer setting and public arena

Solna is a suburb north of the city centre of Stockholm, the capital of Sweden. Sweden has a population of nine million inhabitants, and close to two million live in the greater Stockholm area. Coincidentally, nine million is also the number of customers who pass through the shopping mall Solna Centrum each year. Solna was previously a city in its own right (it received city status in 1943), but recently it has been incorporated as a municipality within the thirteen municipalities that make up greater Stockholm. It has a strong working-class base, and the Social Democrats hold the majority of seats on the municipal council. Solna can be viewed as representative of the Swedish model, the 'People's Home' (*Folkhemmet*). The concept of the 'People's Home' has strong symbolic value in Sweden, to an extent representative of the welfare state itself. *Folkhemmet* was at its height in the 1950s, and it was around this period that most of the buildings in Solna were built. The idea of *Folkhemmet* was established in the 1920s when the Social Democratic Party, in competition with the Conservatives, won the discursive battle over the term *folk* – a battle that, for example, in Germany was won by the Nazis (Becker et al. 2000: 9). From the 1930s to the 1970s the Social Democrats dominated Swedish politics, combining 'modernism with tradition', with an emphasis on, among other things, a high level of 'social engineering' (ibid.: 11). This form of social engineering centred largely on the concept of 'home', with the political programme stressing the need for new housing conditions. Efforts were made to replace the old and often poor housing areas with new, light, spacious, functional homes in the inner cities and their surrounding suburbs.

Television as a medium is traditionally also strongly connected to the home. Home is a powerful metaphor in most cultures of the world. In Western society, home has, at least since the seventeenth century, essentially been considered a private place (Rybczynski 1986/1987: 51ff), in contrast to *Heimat*, which has been regarded as public and collective (cf. Morley 2000: 4). As I will show in greater detail, this has consequences in terms of how to interpret television as a medium in Sweden, particularly when it is situated outside of the home in public settings.

Solna is one of the smallest municipalities in Sweden, with around 57,000 inhabitants (in 2002), distributed over 19 square kilometres. However, it contains a lot of large work places, and a considerable number of people travel from other parts of Stockholm to Solna each day. Because the municipality is well established, the in and out migration is small (approximately 3,000 to 4,000 people each year). The gender structure of the area is to the advantage of women (some 3,000 more women than men), and the age range, compared to Stockholm, comprises slightly fewer young people and slightly more between the ages of 25 to 65 years (i.e. those among the active work force). In comparison to the rest of Sweden, it has a large immigrant population.[3]

Solna Centrum was originally an outdoor centre, as were many other suburb centres that were built in the Stockholm area in the early 1950s. The population growth of Stockholm resulted from structural changes within the economy after the Second World War due to, among other things, the exodus of people in the agrarian sectors who moved to the service sectors in the large cities. This 'flight from the land' to the city called for a new housing policy to accommodate the growing number of urban residents. As a result, many large suburbs were built around Stockholm's centre and other large towns in Sweden. The centres in those suburbs often have shops on both sides of a pedestrian street.

The establishment of new suburban centres in Sweden coincided with the rise of the department store. Although the history of the department store can be traced back to the establishment in the early 1930s of Enhetsprisaktiebolaget EPA (roughly translated, 'The Standard-Price Corporation'), the new suburban centres of the 1950s were the end result of this process (cf. Fredriksson 1998). It can thus be said to be an important part of the development of contemporary Swedish shopping malls, as exemplified by Solna Centrum in this chapter.

As one of these new centres representing the 'People's Home', Solna can, according to definitions in trade journals, be described as a municipal centre, since it is situated in the middle of a municipality and has services such as banks, post offices, employment offices, etc. However, Solna Centrum is larger than most municipal centres, and has more shops and more service facilities than most. It can therefore also be described as a regional centre, as it also attracts customers from neighbouring areas (Karlsson 1996: 6). In the mid-1980s, a glass roof was built over the street, and the centre now stretches out in two directions in a V-shape form. In one of the 'legs' of the V-shaped building, the glass cover has been designed to resemble a Paris *passage*, for example Passage des Panoramas. It is situated close to a subway station, and has an intersection for buses that reaches all the northern suburbs of Stockholm. Close to the centre is Solna Football Stadium, where AIK, one of Stockholm's three major football teams, has its home ground. The stadium is the largest in the Stockholm area, and is also used for international matches. The team has a shop in the mall, selling scarves, posters, videos and other fan-related material.

Another cultural feature that sets its mark on Solna Centrum is Filmstaden, the site where around 350 Swedish films were produced between 1920 and 1970. Filmstaden is situated not far from the mall, and many of the advertisements in Solna Centrum allude to film-making. The famous Swedish actress Greta Garbo is portrayed in a mural painting inside the centre. (Although Garbo's Swedish career was mainly as a mere extra. The only leading part she played before she left Sweden in 1925 was in *Gösta Berlings Saga*, in 1924.) Allusions to the historical past of film-making is also institutionalized in 'the Hollywood stairs', the name given to the main stairs that lead from the ground floor to the upper level of the mall.

A third cultural feature in Solna is Hagaparken, a large public park that stretches out around a bay, and which houses several pavilions and pleasure palaces belonging to the royal family. The park was established by the culturally minded King Gustaf III, and has been immortalized in the many songs by Carl Michael Bellman (1740–1795), a popular Swedish singer and musician who wrote songs about the pleasures of life which are dear to numerous Swedes. Bellman was for many years court singer in the service of Gustaf III. Among the most popular of his songs is 'Fjäriln vingad syns på Haga', a pastoral in which the first verse tells of the butterflies that rise in the dewy morning in Hagaparken. It was written in praise of the newly founded park, and in Solna Centrum there is a chime of bells that strike every hour to the melody of 'Fjäriln vingad'.

One thing that sets Solna Centrum apart from many other shopping malls in Sweden is the fact that it also houses the municipal council. This means that the centre has both an economic and a public function, and this has resulted in a constant struggle between municipal and commercial forces. The drift towards privatization of public property has been a prominent feature in the history of Solna. The trend in recent years has been for publicly owned property to be privatized, and today the only publicly owned buildings are the town hall and the library (cf. Gustavsson 2001: 64ff).

In the mall there are almost 100 stores and shops, and around twenty-five cafés and restaurants (figures from the mall's web page, March 2002).[4] There are nine entrances on the main floor, and two entrances on the basement floor leading from the parking space. On the ground floor four of the entrances are from parking areas. The mix of shops is similar to other Swedish malls (with the exception of the municipal buildings). There are department stores, banks, florists, jewellery stores, as well as several stores for toys, shoes, sportswear, food, etc. When it comes to media, there are two book stores, one record store, a video rental store, a cinema, several photo shops, shops selling television sets, radios and mobile phones, and stores for computer games, etc.

Moving images in consumer settings

Television as a medium is principally thought of as belonging to the home, the routine, everyday intimacy of the family, and the cosiness of the evening's habits. Although many commentators have pointed to its first appearance in public surroundings during the first experimental years (e.g. Björkegren 2001: 104), television soon found its place within the environment of the home. This is also the way in which audience research on television typically has engaged with the medium (e.g. Morley 1986; Ang 1996). However, late modern consumer settings, such as shopping malls and airports, as well as other public settings that are not primarily consumer oriented, such as waiting rooms, train stations, etc., are increasingly permeated with moving images via screens and television sets.

Historically, moving images have been used as commercial tools since the end of the nineteenth century. Between 1896 and 1898, a department store in the Galleria Umberto I, in Naples, Italy, sponsored public screenings of films to attract customers (Bruno 1993: 38f), in what can possibly be labelled an early form of event marketing. The rise of *gallerias* and department stores in the 1890s can be related to strategies for corporate advertising at the end of the nine-teenth century. An indication of the interest in developing the new commercial culture can be seen in the tremendous growth in investment in advertising. In the United States between 1880 and 1910 annual corporate advertising grew from $30 million to $600 million (Budd et al. 1999: 6ff).[5] The focus on adver-tising as a marketing strategy followed from the newly introduced system of self-service, which required that 'the product "speak" directly to the buyer' in the absence of sales clerks (McCarthy 2001: 68). This absence of staff set higher demands on the designation of space, and the ability to attract customers and ultimately to make them purchase the goods on offer.

The research that has been done on social behaviour in relation to television in public places can help us to examine the televisual and aural landscape in Solna Centrum. Friedrich Krotz and Susan Tyler Eastman (1999; cf. Krotz 2001), for example, have in a comparative study of social orientations towards television viewing in malls, airports and restaurants in Hamburg, Germany and

Indianapolis, US, analysed commercial functions of television for users and for site managers respectively. For users, television functioned as a convenience, as atmosphere and as entertainment; for site managers, television simultaneously functioned as diversion, decoration and attraction. These functions can be paired together: what functions as convenience for site managers, for example, functions as diversion for users.

The *convenience/diversion* function is activated and practised in places where people wait, and aims at filling in waiting time in transportation centres, hairdressers, health clubs, and other waiting areas. In Solna Centrum, for example, several stores have television sets that show children's films, allowing parents to leave their children and go off and shop. The latest Disney release on video or children's cartoons are often shown. The *attraction/entertainment* function is employed to draw customers for food and drink sales, according to Krotz and Eastman (1999). This function can be found in bars, restaurants and pubs. The *decoration/atmosphere* function is intended to enhance the mood of customers, encouraging sales of music, youth clothing, shoes, hardware, sporting goods, cosmetics etc., and it can easily be concluded that this is a valid description of television use and function in Solna Centrum as well. As an aesthetic device, television is, for example, used by audio-visual retailers such as Expert or Thorn, who mix the programmes shown on their television sets on display, so that they resemble moving wallpaper in the store.

However, although these three pairings seem to exhaust all possible combinations, there are several other functions that can be attributed to television in Solna. For example, it is used for *information* in the form of teletext in banks, at the employment office and in the town hall. It is also employed for *point-of-purchase advertising* for commodities for sale, as in the toy store Lekplaneten where television sets display the latest video films for sale, as well as other toys on offer, under the guise of demonstrating their use. Further, monitors at the post office display the numbers in the queue system, while simultaneously the other half of the screen displays things to buy, such as CDs (that are, interestingly, not sold at the post office). The point-of-purchase advertising is similar to the attraction part of the attraction/entertainment function, and only differs from that function in that it is seldom entertaining in the way Krotz and Eastman describe. A third additional function is as a *surveillance device*, in the form of surveillance screens inside shops.

Dafna Lemish (1982), taking an action-oriented approach inspired by Erving Goffman and using ethnographic methods, studied rule-bound behaviour in relation to television viewing in student lounges, bars, dining areas and shopping areas. In her analysis she reveals four types of behaviour. First, public viewers adjusted to the physical setting or milieu. This was the most obvious of all rules, according to Lemish. Second, public viewers related themselves to other viewers by physical adjustment (for example, by not blocking another person's view), by fitting in (not being obtrusive), by censuring deviant or inappropriate behaviour (often in subtle forms such as exchanging glances), and by negotiations of programme selection. Third, public viewers adjusted themselves to the television set. Commercial breaks in fictional programmes indicated that it was acceptable to leave, for example, and solo viewers seemed to be the group most engaged in viewing. Fourth, Lemish observed that public viewing implied openness for 'television-related social interaction' (ibid.: 767f), meaning that television viewing stimulates conversations between strangers. A related function of public television viewing was 'stranger avoidance', which meant that intense engagement in viewing indicated a desire to be left alone.

Lemish's examples of behaviour, however, are only partially relevant for descriptions of viewing practices in Solna Centrum. They are of course relevant in describing the television behaviour in the bar Solna Krog, with its two monitors hanging from the ceiling, and its large-screen television set occasionally brought in for important sports events. But they do not fit so well when describing the relations between those who walk past the teletext, giving a quick glance to the latest share prices in the window of the bank opposite to the Hollywood stairs.

In her exhaustive study of the shaping of the architectonic landscape in public places with the aid of television, Anna McCarthy (2001) has pointed to several important features of 'out-of-home television'. Of note is the way that she describes how the medium helps define public space and contributes to the 'site-specificity' of everyday arenas, such as bars, airports, waiting areas and shopping malls. In the following section, I use some of McCarthy's ideas in order to describe further the symbolic landscape in Solna Centrum. Although my example of the mall might seem a very specific one, I argue that the way in which television is used in Solna Centrum is in concordance with how television is used in most shopping malls, at least in the West.

Solna Centrum as symbolic landscape

As a visual and aural landscape, Solna Centrum is characterized by a range of media that, combined with each other, create a symbolic space for consumption. Audio-visual media can of course be found in stores that sell television sets, CD-players, computers, and in music stores, etc. But there are also screens and television sets in other stores and places, like the teletext in the bank, or the sets to amuse customers in the bar described above. Television is also used by shop owners as a way to contribute to the aesthetic atmosphere around the commodities for sale. This is often the case in cosmetic shops, where small-screen monitors are stuck in-between posters, mirrors and cosmetics for sale. Or in music shops, where the television sets in the ceiling are tuned into MTV. In a similar way, when the television sets are off, the latest records (or the favourite records of the staff, depending on the genre and 'niche' orientation of the store) are played. In this way, music stores can thus either use audio-visual media to create mood, or to restrict the mood generator to 'mere' music. In a corresponding manner, the two stores in Solna Centrum that sell television sets arrange these in clusters to create the effect of 'moving wallpaper', showing a combination of set broadcast channels.

As Anna McCarthy (2001: 121) has argued, there are three main ways in which television is positioned in public places: 'overhead screens, single viewer settings, and screens in store windows'. These are also the ways in which most of the screens are arranged in Solna Centrum, if one expands on the store windows to include also those aesthetic arrangements that are inside television retail stores. In what follows, I use this categorization to explore in greater detail the relation between placements of the television sets and functions in Solna Centrum (working with the six functions described above). I will do this mainly on the basis of my observations in Spring 1999, when all the television monitors were systematically counted and mapped, but I will also draw on more recent observations.

On one specific occasion in June 1999, there were just over 100 television monitors in the centre (I counted only those that were active at the time).[6] Not only were these sets placed in a variety of ways, they also served various functions for mall managers, shop owners and customers. By far the most common placement of television sets was *above the head*. This was, and still is, a position that seems to serve all of the functions described earlier. It can serve as diversion for customers waiting in clothes or sports stores (e.g. while waiting for a friend or family member to try on clothes or shoes). The placement 'above the head' can also function as attraction/entertainment, to draw customers to a store. This was the case with several sports stores that showed live footage of Eurosport, and record shops and department stores that broadcast video clips from MTV. High positioning can also be decorative and provide mood via music videos, as displayed in record shops or in the record sales area of larger department stores. Information monitors are almost always placed in high positions, making the voice of information authoritative. The same is true of surveillance monitors, which are frequently placed above head height at entrances, apparently addressing entering customers with the reminder that they are being watched and that theft will not go unnoticed. The same is true inside a store, where the above the head position is common for surveillance monitors, fulfilling the same reminder function as the entry cameras.

If the above the head positioned television sets seem to serve all functions, the opposite is true of the *single viewer setting*. The only single viewer setting that is situated above head height in Solna Centrum is in the shoe repair shop. This small shop has one small screen placed above head height to the right of the counter, and functions as convenience and/or diversion. The positioning is obviously aimed at the person working in the shop (customers have to almost bend over the counter if they want to watch the sports broadcasts from Eurosport, to which the set is most frequently tuned). A more common placement for single viewer settings is exemplified by the sets in the children's section of Hennes & Mauritz, a large Swedish chain store (with branches in many European cities). This acts as a diversion function. In order to make the shopping more convenient for parents with small children, Hennes & Mauritz screen the latest video release for children. Most often, the film is the latest release from Disney, and the screening of a film like *Pocahontas*, for example, is surrounded by a display of children's socks, shirts and underwear adorned with characters from the video, thus making the screening take on features of point-of-purchase advertising.[7] The screen is typically placed in the middle of the children's section of the store, so that parents can see their children and make sure that they do not walk away from the screen (which, of course, they do not, but the central placement has a seemingly reassuring function for the shopping parent). Some Hennes & Mauritz stores have also made small rooms for children to sit and watch a video. These rooms are decorated with film posters, creating a cosy club-like surrounding for the children. Although these settings allow for more than one person to watch at a time, there is always a limit to the number of children able to sit in front of the screen. In this manner, the setting is similar to the way in which people have their television sets at home – that is, adjusted to a small family group viewing. Otherwise, as Krotz (2001: 123) has observed in Germany, television sets in public surroundings are seldom arranged the way they are in private households.

Another single viewer setting aimed at children in Solna Centrum is the single screen under the stairs that lead down to the supermarket in the basement. The screen is directed towards a three-row bench where children can sit and watch cartoons while their parents are shopping for food, in a similar arrangement to the one at Hennes & Mauritz. However, this set is often out of order, although on one occasion I spied an extremely bored child, half-lying on the bench, staring disinterestedly at the blank screen.

Another kind of single viewer setting, fulfilling another function, is the teletext screen inside one of the banks. One of the public telephones also has a digital screen (with authoritative, exhortative messages, such as 'Phone!', 'Fax!', etc.). Obviously single viewer settings tend to be situated more in private areas than in public ones, hence the lack of this positioning in the public parts of Solna Centrum, where the observations for this research were made.

The television sets in shop windows and inside the stores do not fulfil the function of convenience or diversion. Further, they are seldom used for attraction purposes in the way described by Krotz and Eastman (1999). However, one television and audio-visual retail store in the mall has a video camera directed outward from the shop, which is connected to a large television screen where passing customers can catch a glimpse of themselves. Although this arrangement has some similarities with surveillance screens that meet customers when entering into several of the other stores, this screen has a different function. First, it is not placed above head height; instead it is positioned below head level, in the way that television sets are positioned in the home. Second, it does not capture the customer on his or her way into the store. The main function is attracting the gaze of those who pass by, but the effect seems to be restricted to children, as few grown-ups seem to pay much attention to the screen. This is possibly a result of the low positioning, which would suit a sitting grown-up but not one who is standing. For children, who are shorter, this position is of course more appropriate. However, television sets in shops and store windows often have decorative, aesthetic functions, shaping the commercial mood in those shops that sell television sets, videos and other audio-visual equipment. These shops, of which there are two in Solna, have similar arrangements, where television sets are stapled against two or more walls, and where channels are set to form an overall pattern of images.

In the mall, there are also other shops and boutiques that use television screens for aesthetic purposes. The cosmetics shop has placed small screens among the cosmetics on the shelves, screening advertising clips for the surrounding goods for sale. As has already been described, music stores often engage television for aesthetic decoration and atmosphere. Television sets in music stores are usually placed above head height, displaying video clips from the niche genres of the store, or, in the case of the music section of the department store Åhléns, from the top ten list (as a matter of course, department stores always emphasise the mainstream).

Television sets in stores only function as information points if they are placed above head height, and these are mainly to be found in banks, post offices and similar institutions, where they are often used to give information on which number in line you are, or, when in grocery stores, about which goods are sold for reduced prices. A more frequent use of television screens within stores is as point of purchase advertising. Some stores have developed this extensively, for example the hardware store, where at times there can be up to ten screens in different parts of the shop, displaying the different uses of certain tools which are displayed to the side of the television set.

In summary, then, one can say that above head positioning of television sets is the most common arrangement in the mall, and it fulfils all six functions discussed here. Television sets in store windows and inside shops are mainly used for *attraction/entertainment*, *decoration/atmosphere* and sometimes in specific places for *information* and *point of purchase advertising*. In the main, single viewer settings have the function of *information* and sometimes *convenience/diversion*, but they are on the whole the least common arrangement in public areas, at least in Solna Centrum, but probably this is the same in other malls as well. Screens above head height are mainly used for *surveillance*, although they can also be used for *decoration/atmosphere* and for *information*.

Positioning the customer

The placement of the television set above the head, which is the most frequent position, forces, or lures, the customer to look up at the screen. In such stores, which are not usually television retail stores, screens above head height function as information services (at the post office, gambling shops and tobacconists displaying sports results, etc.), but they are mainly used for surveillance. The authoritative address from above, in combination with the lack of sound from the screens used for information and surveillance, address, or interpellate, the subject in a position wherein the only reaction is either to comply with the address or to ignore it. The surveillance screens of course display live footage from stores and store entrances, but the information screens are purely text-based: occasionally, some screens at gambling places display sports games, but most have a more informative function, which is not reliant on sound.

The placement of surveillance screens in different parts of the shopping centre thus reveals something of the relation between staff and customers. Surveillance screens that are situated in the areas where customers can move about freely among the merchandise are almost always situated above head height, addressing customers from an authoritative position. Surveillance monitors that are situated in single viewer settings, intended for only the staff to see, are, on the other hand, often placed low – for example, beneath a counter, so that the staff look down at the customers. In this way, the angle of the surveilling gaze is closed (cf. Fyfe & Bannister 1998).

From this research, it might be possible to claim that above head positioning always indicates authoritative positioning. However, leaving behind the phenomenon of surveillance screens, and looking instead at those above head height screens that have an aesthetic function, the degree of 'authoritativeness' becomes highly dependent on the content of what is displayed. If live footage from inside of stores and public areas have the most authoritative connotations, other contents are less so, or at least, interpellate customers in different authoritative voices. If surveillance screens engage with moral authority, seemingly reminding customers to subject themselves to the legal framework of private ownership, then music video clips, sports broadcasts or entertainment shows interpellate with the tempting voice of desire, reminding them of the duty to consume (cf. Baudrillard 1970/1988). If surveillance screens remind customers of what *is not* theirs, most other fictional or entertainment content speaks of what possibly *could be* theirs.

We have seen above that there are systematic ways in which television is dispersed throughout the consumer milieu in Solna, privileging above head height positioning. How, then, can we interpret this symbolic landscape, and how is it used by site managers, shop owners and staff?

Dreaming the administrative rationality

In the mid-twentieth century, Adorno, Horkheimer and other representatives of the Frankfurt School lamented the ways in which spheres within the lifeworld became subsumed under an administrative logic or rationality that permeated large areas of social life. The historical background, with mushrooming totalitarian societies in the form of Soviet 'state capitalism' and the fascist states of Germany and Italy, as well as the extreme capitalism of the United States, inspired the fathomless pessimism of the forces of capitalism in relation to the life spheres of individuals. This was expressed forcefully in Adorno and Horkheimer's (1947/1979) essay on the culture industries.

This administrative rationality can also be applied to an analysis of television in consumer settings. However, while it is hard to deny that there is an administrative logic to the ways in which television and other components of the symbolic landscape are used, it does not always follow that the strategies of the site managers, store owners and staff always fulfil their intended purposes. In interviews, the site manager, for example, points to the difficulties in organizing the flow of customers. On the one hand, he wants to have a substantial flow of customers through the aisles of the mall, and thus he encourages shop owners to develop event marketing strategies to attract customers. On the other hand, however, the flow of customers can be 'too heavy', creating a form of 'chaos' that is counterproductive for the task of distributing goods to customers (Bolin 2001: 334f). In the eyes of the mall manager, events that are too spectacular distract customers and take away their concentration from the merchandise. Thus he prefers more subtle events, such as having a piano player in the lobby, accompanying the flow of customers and providing a sense of 'mood'. He also has quite elaborate thoughts about how to control the flow with the help of muzak (cf. Sterne 1997), and once ordered a special composition that was supposed to 'follow' the customers through the site, bringing popular connotations and 'smoothing' the movements of the customers. He described the composition as having a 'soft Cuban rhythm'.

The administrative logic concerns both the architectonics and the symbolic space in the mall. The 'hard' architectonic structuring attempts are illustrated by the fact that benches inside the mall have been removed in order to keep people on the move. Combined with the 'soft' symbolic structuring devices, in the form of music and visuals, the management tries to regulate the flow in the centre. This is, however, far from uncontroversial. Older customers, especially, want to have somewhere to sit when visiting the centre (cf. Lövgren 2001). This makes public space also contested space, where the dream to rationalize shopping behaviour is confronted by the wishes of individuals, not only to be addressed as customers, but also as visitors. If the administrative logic of the economic system turns the environment into 'instrumental space' (Goss 1993: 29), this becomes confronted with the social and expressive logic of the life-world, with its insistence on needs that lie outside of the economic rationality. The aim is to establish what could be called 'communicative space', a kind of space that is not commodified, as are the waiting or resting spaces in cafés and restaurants, where you have to buy in order to be able to sit.

The kinds of rationales that result in the removal of benches, and the adaptation of musical genres that shape the background soundtrack to the shopping, are expressions of the will to control the movements of customers in the shopping centre. To this should, of course, also be added the fact that the shopping centre has its own guards that control the premises, deciding who can move about and who are not particularly welcome (e.g. substance abusers who supposedly disturb customers). The hiring of guards, and removing benches, means that the mall managers are involved with the administration of bodies in space (cf. Foucault

1975/1979: 135ff), helping these bodies to come in contact with consumer prod-ucts (which are also distributed in space in different ways). With the help of event marketing and other marketing strategies, the mall manager and the store owners and staff try to develop techniques for controlling bodies in space, to shape a 'ductile mass' (McCarthy 2001: 74f). The wish of sales-floor managers is to control flows of customers, to administrate movement. To control the flow of people by means of structuring the symbolic environment becomes a way of controlling economics and, as a result, the customers become subsumed under an economic rationality. The 'art of distributions' becomes directed towards the consuming body (Foucault 1975/1979: 141ff). The way that the symbolic land-scape addresses the consumer subject can be seen as part of this art. However, this art takes on different forms in different consumer settings.

The art of distribution involves the movement of bodies around the premises, in order to make bodies meet merchandise, be exposed to their symbolic qualities, subjected to the authoritative address of temptation, and tempted to buy. Bodies, however, are not things that automatically respond to stimuli from outside (cf. du Gay and Negus 1994: 405). Bodies react to the movements they are drawn into, for example by perceptual adaptation to the visual environment. As Anne Friedberg (1993) has eloquently shown, since the late nineteenth century there has been a shift in perception whereby a 'mobi-lized gaze' has developed as an answer to the changing characteristics of visual media, not least to film, and to new vehicles of transportation such as cars, trains, elevators and escalators. If one considers this mobilized gaze an effect of the new visual and transportation phenomena, the meaning of this effect is seldom restricted to the total submission under the authoritative interpellation. It is, rather, an effect of the negotiations between this interpellation and how individual subjects interpret this address and the meaning structures it carries. In conclusion, I now want to discuss those meaning structures, taking as my example the slogan, 'Make yourself at home in Solna Centrum.'

At home in the era of economic rationality

As an overall strategy for the administration of space in Solna Centrum, and for the administration of bodies within that commercial geography, the mall manage-ment has chosen to adjust to the historical background of the municipality, and relate to its roots in the Swedish concept of 'People's Home'. Thus one of the mall's slogans reads: 'Make yourself at home in Solna Centrum.' The slogan is reworked in several versions, for example: 'Make your home in Solna Centrum', or 'Make yourself at home.' The visuals that accompany the slogan also vary over time, as does the medium for distributing this message (e.g. ads in the local paper, posters inside the mall, stickers, the web pages of the mall, etc.). The slogan is often accompanied by pictures of families, often young families with children, or young couples holding each other's hands. In that respect, the slogan is addressed to these consumer groups, which incidentally are the very same groups of consumers that

139

television advertisers want to reach via broadcast television on the commercial channels (cf. Bolin 2002). The analogy with broadcast television is not incidental. Just as mainstream mass media addresses their audience in a rhetoric that supposedly offends as few as possible, and thus are reflecting the dominant ideology, the consumer address in shopping malls also reflects broad individual and group identities, to the neglect of groups and individuals that deviate from the mainstream.

As noted earlier, in Sweden the home is strongly connected to post-war political ideals through the concept of the 'People's Home', which like the concept of Heimat, highlights the collective society. This Swedish model was, as Peter Dahlgren (2000) points out, predicated on corporatism with a high degree of co-ordination and consensual agreement between state, capital and labour. These are agreements between, on the one hand, the political and the economic system, and on the other hand, those less intimate parts of the lifeworld to which labour belongs (cf. Åker 1998: 30ff).

Television is a medium with strong connections to the private home as a symbolic category. As Lynn Spigel (1992) has shown, television and home are strongly linked to domestic and family ideals. Thus it is most often connected to the intimate sphere of the lifeworld. But a shopping mall is part of the economic system, and thus far from integrated into lifeworld practices. However, as Jürgen Habermas (1981/1991 and 1981/1992) has discussed, there has always been a tendency for the systems to grow stronger in relation to the lifeworld, striving to colonize spheres within it. Examples of this include economic rationalization, where parts of our private and intimate relations, even if never having been totally freed from system demands and intrusion, are to an increasing extent addressed as markets.[8] And this economic rationalization also includes the attempts to redefine the discourse on home.

Home is a contradictory term in relation to spaces such as shopping malls, as malls are by definition sites of departure and destination that have become 'depots for temporal tourism produced by a mobilized and virtual gaze' (Friedberg 1993: 91; cf. Lash and Urry 1994). However, as a medium, television has the capacity for transgressing the border between systems and the lifeworld. Television screens have the potential to address more effectively the consuming subject in public spaces, as if he or she were at home, as opposed to more traditional media, such as outdoor advertising or window displays. Since television strongly connotes home and intimate relations, the medium is well suited to accompany such slogans as 'Make yourself at home in Solna Centrum.' Television is a medium that became widespread in Sweden (and in many other parts of the world) in the 1950s, which also firmly anchors it within the Swedish context of the 'People's Home'. Arguably, television is the only medium that symbolizes this era in Swedish political and cultural history. It could also be argued that the connection between television and the intimate sphere of the home is stronger in Sweden than it is in the United States, or other countries where television was organized commercially from the start, as commercial funding makes it more strongly connected with the economic system.

However, because of this, the economic system is in the process of incorporating the concept of home into an administrative-economic rationality. And there are good reasons for this, when seen from the point of view of the system. If the logic of capitalism is built on the premise to continually produce more profit, this expansion has to be gained from somewhere. This somewhere can take two forms, one of which can be further subdivided in two. The first is in the form of an *external extension* of the market – an expansion to include new national markets, which have not yet been exploited. The second is in the form of an *internal expansion*. Internal expansion can, on the one hand, be realized by making the production–consumption circuit more effective, for example by turning over commodities faster. This is exemplified by the pressure from the fashion industry to have people update their wardrobes each season, or for children to adopt new toys to replace last month's favourite, or to replace last week's hit song, etc. On the other hand, one could make the old market take on more areas of hitherto unexploited parts of the lifeworld, for example the private areas represented by the home and the commodification of those signs connected to it. And as an aid in this internal expansion, symbolic environments such as Solna Centrum have become tools to further lubricate the wheels of capitalism (cf. Slater 2002).

If one could say that the nineteenth-century *flâneur*, or observer, of modern life was offered the illusion of mobility in the shape of experiences of temporally and spatially remote times and places in the passages, panoramas and department stores (cf. Friedberg 1993: 38), it could be said of his or her late modern cousin that he/she is offered home, rootedness and intimacy in shopping malls such as Solna Centrum. Paradoxically, television, which has been one of the media that have fuelled the development of the mobilized gaze, has at the beginning of the twenty-first century turned into a tool also for the opposite tendency. For Raymond Williams (1974/1979), who inspired Friedberg's concept of mobile privatization, television was a medium that could take the viewer places, from the private sitting room to the world outside. In Solna Centrum, television is taking home into the world.

Notes

1   Although sound has been underprivileged in relation to sight, this is even more significant when it comes to smell (cf. Classen et al. 1994). Sound and smell have, perhaps unfortunately, not been at the focus of this study either.

2   The research has been conducted within the project 'Popular Passages: Media in the Modern Consumption Space', financed by The Bank of Sweden's Tercentenary Foundation. The head of the project was Johan Fornäs, and co-researchers were Karin Becker, Erling Bjurström and Hillevi Ganetz. I will also use some observations made by anthropologist Hasse Huss, who worked with the group to study specifically the soundscape of Solna Centrum (cf. Huss 2001). For this chapter, I have used material from the collective empirical data collection (observations and interviews) carried out between 1998 and 2000. Project reports include Bjurström et al. (2000) and Becker et al. (2001).

3   Statistics come from www.solna.se (where information is also available in English). See also www.solnacentrum.se
4   Because the mall is constantly changing, the number of shops and restaurants varies from year to year. The most recent years have seen an expansion of the centre, with the addition of another pedestrian street covered with a glass roof. For further information, refer to: www.solnacentrum.se
5   Corresponding statistics are not available for Sweden before the 1950s, and even at that time they were quite vague. However, one source mentions SEK 981 million for the year 1961, where advertising in the press amounted to SEK 572 million (Albinsson et al. 1964: 13).
6   In the television retail stores, there were obviously many more sets stacked around the walls. However, they were not included in this research count.
7   This extremely well-organized and integrated commercial strategy is one of the most sophisticated ways in which Disney and its numerous affiliated companies have conquered world markets. The integrative strategy is also accompanied by the throwing of release parties for children, special agreements with Swedish television to include the latest release for TV Christmas specials, joint advertising campaigns with department stores, etc. (cf. Bolin 1996).
8   To give but one example: the time away from work, when the working body is supposed to be recreating and resting in order to be able to produce surplus value more efficiently, has increasingly been turned into market participation. Holidays, health products, entertainment offers, Father's day gifts, etc., address the individual through advertising – not least via commercial television in the private home. In this sense, the recreating body is made into a consuming body. For a more elaborate discussion, see Bolin (2002).

Bibliography

Adorno, T.W. and Horkheimer, M. (1947/1979) *Dialectic of Enlightenment*, London: Verso.

Åker, P. (1998) *Vår Bostad i folkhemmet. Bilden av hemmet i en organisationstidskrift*, Nora: Nya Doxa.

Albinsson, G., Tengelin, S. and Wärneryd, K.-E. (1964) *Reklamens ekonomiska roll*, Stockholm: Almqvist & Wiksell.

Ang, I. (1996) *Living Room Wars. Rethinking Media Audiences for a Postmodern World*, London: Routledge.

Baudrillard, J. (1970/1998) *The Consumer Society. Myths and Structures*, London: Sage.

—— (1972/1981) *For a Critique of the Political Economy of the Sign*, St. Louis: Telos.

—— (1973/1975) *The Mirror of Production*, St. Louis: Telos.

—— (1985/1986) 'Massorna: det socialas implosion i medierna', in M. Löfgren and A. Molander (eds), *Postmoderna tider?*, Stockholm: Norstedts: 327–43.

Bauman, Z. (1998) *Work, Consumerism and the New Poor*, Buckingham: Open University Press.

Becker, K., Ekecrantz, J. and Olsson, T. (2000) 'Introduction: Picturing Politics in 20th Century Sweden', in K. Becker, J. Ekecrantz and T. Olsson (eds), *Picturing Politics. Visual and Textual Formations of Modernity in the Swedish Press*, Stockholm: JMK: 8–25.

Becker, K., Bjurström, E., Fornäs, J. and Ganetz, H. (eds) (2001) *Passager. Medier och kultur i ett köpcentrum*, Nora: Nya Doxa.

Björkegren, D. (2001) *Glädjens mekanismer. Sveriges Television*, Stockholm: Carlssons.

Bjurström, E., Fornäs, J. and Ganetz, H. (2000) *Det kommunikativa handlandet. Kulturella perspektiv på medier och konsumtion*, Nora: Nya Doxa.

Bolin, G. (1996) 'Länge leve Disney! – så länge du kan köpa', in *Filmhäftet. Kritisk tidskrift för analys av rörliga bilder*, no. 3: 44–8.
—— (2001) 'Konsumentflöden', in Becker et al. (eds), *Passager*: 329–35.
—— (2002) 'In the Market for Symbolic Commodities. Swedish Lottery Game Show *Bingolotto* and the Marketing of Social and Cultural Values', *Nordicom Review*, 23:1–2: 177–204.
Bruno, G. (1993) *Streetwalking on a Ruined Map. Cultural Theory and the City Films of Elvira Notari*, Princeton: Princeton University Press.
Budd, M., Craig, S. and Steinman, C. (1999) *Consuming Environments. Television and Commercial Culture*, New Brunswick, N.J. and London: Rutgers University Press.
Classen, C., Howes, D. and Synnott, A. (1994) *Aroma. The Cultural History of Smell*, London and New York: Routledge.
Dahlgren, P. (2000) 'Media and Power Transitions in a Small Country: Sweden', in J. Curran and M.-J. Park (eds), *De-Westernizing Media Studies*, London and New York: Routledge.
de Certeau, M. (1984/1988) *The Practice of Everyday Life*, Berkeley, Los Angeles and London: University of California Press.
Foucault, M. (1975/1979) *Discipline and Punish. The Birth of the Prison*, Harmondsworth: Penguin.
Fredriksson, C. (1998) *Ett paradis för alla*, Stockholm: Nordiska museets förlag.
Friedberg, A. (1993) *Window Shopping. Cinema and the Postmodern*, Berkeley: University of California Press.
Fyfe, N.R. and Bannister, J. (1998) ' "The Eyes Upon the Street". Closed-circuit Television Surveillance and the City', in N.R. Fyfe (ed.) *Images of the Street. Planning, Identity and Control in Public Space*, London and New York: Routledge: 254–67.
Goss, J. (1993) 'The "Magic of the Mall": An Analysis of Form, Function, and Meaning in the Contemporary Retail Built Environment', *Annals of the Association of American Geographers*, 83:1: 18–47.
Gustavsson, M. (2001) 'Markägare och mötesplatser', in Becker et al. (eds) *Passager*: 53–86.
Habermas, J. (1981/1991) *The Theory of Communicative Action. Vol. 1: Reason and the Rationalization of Society*, Cambridge: Polity Press.
—— (1981/1992) *The Theory of Communicative Action. Vol. 2: The Critique of Functionalist Reason*, Cambridge: Polity Press.
Huss, H. (2001) 'Passagernas ton', in Becker et al. (eds), *Passager*: 209–28.
Karlsson, H. (1996) *Köpcentrumkatalogen*, Stockholm: Centrumutveckling.
Krotz, F. (2001) *Die Mediatisierung kommunikativen Handelns. Der Wandel von Alltag und sozialen Beziehungen, Kultur und Gesellschaft durch die Medien*, Wiesbaden: Westdeutcher Verlag.
Krotz, F. and Eastman, S.T. (1999) 'Orientations toward Television Outside the Home', *Journal of Communication*, 49:1: 5–27.
Lasch, S. and Urry, J. (1994) *Economies of Signs and Space*, London: Sage.
Lemish, D. (1982) 'The Rules of Viewing Television in Public Places', *Journal of Broadcasting*, 26:4: 758–81.
Lövgren, K. (2001) 'Batonger och bänkar', in Becker et al. (eds) *Passager*: 130–50.
Marx, K. (1867/1974) *Kapitalet. Kritik av den politiska ekonomin. Första boken: Kapitalets produktionsprocess*, Lund: Arkiv Zenit.

McCarthy, A. (2001) *Ambient Television. Visual Culture and Public Space*, Durham, N.C. and London: Duke University Press.

Miller, D. (ed.) (1995) *Acknowledging Consumption. A Review of New Studies*, London and New York: Routledge.

Miller, D., Jackson, P., Thrift, N., Holbrook, B. and Rowlands, M. (1998) *Shopping, Place and Identity*, London and New York: Routledge.

Morley, D. (1986) *Family Television*, London: Comedia/Routledge.

—— (2000) *Home Territories. Media, Mobility and Identity*, London and New York: Routledge.

Murdock, G. (2000) 'Peculiar Commodities: Audiences at Large in the World of Goods', in I. Hagen and J. Wasko (eds) *Consuming Audiences? Production and Reception in Media Research*, Creskill, N.J.: Hampton Press: 47–70.

Rybczynski, W. (1986/1987) *Home. A Short History of an Idea*, Harmondsworth: Penguin.

Slater, D. (2002) 'Capturing Markets from the Economists', in P. du Gay and M. Pryke (eds) *Cultural Economy. Cultural Analysis and Commercial Life*, London: Sage: 59–77.

Spigel, L. (1992) *Make Room for TV. Television and the Family Ideal in Postwar America*, Chicago and London: University of Chicago Press.

Sterne, J. (1997) 'Sounds Like the Mall of America: Programmed Music and the Architectonics of Commercial Space', *Ethnomusicology*, 41:1: 22–50.

Williams, R. (1974/1979) *Television. Technology and Cultural Form*, London: Fontana.

Zola, É. (1883/1927) *Damernas Paradis* [The Ladies' Paradise], Stockholm: Bröderna Lindströms förlags AB.

8

DOT.COM URBANISM

Andrew Ross

In his book *Bobos in Paradise*, David Brooks offers an extended description of a 'new upper class' which fuses bourgeois and bohemian values, and whose apotheosis is the blue-jean capitalist, preaching liberation management and ingesting organic food. Most of the story Brooks tells about this truce between traditionally warring parties focuses on patterns of taste, consumption and habits of self-expression. 'Marx', he writes, 'told us that classes inevitably conflict, but sometime they just blur.' 'The values of the bourgeois, mainstream culture and the values of the 1960s counterculture', he concludes, 'have merged' (Brooks 2000: 43). Yet Brooks' warring parties have little to do with what Marx meant by class conflict. The conflict between bourgeois and bohemian has always been the result of generational friction or sibling rivalry within a dominant class. Bohemians, then and now, have been attracted to the cause of class conflict as much for aesthetic as for political reasons, but their anti-establishment interests are usually much better served by the maintenance of the bourgeois status quo than by the often repressive outcome of class wars. In this regard, Brooks, as a self-defined bobo, seems no less confused about class identity than Gustave Flaubert or Jack Kerouac had been.

Brooks' cheerful depiction of the bobo is basically an elaborate market profile of an upscale consumer, and could be used as such by the marketing departments of any Tom, Dick and Harry in the gourmet retail business. If we look beneath these alterations in the sumptuary style and etiquette of individuals we will find a much deeper revision of industrial personality. A portrait of the work process ought to provide more telling evidence of this change than Brooks' vignette of the bobo consumer. It will show us what happens when the routine pace and rhythms of industry are reprogrammed to accommodate an artist's work mentality that once flourished in defiance of industrial routine.

To recount this story properly, we must begin with the traditional urban habitat of artists, and consider the changes wrought on this environment by their new industrial recruiters. For most of the post-war period, urban downtowns were the last places you might have expected to see signs of industrial growth. By the late 1980s, some pundits were wryly suggesting that commercial property values might be saved if portions of center cities were allowed to revert to pasture. Yet within a decade, many of these city economies were prospering, and had seen the appearance of new urban industries for the first time since the 1960s. Ever since the flight of manufacturing, city managers had been full-time supplicants, ever vigilant in wooing companies that showed any interest in locating within their borders. By the 1990s, there were clear winners and losers of this courtship game. The losers were scrambling to make room for casinos, and their downtowns, if they were alive at all, were stamped by the mammoth footprint of sports stadiums, museums and retail entertainment centers. The winners had capitalized on niche opportunities in the value-adding economy. Their growth industries, grouped in the high-end tier of producer services, were generating jobs in spades. This growth was less evident in the high-rise enclaves of their central business districts than in the old manufacturing downtown neighborhoods, where the facial marks of dilapidation were profiled and accentuated as indices of vitality, youthful regeneration and glamour.

The new media companies that moved into these zones could not afford prime commercial rents, but their no-collar employees did not want, in any case, to work in plush corporate towers. The bare-plaster, low-rent ambience was as much an aesthetic virtue for the employees as it was an economic necessity for the owners, and it proved an effective and visible way for the companies to advertise themselves as grassroots alternatives to corporate America. Like two generations of artists before them, they would be playing an equivocal role in neighborhood gentrification. The same formula that had driven residential gentrification for three decades would now be applied to the commercial zones of these old neighborhoods, where depressed rents made property ripe for speculative development. From the perspective of city landlords, the digital economy was not a messianic movement bent on delivering a millenial future. It was a high-protein stimulant for zones in transition, and the shabby chic of its boutique companies and human capital was a perfect engine for pumping value into depreciated land assets.

Nowhere was the cost of this transition more deeply felt than in San Francisco, where, in the late 1990s, 70,000 new jobs were being created each year. The city had become an annex of Silicon Valley, and the hub of a New Economy commuting zone that stretched from Santa Cruz in the south to the Russian River in the north, and as far as Stockton in the east. Twenty million dollars of venture capital were washing daily through the city's economy by the fall of 1999. Unlike in New York, the new media sector had become the largest single source of employment, and the high-price growth of this monocrop was crowding everything and everyone else out. Residential rents had already inched above Manhattan's nosebleed prices, and, as downtown leases ran out, landlords quintupled commercial rents (to highs of $80 per square foot for Class A space, the highest asking rate in the nation). Longtime residents of bohemian and working-class areas, like the industrial warehouse sector below Market Street (SoMa), the South Park quadrant and the Mission district to the south, were being squeezed out daily. Artists of all stripes, along with other low-income groups, were faced with extinction in a city renowned for its maverick, counter-cultural spirit (See Chonin and Levy 2000; Nieves 2000: 27; Selvin 2000: A8).

The irony of this predicament escaped few, least of all those employees who had been attracted to the Bay Area for its natural and cultural advantages. Like discerning tourists looking for an unspoiled beach, they had arrived on a surge of people and money that threatened to destroy the very reasons for being there. Barry Christgau, an engineer who had moved from the Mid-West in the late 1980s to work for Sun Microsystems, acknowledged the contradiction: 'I came here for the mountains, ocean, and the liberal lifestyle, and to be with the brightest of the breed. Now people come for the money – the city is full of MBAs and BMWs – and the environment is being ruined. I'm by no means not guilty, and it's a strange feeling to know you are a vehicle for things you don't really agree with. I wish the boom would end.' Christgau could see how turbo-capitalism was making the city unaffordable for those with no stake in the gold rush. He lived in the lower Mission district where neighborhood activists had taken to occupying the buildings of companies that were displacing nonprofits and artists' spaces. Incidents of arson were being reported. 'You have the right to choose to live and work anywhere,' Christgau remarked, and added, cryptically, 'but you don't have the right to live and work anywhere.'

Gulch of pain

In late November 2000, Proposition L, a city ordinance that would curtail the expansion of office space for the Internet industry, was narrowly defeated. Most new media employees were aware of the growing conflict around office expansion, and were deeply ambivalent about the move. 'I'm doing this job to fund my art work', explained a web developer who also made what she calls 'community sculptures'. 'But the way things are going, there won't be anywhere left in this city to do my stuff.' Like many other progressive, arts-minded Internet employees, she had found herself with one foot on either side of battle lines that criss-crossed a landscape in the throes of another gold rush.

In a city with an unrivaled record as a laboratory of social and cultural innovation, the species of gentrification that blew in with the Internet business models had a complex make-up. For one thing, the Internet economy took root in San Francisco rather than Silicon Valley precisely because it was a refuge for alternative thinking, and boasted a resident labor pool of creative workers. Community use of the Internet had been pioneered in the rave scene, on listservs like the Well, and in a frankly non-commercial climate of experimentation. The city was home to *Wired*, which broadcast a glamorous fervor in all things hi-tech, and was heir to a legacy of homegrown utopia in influential publications, from the *Whole Earth Review* of the 1960s to the *Mondo 2000* of the 1980s. Everyone who was not a Bay Area newcomer could say 'it was a culture before it was an industry', and it was common among scene veterans to make a distinction between web people – devoted to the ideals of transforming communication, shareware and free information – and dot.commers – who were widely regarded as gold-diggers.

But San Francisco had also been built on land speculation, beginning with the grabbing of lots in the two years between the raising of the American flag and the chartering of the city in 1850, and continuing with the gold rush and wave after wave of railroad speculation. Portions of the city had a long history of real estate inflation in boom times. South Park itself was a working-class Filipino quarter before it became the epicenter of Multimedia Gulch (Mayor Willie Brown's name for the Internet district north of Portrero Hill), but its origins lay in a much earlier land boom, in the 1860s, when it was developed as an elegant enclave for the city's pioneer mercantile and professional elites (Shumate 1988).[1]

When city artists were last faced with displacement – during the boom of the 1980s – they had fought back and won from City Hall a special live/work ordinance that permitted the conversion of formerly industrial space into studios. This 1988 measure bypassed building codes and affordable housing stipulations. In the course of the next decade, however, it became the loophole of choice for developers to circumvent the city's annual cap on new office construction.[2] Through a loose interpretation of this ordinance, new media companies could define their new premises in SoMa (where development had been all but frozen since 1986) as something other than office space (Blackwell 2000). As Rebecca Solnit and Susan Schwartzenberg point out in *Hollow City*, their passionate account of the 'Siege of San Francisco', Internet companies and their employees looking to locate in a cool district with industrial lofts and warehouses were the ideal clients for landlords who had learned how to manipulate the live/work ordinance (Solnit and Schwartzenberg 2000).

In response, anti-gentrification sentiment ran high. Some of the street protests had a carnivalesque air, recalling an earlier ritual declaration of the demise of a counterculture: Death of Hippie, in Haight-Ashbury, in October 1967.

DEATH NOTICE

It's time. ... Please join us in person or in spirit as we mourn the passing of San Francisco Culture. At two o'clock on Saturday October 21th we will convene at Union Square and proceed up Market Street bearing a coffin to the Steps of City Hall. The procession will include a marching band and police escort ending with speakers, performances, and celebration. Maybe you've watched this unique city's culture, built on diversity and a thriving art community, being strangled by blindly managed growth in recent years. What happened? How can we influence the social impacts of our new economy? (We request that all participants wear somber attire befitting a funeral march).[3]

Other protest groups, like the Mission Yuppie Eradication Society, were less polite, encouraging the aggrieved to vandalize SUVs parked on the street, or to trash and torch 'yuppie bars'. Formed as a unity lobby, the Mission Anti-Displacement Coalition focused on the industry's penetration of the predominantly working-class Latino (and formerly Irish) district that had recently seen the invasion of avant-garde sushi restaurants with valet parking.

In the Mission, for example, landlords (mostly non-Latino) rented on a month-to-month lease, and could quadruple their asking prices at will. It had become common for SoMa landlords to demand company stock before they would lease to start-ups. Unlike the highly visible Internet entrepreneurs, whose business profile required them to seek publicity and to cultivate flamboyant personalities, landlords knew how to remain faceless, and had a long history of evading public scrutiny. All the same, there were few participants in this citywide drama who could claim the moral high ground. Even the anti-gentrification activists were derided by Mission locals as 'old yuppies', who had arrived twenty years before, with their Apple Macs and mountain bikes, and were now trying to drive out the 'new yuppies' with their SUVs, cell-phones and East Coast MBAs.

Like the artists, performers or writers who were also Net employees, community art groups had scant reason to turn their backs on the Internet sector, since so many of their clientele worked for new media companies. Jonathan Youtt, co-founder of CellSpace, which occupied a sprawling, multilevel, 10,000 square foot warehouse in the Mission, estimated that half of the people who used the facility depended on paychecks from the New Economy. CellSpace had grown out of a puppetry collective into a center for collaborative arts that was 95 per cent volunteer run, and had broad ties with community initiatives in the Mission and beyond. Offering performance and exhibition space for dance, art, opera, spoken word, film, music and rollerskating, the warehouse was also a hive of artisanal activity, hosting workshops for metal, sewing, wood, sound, food, digital connectivity and multimedia production. In a venue like this, it was easy to see the continuity between the pre-industrial and the post-industrial arts and crafts. Digital activity was not a distinct realm of gee-whizzery, eclipsing all that had gone before. It was simply one among several crafts for creative expression that had evolved over time, and was made available here as just another medium for community use.

On the night I visited Youtt, yoga and kung fu classes were in session, along with 'tango for protest', and a benefit for groups pushing for the city to create a public power utility. Locals were lining up to use the computer terminals. Youtt, attired like a whimsical magician with streetwise trappings, acknowledged that 'artists are often quite unaware of their role in gentrification, and don't see themselves as a problem'. Those most devoted to their own personal growth (the practitioners of 'art for art's sake') are the ones who 'end up having the most physical impact on the city'. The community arts movement had a different record, because of its direct involvement in neighborhood initiatives and its view of art as a vehicle for community initiatives and empowerment.

Youtt was optimistic that the digital medium would prevail over the dark side of its commercial exploitation. 'There are enough hackers and other Web originators', he estimated, 'to make sure it stays true to their liberating, commercial-free intentions.' As for the developers and entrepreneurs who had colluded in the evictions, Youtt turned necromancer in forecasting their ruin: 'if you enter into this kind of deal with the devil, it means that your whole business is doomed, as far as I can tell. Karmically doomed.' Over the next several months, his prophecy would bear fruit, with or without help from the spirit world. By the end of 2001, failing dot.coms had produced a large surplus of available office space, and rents were dropped as much as 50 per cent in the SoMa submarket (Cushman and Wakefield 2001).

Silicon footprint

Techno-futurists, from Alvin Toffler to Nicholas Negroponte, had forecast that computers would have a decentralizing impact on work. Power, population and wealth would no longer need to be concentrated in metro centers. For many purposes, and for many types of employees, it was predicted that the physical sense of place might become obsolete. Yet this scenario of dispersion had not materialized, as a quick glance at the overheated economies of urban downtowns would show. The dramatic job growth and soaring rents in older metropolitan centers like New York and Chicago had been nearly matched by smaller cities like Boston, Seattle, Toronto, Denver, Portland, San Jose, Salt Lake City, San Diego, San Francisco and Atlanta. It was the same story in Los Angeles, where a combination of unemployed IT workers from the decimated aerospace industry and a glut of underused warehouse space on the West Side had fueled the digital build-up. If anything, there had been an over-concentration of new producer service industries in downtown venues, along with a recentralization of human capital and know-how. In principle, much of the New Economy could be run and serviced by virtual means. In practice, the physical footprints of its geographical division of labor were very tightly mapped onto the existing infrastructure of high-speed backbones and data hubs: the old Arpanet centers of Boston, San Francisco and Washington, or at the termini of intercontinental fiber-optic cables, in Los Angeles, New York, San Francisco and Washington (Cohen 2000).

Outside of the media, fashion and culture industries, most large corporations still had no explicit need for central urban locations, but that had more to do with cost accounting than with the introduction of advanced technology. Science-based knowledge industries, including hardware and software complexes, continued to concentrate on the high-end suburban periphery: Santa Clara County, Irvine and La Jolla in Southern California, Raleigh-Durham in North Carolina, Route 128, outside of Boston, suburban Austin, Redmond, Washington and the Colorado front range. The urban growth in jobs and digital industry was a result of several factors: a ready supply of underemployed creative workers, an available network of web-based skills pioneered by urban artists, and a temporary supply of substandard office space at depressed rental prices. In some cities, like New York and Chicago, financial industries, along with their attendant business and legal services, also saw a boost in growth. If this build-up had anything to do with IT, then it was a result of feedback from the centrifugal impact of technology. Saskia Sassen has argued that the technology-driven dispersion of operations across the global economy made it all the more necessary for transnational firms to have links to centers of coordination for managing their far-flung production units and diversified product lines. These urban service centers were composed of layers of specialized firms – legal, accounting, consulting, business and IT – which needed locational access to key resources. The central agglomeration of these supplier services and activities coexisted with the tendency to distribute production offshore (Sassen 2001).

It would be wrong, however, to see this urban growth solely as the outcome of new technologies playing out their industrial potential. Nor, in the case of the Internet companies, were they merely the fabrication of investors and analysts pumping hot air into the Internet stock bubble. Silicon Alley was as much the result of precision boosting by an urban growth machine calibrated to cycles of real estate speculation that depend on the periodic obsolescence and rehabilitation of building stock. In New York City, the real estate slump of the early 1990s presented a clear opportunity for new kinds of business, and it also promised a huge return to everyone with a vested or peripheral interest in the subsequent inflation of the city's real estate market.

Aside from the boosterism of the industry's own media (the *Silicon Alley Reporter*, *@NY*, *New York Software News* and *Alleycat News*) and trade groups (New York New Media Association, New York Software Industry Association, and the New York eCommerce Association), the city's newspapers, magazines, politicians and lobbyists all played a loud role in cheerleading the rise of Silicon Alley. The idea that New York was a silicon boom town could not get enough press.[4] City and state government also stepped in to subsidize the industry, offering attractive tax abatement packages, and Internet-ready space to promote industry spin-offs in other parts of the metro region (BronxSmart, Silicon Harbor in Brooklyn's Red Hook, CyberCity in Long Island City, SI Hub on Staten Island, HIWay 125 in Harlem and Info River Valley in the Mid-Hudson Valley) that were deemed in need of economic stimulation and regeneration.[5] At an NYSIA 'Software Summit' which I attended in November 2000, the keynote speaker Senator Charles Schumer delivered a typical tribute to the digital faithful: 'When they look at the future of New York, they should look at this room. Ten years ago, this city was near the bottom of any company's list, and we were bleeding jobs. Now we are the world center of ideas, and ideas have become the dominant economic force. In short, you have been a godsend to New York.'

Many moneyed interests happened to converge in applauding the rise of the new media sector. Typically, in a boom economy, a point is reached when the interests come into conflict with each other. As rents explode, so does the cost

of doing business. The return on corporate investments is threatened by the
dizzy return on rents and land speculation. One fraction of the capitalist class,
investing in land, is at odds with another, investing in companies or their
stock. In the newspapers of record, editorials begin to agonize about the
evolving conflict. The city is too expensive for new business, they warn, and
companies hit with rent hikes begin to make noises about relocating.[6]
Regardless of its other dimensions, the correction that began with the Nasdaq
crash in April 2000, and snowballed into a general recession, proved to offer
the only market solution to this growing conflict. Rents stabilized, then
dropped, and stock valuations swooned as the down-cycle of depreciation
kicked in, seeding the way for the soils of opportunity to play host to the next
boom. Because of its monocrop Internet economy, San Francisco was the
hardest hit by the technology slump. Less than two years after the Nasdaq
crash, commercial rents had fallen by up to 50 per cent, and prices were back
at their 1998 asking rates. Yet they still retained a massive appreciation from
pre-dot.com levels.[7]

In New York, where the new media sector only accounted for 5 per cent of
the city's income and employment, the loss of the World Trade Center (erasing
a full third of Lower Manhattan office space) proved to be a much greater blow,
since the financial services industry accounted for over 25 per cent of the city's
economy. Again, however, it was necessary to take a long view. While its firms'
fortunes had been mixed, Silicon Alley was a serendipitous response to a
problem posed by the report of the Wagner Commission on the future of the
city in 1987. The Wagner report, commissioned by Mayor Koch and issued just
three months before the crash on Wall Street, challenged the city to come up
with ways of developing the commercially depressed valley between
Manhattan's two Central Business Districts (*New York Ascendant* 1988). This
challenge loomed even larger in the course of the real estate market collapse of
the early 1990s. The interactive companies of Silicon Alley – spreading out
from the mid-point of the Flatiron District – fitted the bill perfectly. Not only
did their entrepreneurs covet scruffy space, they retrofitted the old building
stock with high-tech infrastructural improvements that boosted its value permanently. Best of all for the building owners, most start-ups quickly outgrew the
space they rented, moving on to larger premises before their leases ran out. This
allowed landlords to rent again, at higher prices, fast-forwarding the market into
a high-altitude bonanza.[8]

The value of street life

Boom times come and go, mostly to meet the appetite of investors and speculators for prodigious short-term returns. In the case of Silicon Alley, however,
New York had not just played host to a boom industry. The stuff of urbanism
was a prime ingredient of the industry's growth, because Silicon Alley companies turned city rhythms and urban attitude into profitable product in much the

same way that realtors had turned ex-industrial grit into added property value. In *The New Geography*, his book on the spatial impact of the digital revolution, Joel Kotkin agues that location still matters in the New Economy because skilled high-tech employees have become 'sophisticated consumers of place'. Companies that need innovative no-collar employees are obliged to locate where these workers want to be – in vibrant urban centers which offer them high-quality stimulation and services (Kotkin 2000). Yet the value of these urban qualities far exceeded their role in services consumed by workers off the job. Urbanism was also playing a significant role in production itself. The best place to view this was in the offices of new media companies like Razorfish (a consulting firm that served as my primary case-study),[9] which tried to capture some of the hum, scurry and sociability of urban streetlife, not to mention its surface transport – rollerblades and scooters.

In an October 2000 *New Yorker* article, Malcolm Gladwell noted that the qualities of street vitality which Jane Jacobs had celebrated in *The Death and Life of Great American Cities* were increasingly prized within office workplaces. Open-style offices were now busy public spaces where 'ideas arise as much out of casual conversations as they do out of formal meetings'. In order to get the most innovation out of employees, the office space had to be very social, with employees from all professional groups interacting regularly. In other words, the office had to host the diversity of uses that Jacobs had once argued for in urban planning: 'the workplace equivalent of houses and apartments and shops and industry' (Gladwell 2000). Some companies had run a long way with the mixed-use neighborhood idea. Gladwell cites the Los Angeles office of Chiat/Day, designed after the ad agency's disastrous New York experiment with 'nonterritoriality'. Boasting a Main Street, a Central Park with café tables and greenery, and basketball courts off to the side, the LA warehouse office was a conscious effort to emulate a bustling streetscape. Similar efforts were mounted by more traditional companies that had created their own internal e-divisions. In London, the new e-commerce unit at British Airways was housed in glass-walled offices built around a cobblestone walkway known as 'the street' and lined with coffee shops, modern sculptures and waterfalls. There was also an indoor olive grove, for contemplation, where noise was forbidden, to ensure mixed use of the office space. In other corporate offices, street cobblestones became a familiar part of the carpet pattern (Whittle 2000).[10]

Most Internet companies shied away from such cheesy efforts to impose the street on the office, settling instead for a spontaneous, disorderly feel, as if ideas were more likely to walk in from the street itself. While the principle behind the idea of the urbane office seemed to make sense, employees had their own preferred patterns of society, often favoring the camaraderie of their professional microcultures to the diffusion model of knowledge-sharing championed at places like Razorfish (a high-flying media company that I studied for eighteen months, from 2000 to 2002). This was a point somewhat replicated in the geography of domiciles – the technologists tended to live in suburbs and commuted, while the creatives lived in Brooklyn, and the MBAs in Manhattan). So, too, employees working together on a long-term project tended to end up seated together, so that big clients had their own 'company towns' inside the office, where knowledge and ideas were shared mostly among the team members rather than among the fish at large. Project employees from those client firms were often happier to work there than in their own corporate offices, and their presence helped to ensure that Razorfish ideas also flowed in the client's direction. As a result, any model of how information and ideas circulated within the office would have to show the drag, or gravitational pull, of territorial neighborhoods as well as the eddies formed around proprietary pockets.

But the analogy that Gladwell drew with the urbanism of Jacobs had a larger social dimension he had not quite allowed for. In her book, Jacobs had adopted the standpoint of the cosmopolitan intellectual, fiercely opposed to 'dullness' in all of its forms. As a result, *Death and Life* was a natural, if sentimental, advocate of diversity and disorder in streetlife, qualities which its author, like most cosmopolitan intellectuals, saw as artful and exciting (Jacobs 1961). Like the classic bohemians, then, Jacobs viewed as a virtue what had once been a necessity for working-class residents. In neighborhoods like her own Greenwich Village or Boston's North End, family life had been conducted on the stoop or the street because the tenement homes and apartments were often overcrowded. For these families, public street life was obligatory, and suburban privacy, when it was offered, proved to be quite inviting by comparison. From the 1970s onward, professionals in the new urban service industries, who could otherwise afford the privacy, embraced in full the principle of urban vitality in neighborhoods their parents might have abandoned a generation earlier. Their ability to pay a premium for the urban principle made mixed neighborhoods like Jacobs' Greenwich Village largely unaffordable for the lower-income population that had been the original source of diversity, and with whom déclassé bohemians had always peaceably coexisted.

By the 1990s, New Yorkers had long grown used to seeing artists' communities serve as a beachhead of choice for residential gentrification. In areas like Greenwich Village, SoHo, the East Village, Tribeca, Chelsea, Dumbo, Williamsburg and Fort Greene, the pioneering of bohemian enclaves had become an indispensable element of the real estate industrial cycle (Smith 1996; Smith and Williams 1986; Wallis 1991; Mele 2000; Abu-Lughod 1994; Deutsche 1996). In the 1990s, a similar cycle of gentrification began to work its way through commercial real estate, with Silicon Alley as one of its leading edges. Just as the new urbanites had made the cost of a Village address prohibitive for low-rent residents, so, too, the Alleycats' taste for raw urbanity in the workplace would boost commercial rents and price out the broader mix of businesses that serviced lower-income customers. Artists had played a leading role in residential gentrification. Now their presence in the workforce was having a similar impact through the industrialization of bohemia.

The value of the artistic life

In the 1960s, the art-making activities at Andy Warhol's Factory caused a stir by showing how artists could create art by imitating the mechanical principles of industrial production. According to Warhol's credo, art was about not only the unique expression of creative individuals, or the one-of-a-kind artifacts they crafted; it had something to say about rhythms of mass manufacturing and the culture of commerce. Thirty years later, by the time Warhol's Factory building on Union Square was being occupied by Razorfish rival, Scient, Silicon Alley managers were moving in exactly the opposite direction. They were trying to fashion a business that imitated all of the attributes of artists – their habitats, lifestyles, clothing, work patterns and custom individuality – and they were seeking to incorporate all of these into a tempo and a work temperament that could be recognized by clients as a reliable industrial process. By then, and partly because of Warhol, the stereotype of the avant-garde artist subsisting on the outer fringes of society was less and less rooted in reality. The art boom of the 1980s had placed artists at the feted center of Manhattan high society, while their art featured as targets of investment for corporate collections. Some were star celebrities, most were a quick study in the business of self-employment, as entrepreneurial in their pursuit of funding as any start-up owner. Stepping into the world of New Economy business was not so much of a culture shock for artists at all.

By the late 1950s, the cheap rents that had sustained urban downtown pockets of bohemia since its mid-nineteenth-century genesis in Paris were beginning to dry up. As manufacturing leached away from the city, artists who took over the vacated factory lofts enjoyed wide-open floors where workspace doubled as living space. This live/work ethos was embraced, to some degree, by upscale buyers who later endowed loft living with real estate allure (Zukin 1982).

Non-artists could now purchase many of the trappings of a creative, bohemian life without having to work at living it. The webshops of Silicon Alley introduced a further phase, when they imported this lifestyle component back into the workplace. The lofts were reclaimed for industry, but the work they hosted looked more and more like play, and employees were encouraged to behave like artists and keep artists' hours. The Alley's neo-bohemian culture helped sustain the belief that this kind of work was a viable alternative to corporate America. This belief (it may be more accurate to call it a willing suspension of disbelief) was especially important to contrarians with an arts background, who had been trained to scorn the conditions of a middle-class work environment, as well as the routine rhythms of industrial time.

Alternative, even subversive, art helped to fashion the profile of companies like Razorfish as a diametrical opposite of Wall Street. In fact, the relationship was more akin to the face-off between classical bohemia and the world of the bourgeois, each needing the other to define its own identity. Bohemia flourished from the 1830s as the seamy flip side of an emerging bourgeois order that was based on tradition, stability, rationalism, conformity and formal convention. It

was a place, elusive even then, where the unbridled energies of modern individ-
ualism could be more fully expressed. Many a young bourgeois, unsatisfied with
the social expectations that came with his inheritance, would find his way
there, temporarily, to test the waters (see Siegel 1986). For the temporary
bohemian, voluntary poverty evoked freedom, to be enjoyed among lower-class
residents whose involuntary poverty, by contrast, constrained their freedoms.
For artists who stayed longer, the low rents of bohemia would begin as a necessity, but, in time, they became a virtue of sorts, a conventional passage to
recognition and success in the art market.

Almost all of the personality traits attributed to companies like Razorfish and
their employees could have been lifted from Henri Murger's portraits of the
Water-Drinkers and grisettes who were playing hide-and-seek with their sober
Parisian elders one hundred and sixty years earlier: rule-breaking, undisciplined,
self-dramatizing, sexually free, drug-using, youthfully merry, inadvisably honest,
unorthodox in their narcissism and neo-socialist in their sense of community. By
the 1990s, la vie de bohème had become part of the standard package of 'hip' and
'cool' in the consumer marketplace.[11] By the end of the decade, the
bohemian–bourgeois family fracas had migrated into the business world, and had
become central to the civil war advertised as New Economy versus Old Economy.
In this briefly fratricidal quarrel, there were many defectors to the rebel side,
corporate regulars who cast aside their suits and ties to take 'the great leap', as it
became known, and join the militias waging insurrection from the guerrilla
strongholds of their lofts. In the softer, less militant New Age version, depicted in
a hundred company ads of the period, a luminous, boho youth explains the
Digital Way to a group of Brooks Brothers-clad executives, gathered together in a
wilderness setting. In both scenarios, the corporate bohemia promised not only
hedonistic enlightenment, but also the potential of vast riches, a far cry from the
traditionally penurious condition of the peripheral artist.

Why were artists and their trappings so important to the industrial process of
New Economy companies? For one thing, artists had been early adopters of web
design tools like HTML, and were indispensable as sources of artisanal knowledge, at least until the digital crafts became a credentialed part of the academic
curriculum. In addition, artists were an accustomed source of creativity and
independent ideas, assets that became central to the ethos of the fast company,
trading on innovation and initiative. By the 1990s, conventional managerial
wisdom held that employees were looking for more than money or benefits;
they wanted 'self-actualization', the quasi-spiritual quality that psychologist
Abraham Maslow had placed at the top of his influential hierarchy of human
needs (Maslow 1954). Employees could now treat their own jobs as if they were
works of art, expressing their own most uniquely cultivated qualities.

Just as relevant, and more lasting, was the work mentality associated with
artistic producers. Artists (in the broad sense of the term) come with a training
in what could be called sacrificial labor. This means they are predisposed to
accept non-monetary rewards – the gratification of producing art – as partial

compensation for their work, thereby discounting the cash price of their labor. Indeed, it is fair to say that the largest subsidy to the arts has always come from arts workers themselves, underselling themselves in anticipation of future career rewards. This disposition was a blessing to a start-up economy that demanded of its workforce a legendary outlay of time and energy on the promise of deferred bounties. Employees invested a massive amount of sweat equity in the mostly futile hope that stock options would be realized. Industry bulletin boards were soon chock-a-block with tales of exploitation (sometimes called geeksploitation) penned by employees who became so complicit with the culture of overwork and burnout that they developed their own insider brand of sick humor about being 'net slaves'; that is, it is actually cool to be so badly exploited. Industrial capitalists used to dream about such a workforce, but their managerial techniques were too rigid to foster it.

In their early book-length exposé of working conditions, entitled *Net Slaves*, Bill Lessard and Steve Baldwin sketched a portrait of an industry that benefits from the hagiographical 'myth of the 22 year-old codeboy genius subsisting on pizza and soda and going 36 hours at a clip'. Employees' quality of life, they concluded, approaches zero as a result, in 'the complete absence of a social life, a lousy diet, lack of exercise, chain smoking, repetitive stress disorders, and, last but not least, hemorrhoids'. 'There's going to be a lot of sick people out there in a few years,' they forecast, 'and worse, they won't even have any health benefits' (Lessard and Baldwin 2000: 246).[12] Industry insiders often traced this chronic burning of midnight oil back to the ritual of crunch-time in Silicon Valley, when programmers pulled all-nighters as part of a 'death march' to meet a software release date. But the technologists were not alone. The impulse to put in overtime for the sheer pleasure of solving a design problem came naturally to those with an arts background.

The flexible ideal

More important, even, than this apprenticeship in sacrifice was the flexibility of artists' work patterns. Ever since flexibility was promoted in the late 1970s as a central principle of the postindustrial economy, the number of artists employed in the general labor force, as defined in census data and annual Bureau of Labor Statistics (BLS), has swelled from year to year. This number more than doubled from 1970 to 1990, crossing the threshold of 2 million in 1998. In 1997, artists (defined by the Department of Labor as eleven occupations: artists who work with their hands, authors, actors and directors, designers, dancers, architects, photographers, arts teachers, musicians and composers) were enjoying a growth rate in employment (at 7 per cent) that far outstripped the general workforce (1.4 per cent) and even that of other professional specialists (3.4 per cent).[13]

These are impressive numbers, notwithstanding that estimates of artists' employment and earnings are notoriously unreliable. They reflect the expansion of economic sectors devoted to the commercial and nonprofit trade in culture, with the consequence that more and more people are able to sustain a living from the arts as a primary occupation.[14] Many of these jobs sprang into existence because culture is perceived as value-adding, and thus increasingly offers a return on investment. Culture has become a major stimulant to urban economies in particular, and a controversial instrument of urban regeneration. Whether for purposes of tourism, or to boost property values of marginal neighborhoods, or simply to satisfy the consumer tastes of urban professionals, every city of middling size now claims its own artsy district, modeled after Manhattan's SoHo, with bohemian status conferred on the neighborhood's nonconformist residents.

But there may also be a more general trend that supports the figures. Artists are more and more in demand because the mentality of work within the knowledge economy conforms more and more to the way in which artists customarily work. Indeed, the traditional situation of the artist as unattached and adaptable to circumstance is surely now coming into its own as the ideal industrial definition of the flexible knowledge worker.[15] As a result, artists are migrating from their traditional position at the margins of the economy to roles much closer to the center. Consider that by 1999, the trends in job growth had reversed, with professional speciality employment now growing at 5 per cent, as companies absorbed many of those trained in the arts, while the growth for artists had dropped to 3.9 per cent.

What is the profile of this new kind of worker who behaves and thinks like an artist? Someone who is comfortable in an ever-changing environment that often demands creative shifts in communication with different kinds of employers, clients and colleagues; who is attitudinally geared toward work that requires long, and often unsocial, hours; who dedicates his/her time and energy to distinct projects, rather than to a steady flow of production; who exercises self-management, if not self-employment, in the execution of his/her work; and who is accustomed to a contingent and casual work environment, without overt supervision or judgment from above. Academic readers will recognize much of their own work mentality in this description. Indeed, their own traditions of sacrificial labor have helped to create a vast tier of contingent teachers in higher education, a sector that more and more resembles the casualized patterns of employment in corporate America. It is no small irony that the heavy hand of administrative management has descended hard upon the arts and education at the very moment it is being lifted from a corporate sector that has declared war on bureaucracy and is busy importing the work mentality of artists and intellectuals.

In the workplaces I observed, employee concentration on the job was variable, often erratic. It was a style of work (which the casual observer could easily misconstrue as goofing-off) where stints of driven self-application alternated with periods of vivid socializing and with those intervals of undirected play and dreamy indolence that Henry James once called the 'unstrenuous brooding sort of attention' that is required to produce art. Razorfish employees were not producing anything that Henry James would have cared to acknowledge as art, but they were doing their work in a way that he might have recognized. Company managers also recognized the benefits of accommodating these spasmodic rhythms. This is how the firm's Creative Mission handbook described it: 'What is needed is an occasional, carefully timed disengagement from the intensifying focus that concentration on creative work requires. With efficient project planning in place we can leave room for this sort of distancing. Those responsible for scheduling need to continually facilitate this.'

Managerial planning at Razorfish never attained the efficiency recommended by the handbook, and so the creative disengagement of employees was neither carefully timed nor was it built into project schedules. Instead, the fish took their cues from the oxygen of permission that circulated through the office. But the managerial dream of efficient scheduling outlined in the handbook is a potent illustration of how the daily work routine might be adjusted to absorb the fitful rhythms of creative labor: twenty minutes of doodling, followed by ninety minutes of application, a fifty-minute break for kibitzing, focused reapplication before a mobile lunch and visit to a nearby art gallery, and then a full hour of surfing and daydreaming, before the first half of the project is complete (repeat or vary the cycle as required). Nor was this kind of tempo confined to the professional creatives on staff. At no-collar companies, every kind of employee is considered to be creative, and is regarded as a potential source of ideas and innovation. In effect, the entire workforce functions like a suggestion box writ large, where the contributions of employees are systematically collected rather than voluntarily offered. In some offices, the walls themselves did the collecting, in the form of interactive whiteboards which converted employee notes and doodles into computer script and data.

Nor was the work day bounded by what happened in the workplace. Ideas and creativity were as likely to surface at home or in other locations, and so employees were encouraged to work elsewhere as and when the spirit took them. A traditional industrial model derives value from workers where and when the company can control their labor. In the realm of no-collar work, the goal is to extract value from any waking moment of an employee's day. In return for ceding freedom of movement to employees along with control over their work schedule, a no-collar company exercises the right to collect returns from areas of their lives that lie far beyond the physical workplace.

Perhaps the most insidious occupational hazard of no-collar work is that it can enlist our most free thoughts and impulses in the service of salaried time. In knowledge companies that trade on creative ideas, services and solutions, everything that employees do, think or say in their waking moments is potential grist for the industrial mill. When elements of play in the office or at home/offsite are factored into creative output, then the work tempo is being recalibrated to incorporate activities, feelings and ideas that are normally pursued on our own free time. For employees who consolidate office and home, who work and play in the same clothes, and whose social life draws heavily on their immediate colleagues, there are no longer any boundaries between work and leisure.[16] Their occupation becomes a support system for everything else. No one who held a New Economy job was immune to this biohazard, unlike in a traditional corporate organization, where it primarily affected the senior managers and executives.

Notes

1 By the early 1990s, South Park resembled a homeless encampment, and seemed destined for upscale redevelopment. By the end of the decade, its commercial landlords were asking for rents almost as high as Class A space in the city's downtown Union Square.

2 The cap of 950,000 square feet was imposed in 1986 as a slow-growth measure to stave off the Manhattanization of the city. Proposition L, created as part of a citywide anti-gentrification crusade, would have closed the loophole, but the damage was already extensive. Many key rehearsal spaces for dancers and musicians, along with dozens of galleries, museums, and community centers had already been turned into dot.com offices.

3 'Death Notice', circulated by Bryan Lee, of the Stain Gallery.

4 *New York* magazine was the most strident organ for boosting the cause of Silicon Alley, with a succession of cover stories – from its 13 November 1995 issue cover, which proclaimed 'High Tech Boom Town' ('It's 1995, and suddenly New York is Cyber City'), to the nostalgia-laden chronicle of the 'Early True Believers' in February 2000.

5 In Lower Manhattan, where 60 million square feet of office space stood vacant at the beginning of the 1990s, the 'information city' was one of the concepts the Alliance for Downtown New York pushed to revitalize commercial rents in the ailing financial district. 55 Broad Street, formerly the multistorey home of the junk bond avatar Drexel Burnham, was retrofitted as a cyber showpiece, and renamed the Information Technology Center to serve as an anchor for other 'plug 'n' go' Internet-ready offices in the immediate vicinity. Renters were offered a lucrative range of tax abatements, rent exemptions and up to 47 per cent energy rate discounts.

6 At the height of the Internet boom in New York, the pursuit of relatively cheap office space had reached 40th Street, as the factories in the garment district and the flower district were increasingly being converted for office use (Calem 2000). By 2000, the industry had all but exhausted the abundant inexpensive space between Midtown and Wall Street that had created the conditions for Silicon Alley's growth just five years earlier.

7 In figures supplied by the San Francisco office of Grubb and Ellis, a commercial real estate firm, Class A space in SoMa/Multimedia Gulch stood at an asking rate of $30.82 per square foot ($21.86 per square foot for Class B) by the end of 2001, down from a high of $73.63 ($61.17 per square foot for Class B) the year before. Since commercial space was not much in demand in the early 1990s, their earliest figures were from 1996, showing a much lower rate of $18.25 per square foot ($13.75 per square foot for Class B).

8 By the end of 2001, commercial rents in Midtown South had fallen from their boom high of $45.65 per square foot to $38.74, but the appreciation from 1995 levels (at $15.24 per square foot) was considerable. These figures were supplied by the New York office of Cushman and Wakefield, a commercial real estate brokerage. In Boston, Class A commercial space fell 15 per cent (less than New York) over the course of 2001 (Kerber 2002).

9 This chapter is drawn from an ethnographic study of two new media companies, Razorfish and 360hiphop, conducted over a period of eighteen months, from the Summer of 2000 to the Spring of 2002. The book-length treatment is *No-Collar: The Humane Workplace and Its Hidden Costs* (New York: Basic Books, 2002)

10 David Brooks (2000: 128) describes the offices of Pitney Bowes Credit Corporation in Connecticut, designed to 'resemble a small village, with cobblestone-patterned carpets, faux gas lamps, a town-square-style clock, and street signs at the intersection of the hallways'.

11 Ann Powers (2000) charts some of this recent history.

12 For an active website, see NetSlaves ('Horror Stories of Working on the Web') at <www.disobey.com/netslaves>

13 See Note 78 on the NEA Research Division Reports on 'Artist Employment in America', at <www.arts.endow.gov/pub/ResearchNotes.html>

14 To be included in the BLS survey, 'one must be working during the survey week and have described that job/work as one of eleven artist occupations'. Respondents are asked to describe the job at which 'they worked the most number of hours in the survey week'. Artists working more hours in other jobs outside the arts are classified as employed in those other occupations. By 1999, these amounted to an additional 295,000, for a total of 2,324,000 artists employed in the workforce (NEA Research Division Note 76, June 2000).

15 Emily Martin (1994) analyzes the broader social and cultural contexts of the flexible industrial ideal.

16 See Christena Nippert-Eng's (1996) study of workplaces where employees either integrated or segregated their workplace and domestic lives.

Bibliography

Abu-Lughod, J. (ed.) (1994) *From Urban Village to East Village*, Oxford: Blackwell.

Blackwell, S. (2000) 'The Battle for San Francisco', *San Francisco Bay Guardian*, 18 Oct.

Brooks, D. (2000) *Bobos in Paradise: The New Upper Class and How They Got There*, New York: Touchstone.

Calem, R. (2000) 'Up, Up, and Away (per square foot)', *New York Times*, 16 Jan.: C4.

Chonin, N. and Levy, D. (2000) 'Culture Clash', *San Francisco Chronicle*, 17–19 Oct.

Cohen, H. (2000), 'Invisible Cities: Is the Internet Making Urban Centers Obsolete?', *The Industry Standard* (online), http://www.thestandard.com (2 Oct.).

Cushman and Wakefield (2001), 'Year End – 2001 Report', *MarketBeat*, San Francisco.

Deutsche, R. (1996) *Evictions: Art and Spatial Politics*, Cambridge, MA: MIT Press.

Gladwell, M. (2000) 'Designs for Working: Why Your Bosses Want to Turn Your Office Into Greenwich Village', *New Yorker*, 8 Dec.: 50–67.

Jacobs, J. (1961) *The Death and Life of Great American Cities*, New York: Basic Books.

Kerber, R. (2002) 'Tech Fallout Lowers Commercial Rents', *Boston Globe*, 28 June.

Kotkin, J. (2000) *The New Geography: How the Digital Revolution is Reshaping the American Landscape*, New York: Random House.

Lessard, B. and Baldwin, S. (2000) *NetSlaves: True Tales of Working on the Web*, New York: McGraw-Hill.

Martin, E. (1994) *Flexible Bodies: Tracking Immunity in American Culture – From the Days of Polio to the age of AIDS*, Boston, MA: Beacon Press.

Maslow, A. (1954), *Motivation and Personality*, New York: Harper.

Mele, C. (2000), *Selling the Lower East Side: Culture, Real Estate and Resistance in New York City*, Minneapolis: University of Minnesota Press.

New York Ascendant: The Commission on the Year 2000 (1988) New York: Harper & Row.

Nieves, E. (2000) 'Mission District Fights Case of dot.com Fever', *New York Times*, 5 Nov.

Nippert-Eng, C. (1996) *Home and Work: Negotiating Boundaries through Everyday Life*, Chicago: University of Chicago Press.

Powers, A. (2000) *Weird Like Us: My Bohemian America*, New York: Simon & Schuster.

Sassen, S. (2001) *The Global City: New York, London, Tokyo*, 2nd edn, Princeton: Princeton University Press.

Selvin, J. (2000) 'No Place to Play Anymore', *San Francisco Chronicle*, 17 Oct.

Shumate, A. (1988) *Rincon Hill and South Park*, Sausalito: Windgate Press.

Siegel, J. (1986) *Bohemian Paris: Culture, Politics and the Boundaries of Bourgeois Life, 1830–1930*, New York: Viking.

Smith, N. (1996) *The New Urban Frontier: Gentrification and the Revanchist City*, New York: Routledge.

Smith, N. and Williams, P. (eds) (1986) *Gentrification of the City*, Boston, MA: Allen and Unwin.

Solnit, R. and Schwartzenberg, S. (2000) *Hollow City: The Siege of San Francisco and the Crisis of American Urbanism*, New York: Verso.

Wallis, B. (ed.) (1991) *If You Lived Here: The City in Art, Theory, and Social Activism, a Project by Martha Rosler*, Seattle: Bay Press.

Whittle, S. (2000) 'Keeping the Team Together', *Industry Standard*, 24 Apr.

Zukin, S. (1982) *Loft Living: Culture and Capital in Urban Change*, Baltimore: Johns Hopkins University Press.

9

INDUSTRIAL GEOGRAPHY LESSONS

Socio-professional rituals and the borderlands of production culture

John T. Caldwell

'Building a Small Studio: Basic Concepts in Digital Video *feng shui.*'
(Trade article on how to organize production space, *DV*, 2001)[1]

In film and television, space is more than simply a site, a mere physical location, or a material world where production takes place. It is also a highly codified arena for status ranking and a public–private rhetorical construct used by practitioners to reflexively make sense of both the creative task and the ever-changing industrial landscape. Consider in this regard producer and CEO Peter Guber's summary description of the industry given to hundreds of eager career trainees at a 'making it in Hollywood' panel presentation:

> In the sixties, change was linear and incremental. In the eighties, change became spatial – and developed like a Polaroid picture. In the new millennium, change is like a stack of Polaroids – with everything developing all at once and on all levels. To make it now, you need a completely new set of skills.[2]

Guber's cogent metaphor of the shared, instantaneous development of a stack of Polaroids fits perfectly the business plans of both of the studios that he has run: Mandalay Pictures and Sony/Columbia. Both studios, after all, have made cross-platform multimedia 're-purposing' (that is, developing 'content' simultaneously for film, television, new media, video gaming, music, publishing and sports) an obligatory, corporate house rule. In what some have termed the 'post-network' age of television and the 'post-studio' age of film, ancillary markets, merchandizing and consumer applications are no longer afterthoughts or 'secondary' considerations in the creative process. Rather, marketing, distribution and merchandizing personnel are brought in at the earliest stages of script development, and work to prefigure the final narrative and presentational form that any 'primary' film or program now takes. But not all spatial allegories of industry are as organizational in nature. Consider 'super-agent' Arnold Rifkin's formulation of space to the same aspirants:

> I became very good at talking by phone. At knowing by the voice and intonation at the other end how good a project or a pitch or a personal relationship might be. Talking must be a part of an agent's skill set. ... [But] when you finally get 15 minutes or an hour for a meeting, yes, show up. But then be clear: that it is your space. Take it. Hone it. Use it.[3]

Rifkin's career road-map, by comparison to Guber's, suggests that a Zen-like mastery is required of the sensitive, discerning, and finally decisive super-agent. Rifkin's earlier comments at the same event do show him to be aware of the necessary complications of the contemporary cross-platform multimedia imperative (i.e., the differences between film and television, for example), when he acknowledged that 'Movie Raisenets simply don't taste the same when you eat them at your house and watch videos'. Yet in elaborating the career proverb cited above, Rifkin lays out a model of agency packaging that is almost mystical in nature. Like a martial artist, the true agent, we are led to believe, sifts through and touches the souls of his workaday phone contacts, but disarms all comers during high moments of appointed 'face-time'. With public allegories, anecdotes and truisms like these, Hollywood provides what are in effect institutional geography lessons for its apprentice players, mentees and wannabes alike. Some of these spatial lessons, like the current public relations boosterism in film/television trade publications surrounding issues of media 'globalization', are macroscopic in function, since they help orient and inform strategic business decisions about the nature and significance of synergies, conglomerations, antipiracy practices and free-trade agreements. Other geography lessons, by contrast, are microscopic, and can be used to guide media career pilgrims through the often-contested corridors of human–corporate relations in a manner that is more therapeutic and developmental in nature.

This chapter examines both the symbolic and material ways that US media production cultures rationalize and sanction specific spatial practices and norms – a production geography as it were – for the production enterprise. The spatial organization and physical presence of a production unit (whether on location, in the studio or in post-production) has always been integral in coding, announcing and interpreting the significance of production. Utilizing Clifford Geertz's notion of 'local knowledge', the chapter describes the ways that the production culture reflexively makes sense of itself – to itself – through its systematic organization and interpretation of space.[4] Methodologically, the chapter stands between, and at times synthesizes, two approaches that are typically seen as divergent: ethnography and textual analysis.[5] Arguing that either approach fails to account for important aspects of spatial practice (with ethnography susceptible to vested

disclosures by industrial informants or, worse, disinformation; and with textu-
alism typically blind to industrial and technological determinants), this
chapter intends to map the critical spatial practice of production through the
close examination of what I call 'deep industrial texts'. Many of these
workaday or 'low' texts' – visual icons, social and professional rituals, demo-
tapes, recurrent trade and union narrativizations, and machine designs that
audiences and viewers never see – circulate in a greatly delimited public sphere,
but a public sphere nevertheless, as promotional and industrial artifacts and
professional events. All of these 'deep texts', as I term them, precede and prefigure the kinds of film/television screen forms that scholars typically analyze,
and all offer dense and over-determined interpretive schemas that serve to
regulate and make sense of the meanings and significance of the spaces of
production, and the spaces of culture.

In taking this approach, I intend to build on and respond to the important,
recent work of both Nick Couldry (Couldry 2000a), and Anna McCarthy
(McCarthy 2001), on Mediaspace. Couldry's *The Place of Media Power* is particularly good at demonstrating the flaws of postmodern theory, which tended in
figures like Baudrillard (1983) to 'erase' space as a meaningful category. A close
examination of the deep spatial texts from industry that I have referred to above
underscores, to use Couldry's terms, media's 'complexification' rather than postmodernism's 'erasure' of space as a meaningful category. Far from offering mere
simulations, industrial rituals and demo-tapes (the deep texts I consider here)
betray an obsession with space and place, often reinforcing the notion that
production spaces, far from being illusory simulations, are physical, tangible,
robust and demanding. Whereas Couldry elaborates on the physical boundaries,
symbolic boundaries, institutional edges and the journeys by lay audiences to
and from industrial space, I take as my focus the faux- and modified public and
private spheres that are constructed for professional community members *inside*
or *within* those institutional boundaries and edges. McCarthy's *Ambient
Television*, in turn, serves to unseat the traditional privilege assigned to the
home and the domestic sphere by media scholars in accounting for television.
She demonstrates, instead, how site-specific uses of television outside of the
home and in social spaces transform and mediate audiences in ways that
complicate conventional understandings of gender, class and consumption. Like
Couldry, McCarthy works to explicate what might be termed the 'borderlands'
of television consumption. The kinds of industrial, spatial and textual practices
that I describe and analyze in the pages that follow similarly complicate the
place of viewership and agency – but do so not from the perspective of the lay
audiences, viewers or consumers that Couldry and McCarthy focus on, but
rather from the perspective of professional media *practitioners*, who also daily
manage, traverse and negotiate institutional borderlands from the other side.

Much of my work has focused on the critical-theoretical competencies and
practices of media production communities. This has included the idea that media
production technologies are 'critical spatial practices' used for status-ranking,[6] that

media producers/encoders are also audiences/decoders (Caldwell 2000), and that production technologies, professional practices and industrial iconographies can be viewed as 'theorizations-in-practice' (Caldwell 1993 and 1995). The studies that follow show how recurrent professional rituals, the use of space, and exchanges of industrial texts and trade icons constantly negotiate what it means to make media, and what it means to form institutional alliances. They also dramatize what and how changes in economy, technology and public taste stand both as threats to career and corporation, and as forces that can be 'leveraged' by foresighted and resilient artisans. Workspaces and depictions of space frequently serve as terms used to rationalize, understand and make sense of change, or even the threat of change. Fully understanding this dynamic means following Foucault's (1983) and Lefebvre's (1991) calls to focus on the materiality and social use of actual spaces, rather than on space as an idealized or conceptual category. A close examination of a range of deep texts in production culture suggests that film/TV practitioners are as versed in deploying space as they are in producing the spectacle of two-dimensional visual images on film and television screens. Yet it is difficult to talk about the geography or spaces of production culture without examining what goes on within those spaces. Understanding the logic and function of these production spaces, that is, cannot be meaningfully done, without understanding as well the conventionalized social interactions and professional rituals that define these spaces.

Deep textual topographies

Self-representations: the digital sweatshop

As a starting point, it is useful to consider a recurrent kind of self-representation in below-the-line work worlds.[7] Many demo-tapes cultivate the perception that the digital and post-production artisan labors alone, in the darkness, in anonymity; cut off from human contact and driven to anxiety by long hours of desperation. A number of demo-tapes bring this spatial 'self-portrait' (i.e., of the digital artist/editor as a bunkered, solitary figure) to life. A flashing emergency light in the image, explosive effects on a synthesizer track and 'Do Not Enter' warning signs cue the viewer of 'ProMax's' Final Cut Pro equipment demo as a hand-held camera races through a security door into a basement-like room that houses a meager pile of computer hardware. A sign, framed in close-up, shouts what can only be a fantasy for the daylight-challenged worker in this subterranean work-world: 'Warning: Extreme Editing Ahead.' The frenetic but low-budget production values of the tape, however, show this to be far from evocative of ESPN's 'The X-Games'. The 'VIP' demo by Lightworks goes one step further, equating the frantic, shouting world of the aggravated male editor with anxieties over bladder control and urinary function. A rapid-fire voice-over succession of the lines 'Gotta go, gotta go, gotta go ...' hounds a traumatized editor shot in fish-eye lens. His predicament? 'Next time *go* Lightworks VIP.' The non-linear manufacturer of Blue (a high-end post-production system that is 'format independent') furthers the mythoi of the editor as alienated man and tortured artist. In low-key, blue tinted nocturnal lighting, a lone man in an edit suite paces nervously under the repetitive chop of an overhead ceiling fan. An empathic male narrator steps through a litany of ulcer inducing pitfalls that haunt the user, including threats of standards incompatability, equipment obsolescence and crushing loan arrangements needed to keep pace with the competitors that hound the post-house manager. Lingering shots of the sweating, twisted body of the (now) T-shirt clad editor – shown tangled in endless cables as he troubleshoots – build after three minutes to a crisis and major plot point. 'How do you know that you're not going to encounter time-consuming and annoying problems?' the narrator intones. The viewer confronts a tortured male face à la Edvard Munch's painting 'The Scream', as the voice-over prophet builds to a climax: 'How do you know you're not going to encounter *non-linear nightmare*' (emphasis theirs). The demo quickly cuts to a sunny room, accompanied by an upbeat techno-music track, where a smiling young woman effortlessly works the editing controls that manipulate the now-dead freeze-frame of the manic-man-with-nightmare. The not so subtle message of the tape: 'It's so easy to use – even a girl can do it.' Over and over, these deep texts and many others create a picture of alienated and isolated male trauma – usually unfolding inside lightless post-production bunkers – as the work-world status quo from which video editors (apparently) need to be freed. In these dramatizations, the relatively private sphere of professional artisan-technicians is theatricalized as a digital sweatshop. The recurrent mythoi are then circulated to the broader (yet still delimited) public sphere of professional peers that exchanges on a regular basis and evaluates demo-tapes.

Solicitation rituals/space

The television and media industries are defined by a Darwinian imperative to survive by gaining advantage and market share over rivals and competitors in a given market sector. Survival of any production company depends upon convincing prospective clients that the company stands as a cost-effective and cutting-edge setter or exploiter of trends. The flip side of this competitive jockeying presupposes an end state of decline, obsolescence or bankruptcy for competitors. Media production is by definition, therefore, a contentious world, but one, ironically, that depends upon the ongoing ability to forge flexible alliances for survival. Hence the need for picking up those partners that can fill your needs, and avoiding those that can shipwreck your future. Production trade shows – such as the National Association of Program Executives Convention (NATPE), the National Association of Broadcasters (NAB) and ShowBiz Expo – function as bracketed moments during which time players in the field seek out partners for imagined 'synergies' of one form or another (with suppliers, clients, manufacturers, purchasers, syndicators, contractors, etc.). The NAB convention in Las Vegas typically has over 100,000 attendees, and regularly offers events within this professional-communal setting aimed at soliciting partners out of the morass of potential competitors. These events, or special mixers, include contests to produce original video spots using equipment from manufacturers who offer cash and new equipment prizes as well as a showcase for screening the winning productions at the convention. These projects are not pre-produced or canned sales or demo-tapes, but are in essence 'spec' art projects made by independent practitioners without the burden of an apparent cost- and product-obsessed client in sight.

One winner of such an award at NAB 1995 produced a rapid montage spot depicting life in the edit suite that loaded up layers of inane audio comments ('I'm thinking of something *organic*' … 'what about – *cactus?*' … 'no, the other way' … 'we can't use it' … 'no' … 'how long is this going to take?' …) shouted by the shallow and callous hangers-on (producers, directors, clients) who (apparently) live to harass post-production workers. The spot ends by showing an editor saying 'done' after smirking through the harangues from the above-the-line folks who can only retort 'that's impossible'. A practitioner's self-fantasy of wizardry plays out here: a resilient motif deployed by technical workers since the earliest days of silent cinema and Méliès. Here, however, the pose also stands as a form of cynical and symbolic resistance aimed at overpaid and vacuous bosses. Such solicitation rituals look like opportunities for free-thinking, but they also work to wed master-artists-trying-to-shed-their-technician-identities to pieces of proprietary and costly production equipment.

One of the most elaborate demo-tapes cultivating the need to solicit career-saving partnerships was produced by Lightworks for their VIP system. The demo sounds and looks initially like an episode from the television series, *The X Files*, but ends up feeling dramatically more like low-budget porn. The demo opens in the crowded hallway of a fairly large-sized post-production house. A brooding woman (an Agent Scully look-alike) struts toward the camera as two men try to calm her down. Her problem? Her production is over budget (on a 'big-budget doc') and her deadline ('she's got a drop-dead date of Friday') looks impossible to make. A weasely male off-line editor (a Dana Carvey look-alike) tries to attract her attention in the photocopy room ('I'm pretty quick'), by offering to edit it on an underpowered off-line system. She passes ('I'll blow a budget … or a blood-vessel'). An older man, pretending to be fatherly, tries to console her with a reality check ('I'd like to help. But as your on-line editor, I can't do what's not in my vocabulary'). As the two men try to settle her down, in a soft sepia-toned lounge with leather furniture and abstract art on the hall, she erupts: 'I mean – this project is a career maker, or breaker. Hello Scott! I need some help here.' The two escorts exchange a succession of glances in close-up, recognizing non-verbally that they must acquiesce and refer her to a man with more power. As a swarthy young man discards his black leather coat and enters the room in a wide, low-angle shot, the online editor ambivalently confides his secret to Lauren (the Scully look-alike): 'Meet Chris Carter – the hottest freelance editor in town.'[8] At first curt, but then intrigued, Lauren listens to the mystery man, as he begins to reduce the altered state soap opera to a lengthy (but oddly out-of-place) tech-writer's monologue about the various benefits and downsides of on-line versus off-line editing. The generic transmutation in this demo does not just explain how one can save one's career technically, it also models the interpersonal and heterosexual mannerisms needed to solicit and tap into off-shore, freelance production potency. Here, Lightworks VIP poses as the strange new man in town.

Spaces for solicitation include pavilion-size corporate tableaus as well as the fictional worlds dramatized in moving image demo form described above. At major trade shows, like ShowBiz Expo and the NAB, key transnational media corporations, such as Sony, Panasonic and Quantel pay for acre-size display floors that dominate the center of vast convention complexes. Sony recently channeled its thousands of attendees through as many as fifteen different sub-areas for Sony products and services, with massive video walls. Stretched across numerous monitors, satisfied partners and clients gave pseudo-religious personal testimonies of devotion and gratitude to Sony: for rewarding their small business; for responding sensitively and intuitively to the product and supply needs of end-users; and for developing, as the video walls confessed, personal, 'long-term relationships'. In a proprietary Sony arena, that was so vast that attendees were given road-maps to navigate by, these ubiquitous video walls underscored to newcomers a motif recurrent in other transnational corporate pavilions and displays as well: far from focused on the bottom line, Sony's partners and clients, as it were, comprised a close and intimate 'family'; one based on apparently selfless care and mutual trust.

Professional solicitation rituals also function at a third level beyond the fictionalized or allegorical space of demo-tapes and the therapeutic family-building space of the trade pavilion. Production trade conventions are so big, in fact, that entire 'television networks' – like Testa Communication's 'Convention TV' – have sprung up to 'cover' and cablecast the limitless activities of these important moments of vast group consensus in the field. Many attendees with next-morning hangovers might identify such networks as the purveyors of the rote trade show and booth information scrolling on the closed-circuit hotel room TVs at the Las Vegas Hilton, the Sands or the Sahara. Yet Convention TV's aims, and logistical footprint, are much more prime-time. Complete with 'dawn to dusk' coverage, ENG crews 'capturing late-breaking news on the floor' ('events' usually triggered by a stack of pre-planned corporate press-releases), and a three-camera studio operation with bantering news readers and anchor persons, Convention TV stages contests and on-air giveaways that it organizes as participatory and interactive parts of what it terms 'the convention experience'. Enjoining editors of the trade publication *Post Magazine* and the NAB 'to serve as judges' at one convention, Convention TV promised that a 'winner would be announced live', on camera and on the floor, 'at the Tektronix corporation booth'. Making media events of this kind also provides other opportunities to cover and report them. 'And our crews were there to catch all of the excitement', the network plugged in a lead-in to a later 'news-cast'. The winner, now caught on camera, gave an 'aw-shucks it was nothing' explanation of his prized contribution. 'We just shot what happens in an edit suite during a worst-case scenario. ... We literally had only an hour to put the thing together before we hit the FedEx delivery. ... We just squeaked it in.' Convention TV then cut back to the studio anchor for the wrap-up: 'And that's our show for tonight. We'll be back tomorrow with a special highlight edition. I'm ... . Thanks for watching.'

These examples show just how focused trade groups are in cultivating what they consider to be essential forms of solicitation, networking and professional 'hooking-up'. First, fictionalized and allegorical demo-tapes 'project' professional viewers into hypothetical scenarios that establish the high stakes involved in successfully building and managing human relations in the work world. Second, exposition pavilions provide what I would term ambient and ubiquitous media commentaries that narrate a potential buyer as he or she navigates the maze of sub-products within each corporate acre of the mother-brand – and this ambient narration is typically done in 'real time' via audio or video walls that electronically augment physical space. Third, on an even broader topographic level, convention television networks script, stage and then report and interpret the entire experience as 'news'. The hypothetical 'what-if' future state of the demo-tape, the 'here-and-now' augmented present state of the pavilion, and the 'there-and-then' network mapping of the trade cohort's recent past, therefore, together provide an over-determined temporal heuristic. These deep textual and ritual forms, that is, attempt to underscore the (vested) 'meanings' and 'insights' of the convention experience – along with the state of the production industry – in future, present and past tenses. In this sense, these conventions are not merely grand industrial singles bars, or personal columns, for corporate players with precarious profit margins or, worse, takeover prone debt. Yes, organizers stage and facilitate vast, shared trade events as necessary mixers for professionals who need to network and schmooze, but the deep texts and rituals that circulate in these spaces do something far more. As personal–professional guide books, they interpret and chart the cognitive meanings, the social significance and the economic logic of these trade spaces even as the practitioners walk the vast and disorientating physical floors of the exposition halls.

Cultivation rituals/private–public space

The film, television and digital media industries are characterized by an extreme stratification and division of labor, a pyramidal, top-down management struc-ture, and winner-takes-all business plans. Yet many of the favored industrial rituals act blind to the group-based contestation that inherently defines the production enterprise. Indeed, many deep texts and socio-professional rituals work (sometimes incessantly) to promote an antithetical idea: that the industry is collaborative, personal and humane. To cultivate this perception, the industry makes an over-determined effort in press releases and trade publications to underscore the many critical 'private' moments and 'interpersonal' spaces that drive effective film/TV producing and content development. One set of critical industrial practices works to bring those important moments of privacy 'out into the daylight', in enabling, social gestures ostensibly intended to 'help' others in the field. This impulse to make the private sphere public shows that the appetite for 'behind-the-scenes' information and 'secrets' is not unique to fandoms, gossip columnists, *Entertainment Weekly* or show-biz reports broadcast on *Access Hollywood*. Rather, the same appetite for 'useful' trade and career secrets circulates in the professional sphere, in the form of semi-public panels on 'how to make it in the industry', and in various mentoring initiatives and apprenticeship schemes.

Many experts and seasoned veterans in Hollywood, for example, frequently explain success with all of the rhetorical tools and themes that a motivational speaker or revivalist might use. 'Integrity', 'humanity', 'dedication', 'self-sacrifice', 'face-time' and 'personal vision' are all repeatedly lauded (in public rhetoric at least) as keys to getting ahead. Even those 'players' who might be infamous for years of budget-busting excess, bad-bet developments, derailed productions, colleague back-stabbing and corporate 'exit strategies' due to 'irreconcilable creative differences' regularly pose in public, oddly enough, as altruistic mentors and facilitators. Those offering 'to give something back' to the field, that is, frequently posture (or are publicly packaged) as seasoned veterans, guiding hands, wise sages and noble moralists. This acting-out (and demeanor overhaul) furthermore, frequently takes place in what might be termed 'half-way spaces' that exist between the private and the public spheres of the professional: guild halls, film festivals, cinematheque retrospectives, film/TV museums, summits and panels, industry conventions, trade shows and universities. Even a cursory glance at the material, physical barriers erected around the entertainment industry in Los Angeles (fortress-like studio walls, security details, bodyguards and cul-de-sacs) makes it eminently clear the extent to which business interactions are highly proprietary and sequestered away from those on 'the outside' by design. Cultivation rituals and mentoring activities in these half-way spaces, ironically, often pretend to bring the heretofore hidden secrets of the bunkered practitioner out into the light of day.

The NATPE Convention in New Orleans in 2000 employed a diverse range of intermediate spaces in which private workings from the highest levels of industry were 'performed' as semi-public events. These staged self-disclosures (panels, keynotes and special events) were presented at the city's convention center and hotels, and were covered by the trade press, but could be seen and heard only by registered, fee-paying, professionals and buyers from the field. The keynote presentation by the organization's chairman provides some context for this process. The syndicated television producing and selling industry that NATPE represents had entered a period of great crisis and instability before the convention. This state of affairs was caused in part by the impact of new technologies, newly cut-throat competition, government de-regulation and threats by many of the major syndication studios (who now openly questioned the value of the long-standing association) to pull out of NATPE altogether, in order to go it alone. Yet one would never have suspected this level of contention and business chaos based on the suave and comforting appeals to attendees in the audience by NATPE's chairman, or the rousing cheers that answered him when he stepped through what was essentially a multimedia pep rally for the state of television at the dawn of the new millennium. After an introduction, the curtains parted, the lights dimmed and a hi-resolution, widescreen video un-spooled. As a rapid-fire montage of clips represented the history of the United States (in thirty seconds), a gray-haired African-American actor spoke with nostalgia:

> I was there when Dr. [Martin Luther] King shared his Dream with the world ... and I was there when Mark McGuire broke the home run record. ... Yep, I've seen a lot in my day. Thanks to television, of course.[9]

When the lights faded up, the chairman surmised, 'We think this PSA says it best'. He then vocally repeated the final graphic of the spot, 'Television: The World's Best View', and the syndicators in the audience – almost all white, male executives – roared approval. Now, this high-production value spot by the trade organization appeared a few weeks after the NAACP and other civil rights organizations had attacked the television industry, in press conferences and policy documents, for its exclusionary racial practices and for making programming almost entirely 'white'. It was not clear whether the nostalgic tear-jerker on the screen worked in this room because the executives in the audience longed for simpler and more stable times in television, or because they feared for the impact of yet another broadside (this one racial) against an already faltering industry. Yet this production was more than just a Geertzian self-reflection, a demo to be circulated internally inside the production and syndication culture. The chairman announced that the tape was 'available in standard NTSC, DTV, and, we're proud to say, in HDTV [applause]'. *Television: The World's Best View* was also given freely to attendees and broadcasters for use as a 'public service announcement' to air back at their home stations. Such a transformation, from a demo (of the industry speaking to itself) to a PSA (of the industry allowing the lay public to hear the industry speaking to itself) carried both internal and external benefits. On one register, the deep text serves to calm self-doubts about the possibility of exclusionary and regressive practices; on another register, as a quasi-public text, the spot intends to underscore the long-term value of the trade organization's commitment to a race-free logic of the 'human spirit'. The meanings of deep texts are not fixed. They shift according to the industrial, regulatory and cultural spaces in which they are allowed to circulate.

While most professionals in the various production cultures pose as 'insiders' (whether or not they are), group marketing events like NATPE and the NAB are odd in that they offer opportunities for a large mass of attending 'insiders' to role-play as 'outsiders' or as aspirants to the field. One striking example of this impulse to theatricalize the intensely private sphere of the practitioner – and to re-segregate the field into graded categories along an insider–outsider spectrum – is something called the 'Pitchfest'. At the NATPE Convention 2000, between 800 and 1,000 participants and attendees (professional program producers and buyers) served as 'audience members' in the syndication association's annual Pitchfest. They watched as other producer/buyer attendees, 'chosen randomly', were asked to 'come-on-down' in front of the audience to pitch proposed projects (mostly television series) to heavy-hitter talent agents from CAA, Endeavor and the William Morris Agency.

After each number was called, shrieking and ecstatic independent producers came down to demo their pitching abilities on an elevated stage that looked not unlike the game show *Wheel of Fortune*. A large time-clock to the left marked down the few seconds each pitcher had to present his or her projects to a series of three Hollywood agents, who sat, chair-bound with dark suits and clipboards, to the right. The aspiring producers were given three minutes to make the hard sell (one minute to summarize the project; one minute to answer questions from the agents; and one minute to take suggestions about how to improve the project and presentation). Those that faltered or fell far short of expectations were 'gonged' prematurely off of the stage by the agents. Pitcher no. 48, an African-American producer named Sabrina Lamb, uncorked what was to be the winning pitch for a show entitled *Kahlalu and Cornbread*. She began by singing and altering an old stand-by: 'Day-Oh, day ay ay-Oh. My TV show needs a network home.' Lamb cut from the lyrics, then hollered 'Kahlaluuuuu and Cornbread' and licked her fingers emphatically, 'umh, umh, umh'. She then sketched out the plot summary in short order:

> A half-hour romantic comedy set in Brooklyn. It's *I Love Lucy* meets *Ally McBeal* with Caribbean seasoning. [Audience howls.] *Kahlalu and Cornbread* is a story of Kim – a small-town southern gal and her adventures in the big city. Where she takes on life, love and law school. She gets a job in the Caribbean restaurant where she forms a love-hate relationship with the boss, turns-off the Law School Dean, and eats … bull … penis … soup! It's [as if hollering from the plantation fields] *Kahlalu and Cornbread* …

With the audience in an uproar, and the emcee warning 'That's one minute!', the agents then jumped in with attempted witticisms ('What does he eat in the next episode?') and suggestions for improving the pitch. 'Q: What network? A: NBC, 8:00 o'clock, Thursday night.' More applause. 'Q: Who do you see in the lead? A: Lauryn Hill and Chris Rock!' Agent: 'If you get Lauryn Hill and Chris Rock, you'll have a bidding war [pointing to himself and the other agents on stage] between Endeavor, CAA and William Morris.'

Winners were promised a trip to Hollywood, face-time with studio and network executives and the chance to pitch their show and see it developed for prime-time. Yet, after a hard day of selling on the convention floor, there were cracks in the general euphoria and adrenaline in the room. Although the names of CAA and William Morris were tossed around conspicuously, the agents themselves were not household names. The power and ostensible experience of the white-men-judging-in-dark-suits was sometimes suspect as well. One agent compared the uniqueness of the winner's pitch to the many that he had heard 'over the years' – a career which turned out, oddly enough, to be a mere two years as an agent. Many of the pitchers, in fact, seemed to have had more years of experience in the media than the agents, even if that experience may have been in the lower castes: independent production or regional broadcasting. Yet the aura of, and lure of access to, 'Hollywood' bewitched even these seasoned professionals, who at times appeared as no more than desperate outsiders. The fragile nature of this façade, based on an artificial cultural geography, finally began to break as the emcee and judges paused to allow last year's winner to appear on stage. Intended to underscore the substantial and valuable nature of her experience in Hollywood, last year's winner instead drifted off into a rambling litany about the ways that her trip had actually been a failure. Her meetings were not with real players, her pitches were not bought, and her winning project from last year's Pitchfest was never developed. All of the participants on stage smiled in denial. Last year's winning malcontent was eventually pulled from the stage, and the ecstasy of pitches and possible 'discoveries' continued unabated. Even if the actual results of this large group performance by professionals accomplished little in the way of actual or new TV programming, the Pitchfest itself clearly fulfilled an important and affirming symbolic function for the trade organization. Identities and hierarchies were broached and bartered out in the 'open' in a way that reaffirmed a long-standing cultural geography in the United States; one that places Hollywood and the West Coast in the big leagues, and broadcasters in the heartland as the farm system for talent.

As with the 'how to make it' events and semi-public panels intended to mentor newcomers, public pitchfests (even for professionals) construe the powerful in moments most candid. These 'super agents' and judges are, apparently, merely sensitive and caring lay colleagues willing to share secrets, and provide the kind of 'face-time' never possible in the overpopulated, agent-inaccessible, world of Century City and Hollywood. But all of this pitching, mentoring and sharing of secrets also functions like gossip traditionally has in neighborhoods. It functions, that is, as a way to create solidarity, community and a (perhaps false) sense of empowerment through 'insider' trade association knowledge about 'how things are really done'.

Maintenance rituals/spaces

To get to and participate in the solicitation and cultivation rituals found at industry conventions like NATPE and NAB described above, many media practitioners journey from their regional offices to such places as Las Vegas or New Orleans. Once business relationships are solicited and initiated, the strategic importance of repeat business means that large media corporations must work hard to create the spaces and social interactions necessary to 'maintain' those clients. These spaces for relationship maintenance are as important for 'below-the-line' personnel as for executives. Sony Broadcast regularly stages subsidiary events around larger trade conventions for this purpose. At NAB in Las Vegas, Sony invited camera operators and potential Sony buyers to participate in an annual retreat and 'shoot-out'. These activities were filmed one year, and then edited into promotional videos that were circulated the following year at NAB.[10] One result was a demo-tape for Sony's new 'Betacam PVW-537' broadcast ENG camera, that looked (sans Clint Eastwood) and sounded (complete with haunting whistling) earnestly like a spaghetti western directed by Sergio Leone. A deep, gravelly male voice spoke the rugged poetry of camera-operator bonding, over long shots of the western landscape:

> Below the solitude of the last spring snow. ... Down through the rugged canyons carved by time. ... Came men and women of a special breed. Known to shoot first and ask questions later, they came for something wild – and they found it – in Las Vegas!

The video then cuts to the bright lights of Vegas, as limo-borne cameramen (using the PVW-537, of course) cut through the city-scape at night. This segment ends with soft-core images of screaming, bikini-clad women shooting through nearby waterslides as a keyed graphic zooms toward the viewer: 'Going Wild in Las Vegas: The PVW-537.' Littered throughout the technical discussion of the new camera's features that follows, are other examples of what these technicians might call 'eye candy'. The net effect of the tape, however, is to show Sony benevolently inviting regional cameramen to Beta-test their latest cutting-edge rig from helicopters, limos and horses provided at the shoot-out and retreat. The promotional video as a whole, however, suggests that male bonding and partying (with those you share a technical affinity) are as important to maintaining user-ship as are any purely technical descriptions of product. Going Wild in Las Vegas provides a troubling image of the aggressive (rugged, tough, masterful) and masculinist (moving, mounting, going wild) ideology of what is apparently an ideal camera operator in the business and marketing plans of multinational equipment manufacturer Sony.

Other ritual spaces used by practitioners, however, reverse this spatial dynamic and direction of travel. Several conventional practices, that is, have Muhammad (the networks) 'going to the mountain' (the business affiliates) rather than vice versa. Three highly publicized industrial 'pilgrimages' help the networks maintain their precarious relationships with key partners – advertisers, the press and the affiliates respectively. The annual May preview and presentation of the new Fall programming season to advertising agencies in New York – called 'up-fronts' – has become an obligatory high-point and organizational target in the calendar for each of the six major television networks. Shortly after the up-fronts, and then later in the year at syndication markets, the networks reach out to affiliates and independent stations in meetings intended to secure local broadcasts for the coming year. Finally, each December in Pasadena the television industry reaches out to provide 'inside' access to the activities and programming strategies of the major networks. These television critics' meetings provide human contact and access to new shows, but they can also touch the lives and stroke the egos of the press. Television journalists form a cadre that has always had an uneasy relationship with the networks and the studios. Critics and reviewers are sanctioned as journalists to cull and dredge through both the good and the bad of programming during the year. Yet they are very much dependent on the studios and networks to gain access to the very stars, shows and personnel that make this back-story possible. Critics' meetings serve the networks, therefore, as a carrot, rather than a stick, an incentive used to cultivate a climate conducive to positive critical reception.

In some ways, these journeys out of the executive suites and studio walls in Hollywood and Century City are faux-pilgrimages – intended to symbolically honor the subjugated (those dependent on the Hollywood pipeline). With affiliate anxiety over the benefits of affiliation always in doubt; with fickle critics in position to financially kill or renew series; and with advertisers always threatening to jump ship to other networks and media forms when superior ratings are found elsewhere – these pilgrimages are really attempts at reconciliation. The success of the network 'family' depends upon effectively communicating concern for the business associates and advertisers normally dispersed across the country. While press conferences are part and parcel of these maintenance rituals, so too is a graded, hierarchical system of parties. UPN, for example, faced with precipitously declining viewership only a few years into its launch as a network (and trade rumors about the job insecurities of UPN executives Valentine and Nunan), worked overtime at NATPE 2000 to keep its local broadcasters on board for the coming season. UPN threw a lavish invitation-only party for its affiliates and partners, with ample catering and an exclusive concert performed by the group the B-52s. Higher floors in the Hilton that week hosted even more exclusive network and corporate parties. Lower floors and suites hosted cash bars and generic and obligatory association receptions sponsored by those less anxious to seek reconciliation or to cultivate and maintain new business relationships. The harsh economic situation in the syndication industry became so bad by January 2002 that all of the major Los Angeles studios (Columbia Tri-Star, Paramount, etc.) had pulled out of the NATPE convention floor entirely, 'as cost-saving measures'. What they booked, instead, were entire floors and suites in nearby luxury hotels. In this way, the majors shifted sales away from the leveled, democratic chaos and the bazaar-like nature of a convention-floor television market. They now focused on more personal forms of relationship-building, deployed perks and managed the graded hierarchies inherent in more exclusive parties, meetings and receptions. From a political-economic perspective, these changes in industrial and marketing behavior have come alongside increasing corporate conglomeration that has forced many independent stations and 'mom-and-pop' syndicators out of business. The trade culture shift – from the more democratic interactions of a convention floor (a horizontal scheme based on multiple points of access) to the individuated solicitations of the hotel suites (a vertical scheme based on exclusivity) – mirrors an ongoing constriction of diversity, competition and content in the syndication industry as a whole.

Monitoring rituals/spaces

The solicitation, cultivation and maintenance rituals described above all work in public relations to build consensus, solidarity and a sense of commonality, and by so doing cover over the anxieties that threaten productive corporate relations. Other workaday rituals in television, however, work in antithetical ways by producing and instilling anxiety in the community of production professionals. The process of 'giving notes' occurs when an executive or producer sends suggestions to directors or writers about how to 'improve' the direction of an ongoing project, program or series. While such incursions by 'the suits' into the aesthetic domain rankle with most directors, the process has a far more fundamental function. The now ubiquitous ritual of giving notes underscores the sense that the proprietary and private world of the studio and soundstage is actually very much in doubt, monitored as it is daily by an amorphous but ever-expanding ensemble of seldom seen but always present producers, executives and their assistants. Production personnel internalize this sense of being watched, much as the prisoners of Bentham's 'panopticon' are disciplined by the continual threat (real or imagined) of always being under surveillance; a sense that many inmates internalize. Curse the notes if you will, but you are being watched and evaluated.

Other monitoring rituals always keep the production space and enterprise from stasis and balance. Many independent program productions involve the daily reconciliation of costs spent versus projected budget estimates. The obligatory production and post-production meetings during works-in-progress also inculcate the personnel with the sense that the project is always 'incremental'; that their future is always tied to successfully meeting projected benchmarks throughout the shooting schedule. Most independent program productions also contractually tie financial disbursements to the necessary approval of each major stage in the production by executive producers, or studios. Television ratings, like box-office, have also become the basis for ever-present monitoring rituals. Ratings provide a set of benchmarks for all competitors, since accurate viewing numbers and demographics are the basis for rationalizing the success or failure of a show or

177

series. For this reason, endless tactics are devised to spike or hypo ratings in dayparts across the country. The high season for this kind of ritual interchange occurs three times a year during 'sweeps weeks', when viewer numbers are codified as the basis for ad rates for the months that follow.

Other monitoring rituals spin out from these kinds of ever-present forms of ritualized surveillance and response. Each May and June, after the Fall season has been unveiled for advertisers and affiliates, bets are taken on which network programming heads will roll first. This sense of an 'executive revolving door' ritual further underscores the fact that despite all of the over-determined attempts to build consensus among industrial participants, the daily spaces of the production and producing worlds are characterized by great instabilities and anxieties about duration of employment. Inculcating this impending sense of inevitable temporariness works perfectly to legitimize the vast system of 'contract' rather than permanent employee labor that has come to be known as the Hollywoodization business in the United States.

Spatially, monitoring rituals unsettle the ostensibly private and proprietary nature of studio and production space. Studio and soundstage walls evoke walled off privacy. But note giving, ratings, endless in-progress production meetings, daily budget reconciliations, incremental production funding and disbursement, and the executive revolving door all betray just how 'porous' those proprietary walls are. This porosity – providing a one-way vantage point to those controlling both the bottom-line and the possibility of project green-lighting – serves to discipline psychologically the community of production in cost-effective ways.

While maintenance rituals appear to extend the private and proprietary executive suites out into a semi-public space for purposes of affiliate or client reconciliation, the monitoring rituals described here tend to keep the possibility of reconciliation always in doubt. The complicated network of contract labor that defines Hollywood knows by these regularized incursions just how precarious practitioner futures are and will be.

Contestation celebrations/spaces

All of the industrial ritual spaces examined thus far can be understood by their placement within a model of socio-professional formation and affinity. That is, they articulate fundamental tensions between industrial forces of consensus, commonality and inclusion, on the one hand; or, they serve as industrial forces of dissent, instability and exclusion, on the other. As contentious and divisive industries, broadcasting and cable in the age of digital and deregulation count the pre-merger life-spans of many corporate players in months and years rather than decades. It is within this climate of ever-increasing instability (for both career and corporation) that regularized, annual trade or industrial gatherings somehow strive to celebrate a common purpose and identity.

With over 110,000 participants annually, the NAB convention in Las Vegas discussed thus far looks like a grand, group hand-holding exercise. In actual fact, behind all of the consensual hype about consolidation and 'convergence', the NAB is actually a brutal marketplace, peopled by thousands of vendors, companies and manufacturers intent on eclipsing and/or bankrupting their competitors. Early adopters battle late adopters. Patent holders threaten and selectively licence to highest bidders. Because of its legion of product models, complimentary gifts, demos, special effects and hype, the NAB might be construed, à la Bahktin, as a 'carnivalesque' moment of celebration. Yet the smiling corporate competitors also stand side by side and hawk damning theorizations about enemy technologies and the shortsighted plans and practices of competitors. Together these workaday barbs and diatribes comprise a set of behaviors that makes the convention more like a bloodletting coliseum than a carnival. The NAB liberally expends public relations energy leading the cheers of an industry by announcing, year in and year out, that it is helping to forge a common future. In fact, this rote public relations optimism of the NAB about a common industry seldom conceals the yearly absence of many former industrial players that went bankrupt, were hostilely taken over, or simply made obsolescent.

The trade media infrastructure covering such shows helps provide a sense of rationality, fairness and order, thereby suggesting that even technical competitiveness helps forge a common future. The studio anchors of Convention TV, for example, repeatedly and regularly reassert their 'expertise' and 'objectivity' between stories from the floor: 'Our reporters and production personnel are experienced professionals. Bringing you the news with integrity. Keeping you informed and up-to-date.'[11]

This kind of rhetoric appears to level the field fairly, as the networks cover the latest 'digital effects', 'curl packages' and 'corner-pinning' graphic technologies, but as formal and scientific – rather than proprietary – breakthroughs in the field. Yet Convention TV's on-air tactic of constantly reasserting its 'integrity' tends to have the same impact as a used-car salesman who feels the need to say repeatedly that he is honest, and that there is no need to worry, to an anxious or suspicious buyer. The blatant promotional and marketing motifs that spike the network's flow of convention news further places the façade of a level playing field, of agreeable affinity, and of common cause in question.

Whereas the NAB serves to stage, celebrate and civilize the grand contestation between equipment and technology firms, the NATPE market serves to celebrate and civilize the contestation between warring first-run syndicators, buyers, and broadcasters for both domestic and foreign markets. Behind the glitz, models and cameo appearances at the show by prime-time stars like David Hasselhoff from *Baywatch*, or Ray Romano from *Everybody Loves Raymond*, or Pamela Anderson from *VIP*, lies the ulcer-inducing high-stakes game of 'clearing' enough broadcast markets to successfully launch or keep a show the following year. File footage from past conventions shows just how contentious this world under-the-surface is. Images of the 'highly successful' and 'legendary' syndicator Sandy Frank, at work in a market pavilion, show him barking out orders at his frantic assistants to get buyers and program reps 'here, immediately!'[12] Exasperated station buyers describe how they would finally 'cave-in' to Frank because he was so physically aggressive and 'obnoxious'. A younger Frank, in his prime, is shown with his hands around the neck of a startled buyer, threatening to strangle him. He retorts, cockily, to an interviewer: 'It's trench warfare out there (on the sales floor). It's either kill or be killed. ... [Frank physically grabs a buyer by the throat] ... So I go for the jugular vein, like this!' This celebration of kill-or-be-killed sales militarism might simply be explained as a result of one syndicator's self-promotion as an abrasive personality. But other examples of file footage from 1994 show the kinds of institutional 'cracks' that tend to break open when a single trade organization tries to embrace segments of the industry that are clearly at odds with each other. One local station buyer goes ballistic in a tirade directed at the encroachments of a major syndicator from Los Angles: 'I'm sick and tired of you coming in here and taking over my business. You are in the supply business, and I'm in the broadcasting business. Don't barter away advertising slots in the shows I buy. That's my business.'[13]

Although trade panels usually include a range of vested interests, staged together to show common cause, such volatile panels, however, could not possibly mediate the fundamental differences in roles. In the past, syndicators sold first-run series to local stations, which then were allowed to sell advertising time in the show to recoup their costs. At this point in history, however, syndicated program producers themselves had begun to preemptively sell some of the spots in advance, well before shows were ever delivered to local broadcasters. By encroaching on a client's turf in this way, sellers were not simply raking-off someone else's profits in advance, they were seen (by broadcasters) to be stabbing their loyal long-standing 'partners' in the back. File footage from the market shows how much NATPE acknowledges this contestation and vitriol. Yet the organization also promotes something that is more crucial to the effective operations of any 'fair market' – a more orderly image of rule-governed proficiency, equity and rationality.

With the future of first-run television syndication increasingly in question, the National Association of Television Program Executives produced a feature-length video, entitled *The Legends of Syndication*, in 2000 to help orient newcomers to the syndication industry, to explain the logic and practices of syndication, and to provide an oral history of the many (now ageing) 'stars' of syndicated selling. More than simply a history of the 'traveling salesmen' who go from independent station to independent station to sell first-run syndicated shows, *Legends* provides particularly good insights into the ethos and self-perceptions of syndicated personnel. Story after story focuses on hardships of the early days. Old-timers note that 'long before video projectors and power point presentations', they had to lug '100s of pounds of heavy 16mm projectors and reels' in order to make a broadcast sale. Veterans speak of vast rural distances covered, and hard-sells made despite excessive evidence of sweat and fatigue from the obligatory AV gear, which they carried into everything from formal pitches at TV stations to presentations made to station owners on 'dairy farms'. Executives reminisce about their original sales territories (southern Indiana, Ohio, rural Nebraska) in a montage of visual maps of those remote areas which slide through the image. One ex-salesman, after having lied about not being underage, boasts of braving a blizzard by foot in order to get to the first sale of his career. A succession of syndicators in the production offer their best anecdotes of missed appointments, odd coincidences and quirky behaviors by competitors and clients.

The themes and motifs in this material create a composite self-portrait of these practitioners as hardy, tough-traveling, confident and aggressive competitors. Pioneers who stuck with the task long enough to have advanced to executive positions in management and entertainment. The below-the-line folks in Sony's shoot-out initiative described above celebrated a tough form of raw masculinity as a foundation for proficient camerawork. And this is perhaps logical, given that film/video field production *is* physical labor. But these (now) above-the-line syndication executives also create a self-portrait with many of the same sorts of traits. Viewers might consider programming to be the result of an abstract sequence of decisions, but behind television (according to these archival tapes and oral histories by practitioners) lie physical and emotional struggle, doubts and fortitude. Perhaps the most gripping scenes in *Legends* involve a dramatization and re-creation of the abduction, robbery and near murder of one syndicated salesman. The segment is shot in the best tradition of reality television (it is a dead-on clone of *America's Most Wanted*) – complete with look-alike actors, fake hand-held cameras, slow-motion footage, and a dissonant synth track. The segment includes repeated loops of the criminal reenactment, which are inter-cut with the pensive but knowing head-shots of the sales veteran telling his story. The story arc builds to a climax, and viewers learn that the salesman proved so persuasive to the abductors (he offered to exchange his credit cards for cash if they took him back in his hotel room), that he was spared the fate of several previous victims who had been abducted and killed a few days earlier on these same roads in Ohio. The message of this reenactment, made by practitioners for practitioners, was that one syndicator was so go at persuasion and selling that he convinced even his 'hijackers' not to kill him. So goes the moral about a syndicator with (as the tape by practitioners terms it) 'nerves of steel'.

Monitoring rituals betray the ostensibly walled and proprietary film/TV production worlds as, in actuality, 'faux-private spheres'. Competitive celebratory rituals like NAB and NATPE, by contrast, transform the semi-privacy of a gated trade show into a 'faux-public sphere'. The Las Vegas and New Orleans convention events might look like the bracketed-off, in-between border spaces of Bahktin's 'carnivalesque' (i.e, the NAB like Mardi Gras) or of Victor Turner's liminal rituals (NATPE like a Papuan sing-sing). In actuality, however, these huge socio-professional events are contestatory tournament sites, staged in artificially walled off and sequestered public spheres. In competitive, celebratory rituals like these, corporations drag out their proprietary content, technologies and vaporware in order to hype or overwhelm the competition into genre, standards or programming obsolescence.

Conjugal celebrations

In the contemporary, de-regulated mediascape, corporate conglomeration has increased and accelerated in the last ten years. The original promise of the 500 channel market was that diversity of programming would guarantee diversity of viewpoint, opinion and aesthetic taste. It was also to have provided for a far more democratic landscape for media consumption. The scores of new corporate players that entered the growing multichannel market since the early 1980s, however, have re-aggregated into but six giant multinationals. This renewed acceptance of (or appetite for) vertical integration has been fueled by a set of broad cultural and political changes. But it has also been sanctioned and symbolically legitimized through the recurrent staging of industrial 'conjugal celebrations'. Mergers are announced and pitched to the trades as synergistic 'win-win' marriages between lonely but growth-hungry corporate components. The Time-Warner/AOL merger, for example, was self-consciously pitched by the mega-corporations as a 'marriage' of two diverse but now eager partners: the geek-caricatured hi-tech boys' club of AOL with the Hollywood insider pretense of Time-Warner. Merging CEO's posed in culture-specific clothing (at press conferences, Time-Warner executives donned the shirt-sleeve, casual look of computer culture, while AOL execs adopted the business attire of the film industry). The trades then mapped out the intermingling of practitioner cultures that had been set in motion. This same critical interpretation (the marriage of strange bedfellows motif) ran through the trades when financially ailing Yahoo.com snagged Hollywood executive and 'insider' Terry Simel. Simel left the major Los Angeles studio for the Bay area to serve as Yahoo's suitor and savior (he was deemed a master of management, well versed in old media, rather than dot.com, wisdom) in April 2001. By the time the grand Time-Warner/AOL conglomerate began to drag itself down in the financial markets in 2002, and angry stock-holders asked for the heads of the executives, the trades invoked the darker side of the conjugal paradigm. These circumstances had now become contentious 'divorce' proceedings. The failed corporate marriage (according to financial analyst Merrill Lynch, which had earlier hyped the marriage), now brought the earlier myth of broadband convergence to a premature and sorry end.

Like press conferences that announce and justify corporate mergers, award shows by the various professional organizations and guilds also create spaces of industrial cohabitation. That is, award shows bring together in the same giant space (which is frequently televised) long-standing sparring partners who suspend their competitive relations or who leave aside their 'irreconcilable differences' to participate in a common event. Regardless of what various professional production communities are like in real life, conjugal celebrations serve to spotlight the existence of bounded 'communities' comprised of practitioners. Through television, these same industries and professional groups usually grant lay audiences a keyhole view of the community. Even if it is a virtual stage on which the televisual eye gazes, the net effect is of a singular monolith or unity that can cheerfully laud its elites. Unlike contestatory celebrations (staged for practitioners by practitioners), conjugal celebrations and awards events overproduce an aura of consensus for a broader, non-professional public. This staging for a popular or lay consciousness shows the industry to be extending its borders out into culture. But it also shows just how well the industry controls access to those borderlands – through limited electronic keyholes to the event-worlds, and via show business reports. Less focused on exclusion or on streamlining the marketplace, conjugal celebrations theatricalize industrial practice for the public, and attempt to promote 'quality', 'vision' and common cause as industry-wide business principles.

Therapeutic rituals/spaces

A series of factors – contract labor abuses, long hours, technical obsolescence, alienation from factory-like production conditions and ageism – have taken their toll on perceptions of media management practice. As a result, new types of business consultants have begun bringing into corporate institutions practices and exercises that are more 'therapeutic' in nature. A concern with human and career development has become almost as important as product development, at least for some companies that consider themselves progressive. Retreats, team-building workshops and even sabbaticals have emerged on the radar of management experts, although many would still voice the sentiments of the John Travolta character in the film *Come On, Trust Us*: 'I'm not sure what a retreat is. ... I think it's a religious thing.'[14] The Las Vegas 'shoot-out', cited earlier, included a 'retreat' where camera operators from around the country were brought together to mix and mingle in a rugged wilderness setting. But retreats are also offered for executives, and not just technicians; and are sponsored by corporate employers, and not just third-party vendors, like Sony.

From a structural and conceptual point of view, retreats promise above-the-line and producer personnel the chance to 'escape' the claustrophobic confines of the offices and executive suites in Los Angeles in favor of the group sessions, mud-baths and clear air of, say, Palm Springs. Retreats also presuppose and strategize how to allow media players or professionals (in standard parlance) to 'step-outside-of-the box', to 'brainstorm' and to make creative decisions; all of which function as industrial allegories for psychologistic concepts like 'finding one's inner child'. A less obvious goal or result is that retreats (which sometimes are synonymous with 'team-building exercises') also provide an apparent escape from the contentious 'division of labor' that under-girds most studios and soundstages. By turning a cadre of office-bound executives and producers into participants in a group therapy session, media corporations also intend to create an industrial space that allows for intimacy and rebirth. Retreats work, obviously, in a manner far less sinister, on the face of it, than the panopticon-effect evident in the monitoring rituals discussed earlier. While monitoring rituals constantly underscore the presence or possibility of surveillance, thera-peutic rituals are far more deceptive. For while the official demeanor of a retreat is enabling, the discussions and brainstorming that take place in a retreat also proceed under effaced forms of surveillance or documentation. The therapeutic spaces of retreats look far more benign than the conventional prac-tices of note-giving. But both ritual forms always circulate within the constraints of the corporation gaze and/or its sponsorship. Compared to the corporate retreat, dealing with or responding to network 'notes' probably simply produces more overt forms of cynicism and on-set bonding than it does a tan from a retreat. One set of spatial practices is organized on a top-down model (note-giving); the other on a ground-up model (retreats and team-building exercises). Both allow commercial organizations to process additional information in a way that keeps the company more flexible (or more unstable) in the face of change.

Retrospective memorial/space

Other ritual spaces regularly staged by practitioners include the 'homage' or 'retrospective memorial'. At NATPE 2000, the ageing 'golden age' patriarch, Sid Caesar, was feted in the market's keynote event. With an elaborately edited, large-screen montage, with testimonials, and then standing ovation, the association pitched Caesar as if he was the single most important figure in television history. Immediately following this near-religious homage to a visionary patriarch, the event organizers called out (and thus linked him to) what NATPE apparently considered to be today's front-line players in contemporary television: Bill Maher, host of *Politically Incorrect*, Robin Givens, Jerry Springer and a host of also-rans from the very margins of early prime-time and daytime television. This group was marshaled on-stage to discuss the current state of television. But in updating the audience as to how television had changed since its golden age, one thing became painfully clear. With Jerry Springer and Bill Maher ostensibly carrying on the tradition of Sid and the golden age, the current state of US television programming is, obvi-ously, in big trouble. History is regularly 'performed' by instititutions as a way of establishing credibility and legitimacy. The 'exhibitionist history' performed with a straight face here, worked to grossly 'over-produce' the trade association's significance.[15] By retrospectively attaching and glomming the troubled syndica-tion association on to an earlier period marked by high consensus, the organization was actually betraying its uncertainty and instability. By 2000 the US television syndication business was in trouble. To counter such troubles, the institutions that represent professional media cultures work hard to establish their own distinctive 'genesis narratives'. Intended to boost member morale and justify present directions, however, this particular re-creation of the history of syndication's genesis (including Sid Caesar's disoriented early morning talk, following his red-eye flight from LA) made it painfully clear just how far syndication had fallen from live anthology drama; and how far the syndicated sellers of *Baywatch*, Jerry Springer and Judge Judy, gathered in Louisiana, were from New York or Los Angeles.

Conclusion

A cultural geography of the production culture cannot be charted by reference to conceptual notions or physical spaces alone. A rich and complex set of deep texts (made by practitioners for practitioners) circulates and helps orient users to the work-worlds and career spaces that workers confront. These deep texts are coexistent with the spaces themselves and serve as user-guides and road maps for practitioners. They also help rationalize and script the socio-professional rituals that inhabit and define production spaces. And this situation means that any effective topography of production must also include and integrate an analysis of the specific socio-professional rituals, events and human interactions that are deployed in those spaces. A summary survey of the deep texts and industrial rituals described in this chapter reveals at least three areas in which the cultural significance of this geography can be noted:

(1) **Narrativization/war stories** Inevitably, industrial rituals in the production culture work by 'narrativizing' the context for rituals, meetings, conventions and networking. The narratives operative in deep texts establish idealized stories of the origin of various trade groups; they help to script group professional events that follow their circulation as texts; and they help practitioners to decipher trade events as they unfold. A cursory summary of the themes employed in these deep text narrativizations shows a systematic pattern of assertion and denial. Recurrent plot themes promote the idea that: (a) the trade task is about creativity, when it seldom is; (b) the trade task is regionally or locally specific, when it seldom is; (c) the trade task is physical, muscular or masculine, when it seldom is; and (d) the trade task is about moral integrity and the human spirit, when it rarely is. These transformations stand as textual themes – institutional self-portraits, as it were – through which practitioners convince themselves of the significance of their work.

(2) **A taxonomy of social spaces** More than simply cognitive meditations that help build and maintain morale (which is an essential component for career longevity in any craft), these narrative contexts and arcs help demarcate a graded taxonomy of social spaces. This taxonomy can be placed on an institutional map of the production culture, comprised of concentric rings, whose boundaries are meticulously managed. These concentric zones can be summarized (from the innermost region to the outermost border) as follows:

185

- The highly *proprietary private sphere* of the pitch and the high-level development meeting; a studio/network inner sanctum, as it were. To:
- The *therapeutic private space* of the corporate retreat and the team-building workshop. To:
- The *faux-private space of the workplace*, studio and soundstage, wherein constant discursive interventions (like note-giving and production meetings) by management create instability and anxiety through implied surveillance. To:
- The *faux-public space*, or the *sequestered public sphere*, created at professional trade shows, conventions and meetings where contestation and celebration are staged for professionals in the community. To:
- The *semi-public space* of advertiser up-fronts, Fall preview meetings for affiliates, professional awards shows and press junkets where a place for access is extended to intermediaries for the public. Critics, journalists and television are allowed to 'cover' the industry in these highly controlled ways. These practices tend to sanction audience consumption from a specific, regulated vantage point. The public nature of these 'stages' (ocular or virtual keyholes) is typically over-announced or over-marketed in public relations. The aura of consensus and perception of common cause that result frequently cover over severe contestation and dissent within the guild, the association or the trade organization in question.
- Finally, *contact zones for mentoring and recruitment* emerge at moments in which those with 'insider' knowledge venture out to half-way spaces to share personal insights on 'making it in the business', 'how the business works', 'how to pitch', 'how to take a meeting' and 'how to start a career'. These contact zones provide one of the few points of human contact, and promise to help aspirants achieve more effective 'skill-sets', but they exist at the furthermost ring of the studio/network maze.

With the 'insider–outsider' binary as the central ideology marking these zones, *travel or movement* between zones emerges as the key moments – or demonstrations – of industrial performance and professional competence. As a result, many of the deep texts and socio-professional rituals examined in this chapter are in fact 'primers' on how to 'cross-over' the various concentric borders outlined above.

(3) **Reflexivity** Perhaps most interesting in these graded, proprietary zones of relative ownership and exclusivity is the fact that industrial culture works hard to symbolize and represent itself to itself by emulating and performing the kind and styles of 'content' that film and television audiences see at home or at the theater. Demo-tapes, trade show events, pitch-fests and other forms all show that technical and delivery communities also emulate on-screen 'content' cultures as well. In this way a practitioner's competence (his or her accumulation of cultural and aesthetic capital) can be used to leverage projects, partner with affiliates and influence clients. Demos look like soap operas, or westerns, or film noir.

Pitch-fests cultivate stage presence, Stanislavski, gameshows and Aristotelean poetics. Video equipment manufacturers use 'visits' (real or virtual) by higher cinema auteurs like George Lucas to explain their engineering aims to production staffers in the lower castes (industrials, commercial, infomercials). Corporations employ product models, modern art and eye-catching set designs to physically demonstrate technical performance. Spokespersons and heads of NATPE, the NAB and SMPTE pose in a sometimes awkward attempt to find a presentational style that mirrors the mission of their associations. In these ways, the private, off-screen, production and distribution communities create spaces for themselves in which they can masquerade as the (higher-caste) on-screen content worlds (in prime time and theatrically) that they normally defer to and produce for.

Through these practices, production personnel close ranks to weather change. By circulating highly reflexive forms among themselves, practitioners do not simply learn new things. They also work to convince – and to acknowledge to themselves – that their distinctive value to the industry lies in some unique specialty of their guild, or craft or trade association. This constant reaffirmation of trade distinction is more than just a turf battle. It helps market the relatively hidden guild, craft and proprietary worlds to various publics as unapproachable and unassailable. Just like 'the industry' as a whole. Socio-professional communities produce content spectacles for their own consumption, and organize semi-public spaces and events to manage that consumption. This tendency can at times evoke the quality of a secret society, one that possesses the alchemy that everyone else wants, but can't ever quite get to. The graded industrial contact zones of the production culture, therefore, are not controlled lock-step by bunkered executives in studio sanctums. A large coalition of practitioner communities – held loosely together by a sense of willed affinity and an unstable economic climate – work together to guard their own turf as well as the key access points leading to adjacent zones. This boundary maintenance helps ensure that all comers – insiders, outsiders, apprentices, mentees and the curious public – have the proper deference and respect. Mystique and profits both depend upon the vigilant management of production space – and especially its borderlands.

Acknowledgement

This chapter was originally presented as 'Liminal Industry: Ceremonial Rituals of the Production Culture' at the University of Copenhagen, Denmark on 25 September 1997, and later at the Society for Cinema Studies conference in Washington, D.C., on 24 May 2001. I thank Klaus Bruhn Jensen, Lennard Hojbjerg, and Nick Couldry for their invitations and comments on these occasions.

Notes

1 *Feng Shui* is the ancient (and now modernized) Chinese art or way of organizing living space and architecture. *Feng Shui* focuses on designing a room or building according to the optimal arrangement of life-forces (yin and yang, light and dark, directional orientations) that bear upon or permeate any space. *DV* (*Digital Video*) is a trade publication for digital cinematographers, editors and post-production artists. This article, authored by a 'video systems designer', seeks to help orient user-practitioners to design-of-space issues that are important but often overlooked in the daily work worlds of production companies (see Henage 2001).

2 Peter Guber is CEO of Mandalay Pictures in Los Angeles, and former President of Sony/Columbia Studios (Guber 2001).

3 This comment is from Arnold Rifkin, an agent, and formerly of CAA (Rifkin 2001).

4 Clifford Geertz discusses his studies of 'the understanding of understanding', or 'hermeneutics', in *Local Knowledge: Further Essays in Interpretive Anthropology* (Geertz 1983: 5, 10).

5 The ethnographic fieldwork for this chapter was done from 1997–2002 at a series of professional conferences and trade shows for various production groups. These included research at the following industry conventions: ShowBiz Expo, Los Angeles (1997), NAB, Las Vegas (2000), NATPE, New Orleans (2000), Siggraph (the professional society for computer graphics and animation) (2001), NAB, Las Vegas (2001), and SMPTE (Society for Motion Picture and Television Engineers), Pasadena (2002).

6 These studies of production space as a critical practice were presented in John Caldwell, 'Probe Technology, Push Programming, and the World: Boy's Geography Lessons' (Caldwell 1998).

7 More than just analogous to 'blue-collar' workers in film and television, 'below-the-line' refers, traditionally, to all of the crafts and trades that work on a film/video production, but that are not given credits 'above' or before the title of the film or program. 'Above-the-line' functions (producers, writers, directors) are credited before the title and are equivalent to executive or management ranks in traditional industries.

8 Yes, 'Chris Carter', as in the name of the very successful show-runner and creator of *The X Files* series; a designation that leaves no doubt as to the demo producers' model for emulation.

9 This PSA, produced in 2000 by NATPE, is titled *Television: The World's Best View*. I viewed the screening of the PSA at the event, and examined a BetacamSP version of the tape as the basis for the discussion above.

10 This promotional video from Sony Broadcast was entitled *Going Wild in Las Vegas: The PVW-537*, was produced in 1991, and distributed in the years that followed both at the NAB and through sales and regional operations of the Sony Corporation.

11 From Convention TV's 'off-air' videotape at the NAB convention. VHS, Testa Communications, 1995.

12 This market footage of Sandy Frank, from the 1980s, is included in 'The Legends of Syndication' video, compiled by NATPE in 2000.

13 This footage is from a panel on the syndication and 'barter' business, filmed at the NATPE conference in 1994.

14 *Come On, Trust Us* was produced and distributed in 2000.

15 The notion of 'exhibitionist history' is examined in my *Televisuality*, while the theorization of the 'over-production of history' is found in Mimi White, 'Reliving the Body, Over and Over Again: Popular Memory in Homefront and I'll Fly Away' (White 1997).

Bibliography

Baudrillard, J. (1983) *Simulations*, New York: Semiotext(e).

Caldwell, J. (1993) 'Television as a Semiotic Machine: Emerging Paradigms in Low Theory', *Cinema Journal*, 23: 24–48.

—— (1995) *Televisuality: Style, Crisis, and Authority in American Television*, New Brunswick: Rutgers University Press.

—— (1998) 'Probe Technology, Push Programming, and the World: Boy's Geography Lessons', paper presented at the Society for Cinema Studies Conference, La Jolla, CA, April 1998 and at the Mediating Knowledge Conference, University of Wisconsin, Milwaukee, May 1999. Subsequently published in J. Olsson and J. Fullerton (eds) *Moving Image Technologies*, Sydney/Bloomington: John Libbey/Indiana University Press.

—— (2000) 'Theorizing the Digital Landrush', in J. Caldwell (ed.) *Electronic Media and Technoculture*, New Brunswick: Rutgers University Press: 1–34.

Couldry, N. (2000a) *The Place of Media Power: Pilgrims and Witnesses of the Media Age*, London: Routledge.

—— (2000b) 'Tracking Down the Media: From the Studio to the Doorstep', Paper presented at the Crossroads in Cultural Studies Conference, University of Birmingham, UK, 21–25 June.

Foucault, M. (1983) 'Space, Knowledge, and Power', in P. Rabinow (ed.) *The Foucault Reader*, New York: Random House.

Geertz, C. (1983) *Local Knowledge: Further Essays in Interpretive Anthropology*, New York: Basic Books.

Guber, P. (2001) Public comments at 'Transition' event, UCLA, 25 April.

Henage, C. (2001) 'Building a Small Studio: Basic Concepts in DV Feng Shui', *DV*, 29–31 March.

Lefebvre, H. (1991) *The Production of Space*, trans. D. Nicholson-Smith, Oxford: Blackwell Publishing.

McCarthy, A. (2001) *Ambient Television: Visual Culture and Public Space*, Durham, N.C. and London: Duke University Press.

Rifkin, A. (2001) Public comments at 'Transition' event, UCLA, 25 April.

White, M. (1997) 'Reliving the Body, Over and Over Again: Popular Memory in Homefront and I'll Fly Away', in Sasha Torres (ed.) *Living Color: Race and Television in the United States*, Durham, N.C. and London: Duke University Press.

Part III

NEW MEDIA SPACES

10

THE WEBCAM SUBCULTURE
AND THE DIGITAL ENCLOSURE

Mark Andrejevic

... it is going to be a VERY interesting day indeed, when streaming with sound is available to everyone and EVERYONE has a TV show :) I can't wait!
(From the public diary of webcam celebrity Ana Voog)

Introduction

When Jennifer Ringley first turned an inexpensive digital camera on herself in a college dorm and went live to an audience that would eventually include millions of online fans (and critics), she seemed to demonstrate the revolutionary potential of the Internet. After all, she was but a young woman with paltry resources and no background in media production, and she managed to produce a popular show on a shoestring budget with a production crew of one: herself. Single-handedly she seemed to herald an alternative media model – one that had haunted the imagination of media critics for decades. If the mass media represented the concentration of symbolic power in the hands of a select few, 'Jennicam' demonstrated that an 'ordinary' person could reach millions from the public privacy of her home. Similarly, if the mass media provided a one-way form of broadcasting, Jennicam demonstrated the ability of at least one member of the mass to speak back: not only by putting on her show, but by engaging in ongoing online chats with her audience. Finally, if the networks provided viewers with predigested news and canned entertainment programming, Jennicam promised access to uncut, uncensored and unedited reality. Several years ahead of her time, Ringley anticipated the reality-programming trend. Her occasional critiques of the formulaic products of the mass media and her professed ideals of a community-based medium also seemed to anticipate in some distant form the utopian yearnings of Douglas Kellner's claim that new media enable 'ordinary citizens and activists themselves to become political actors and communicators, to reproduce and disseminate information, and to participate in debates and struggles, thus helping to realize Gramsci's dictum that anyone could be a public intellectual' (Kellner 1999: 109).

Of course, Ringley was hailed not as a revolutionary but as a curiosity, and she became a darling of the mass media, which relentlessly featured her in newspaper articles and news interviews, helping to build her audience around the world and to inspire imitators. In 1999, the *New York Times* estimated that there were approximately a quarter of a million people around the globe 'exposing their lives part-time' and that one million webcams were sold in 1999 alone (Sella 2000: 54). Brian Cury, the founder of Earthcam.com, estimated that there would be some 36 million webcams in operation in North America by 2005, creating an online echo of the boom in reality-based programming (MSNBC Reports 2000). If Jennicam was little more than a curiosity, her followers seemed to have sparked a small movement, which a recent MSNBC documentary dubbed 'The Webcam Explosion' (ibid.). The rhetoric of the information revolution accordingly engulfed the webcam movement, which offered a paradigmatic, if somewhat eccentric, example of the decentralization and democratization of social power promised by techno-utopians like William Wriston and Derrick DeKerchkove (Wriston 1992; Kelly 1996).

As the example of Jennicam suggests, this promise unfolds itself in spatial terms: the development of interactive, networked communication technologies offers to transform sites formerly devoted to passive reception into spaces of production. Digital convergence ostensibly overwhelms the spatial divisions associated with the concentration of power, and with the alienation of consumers and viewers from the production process. Thanks to the new medium, we can all gain access to the means of production by migrating into the undifferentiated, liberating realm of cyberspace.

However, as Robins and Webster (1999) have suggested, such revolutionary rhetoric is misplaced if it is meant to herald a fundamental shift in social relations. On the contrary, interactive media are rapidly being assimilated into an economic framework in which participation has nothing at all to do with power sharing. And yet, media consumption and production are both undoubtedly undergoing dramatic transformations. The networks are gearing up for 'interactive' television and media convergence, or so we are told, while Internet use in the developed nations is increasing at an impressive pace. If these changes are not revolutionary, we have to admit at the very least that they signal dramatic transformations in the way we think about and use the media.

History is rife with examples of dramatic transformations that have fallen far short of being revolutionary in the political sense of the word. Indeed, the notion of revolution itself has been thoroughly de-politicized in such phrases as 'the Industrial Revolution' and 'the Information Revolution'. The problem for media theory, then, is to account for the fact that such dramatic transformations are *not* revolutionary. In somewhat different terms, the problem is to explain how existing social relations are being reconfigured to absorb and exploit dramatic changes in media technology and practice. The goal of this chapter is to attempt to offer one such explanation based on a discussion of the so-called webcam revolution and its reconfiguration of productive space. The promise of spatial de-differentiation is real: webcam pages really do offer a site of media production radically different from that of the mass media, and they also offer a way of reaching potential audiences and creating an interactive forum for public discussion. However, far from being subversive, the use of webcam pages for perpetual self-disclosure (personal 'reality TV', as it were) anticipates the emerging surveillance-based rationalization of the online economy. Far from shifting control over the means of production – media or otherwise – the commercial deployment of interactive media allows for the exploitation of the work of being watched. In other words, the de-differentiation of spaces of consumption and production achieved by new media serves as a form of spatial enclosure: a technology for enfolding previously unmonitored activities within the monitoring gaze of marketers. Spaces associated with leisure and domestic activities do become increasingly productive from a commercial point of view, precisely because they can be more thoroughly monitored. Viewed from this perspective, webcam celebrities like Jennifer Ringley and her various imitators presage not the paradigm of the online public intellectual envisioned by Kellner, but that of the 'fully-documented life' described by Bill Gates (1996).

The day in which everyone will be able to have his or her own TV show is neither as far off nor as utopian as the imaginings of Minneapolis-based webcam artist Ana Voog quoted above might suggest. Although they do not put it quite in these terms, the writings of economic futurists (including Mougayar 1998; Gates 1996; Pine 1993) envision a future in which a large number of content producers – the public – will Netcast the rhythm of their day-to-day lives to a small group of viewers. Perhaps the term 'Netcasting' needs to be recast, since the incipient media model is neither the familiar one-to-many nor the one-to-one model, but rather a 'many-to-few' format: consumers will relay the content of their daily lives to a core group of data miners. This latter group will, in turn, sort, package, re-sell and eventually use this information. In other words, everyone (with some minimal level of disposable income) will have his or her own show. That show will be their 'real' lives: the details of their purchases, of their leisure-time choices, of their advertising and programming preferences – of as much of their private life as can be commodified (which is to say, nearly all of it). In this sense, Netcasting might have a bigger future than even its most ardent fans imagine.

Exploring the social transformations that correspond to this potential future requires reformulation of the terms that media critics generally deploy. It should be fairly obvious by now that those terms have been co-opted by the commercial proponents of new media, who are themselves decrying the shortcomings of the mass media and of mass society in general. Consider, for example, the recent advertisement for the digital television service TiVo: two bouncers charge into a TV executive's office and throw him out the window. The message is that viewers are no longer at the mercy of the programming whims of TV execs: they can watch what they want, when they want (and even bleep through the commercials). The form of the promise is explicitly spatial: thanks to the new technology, the inner sanctum of media control, the headquarters of symbolic power, is breached. Once inside, the viewer is able to seize control of the programming process. The promise of the digital revolution is precisely that it will surpass the shortcomings of mass society: consumers will no longer be faced with homogenized products (media and otherwise) and standardized prices. They will be able to participate in the planning process from which they were excluded, and to purchase customized goods, services and information; to search for the lowest prices, and even to bargain online (consider, for example, the success of online auction sites like E-bay and Priceline.com). Overcoming mass society means overcoming the spatial divisions that constituted and reproduced it, in particular the division between planning, execution and consumption. The promise of a post-mass society thus builds on the thread of pre-mass nostalgia that runs through the mass society critique. Is production too standardized? New information and communication technologies will help customize it. Are the media too one-way, top-down and monopolistic? The Internet will render them decentralized and interactive. Have we become separated and alienated from the production process and from the planners who orchestrate our needs and desires? In cyberspace this alienation can be overcome. Have we lost our sense of community, become disembedded and deterritorialized? We can rediscover community and re-embed ourselves in virtual space.

Since this promise is so pervasive both in descriptions of the online economy and in the mass society critique that it has co-opted, our first task will be to attempt to devise an alternative critical framework and terminology for exploring the deployment of interactive media, which I outline briefly in the discussion of the 'digital enclosure' below. The remainder of the chapter will draw on this framework to explore the transitional or fringe case of webcams. The goal is to suggest a reconsideration of the question of the revolutionary potential of new media technologies. Far from reintroducing political participation into the mediated public sphere, interactivity offers the potential to democratize publicity as celebrity. No longer are we faced with the binary opposition between passive consumption and active (presumably critical) participation, rather with the paradigm of active participation as a form of self-commodification. Kellner's hope for the resurgence of the public intellectual is short-circuited by the false revolution anticipated by Baudrillard, in which 'reversibility' – or what might be termed 'interactivity' in the jargon of the technoculture – merely recapitulates the instrumentalization of publicity by 'proposing, as a revolutionary solution, that everyone become a manipulator, in the sense of active operator, producer, etc.' (Baudrillard 1981: 82).

Spatial transformations and the digital enclosure

If a crucial element of the promise of new media interactivity is that of spatial de-differentiation – of overcoming the boundaries that concentrated power and control in mass society – then debunking this promise requires an alternative interpretation of the de-differentiation process. Instead of promoting power sharing, the contemporary deployment of interactivity exploits participation as a form of labor. Consumers generate marketable commodities by submitting to comprehensive monitoring. They are not so much *participating*, in the progressive sense of collective self-determination, as they are *working* by submitting to interactive monitoring. The advent of digital interactivity does not challenge the social relations associated with capitalist rationalization, it reinforces them and expands the scale on which they operate. Historically, we can trace a three-step progression: spaces of work, leisure and domesticity are first differentiated and then, thanks to the creation of a monitored workspace, techniques for the supervision and rationalization of the labor process are developed and intensified. Finally, this rationalization process is extended into the spaces from which it was originally isolated. Thus, the boundary-breaking character of networked interactivity is not revolutionary in a political sense. Rather it bears the character of what Marcuse (1992) described as 'repressive desublimation': an ostensible liberation that reinforces entrenched social relations. Far from democratizing the production process, participation has the potential to vastly enhance its rationalization.

A spatially-inflected critique of interactive media must therefore locate their deployment within the history of monitored space in capitalist production. The advent of capitalism was predicated upon the spatial strategy of enclosure, which, as Giddens (1981) describes, made possible a transformation in the mode of exploitation from one based on the forcible appropriation of surplus product to the contractual accumulation of surplus value. When workers are compensated in the form of wages rather than in the form of a portion of their product, the need for monitoring is obviously intensified – hence the need for a workspace proper that can be separated out from other social spaces and closely monitored. Giddens notes that this spatial differentiation might be seen as the first step in the scientific management of labor: 'The main phenomenon, in fact, that promotes the separation of home and work-place is the recognition of employers that labour discipline is more satisfactorily sustained if workers are under one roof' (Giddens 1981: 10). The rise of industrialization, as both Giddens (1981) and Foucault (1978) suggest, was predicated on the spatial concentration of workers within the factory where their work could be more easily surveyed. As Braverman (1974) observes, the consequent scientific management of production is predicated on a spatial division within the factory: that between the factory floor and the planning department, where information about workers is gathered, analyzed and used to determine ways of rendering the deployment of labor power more efficient.

The characteristic spatial divisions of modernity correspond not just to the division of labor, but to the divisions between labor and non-labor activities. The social relations of production are reinforced by the spatial segregation of sites of production and consumption. As Couldry (2000) notes, this segregation is carried over into the sphere of media practice, where it reinforces the symbolic power of media institutions. Limited access to the site of media production helps naturalize the way stories are framed and facts presented, precisely because the editing and writing processes whereby media products are constructed remain largely inaccessible to the public.

On its surface, the webcam 'movement' seems to challenge this spatial segregation by allowing a domestic site like a dorm room or household to become a site of production in its own right. However, far from subverting power relations, such a challenge anticipates the reconfigured spatial logic of what Schiller (1999) calls digital capitalism. This reconfiguration is embodied by the double movement of the 'digital enclosure', which can be understood as the process whereby activities formerly carried out beyond the monitoring capacity of the Internet are enfolded into its virtual space. Examples might include the attempt by online booksellers to replace 'bricks and mortar' stores, or the development of digital forms of television delivery. The process is still very much in its early stages, but is being heavily underwritten by capital investment as well as by the enthusiastic and breathless predictions of the mass media.

From an economic perspective, the process of digital enclosure relates to the earlier enclosure movement in so far as it promises to compel entry into a particular social relation – one of surveillance – by pre-empting alternative spaces. A service like TiVo, for example, which promises to empower viewers, serves simultaneously to subject them to an unprecedented level of monitoring. Viewers may be able to choose which shows they watch and when, but in return they supply the details of their viewing habits to TiVo, which can use the information to customize marketing appeals and programming recommendations. The payment for this information is offered in the form of added convenience and customization. To the extent that an interactive digital system becomes the standard for content delivery and not just one more option, as envisioned, for example, by Bill Gates (1996), viewers lose the ability to choose whether or not to submit to comprehensive monitoring. Watching interactive TV, in other words, requires entry into a monitored relationship, which in turn allows for the increasing rationalization of the marketing process. This, of course, is precisely the paradigm of customized marketing envisioned by both proponents and critics of e-commerce (see, for example, Schiller 1999; Gates 1996; Pine 1993).

It is, at the same time, important to note that entry into the digital enclosure promises to *undo* one of the constituent spatial divisions of capitalist modernity: that between sites of labor and leisure. This undoing represents a form of de-differentiation whereby formerly 'unproductive' spaces are rendered economically productive (the scare quotes are meant to acknowledge the way in which notions of economic productivity tend to overlook unpaid domestic labor). Despite the rhetoric of empowerment, the process of de-differentiation tends to work primarily in one direction: it does not make work more like 'free time', but, rather, tends to commodify free time by transforming it into time that can be monitored, recorded, repackaged and sold. If the land enclosure movement helped separate spaces of labor from those of leisure and domesticity so that the deployment of labor time could be more efficiently exploited, the digital enclosure stretches out to encompass what was left over.

The anticipated productivity of this mediated digital enclosure is thus predicated on a self-reinforcing spiral of surveillance and self-disclosure. Entry into this enclosure allows consumption to double as a form of production. Downloading a book or programming a digital television set generates information that can be repackaged, sold and eventually incorporated into customized products whose consumption generates ever more specific demographic information. If, within the digital enclosure, surfing the web doubles as a form of self-disclosure, and if this self-disclosure generates commodifiable information, then the more one consumes, the more one specifies who one is (from a marketing perspective), and thus what one wants. Full attainment of desire is predicated on complete disclosure. Personal webcam sites anticipate this process by providing unedited access to the rhythms of the day-to-day life of their protagonists. However, rather than divulging this information to a select group of viewers who stand to profit from its monopolization, webcam sites offer themselves directly to consumers as a form of entertainment that doubles as a means of advertising the advantages, conveniences and, even, the sociability of the digital enclosure. In this respect, webcam celebrities who profit from their activity represent the entrepreneurs of the digital enclosure.

The digital enclosure of DotComGuy

Since Jennicam first went online from Dickinson College in 1996, hundreds of imitators have followed suit, and many of them have attempted to tap into the commercial potential of home webcasting. One of the most recent imitators, a 26-year-old former computer systems manager who changed his name to DotComGuy when he decided to live his life online for a year, served as a round-the-clock advertisement for the ostensible benefits of the de-differentiation of work, leisure and domestic space within the digital enclosure. DotComGuy's stated goal was to prove to the world that he could order everything he needed to survive over the Internet – without leaving home for all of the year 2000. Furthermore, he attempted to earn a living while shopping, budgeting himself a $98,000 salary based on the revenues he hoped to earn from online sponsorships and advertising. The project got off to a strong start: during the early months, DotComGuy's website boasted an average of one million hits a day (Eldredge 2000), and he built up an impressive list of online sponsors. However, his timing was bad. The dot.com crash was in full swing by the time he had spent half a year in the DotComPound, and he left the house at the end of the year with nothing to show for his efforts but a few of the products that had been donated by sponsors. Despite its failure as an entrepreneurial endeavor, the DotComGuy website made explicit the role that surveillance played in transforming domestic and leisure-oriented spaces into spaces of production. One newspaper account put it succinctly, describing DotComGuy (a.k.a. Mitch Maddox of Dallas, Texas) as 'a guy who sold his own life – whose journals are posted on-line, whose everyday speech is riddled with endorsements, whose movements even in sleep are scrutinized by millions of viewers' (Copeland 2000: C1).

DotComGuy, in short, overcame the spatial divisions of modernity described by Giddens (1981). When he was in the DotCompound (which included a backyard for DotComDog), he was, in some sense, always working. Even when he was sleeping, a viewer who logged onto the site could find an image of him in bed surrounded by the flashing banner ads that helped pay his salary. In addition to turning his life into a series of product endorsements (from online grocery and maid services to software products and even an online athletic trainer), DotComGuy served as a branded advertisement for the promise of the online economy. This promotional function was not a by-product of the project, but its explicit goal, as stated on DotComGuy's website:

> It started with an observation: … E-commerce can provide anything you could ask for, and you'd never have to leave home. … Most people still think the Internet is an infant. This then, is a unique opportunity to help bring that baby up and help others learn to trust it. … This project can help take some of the drudgery out of day-to-day purchases, and even help turn people on to a world they might not otherwise embrace.
>
> (DotComGuy.com 2000)

In short, DotComGuy's life became a round-the-clock advertisement for a lifestyle that corresponded to a new way of consuming. It was by no means a fluke that this advertisement took the form of perpetual surveillance, for such is the nature of the lifestyle being advertised. Online, we may well all become DotComPeople, under perpetual surveillance, ostensibly for our own convenience and profit. DotComGuy's advertising campaign, then, makes a pitch not just for the convenience of online shopping, but for the advantages of being watched. By agreeing to live his life on camera, DotComGuy enacted the appropriate attitude of the wired consumer: a thoroughly contemporary, almost 'hip', lack of squeamishness toward surveillance.

This is the attitude of the youth celebrities on MTV's *Real World* and of would-be contestants on reality game shows like *Survivor* and *Big Brother*. It is also the characteristic attitude of the webcam celebrity. Jennifer Ringley, for example, equates the retreat into privacy concerns as a form of self-delusion: 'I honestly think the concept of privacy is a mental fabrication. It's a convenient way to imagine we're hiding the things we like least about ourselves, and therefore negates us from responsibility for them. … Realistically … we should be able to defend our actions to ourselves, to know why we do what we do and to come to peace with it' (Ringley 2000). Perpetual surveillance, in other words, is nothing to be afraid of – so long as we are honest with ourselves. Comfort with self-disclosure signifies a healthy openness and self-awareness. It is no longer surveillance that is stigmatized, but the fear of it. This attitude neatly aligns itself with the marketing promise of e-commerce: that willing submission to perpetual self-disclosure should be viewed neither as an intrusion nor as an inconvenience to be tolerated, but as an advantage to consumers. One of the reasons that the mass market felt like a homogenizing force was that our individual natures were shielded in privacy that failed to let marketers discern the idiosyncrasies of our desires. Thus, if we are to counter this tendency, we must open ourselves up to the process of self-commodification as self-expression.

The virtual workspace

DotComGuy's publicity project anticipates not just the rationalization of consumption via surveillance, it also serves as a rudimentary model of the twenty-first-century workplace envisioned by corporate futurists. Pruitt and Barrett (1991), for example, imagine that workers will be able to go to work without leaving home, by entering a 'corporate virtual workspace' – a virtual reality construct that workers log into from home. This workspace conveniently does away with the wasted time of commuting and even of showering and dressing, when the work to be attended to is truly pressing (in the world they describe, it is apparently oppressively so). Indeed, the workspace is never more than a mouse-click away. The absorption of the workspace by the digital enclosure captures the capitalist imagination for two reasons. First, because it promises to facilitate management monitoring, and second, because it contributes to the fantasy of friction-free capitalism by offering to make labor markets fluid and flexible.

Pruitt and Barrett do not shy away from the implications of this new space for workers. The 'unprecedented freedom' they predict for the workforce of the future turns out to be, in significant ways, a negative form of freedom: freedom from benefits and job security: 'If the individual takes full advantage of cyberspace and becomes an independent economic unit, he will need to become more self-reliant. Health care and financial cushions [by which they presumably mean retirement and unemployment benefits] may become the responsibility of the individual' (Pruitt and Barrett 1991: 406). Ongoing job shifting and retraining would be the norm, and corporations would no longer bear the burden of looking after their employees: 'By releasing workers with no repercussions, a company may find itself rehiring a rejuvenated and enriched worker' (Pruitt and Barrett 1991: 407). Freedom is reconfigured as the natural, Darwinian freedom of the marketplace: the freedom to compete for jobs on an ongoing basis; and it is underwritten by the de-differentiation that transforms the private 'free' space of the home into a workplace.

The fact that DotComGuy's status remains somewhat indeterminate (is he producing or consuming? is his home a workspace, a domestic space, or a public space?) highlights the de-differentiation of space that facilitates the commodification of both consumption and leisure time. Free time in the digital enclosure is not quite as 'free' from commodification as it was 'on the outside'. Within the enclosure every consumption decision represents a double value: that realized in exchange, and that which can be generated by the information about the transaction.

From the perspective of media production, DotComGuy represents not only the indeterminate space of consumption/production, but the erosion of the division between advertising and content that takes place within such a space. Like the character Truman Burbank in the film *The Truman Show*, DotComGuy is both the site's protagonist and a round-the-clock male model for the products it endorses. He wears the clothes and eats the food he orders over the Internet – and he does so online, providing viewers with links that allow them to do the same. He thereby extends the process of de-differentiation to the boundary between advertising and content – a boundary that has long been contested in the US commercial media, but whose dissolution has become an explicit goal for advertisers in an era when digital VCRs promise to make ad zapping easier than ever before. The reality TV trend has been at the forefront of this de-differentiation process, as evidenced by the integration of sponsors into the content of such successful shows as *Survivor* and *American Idol*. As *Survivor* producer Mark Burnett observed, the show 'is as much a marketing vehicle as it is a television show. My shows create an interest, and people will look at them, but the endgame here is selling products in stores – a car, deodorant, running shoes. It's the future of television' (Reiter 2002).

Convergence: being watched at work and the work of being watched

DotComGuy, then, stands at the point of convergence of two trends in the online economy: the flexible, interactive workspace, and the monitored space of consumption. It is not the goal of this chapter to conflate these two spaces, but rather to observe the way in which they reflect one another. Interactive, networked media allow both for the development of the spatially 'flexible' workspace and for the increased economic productivity of spaces of leisure and domesticity. These trends represent two forms of spatial transformation: that of the home (or café, or airport, etc.) doubling as an office, and that of non-workplace activities becoming economically productive when they take place within the monitored space of the digital enclosure.

If DotComGuy combines these forms of productivity from the privacy of his home, another webcam site, 'The Nerdman Show' (as in *The Truman Show*), bridges the physical division between work and home with webcams. Nerdman, a.k.a. Vance Kozik, engineers webcams for a living and uses his site to demonstrate his wares, which include twelve webcams in his office and six in his home that send fresh images to the Internet every 60 seconds. Although the site provides very tame Internet fare, displaying mainly office cubicles, furniture and the cat litter box, it nevertheless manages to draw some 1,500 viewers daily (Sella 2000).

'The Nerdman Show', like the DotCompound, is a commercial venture. As Kozik puts it, 'Product promotion was the original concept behind the site, and it continues to be the most beneficial aspect to me' (Kozik 2000). The ads on the site earn him a small monthly income of about $120 a month, and his company supplies him with free equipment in exchange for the publicity. Given the modest profitability of the site, Kozik describes it primarily as a novelty that helps draw attention to the webcams. Indeed, his website reads like the testimonial of a sincere convert:

> The combination of camera technology and the reach of the Internet makes for a great way to check the weather, watch what's going on at your home/office, and of course see if the cat box needs changing. ... The applications are endless ... security, surveillance, tourism, construction.
> (http://nerdman.com/faq.html 2002)

Kozik claims to have little interest in other people's webcams. Instead, he prefers outdoor webcam sites, which make it possible to import vistas from around the world. The availability of thousands of landscape cameras through sites like Earthcam.com seems a fitting complement to the shut-in character of the DotComGuy lifestyle. The worker who telecommutes to the other side of the globe can watch the sun set over company headquarters without leaving the privacy of home.

Being watched as work: VoyeurDorm and CuteCouple

The economic potential of the commodification of self-disclosure represented by commercial webcam sites became apparent early on when Jennicam earned surprisingly high ratings (upwards of several million hits a day) and became the subject of extensive media coverage (Balint 1999). From the privacy of her dorm room, Ringley managed to reach an audience that surpassed the circulation of many small and mid-sized newspapers – a fact that did not escape the attention of advertisers for long. In the wake of the media publicity, Ringley was approached by a soft drink company with an offer of $10,000 a month to leave bottles of its product around her house within range of the cameras. She turned down the offer to protect the authenticity of the site, explaining that 'it would ... make the site about as real as 'The Real World' or any of the other cheesy productions mainstream society produces. Once I start fabricating the content, especially for the sake of money, it's not worth even doing anymore' (Ringley 2000).

If Ringley remained reluctant to exploit the commercial potential of her site, which charges a monthly fee for those who want to receive more frequent photo updates, other webcam producers are more than willing. The CuteCouple.com webcam site, for example, offers paying subscribers an unedited glimpse into the daily (and nightly) life of a college-aged couple in Austin, Texas. The couple,

Chris and Ashley, claim that the site earned about $20,000 during its first two and a half months online. Which is good money for work they enjoy: 'It sounds funny but we really do LIVE for a living. The only difference between us and anyone else is that we post it on the World Wide Web. It's the best "JOB" in the world! "Here's some money to live your life!" We'll take that any day!' (Chris and Ashley 2000).

The people who are really cashing in, however, are the pioneers of the factory model of webcam production, wherein salaried workers sell their privacy in shifts. The founders of a website called VoyeurDorm, which pays college women to live in houses outfitted with a battery of digital cameras, estimated revenues of approximately $15 million in 2000 (Huettel 2000). The VoyeurDorm house in Tampa, Florida, boasts eight 'sexy college girls' and seventy-five live cameras – including at least two in the bathrooms (MSNBC Reports 2000). The VoyeurDorm women are paid laborers, and according to one news account, 'receive free tuition, free rent and a modest salary. They work in shifts that include scheduled parties and lingerie shows. No drugs are allowed. They can show as little or as much skin as they like' (Huettel 1999). The scheduled spontaneity and contrived nature of such a site might seem to undermine its claim to authenticity. However, as in the case of reality television programs, this claim is predicated not so much on a freedom from all contrivance as upon the fact that the site is 'unscripted, unedited, and uncensored' (voyeurdorm.com 2000).

VoyeurDorm capitalizes on the commodification of self-disclosure not only by advertising itself to consumers as a site for unabashed voyeurism, but by promoting itself to prospective tenants as a great way to launch a show-business career. The introductory tour of the site, for example, includes the gushing testimonial attributed to 21-year-old VoyeurDorm resident Alex: 'I love all the attention I have received over the past two years from being a VoyeurDorm girl! I have been on dozens of TV shows and magazines. I was recently on VH1 [a cable music show] for my music talent and now I'm working on signing a record contract!' (voyeurdorm.com 2000). Like other so-called reality formats, VoyeurDorm inverts the relationship between celebrity and surveillance: rather than the latter following upon the former, celebrity becomes the effect of self-disclosure. Therein lies the promise of the democratization of celebrity: the manipulated can become the manipulators.

It is this ostensible penetration into the realm of media production that underwrites the promise of democratization built into the reality genre. Just as access to the means of media production is facilitated by the relatively inexpensive technology of the webcam, the emerging emphasis on unedited 'reality' highlights the perceived diminution of producer 'control' over the show. One of the staples of webcam chatrooms is the attempt by viewers to get webcasters to respond to them in a way that viewers can see by, for example, waving in response to an emailed request. Often the requests – especially those directed toward female web-celebs like Jennifer Ringley – are more salacious, and webcam entrepreneurs have been quick to capitalize on this perceived demand. A now notorious Maryland couple offers a webcam site that combines the appeal of reality and interactivity by allowing viewers to direct their love-making. The self-invoked appeal of the site – what ostensibly distinguishes it from the myriad of other live-porn sites online – is the fact that the couple are 'real' people – an unemployed funeral home employee and a soccer mom – not porn stars. As the couple's web page puts it, 'REAL PEOPLE, REAL SEX … that's our motto' (thewetlands.com 2000). The couple has since recruited other couples to join their site, which made $6 million in 1999 (MSNBC Reports 2000). Thanks to the power of the new technology, anyone with access to a server and a modicum of technical know-how can turn the most intimate of spaces into an economically productive one, bypassing the usual avenues of media production.

Conclusion: the transformation of the publicity sphere

The entrepreneurial potential of personal webcams, erotic or otherwise, remains that of a pyramid scheme: those who get in first are likely to capture the profits and the attention. However, a future in which everyone has his or her own show supported by everyone else remains a zero-sum proposition. Webcams can be viewed as an experiment in home-made media production and perhaps one of those experimental uses that crop up in the transitional period surrounding the implementation and deployment of a new medium, before the dominant model is fully in place. Which is not to say that webcam sites will become extinct any more than, for example, Ham radio became extinct. Rather they are likely to continue to remain a fringe use, perhaps the province of hobbyists and amateurs. Despite the revolutionary rhetoric of such webcam producers as Ana Voog and Jennifer Ringley, who envision a sustainable, home-brewed version of media production, the mass media are unlikely to face any serious threat from this quarter. Furthermore, commercial sites like DotComGuy remind us that we should be wary of formulations that adopt the binary terms of the mass society critique: active production or passive consumption. What we are likely to see instead is active participation that, far from undermining the social relations of production, facilitates the rationalization of consumption. The webcam 'move-ment' is suggestive in so far as it thematizes the value of the work of being watched and the spatial de-differentiation that accompanies it. The sites considered above demonstrate some of the ways in which interactive media blur the boundaries between work and recreation, between spaces of leisure and labor, and between advertising and content. Perhaps most importantly they highlight the overlap between interactivity, participation and labor.

Too often, the critique of the mass media is accompanied by an uncritical celebration of the inherently progressive virtues of participation. The Gemeinschaft-nostalgia that characterizes much of the writing on media and democracy is particularly prevalent in Habermas-inspired discussions of a pre-mass media public sphere. Typical of such approaches is James Carey's description of the deterioration of public life that accompanied the rise of a mass commercial press, which 'no longer facilitated or animated a public conversation. ... It informed a passive and privatized group of citizens who participated in politics through the press' (Carey 1995: 189). The notion of public participation is central to Habermas' own account of the re-feudalization of the public sphere: 'Thus a public of citizens that had disintegrated as a public was reduced by publicist means to such a position that it could be claimed for the legitimation of political compromises without participating in effective decisions or being in the least capable of such participation' (Habermas 1996: 221). The fate of the public is manifested by the co-optation of the language of publicity, as Peters points out: 'In writings by theorists such as Jeremy Bentham and John Stuart Mill ... "publicity" meant openness of discussion and commerce as well as popular access to government. Today publicity only suggests public relations' (Peters 1993: 543).

Peters goes on to argue that this semantic transformation parallels Habermas' description of the transformation from 'critical participation' to 'consumerist manipulation' (Peters 1993: 543). This opposition, which has become a staple of critical media studies, creates an implicit, natural link between participation and critique that helps to underwrite the ostensibly politically progressive character of interactive media. In the era of one-way, top-down media production and delivery, participation and critique seemed naturally allied. With the advent of interactive media, we need to more closely interrogate and clarify the promise of participation, which has been enlisted by the promoters of the online economy. To put it in somewhat different terms, if there is an acknowledged thread of qualified nostalgia for the de-differentiated spaces associated with a romanticized past, this same nostalgia haunts the digital imaginary. Mass-customized society, or so the business literature would have it, will combine the advantages of handicraft society and its associated community with the efficiency of modern technologies and techniques. The promises of the digital economy, of digital community and of interactive media, are inextricably intertwined with the notion of participatory interactivity. The fact that this promise aligns itself with the critique of mass society ought to inspire a certain wariness on the part of media scholars and theorists toward the opposition between consumerist manipulation and participatory critique.

The example of the commercial webcam site suggests a third possibility: the exploitation of participation understood as the labor of self-commodification. The trajectory of the term 'publicity' traced by Peters, in other words, cannot be undone merely by de-differentiating spaces of symbolic production and consumption. Certainly, the potential exists, as Kellner suggests, for the Internet to create a society of public intellectuals. To assume that it will do so, however, is to fail to appreciate the pressures of history and existing social relations. If publicity has evolved into a commercialized, promotional activity, providing access to the means of publicity makes it possible for everyone to actively participate in his or her own self-commodification. This prospect is reflected in the pessimistic conclusion drawn by Baudrillard in his discussion of reality TV – a discussion that anticipated both the *Big Brother* television franchise and the webcam trend: 'We are exposed to the instantaneous retransmission of all our facts and gestures on whatever channel. We would have experienced this before as police control. Today it is just like an advertising promotion' (Baudrillard 1995: 97).

Webcasters do not necessarily reverse the trajectory of publicity by reclaiming it as a form of open deliberation and access to government (in the sense outlined by Peters above). Instead, they are, paradoxically, democratizing (publicity as) celebrity: access to the means of publicity *as a form of self-promotion* is made more generally available. As Ana Voog, who notes on her FAQ page that she hates politics, puts it, 'I guess it was my goal for a while, and it still is my goal, to become an icon' (MSNBC Reports 2000). This is the language not of Gramsci, but of Hollywood Boulevard. Similarly, one VoyeurDorm resident described her webcam work as her first big break: 'this is just an everyday movie … I'm in a movie every single day of my life, and that's how I look at it. … Like, I'm an actress every single day' (MSNBC Reports 2000). Now that they have gained access to the means of symbolic production, the webcasters are not so much revolutionizing it as reproducing it. Their attempt to co-opt the mass media model leads to a familiar preoccupation with ratings. Even the whimsical Nerdman has adopted the language of the studio executive: 'I have all this traffic now. … You can't just stop at this point. If the ratings go up, you don't cancel the show' (Sella 2000: 68). Within the digital enclosure, the option to cancel may become increasingly remote as we find that being watched was never so much work and, at the same time, never easier.

Bibliography

Baudrillard, J. (1981) *For a Critique of the Political Economy of the Sign*, trans. C. Levin, St. Louis: Telos Press.

—— (1995) 'The Virtual Illusion: Or the Automatic Writing of the World', *Theory, Culture and Society*, 12: 97–107.

Braverman, H. (1974) *Labor and Monopoly Capital*, New York: Monthly Review Press.

Carey, J. (1995) 'The Press, Public Opinion, and Public Discourse', in T.L. Glasser and C.T. Salmon (eds) *Public Opinion and the Communication of Consent*, New York: Guilford: 373–402.

Chris and Ashley (of CuteCouple.com) (2000) 'Interview Request: Finally!' Email (14 November).

Copeland, L. (2000) 'The Cyber-house Rules: Dallas's DotComGuy Makes a Domain Name for Himself', *Washington Post*, 8 July, C01.

Couldry, Nick (2000) *The Place of Media Power*, London: Routledge.

DotComGuy (2000) 'Frequently Asked Questions', Online, Available HTTP: <http://dotcomguy.com> (20 March).

Eldredge, R.L. (2000) 'Peach Buzz: June Looking Good in Profile', *Atlanta Constitution*, 5 July, 2C.

Foucault, M. (1978) *The History of Sexuality: An Introduction*, trans. R. Hurley, New York: Pantheon Books.

Gates, B. (1996) *The Road Ahead*, New York: Penguin.

Giddens, A. (1981) *A Contemporary Critique of Historical Materialism*, Berkeley: University of California Press.

Habermas, J. (1996) *The Structural Transformation of the Public Sphere*, trans. T. Burger, Cambridge, MA: MIT Press.

Huettel, S. (1999) 'Voyeur Dorm is Test of Cyber Law', *St. Petersburg Times* (Florida), 26 April, 1B.

—— (2000) 'Adult Web Site Opens Doors for Owners', *St. Petersburg Times* (Florida), 13 August, 1B.

Kellner, D. (1999) 'Globalisation from Below? Toward a Radical Democratic Technopolitics', *Angelaki* 4(2): 101–11.

Kelly, K. (1996) 'What Would McLuhan Say?', *Wired Magazine*. Online. Available HTTP: <http://www.wired.com/wired/archive/4.10/dekerckhove.html> (18 December 2000).

Kozik, V. (2000) 'Book Chapter', email (12 September).

—— (2002) *The Nerdman Show*. Online. Available HTTP: <www.nerdman.com> (22 August).

Lefebvre, H. (1991) *The Production of Space*, Oxford: Blackwell.

Marcuse, H. (1992) *One-Dimensional Man: Studies in Ideology of Advanced Industrial Society*, Boston, MA: Beacon Press.

Mougayar, W. (1998) *Opening Digital Markets*, New York: McGraw-Hill.

MSNBC Reports: 'Look at Me! The Webcam Explosion', 2000. TV, MSNBC. 2000 29 August.

Nerdman Show, The (2002) 'Frequently Asked Questions'.

Peters, J.D. (1993) 'Distrust of Representation: Habermas on the Public Sphere', *Media, Culture and Society*, 15: 541–71.

Pine, J. (1993) *Mass Customization: The New Frontier in Business Competition*, Cambridge, MA: Harvard University Press.

Pruitt, S. and Barrett, T. (1991) 'Corporate Virtual Workspace', in M. Benedikt (ed.), *Cyberspace: First Steps*, Cambridge, MA: MIT Press.

Reiter, A. (2001) 'Nothing Personal'. Salon.Com. Online. Available HTTP: <http://archive.salon.com/people/col/reit/2001/06/06/npwed/> (6 June).

Ringley, J. (2000) 'Book Chapter Request', Email (14 September).

Robins, K. and Webster, F. (1999) *Times of the Technoculture: From the Information Society to the Virtual Life*, London: Routledge.

Sella, M. (2000) 'The Electronic Fishbowl', *New York Times*, 21 May: 50–57, 68, 102.

Wriston, W. (1992) *The Twilight of Sovereignty: How the Information Revolution is Transforming our World*, New York: Scribner.

11

CROSSING THE MEDIA(-N)

Auto-mobility, the transported self and technologies of freedom

James Hay and Jeremy Packer

Auto-mobility: making MediaSpace for IT

In early December 2001, a few months following the collapse of the World Trade Center in New York, ABC's *Good Morning America* became the locus for the public unveiling of the Segway Human Transporter (SHT). The device had been the topic of very public rumors for at least a year, and no public source had been able to determine exactly what 'it' was. A journalistic 'buzz' about a yet to be published, unauthorized literary account of the device's planning and financing added to the mystery. And through the swarming of speculation, the unidentifiable device became reified; its proper name (temporarily) became 'IT'. Culminating the year of public rumoring, therefore, *Good Morning America* dramatized the device's unveiling as a magic act, the shadowy device back-lit behind a sheer, white curtain that was raised to reveal IT. Pronoun, acronym (Intelligent Transport, Individualized Transport)? No one was sure. IT's capacity to transport in its design's capacity for representing simplicity: 'Is that it?' A pair of wheels supporting feet rests and a vertical handlebar guided and balanced (with minimal visible effort or motion by its human operator) through a system of gyroscopes and computerized relays. This was the advancement of personal transport through 'intelligent' technology, a 'smart' scooter, techno-human 'dressage' for the twenty-first century.

Coupled with ABC's exclusive rights to the telecast, and Amazon.com's exclusive sale three months later of the models unveiled on *Good Morning America*, both the transporter and the broadcast became intertwined *events* (Deleuze 1993a, 1993b; Foucault 1977), IT the latest happening in (*Good Morning*) America's new day, and television and the World Wide Web the vehicles for the unbearable lightness of human transport, as the program's hosts (Diane Sawyer and Charles Gibson) and Dean Kamen (the 'inventor' of the SHT) transported themselves outside ABC's New York studio and into/through Bryant Park amidst the program's fans, many of whom travel great distances to stand in each weekday morning for broadcast television's unscripted liveness and connection to the people of America. The event thus involved a convergence of

209

technologies of transportation and communication: television as a technology of communication and transport (a material and representational mediation of house/home, ABC's New York studio, and a national broadcast range), *Good Morning America* as a technology of communication and transport (the use of a plate-glass window to represent a spectatorial relation between hosts, transporters and the public on the street, or the mobility of cameras, hosts, inventors and transporters to an outside, in Bryant Park), the show's on-location fans (whose signs and T-shirt logos represent their relation to the places from which they have traveled), and the human transporter (whose form and function, whose 'complete subject', are predicated upon the conjugation of techno-human intelligence, balance and mobility).

These intertwined events offer us an opportunity to introduce what this chapter does and does not emphasize about media/communication and transportation/space. While considering the convention and contra-convention of the human transporter as event certainly involves recognizing that technologies of media, communication, and the televisual, are forms of representation, this chapter is not only or even primarily interested in how transportation and events are represented, or in how their representation occurs through the narrative and signifying conventions and contra-conventions of television, or in how televisual representation produces ideological subject-spectators. While we are

Figure 11.1 The Segway Human Transporter.™
Source: Segway.

210

decidedly interested in the linkage and assemblage (the *conjugation*) of media/communication technologies and technologies of transport, and the assemblage/conjugation of the 'complete' techno-human subject-self-citizen through these technologies, all of which the ABC telecast represents, we are relatively uninterested in their relation as an apparatus of illusion, in the power of media to transport – or the power of transport to mediate – as magic, deception, false consciousness, ideological interpellation. In our opinion, this has been an unduly protracted tendency and disposition of literary, film and television criticism and of their relation to a modern logic of mediation – to a preoccupation with two concerns, spectatorship and consumption (understood through the binary logic of codes and signs, base and superstructure, power and resistance). Therefore, while this chapter is interested in a conjugation of communication and transportation as event, it is less interested in event as spectacle. Instead, it is more concerned with event as a timely yet ordinary, everyday exhibition, demonstration and exercise – in this case, of the *advancement* of the technology of freedom, or more precisely the advancement of a technology of the self, which (amidst the current reinvention of liberalism and the governmental discourse about freedoms) also constitutes a technology of governance. This chapter is principally concerned with media/communication's dependence upon and deployment of technologies of transportation, with transportation's dependence upon and deployment of technologies of communication, with ways that media/communication have pertained to *regimes* of mobility (as well as what Foucault called 'regimes of truth') (Foucault 1980 and 1997), and with understanding and diagnosing current reasonings about freedom and governance in terms of how communication and transportation have been and are being conjugated and linked and, in their coupling, advanced – made to *move* and matter.

To become a 'social technology' (a term that Raymond Williams [1992] used to describe television) will involve more than IT's fetishization as a commodity that has acquired value or can be purchased via television or Amazon.com. It will involve adjusting to a regime of mobility and spatial production (the routes and rules of transport), even as its uses call into question and modify these routes and rules. Will the transporter be allowed on sidewalks and streets? How will its regulation redefine and reassemble public and private spheres, and rearticulate the rules governing spaces of sociality, labor and leisure, particularly as these spaces have become governable and ungovernable through practices and rules concerning television and other tele-technologies such as the Internet? Addressing these questions involves considering the mobilization of the transporter, as events and cumulatively as instrumental to a diagram sustaining the advancement, refinement and readjustment of *auto-mobility* in its relation to a reasoning about freedoms and governance. The transporter is one of the latest, most advanced and 'pure' forms of auto-mobility whose form and functions rely upon the convergence of communication/media and transportation technology.

By auto-mobility, we refer not simply to the car. The car has become easily the object most often identified with the term 'automobility'. Our interest in discussing the car in a book about media and space is in part strategic; for us, the car is a strategy for understanding 'media' in a way that is not overly media-centric and for rethinking the importance accorded the relation of cinema, television and other 'media' to places that are assumed to be fixed (e.g., cinema's relation to theaters, and television's relation to the domestic sphere). Auto-mobility thus allows us to focus squarely upon the mobility and 'mobilization' of media – the portability of media and communication technologies, the material attachment of these technologies to technologies of transport, and the mattering of media and communication technologies within changing regimes of mobility. These concerns lead us to consider how the car has been (and is being) reassembled, as forms and functions, through the interdependencies between media/communication and transportation technologies – between the car and the screen, for instance, as technologies of mobility. In this sense, we also are less interested in the car as the most pure form of automobility than we are in auto-mobility as a broad range – an assemblage – of technical devices, applied and social technologies of communication and transportation. Considering these developments of the car and their relation to auto-mobility also allows us to rethink (as we explain below) how car/transportation studies and media/communication studies have developed mostly as objects of separate disciplinary knowledges. Our project, therefore, is (in Bruno Latour's [1993] sense) a translation, thinking about media, cars and communication in their hybridized forms, and focusing on the events where media/communication and mobility/transportation have become integral to one another as a continuous networking.

Our interest, furthermore, in the articulation of the 'auto' to various practices, knowledges and rules pertaining to mobility (i.e., 'auto-mobility') involves a set of concerns that are not restricted narrowly to cars or even wheeled transport. 'Auto' serves as a reference to the self (e.g., auto-matic/self-acting, auto-mated/self-generating, auto-nomous/self-sufficient), and to the various articulations of auto- in modern conceptions/actualizations of the self as free and independent. Understood as an expression of auto-mobility, the car is but one kind of assemblage that has become integral to regimes of mobility wherein specific modes of transport are conceived to be a means to self-sufficiency, wherein self-transport is conceived as a basis for states of freedom and independence, and wherein ideals of self-transport, self-sufficiency, and advanced states of freedom (the fully automatic) bleed into one another. While we do consider the car specifically, and auto-mobility more generally, to be integral to modern conceptions and formations of the social (and of 'civil society'), we thus are interested in auto-mobility as an idea and an ideal, as a desired and valued objective for shaping and governing modern societies and selves. Indeed, our focus upon forms and practices of auto-mobility intends to underscore how modern conceptions of the self, and its relation to forms and practices of sociality, have profoundly been about the mattering of mobility – of freedoms conceived in terms of a complicated conjunction of social and physical bodies in space and in motion. The idea of auto-mobility considered here, therefore, pertains to the self not only as moved, motivated and mobilized (the concern of ideological criticism), but as having certain capacities and expectations about autonomy/freedom (the fully mobile self) that have become inseparable from technical devices, applications and technologies. Our interest in the intersection between technologies of media/communication and transport therefore allows us to consider how the capacities and expectations about the fully mobile self have occurred through media/communication technologies as well as transportation technologies (or rather through the interdependence of these technologies). Finally, our interest in these interdependencies involves a somewhat different conception of power than the one that has tended to dominate media and communication studies, which has focused its attention on fixed enclosures where media are engaged (movie theaters, living rooms), the fixity of media/social subjects (in movie theaters or in front of the television set), on issues of spectatorship and consumption as an effect of media production or transmission, and on freedom as primarily a matter of resistance to the power of media. Our account of auto-mobility emphasizes instead that freedom is predicated upon certain technical and technological dependencies that shape the conduct of audiences/drivers, i.e., the capacity of bodies to be both (mobile) agents and governed–power conductors, in both senses.

The advancement of freedom as vehicle: reinventing human transport and reinventing government

Diagnosing the Segway Human Transporter as event involves recognizing two interrelated issues addressed in the remainder of this chapter. The first concerns the interdependence of technologies of communication and transport as twin technologies of mediation. Although television would be a technology most commonly described as 'medium' (after McLuhan's famous dictum), the transporter also operates as media, not only in its design (its capacity to signify and to move/transport as communication), but also in its capacity to move bodies from one physical location to another (to mediate distance). In this respect, not only is the SHT the latest basis for demonstrating how communication technology *translates* transportation technology (and vice versa), but also how diagnosing their translation involves rethinking what has counted as media and mediation, and rethinking what media studies (media criticism, media-effects studies, political economies of media) have considered appropriate demonstrations of certain technologies' power to mediate. Our project operates through an alternative model of mediation, focusing on translations of communication and transportation technology (e.g., the SHT) in order to develop an alternative to models of power that have shaped media studies.

We therefore suggest that diagnosing the Segway Human Transporter as event involves recognizing a second issue: the event's mattering, not only within a current regime of mobility, but also within a rationality of personal freedom and governance (or personal freedoms and self-governance) – a reasoning about the 'advancement' and 'reinvention' of liberal government through expanding the capacity of bodies and populations to be self-directed, self-responsible and self-sufficient citizens. That the human transporter pertains to a governmental *rationality* was affirmed in part by the *Good Morning America* demonstration, when Dean Kamen reasoned that 'we [self-transporters] are empowered pedestrians here. If you and I were to collide, we would be no more problematic than two pedestrians. ... If the city decided that 8 miles an hour is good ... we can pick the key we want to turn it on for different speeds.' The demonstration of the transporter thus affirms that the well-balanced self is a well-conducted self (and vice versa), especially since the transporting machines involved in this event (TV and Human Transporter) involve inter-dependent technologies of self-correction (e.g., the human transporter's constant mainte-nance of balance through gyroscopes and sensors, and television broadcasting as a cultural technology for improving and expanding the capacities of the self through demonstrations). In this respect, auto-mobility is one way to consider media/communication and transport as twin/hybridized *technologies of citizenship*, and one way to consider how technologies of communication and transporta-tion have been conjoined in fashioning the car as a locus and a technology of citizenship.

Before focusing directly on how media and communication technologies have become integral to driving it is worth considering briefly two events that have linked the automation of self-transport (auto-mobility) to the advance-ment and reinvention of government. We have selected these events in part because each conjugates communication and transportation differently, and because they interdependently have contributed to a current regime of mobility that our project seeks to diagnose. One such event, which occurred contempo-raneously with the unveiling of the SHT, involved the multiform tactics through which the car and other forms of wheeled transport became vehicles for displaying, demonstrating and exercising freedoms and proper conduct following the collapse of the World Trade Center towers on 11 September 2001. Flags were attached to or emblazoned on cars, recreational vehicles, pick-up trucks, fire trucks, postal carriers, police cruisers, buses, motorcycles and trailers. Some flags were affixed to radio antennae and to side-windows so that they flapped vigorously at high speeds; some flags were displayed more decorously (e.g., the arrangement of matching miniature flags, equidistant from one another, just inside the rear windshield of a well-maintained Cadillac sedan – 'flag-under-glass'). The attachment of the flag to forms of wheeled transport thus performed a translation of each, producing a hybrid vehicle: neither purely flag nor car, a flag on wheels, a car that flies. The 'right' to attach flags on any vehicle rejected not only the difference between privately-owned, commercial and municipal carriers, or between everyday travel and the road-rights extended to 'emergency vehicles', but also between civilian, military and attaché forms of transport (e.g., expanding the fleet and the right-of-way of flag-flying 'staffcars').

While wheeled transport was not the only object – mobile or stationary – to which flags were affixed, the streets, highways and driving-rules in the United States became conduits for asserting/linking individual freedoms and responsibilities, and, in so doing, for mobilizing, collectivizing and managing the correct conduct of traffic. Freedom and responsibility constructed through auto-mobility; the auto-mobilization of citizenship as a set of rights, rules and responsibilities. The flag-car thus became a locus and mechanism of translation, the self-fashioning of a common vehicle for driving and for citizenship, enacted *by* U.S. driver-citizens. The flag-car converted a technology of autonomy, free-movement, and self-sufficiency into a technology of self-regulation and self-responsibility, all activated as/through emergency rule and the new regularities of traveling, of transporting oneself, and of organizing/managing/conducting the public aggregation, the 'traffic,' of driver-citizens.

Although this event – these daily occurrences – were responses to the collapse of the World Trade Center, and while they became an activity integral to the mobilization of a citizenry for a 'war on terrorism' (and President George Bush's dictum that '*we* will not let terrorists hold freedom hostage'), they pertained even more profoundly to a new stage of auto-mobility, and its relation to the advancement or reinvention of government, which is a process not specific to the events of September 11, but has been organized through these events. The mattering of auto-mobility in the advancement and reinvention of political government (the car as a technology of neo-liberal government) comes together in a third event that was contemporaneous with the two events discussed above.

In early January 2002, a month after the unveiling of the Segway Human Transporter, and two months before the transporter was auctioned on Amazon.com, the Bush administration's Department of Energy unveiled an agreement between government and car makers and energy producers in the United States to develop a form of transport reliant upon 'alternative' energy sources, and they christened the program's objective the FreedomCAR (an acronym for Cooperative Automotive Research). FreedomCAR was one of several programs that the Bush administration articulated to freedoms during its first two years, so this particular program was but one initiative in a concerted effort by political government to cast itself as sponsors, facilitators, safeguarders of freedoms (even as its various departments sanctioned and undertook a broad reassessment of the rules and limits of civil liberties following September 11). As government policy that links *laissez faire* and *laissez passer* (i.e., the governmental assurance and safeguarding of open and free passages as a condition of open and free markets, and vice versa), the FreedomCAR thus is not a 'freedom-car' but a program for designing/inventing a vehicle capable of advancing or 'reinventing' the objectives of liberal government.

As a program for replacing gasoline-powered forms of wheeled transport, FreedomCAR represented the Bush administration's interest in replacing the Program for a New Generation of Vehicle (PNGV) initiated during the Clinton administration, whose emphasis upon research and development of 'hybrid' cars powered partly by electric batteries was deemed by the Bush administration to be unappealing to 'consumer tastes' (and presumably to the taste of the energy companies represented by the Bush administration). Although the Bush admin- istration's reconception of a 'hybrid' car as hydrogen-powered differs from the technical objectives of the Clinton administration's PNGV, FreedomCAR also continues a reasoning by political government about mobility and transport that, since the 1980s, has envisaged a cleaner, quieter and lighter form of human transport (and for some versions, having to stop less frequently for fueling) – a form that more *purely* represents the independence and self-sufficiency of human transport, even while its acceptance as a social technology will involve a broad rearrangement of the routes and rules of auto-mobility in the United States. It is not coincidental, therefore, that both the Clinton–Gore and Bush–Cheney administrations have articulated plans to 'reinvent' liberal government to programs for refining auto-mobility. Furthermore, it is not coincidental that the ideal of the hybrid car gains traction precisely in the age of virtual forms of trans- port, represented to many by/through digitally-powered and -managed forms of tele-communication such as the cellphone (mobile phone) and the Internet. Gore's plan for an 'information highway' was one objective of a governmental reasoning about 'intelligent transport'. As Jody Berland and others have pointed out, the unbearable lightness of being (and transport) attributed to virtual space, virtual travel and 'going online' has come to imply an evolved/improved state, a state of transcendence through incorporeality, or, as Robins and Webster have noted, of making social distance/difference irrelevant (Berland 2000; Robins and Webster 1999). We would add that the innovation of smart vehicles, in their relation to purer, lighter, virtual forms of transport, also have been about advancing technology of freedom, which is, as well, a governmental technology. The SHT's application at Amazon.com also underscores how the ideal of purer forms of auto-mobility has been supported by online shopping/commerce that has required expanding and expediting modes of transporting physical goods (e.g., overnight delivery services).

In certain respects, the Segway Human Transporter – in its relation to the flag- car and FreedomCAR – represents the technologies and procedures through which auto-mobility has come to be understood and enacted within a (new) reasoning about freedom and government, and an emerging regime of mobility. All three events involve inter-dependent programs/plans for mobilizing civic activity through a rationality about government and liberties; and in the case of the recent applications of the human transporter cited above and of FreedomCAR, these events suggests a framework for more efficient productivity by workers and consumers. We suggest that this new governmental rationality, in its relation to an emerging regime of mobility, concerns a new convergence between technologies of communication and transportation, though (as we explain in the next section) we reject the notion that 'convergence' is a quality unique to recent times. The 'smart' car is one of many 'intelligent' machines and appliances, but its design corresponds to a logic about purer forms of auto-mobility (about freeing and expanding the capacity of social bodies and citizens) which have developed through conceptions and applications of personal computers, portable sound systems and mobile telephony as tele-technologies.

Tracking the smart car in the United States

The events discussed in the preceding sections allow us to consider a diagram: the interdependence of dispersed but concurrent exercises of auto-mobility, each enacting a reasoning about freedom and governance, each contributing to a regime of mobility that involves technologies of communication and transportation as technologies of the self. Our interest in the car as a site where communication and transportation technologies are (in Latour's sense) *translated*, therefore, is imbricated in our interest in the car as a complex of communication and transportation technologies whose efficacy and effectivity as concrete assemblage is developing across the events (and through the abstract assemblage of these mobilizations) that we have been describing (Latour 1993).

In this section we turn to a question implied in the previous two sections but not yet adequately developed: the car as communication-transportation technology. In 1997, *Japanese High-Tech News* ran an article devoted to the convergence of communication technologies in the automobile, entitled 'Are Toyota Automobiles the Communication Medium of the Next Generation?' (Ragano 1997). We phrase the question somewhat differently: how has the car been a site where particular translations of communication and transportation occurred, and through whose translations of communication and transportation technology a regime of (auto-)mobility has emerged? Addressing this question involves rethinking the car as media/mediation and rethinking communication as a form of knowledge/power over mobility.

First, the car as media/mediation. We certainly are interested in how recent car design and application have been considered 'smart' and 'intelligent', alongside a variety of 'smart' and 'intelligent' machines. Although the installation of telephones, personal computers, navigation and tracking systems, and video monitors are still mostly optional features of car ownership (as compared to CD-players), the idea of having these devices in cars has become a more common conception of car design and application, not only as the car's operation increasingly relies upon digital/computerized sensing and relay/communication systems, but also as the car is reapplied within an emerging regime of privacy and mobility (a new stage of what Williams [1992] called mobile privatization) through sites other than the car (Hay 2001 and 2003). The car's design as a complex of technologies of communication and transportation thus has occurred through its application as a means of mediating different spheres of everyday life (coming and going between other sites) organized partly through communication technologies. Furthermore, the 'smart car' has developed through the car's application increasingly as a 'home away from home' (or better, one of many loci of the domestic sphere). For a particular class and taste culture whose activities concern service industries, the car is potentially as much a work-station as is house/home – a feature of the car that already has shaped the initial applications of the Segway Human Transporter (e.g., by postal workers, meter-readers and park rangers).

Complicating the current discourse of smart vehicles and road systems, however, is the fact that the car has always 'mediated' (both as a form of transport from one point to another and as individualized moving panorama, through the windshield as screen). Furthermore, the car has developed through and out of other forms of mobility that have altered or mediated the relation to the outside world prior to this, including the train, the coach, the diorama, the movie theater, and so on.

The automobile is then simply one of many technologies of mobility that have mediated experience. Yet it is a little more complex than this. Few if any technologies have mediated time and space more than the automobile. With the exception of agriculture, no other technology has altered the physical land-scape more than the automobile, and in the United States, with the exception of the television, no other technology demands as much screen-time as the automobile. Furthermore, if we think then in terms of how media technologies are often imagined and defined by form, the screen only functions as one of many means of thinking mediation.

Automobiles and their attendant communication technologies are part and parcel of a more general process. In part this would be fulfilling the classic goal of communication by overcoming natural barriers to facilitate the movement of people, goods and culture, thereby expanding networks of interconnection. Armand Mattelart has emphasized that the idea of communication in modern societies was about how to effect a rational, good and open circulatory system – a system consonant with the aims of liberal government and capitalism (Mattelart 1996). Within the modern regime of auto-mobility, communication also has operated as knowledge/power over movement and transport of social bodies. In this regard, movement and connectivity, particularly as they have been bound up with a concern about freedoms (the openness and improvement of circulatory systems designed for auto-mobility), are profoundly matters of governance – of governing oneself, of being governed through technologies, rules, routes and also (though not primarily) by political government.

With the advent of the smart car and the intelligent highway the notion of the automobile as a mobile space for mediation, although increasingly true, can not be summed up as simply an example of another technological convergence. Instead, we will show in the next section that the vogue for convergence is neither new nor adequate for understanding how these technologies have been imagined, governed or used. The question that we emphasize is what the smartness or intelligence of the car (the ideal of driving without hands, of fully automated social bodies) has to do with a new relation between power/ knowledge and a new governmental rationality – new techniques and a new reasoning about governing. We propose that considering the car as media and as a form of communication involves considering how driving smart cars and smart highways (like using the Internet) are caught up in a complex set of questions about power/knowledge – about governing oneself as driver, about a kind of governance that *acts upon* the well-conducted driver (here we borrow from Toby Miller's notion of the well-tempered self), someone who stays within the median (Miller 1993). Communication, as knowledge/power over transport, therefore, has been about establishing rules/provisions that make freedom of self/movement profoundly a matter of safety and security, in Foucault's sense of watching out for and watching over (of recognizing an obligation to) self and other as an objective of government (Foucault 1991; Packer 2003). In this sense, knowledge and communication are integral to a modern regime of auto-mobility and of liberal political government as assuring that everyone plays a role in his or her own governance.

Although Williams' consideration of mobile privatization does bear upon our interest in considering the interdependence of communication and transportation in shaping interdependent social technologies (e.g., television's emergence within a particular stage of mass suburbanization and freeway/highway development), his brief account of mobile privatization lacked attention to questions of security, which not only have been integral to a regime of mobility and privacy, but also to the governmentalization of freedom as auto-mobility. How, in other words, was the regime of mobility and privacy wherein television developed most rapidly involved in the reorganization of spheres of privacy and mobility (e.g., houses and cars) through programs and technologies of safety and risk-management designed to make the enactment or performance of freedoms responsible and thus governable? The following two sections, therefore, emphasize the relation between freedoms and risk-management, privacy and surveillance, as they pertain to the ideal of auto-mobility in the United States.

Whereas the preceding sections have followed some of the events and 'mobilizations' through which human transport has become a technology both of freedom and governance, the next three sections *track* (provide a *genealogy*) of how mediation has been brought to bear upon a number of automotive concerns, how certain provisions and rules (*knowledge* about driving and drivers) have supported the current regime of auto-mobility, and how both communication and transportation technologies have been integral to shaping the conduct of the driving-self. Once communication was physically and discursively articulated to the automobile, thought regarding governmental appropriations of, and technological applications for communication and the automobile have reorganized ideas of mobility, freedom, connectivity, safety and security. These current goals animate discussions of smart cars and intelligent highways. Describing 'smarts' and 'intelligence' produces a value judgment regarding a hierarchy of knowledge. Furthermore, this knowledge is embroiled in a set of power relations regarding what that knowledge should be used for and who should have access to it. Within these definitions lie a desire, a need and an assumed good. This genealogy is organized by three such 'goods' and desires: governmental organization of mobility, automobile safety, and the dream of the automatic. Put simply, what determines whether a smart car passes the test is its ability to produce or relay knowledge that will aid in these concerns.

Productively policing freedom

The police force has been at the forefront of implementing electronic communications technologies into forms of governance since 1845 when the description and whereabouts of a train-bound murderer were transmitted by telegraph to police 18 miles away in London. The suspect was apprehended as he disembarked the train. Quite simply, the telegraph is a faster means of communication than the train. Numerous communications technologies followed the telegraph, but they shared a few key elements. Each allowed for the transmission of greater amounts of information across greater spaces to an increasingly mobile and more organized police force. What began in 1829 with the use of three bursts of a whistle or three taps with a baton indicating the need for help, by 2003 had grown into a vast surveillance network that included two-way radio, belt and pocket transmitters, mobile-relay radio systems, vast Internet databases, satellite reconnaissance photography, automobile Black Boxes, in-car Internet access (and hence all information accessible and record-able therein), computer and phone bugging capabilities, helicopter and airplane patrols, and well-organized automobile patrols.

As noted above, numerous communication technologies were used by police to orchestrate police movement and extend the space that could be monitored. More generally, Andrew Barry (1996) argues, in 'Lines of Communication and Spaces of Rule', that electronic communications technologies have been an integral part of liberal governance. As he points out, Foucault laid the groundwork for thinking about how communications worked to expand the facility of the state and reoriented the model for organizing and governing away from the architecture of fixed places. Yet Barry maintains that communications have ultimately functioned not to increase State surveillance or allow for a 'super-panopticon'; rather they have become technologies of freedom (Barry 1996: 138). To a degree his argument is dependent upon assumptions regarding what forms of conduct are under surveillance and which are left outside purview, but expansion of mobile communications opens new types of conduct to surveillance. Thinking then in terms of how communication facilitates the movement of people and goods, and not just information across space, we can see that communication in the narrow sense facilitates its own expansion in the greater sense. How goods and people are directed and mobilized is not only a vast project for governments, but being able to govern them at a distance in their various states of mobility is of paramount importance. As Barry rightly notes, freedom (and we would argue mobility, a sub-category of freedom) is a necessary part of liberal governing strategies (Barry 1996). By producing a set of circumscribed and discursively legitimated forms of mobile conduct and then allowing citizens to freely roam within those parameters, governing at a distance is ensured.

By organizing the terrain in this fashion, specific communications technologies can be seen as not simply an addition to an already existing technology (e.g., the car plus radio). Rather, they are a sharpening and focusing of governing at a distance. Police radio, as mentioned earlier, aids in orchestrating police movement. Earlier communication technologies had been put to the same use, but were neither mobile, nor in cars. In 1867 a system of strategically placed signaling lights and phone-boxes was first employed to orchestrate the movements of foot police, provide two-way communication with headquarters, decrease response times, and expand surveillance networks. Numerous alterations in the telephone booth/foot-patrol communication network were construed, yet they failed when confronted by the automobile. Vast increases in automobile patrols, necessitated and facilitated by expanded auto-mobility, altered the means and aims of policing. Increasingly, auto-mobility itself was the target of policing efforts and as such new communications technologies were set in place to deal with the new more mobile terrain of policing. The assumptions and questions regarding the importance of radio, particularly as it gained widespread popularity in the late 1920s and early 1930s, are most often of a different order. Yet, this is the very moment that police radio is coming into being and radically alters the nature of police surveillance by expanding the field of vision. It also aids in the orchestration of police at the local, state and federal levels as radio in tandem with telegraph and teletype facilitates the beginning of a quick response national network of law enforcement grounded in an ever-expanding database. By 1940 most police departments in the United States had implemented the most vital of all communications devices – the two-way radio – which connected automobile patrolmen to State and local police headquarters. This followed a short ten- to twelve-year period of one-way radio in which central transmissions were sent out across the FM band to police cars with special radio receivers. It is important to note that these communication technologies were used almost exclusively by police, fire departments and the military. In this way the state had a monopoly on mobile communications. Their ability to orchestrate their own movements and monitor the movement of citizens was vastly increased in the name of crime-fighting and to a lesser degree science and progress, as witnessed by a 1934 *Popular Science* article:

> Sensational new pages are being written into the record of science's war on crime. ... Red-hot telegraph wires flash cryptic messages as the search for criminals is launched in every state. ... Chattering teletype machines and short-wave radio messages outdistance the fleetest car, while police encircle a fleeing criminal in an effort to make escape impossible.
>
> (Gleason 1934: 11–12)

Lastly, the popularity of 1930s police radio dramas, coupled with the almost childlike reverence for radio's magic power, produced a sense that there was in fact a super-police-panopticon (Battles 2002). Examining what radio actually did at this formative stage opens up new spaces for thinking not only about the medium, but about the power/knowledge nexus radio was instrumental in facilitating.

Orchestrating and monitoring remain vital elements of how mobile communications technologies are put to use, but they stretch beyond police departments and governmental security forces. Government is not the only entity driven by this impetus. More individual citizens and private businesses are using auto-mobile communication technologies to accomplish similar goals. Furthermore, governmental apparatuses are increasingly calling upon both the interconnected citizenry and sub-contracted businesses to carry out such monitoring and mobile organization in conjunction with government agencies. A brief survey of some of these technologies and their uses will give a sense of how long this tradition is, the motivations behind it, and how it is coupled with governmental goals.

In 1910, the earliest example of wedding a radio to an automobile was accomplished in order to monitor race contestants in the Glidden Tour, a popular road rally (Homer: 395). Tour officials ensured fair results and added a modicum of safety via the telegraph apparatus attached to a car, which was in radio contact with stabile telegraph towers strategically positioned along the race route. This mating of visual immediacy to transmitted audio is one of two key methods for using the automobile/communication couplet to expand surveillance capabilities. An example of the second method first appears in 1913, the same year Ford is said to have mastered the assembly line, which points out just how early in the automobile century such concerns have ordered thought regarding auto-mobility.

Today they are widely referred to as Black Boxes and justified on the grounds of safety. The first such device was specially built to aid in the fight against working-class inefficiency. The supposed propensity of truck drivers to loaf or take romantic detours while on the clock inspired the creation of a recording drum placed in the engine compartment of commercial trucks: 'Briefly, the instrument records the time a vehicle has been in motion, the number and duration of the stops made, the mileage traveled, and the speed of the vehicle at any moment it is under way' ('The Motor-driven Commercial Vehicle' 1913: 248). This type of monitoring technology is after the fact. Immediacy is not the primary concern, but rather accuracy and accountability. It provides a technological facticity to information that human spectators belie. Such devices, as well as those that followed, were put to use as unbiased witnesses in trials concerning commercial vehicle crashes as early as 1913. The legal ramifications were an immediate, yet secondary, use for the recording drums, but it should not be forgotten that their primary use was that of worker-directed efficiency campaigns via panopticism. This form of panopticism differs slightly from the classic model illustrated by Foucault via Jeremy Bentham's architectural model for his ideal prison, the panopticon (Foucault 1979). In this model, it is the unerring tape-trail, not the immediate presence of surveillance, which internalizes, or simply demands, proper conduct. As Foucault pointed out though, it is not only carceral or criminological ends that surveillance is put to; in this case it is efficiency and economic accountability. These discourses continue to motivate private and governmental initiatives to intertwine new technologies into the automobile/communication couplet.

Furthermore, the two methods of surveillance outlined here, the Black Box and the audio transmission of visual immediacy, have recently been conjoined to facilitate immediate transmission of Black Box data. This has been further tied into communication control and alarm devices so that drivers' conduct can be constantly monitored by Black Boxes, largely unknown to the drivers in question. This use is prevalent in the rescue field (ambulances and fire trucks) and is supplied by Independent Witness Inc.'s black box, The Witness. Recently, Black Box use has spread from and to the familial field. Specially designed Black Boxes are used as electronic parent-speed-traps, marketed by Road Safety International Inc. who aptly named their product SafeForce. They warn teen drivers if they are speeding, exceeding g-force recommendations in turns, braking too fast, not wearing seatbelts, or committing any other form of parent-defined misconduct. The surveillance mechanism in this instance is legitimated via the discourse of safety. The sales literature and newspaper articles that support such technology applications recognize the implicit effect of panopticism, although they are partially skeptical of its ultimate results. 'This is something that every car should have', says Janice Manzer of Camarillo. By word of mouth she managed to get a prototype of the box in her 17-year-old son's car after he had an accident in the school parking lot and received a speeding ticket on a city street. 'It's like having a babysitter in the car' (Davis 2002).

Parenting by proxy organizes such sentiments, but is countered by the more immediate visual demand that Charles Butler, director of safety services at AAA, places on panopticism: 'If the box helps give parents peace of mind, maybe it's worth it. But if you really want peace of mind, don't let your kid drive alone. You can be the black box' (Davis 2002). Both responses point toward increases in the use of communication technologies to discipline children.

Although this brief recounting, fails to do justice to the plethora of surveillance technologies employed by state agencies and private citizens, it does give evidence to place in doubt Barry's thesis that communications has not or is not helping in the process of creating a super panopticon. Furthermore, although there is no means to quantitatively or qualitatively assess the magnitude or effectiveness of such a super panopticon, clearly one overriding desire of mating communications and automobiles has been and continues to be panopticism. But panopticism alone does not tell the whole story, neither for our analysis nor in popular discourse. Rather it is very often mated with and legitimated by another animating sign of 'intelligence', safety.

223

The illuminated hand of safety

As James Carey has noted, telegraphy separated communication from transportation (i.e., communicating no longer depended upon physical transport between two points) while communication and transportation became more interdependent, part of the formation of communication and transportation networks through one another (e.g., railways built along telegraph routes in some areas, and telegraph networks following railroads in other areas) (Carey 1988). This section emphasizes a related, but less recognized, development: how transportation has become dependent upon communication via the demands of safety. Furthermore, safety, as a legitimating discourse, sets the parameters for proper mobile conduct and in the realm of mobility safety equals intelligence (Packer 2003).

Safety is brought into discussions of communication and transportation as lack or excess. Lack of communication leads to accidents, excessive communication leads to accidents. At least four communication technologies make this apparent: signaling devices, radio-stereo systems (manipulating controls, inability to focus on more than one thing at a time, volume too loud to hear other types of communication, used to keep up on traffic reports, weather advisories, keep drivers awake), citizens' band (CB) and cellphones. This lack or excess discourse appears in popular periodicals as early as 1900. One concern is how drivers communicate with each other and pedestrians. A second is, how can rules, regulations and guidance be communicated to drivers in a safe and efficient fashion? Various forms of signage and technologies were imagined and implemented within the short period of automotive introduction into daily life. Horns, turn indicators (which appear first in the United States in 1926, and are arrow-shaped lights attached to the rear license plate), traffic signals, traffic signs, headlights, windshields, windshield wipers, hand signals, license plates and various others were all imagined as devices to ensure the safety of drivers, pedestrians and horse-drawn vehicles in the early part of the twentieth century. Many of these are today not even thought of as communication technologies. The exclusion speaks to a high-tech bias (who cares about horns when you can have GPS?) and provides a means to investigate not so much the claims regarding the effectiveness of these technologies, but rather how safety continues to animate the automobile/communications coupling.

Some of the devices were quite simple. For instance, a series of hand signals were developed to signal such things as 'You have a flat shoe', 'You had better stop and inspect your car', 'Am I on the best and shortest road to the next town?', and the all-important 'Danger ahead' (Skerrett 1930: 305). This system was considered 'an amplification of the one-arm semaphore' (ibid.). It was then a means of overcoming a lack, amplifying the signal to clarify inter-driver communication. A different form of amplification would overcome another lack – night vision. 'How do you signal to other drivers at night?', With an illuminated prosthetic hand (imagine the Hamburger Helper mascot on a flashlight), which allows 'the motorist to signal at night in the same way as he does so naturally and unconsciously during the daytime' ('An Illuminated Hand' 1916: 50, comments added). The blind turn could be better managed by imagining it as a deaf turn and applying a series of horn blasts to make one's presence known (Barrett 1916). It was said that 'the horn scares people instead of warning them, thus inducing nervous disorders of all kinds' ('Ding to Beep to Boo-oom' 1936: 36). Such claims may have been overblown, but they do repeat the logic of lack or excess – blow-hard versus breathless. Elaborate mechanical contraptions were created that linked automobile-triggered lighting systems and warning signs. However, G.H. Dacy warned that, 'When one runs over a road which is posted "Danger Ahead", "Caution", "Run Slowly", etc. at the summit of every slightest twist in the roadway, the best intentioned driver in the world cannot help acquiring a feeling of contempt and disregard' (1920: 468). Thus, the line between lack and excess is a fine one indeed.

With their 1929 introduction of car radio the company Motorola was born. These were after-market units, and it would be a decade before the widespread inclusion of radios on new-car options lists. But before this would take place debates over whether radio was safe were waged. Too much radio was seen as being distracting to drivers, yet radio could warn drivers of inclement weather and other dangerous road conditions, as well as keep potentially drowsy drivers awake. Headphone-wearing drivers and ground-shaking stereo systems in the 1980s were seen as over-amplifying communication, thus drowning out other safety-minded communication devices like sirens and horns.

Concerns over the safe use of citizens' band radio (CB) followed a different drummer (Packer 2002). First used extensively for dispatch service by police forces, fire departments and commercial delivery companies, two-way car radios were seen as a means to create a more efficient and quicker reacting mobile fleet. Two-way radio was thus seen as a useful tool for ensuring not only commerce but also public safety. It remained the exclusive terrain of government and commerce until the citizens' band was created in 1958, which expanded use to private parties who were willing to follow some very specific rules for its use. The overarching ethic of these rules was that only necessary communications, not 'chit chat', were to take place via CB. The intended goal was to aid the efficient and safe movement of people and goods. To this end CB users were called upon to help police monitor roadways and inform them of emergencies. CB was a means to extend the mobile surveillance network of police. It was consistently called the 'greatest safety-device since the seat belt' and its use was justified by such claims. However, the story by no means ends there. Following the doubly constrictive measures of the 55 mph speed limit and the OPEC induced oil-shortage, independent truckers began to use CB as an aid in their efforts to counter police surveillance and speed traps in efforts to maintain profitable speeds on their trucking routes. Not surprisingly, there was extensive police outrage at such so-called abuses. The FCC held hearings to respond to the crisis in order to reestablish proper use of CB, not only by truckers, but also by the increasing number of citizens who had purchased sets in no small part to increase their own ability to speed on the highways, thus

Figure 11.2 Early version of the mobile phone. Smart car or smartly designed fashion accessory?

Source: ImageState.

extending the anti-surveillance communications network. This struggle over the definition of proper CB use recognizes that its intended use and its unintended use were legitimated or de-legitimated according to the logic of safety. Furthermore, it was assumed that what CB could and should be used for was to aid in transportation. It was seen as an addendum to already existing transportation technologies and already existing safety and security agencies. The threat of CB was not so much what was said – 'there's a Smoky under the I-80 overpass at mile marker 99' – rather, how such information was integrated into activities deemed safe or unsafe.

Cellphones (also known as mobile phones) have undergone a similar transition in safety status. Originally they were primarily considered and even called 'car-phones'. They were also used to extend the reach of police traffic information, and the merits of their use as an aid in transportation breakdowns was one of their biggest early selling points – due largely to the female-gendered fear of being stranded alone on the side of the road. In essence, they were said to ensure the safety of transportation. Yet more recent concerns, particularly in New York, revolve around the potential dangers that cellphones pose, with drivers chatting away and thus missing Stop signs and the brake lights of the car being tailgated. But the most extensive and far-reaching connection between communication and transportation has to do with the overarching desire to do away with the greatest threat to safety altogether – the human operator.

No hands required in the Intelligent Transportation Systems (ITS)

Futurama was the imagined city of tomorrow sponsored by General Motors, designed by Norman Bel Geddes, and considered the most popular display of the 1939 World's Fair in New York. Given GM's sponsorship it should not be a surprise that automobiles were an integral part of this 'imagineered' rendition of America circa 1960. There was reason to believe that within twenty years automobiles would be not only 'space-age', but truly automatic; they would drive themselves. Automobiles would, it was imagined, be controlled via a system of communication technologies that would guide individual vehicles and coordinate them into a vast network of highways that criss-crossed rural, urban and suburban areas alike. Through the integration of global positioning devices, video, infrared and microwave monitoring devices, computer-monitored and -controlled engines, car-to-car 'conversation' (not human in a car), 'smart' roads and a plethora of other internal and external communication technologies, the automatic automobile is currently a reality. (Although, obviously, not a publicly available one, and forty years too late according to the 1960 vision of Futurama.) Over the past decade the United States government apportioned over one billion dollars for research, advocating an Intelligent Vehicle Highway System (IVHS) which was to integrate new technologies and new modes of governing mobility. This is certainly not the most advanced form of communications-controlled transportation, especially when we take into account commercial aircraft, space exploration pods and missile guidance systems, but it does point out the overriding extent to which communication technologies continue to be increasingly integrated with transportation technologies. We have explained how safety and surveillance have driven this integration over the past century, but the dream of Futurama and the IVHS do not simply conform to these desires. These dream systems and the attendant struggle to control this future terrain are organized by a strange paradox regarding freedom and control – a subject which we will analyze in the final part of this chapter.

The desire to be free from the constraints of driving demands being tied into communications networks. Intelligent Transportation Systems (ITS, of which IVHS is one example) depends upon communications systems to operate, but also promises greater media possibilities by turning the automobile into a mobile-home-office, where you can watch television and movies, talk on the phone, surf the net, conduct any sort of business-related work, or even communicate with your subconscious while sleeping. Interestingly, two communicative functions that never appear in popular or expert discourse regarding ITS are reading or having a conversation with a fellow passenger. Rightly or not, it is

assumed these smart vehicles will be high-tech personal transportation/commu-
nication machines used for purposes of commuter and sales-staff work efficiency.
The automobile is envisioned as a mobile-domestic or mobile-industrial space,
but also as always a linked, hooked-up, connected space. Its connectivity is
imagined as being most important to creating freedom. Not gaining freedom,
but producing it. Not diminishing connectivity (even though to be
connected/hooked-up connotes being tied, linked or bound), but fostering it, in
fact, demanding connectivity in order to be part of any ITS. Freedom is rightly
seen as being something that is uniquely produced in this new techno-cultural
sphere. This newest of auto-mobilities is both and neither a freedom and a
constraint, an impetus and possibility.

Currently, ITS is a catch-all shorthand for any product or policy that relocates
the human burden of driving to a machine. Like any new set of technologies, the
battle for supremacy in production, implementation, expertise and policy-making
is immense. There were no less than 862 terms in the ITS glossary as of 9
September 2002, almost universally acronyms. In the 'P' section alone there were
sixty-nine entries, with the all too likely clichéd names 'PROMETHEUS',
'PLATO', 'PASSPORT' and 'PLANET', which gives a solid sense of the
grandiosity of the vision, the scope of their mission, the hopes for global monitoring, and the self-advertising of the ITS governmental/entrepreneurial nexus.
This is a multi-disciplinary, international, profit- and control-oriented group of
players. The vastness of terminology speaks to an as of yet set of protocols or
governing bodies and the vast number of players attempting to put their stamp on
the field via dominant technologies and vocabularies.

The burgeoning post 9/11 security-industrial complex has also altered the
nature of this growth industry. The integration of these technologies, mobilities,
surveillance capacities and governing policies has seen its focus aimed increasingly on issues of national security rather than personal safety. Surveillance
capabilities and remote-control truck fleets and eventually all automobiles are
being touted as key players in the fight against terrorism. ITS is seen as a key
element in the 'border of the future'. The present (2003) California Governor,
Grey Davis, is calling for ITS to be used in child abduction cases. The Federal
Highway Administration has shifted safety funds into ITS security applications.
Tom Ridge for one called for an integration of ITS and homeland security.
Delphi corporation has created TruckSecure™, a device to be placed in
trucking fleets that can identify and authorize drivers, track and guide vehicles,
and even shut down a vehicle if it drives into a prohibited area. This leads us
toward our concluding remarks via a scene from the 2002 Steven Spielberg
movie, Minority Report.

Minority Report provides a fairly standard science-fiction critique of the
dystopic possibilities of human reliance upon science, technology and social
control. The loss of free will is presented as the ultimate sacrifice in a world
where future murders are 'seen' by a set of cyborg-prophets prior to happening.
Murders can thus be prevented by special police operatives, Tom Cruise serves as

their leader. When it is discovered that Cruise will commit a murder, he becomes the hunted. And it is here that we come back to ITS and concerns regarding freedom, safety, security, surveillance and communications-enabled connectivity. Cruise, like so many previous cinematic fugitives, jumps in a car to escape what appears to be the misapplied reach of the long arm of the law. Yet, his highly stylized, product-placed, fully ITS-integrated Lexus fails him. Because it is not fast, nimble or gadget-laden enough? No. Quite the opposite. It fails him because the ultimate freedom that will allow commuters to multi-task their way to the office every morning has linked his vehicle into a police-controlled network: a very efficient, very intelligent vehicle/highway system. An Intelligent Transportation System that remotely guides his car to alter course and bring Cruise to police headquarters. His Lexus turns into the ultimate incarcerating machine. It is this merging of auto-mobility and security that we see as the logical endpoint of ITS. Into Tomorrow Swiftly or I'm Truly Scared?

The highway into the future: modernity, mobilization, and a counter-modern logic of mediation

While our chapter is interested in locating the smart car within a regime of (auto-) mobility that has mattered long and hence deeply in the United States, our doing so is intended to bring these 'trackings' to bear on an understanding of the events and mobilizations (a reasoning about freedom and governance) discussed in the first sections. Proceeding this way, however, requires a concluding note about the *modernity* of these events, mobilizations and regimes, and about a counter-modern analytic suited to their effective diagnosis. Auto-mobility (the mobile self) is a 'modern' technical achievement involving communication and transportation. The car's design and application as an assemblage of communication and transportation technologies is one way of considering auto-mobility as a modern technical achievement, but also of considering what it means to be modern, that is, to have developed the machinic assemblages and networks for spatially and temporally 'advancing' the free and autonomous individual and for transporting oneself away from a past horizon and across territory as rapidly as possible.

To describe the car as communication and media is in part to acknowledge that it has been an object and technique of fashioning the modern self as mobile and, in its mobility, free yet responsible. The car (in part as self-fashioning) also has mattered and materialized at a time when technologies of communication contributed to a deepening regime of (auto-)mobility. The car, and the technical achievement of auto-mobility (the modern mobile self), developed through and out of 'tele-technologies' (e.g., telegraphy, telephony, television) whose development and increasingly widespread application during the nineteenth century became technologies of 'modernization' and 'rationalization' for Western societies. Tele-technologies were not only instruments of distance-management ('tele-' referring to the modern ideal of communicating and being transported over distances that previously had depended upon physical transport) but also for *managing* life over greater distances, in the sense of living and governing at a distance. Tele-technologies (or what Foucault has called 'technics of space') were profoundly instrumental to an emerging *arrangement* – a *spatial distribution* of people and resources, and a *contract* about their management that (in both senses) encouraged certain forms of agency and sociality. Although telegraphic networks and railroads developed through one another, the ideal of auto-mobility adhered to relatively more 'advanced' tele-technologization in Western societies during the late nineteenth and, particularly, early twentieth centuries (i.e., amidst the rapid expansion of telephone and broadcasting networks, and their relation to electrical and energy networks). Whereas train travel and trolley travel, as its urban counterpart, were forms of group transport, auto-mobility pertained to a somewhat different conception of the social body and self, and a relatively new regime of privacy. It represented an advancement of freedoms and required a new set of protocols, plans and rules for making car transport (auto-mobility) governable and secure.

In describing the driver as a point of intersection between technologies of communication and transportation, we are interested less in the binary logics of modern (or postmodern) conceptions of subject–object relations (of media primarily as an issue of spectatorship and consumption, of 'mediation' between two autonomous points), and more in an alternative to a modern logic of mediation – a way of thinking about the car as what Foucault would call a 'technology of the self', a set of technical operations and skills necessary for properly conducting oneself within a current regime of mobility, which supports a social arrangement and a moral economy. How is the self conducted – simultaneously made free and managed, brought into a relation with itself as a social body – through technologies, or technological assemblages, such as the 'smart car'? How is freedom predicated upon rules ('medians') for accessing places and routes, for conducting oneself through technologies of transport and communication (telecommuting)? Communication and transportation (as auto-mobility) have been and continue to be part of a moral economy that involves conducting oneself (self-governance) within a socio-spatial arrangement (as map and contract). In this way, the car (as a technology and practice of auto-mobility) has mattered and continues to matter in formations and 'advancements' of liberal government. In societies that have understood themselves to be modern, the technology of auto-mobility (such as the car) moreover has been an objective of liberal government's formation and continuation (indeed of its expansion) – liberal government's promise of assuring that each individual plays a role in its own governance.

If auto-mobility is a condition of citizenship and civil society in the United States, how has it also been a condition for political mobilization for reinventing government? Certainly, the fashioning of flag-cars in the States after September 11 was a technique of political demonstration – demonstrating the car's potential as a technology of citizenship within perceived threats to a *civil* society. In October 2002, as American voters were being mobilized for November elections and as the government mobilized for an invasion of Iraq, a counter-initiative, sponsored by MoveOn, called on its supporters to download through their personal computers a representation of the American flag accompanied by the statement 'Regime Change Begins at Home', and to affix the page-size emblem to the rear windshield of their cars. While this initiative/event vividly attests to the conditions of mobilizing and counter-mobilization in the United States in the early twenty-first century (wherein the intersection of technologies of communication and transport adheres to a new regime of intelligent machines), the event serves as a reminder that contemporary forms of activism are intertwined with technologies and programs of a neo-liberal entrepreneurialism that requires a new regime of auto-mobility. 'Regime change' begins as much through the car as 'at home'.

Bibliography

Barrett, C. (1916) 'The "Blind Turn": Its Dangers and Various Methods of Solution', *Scientific American*, 1 January: 24, 45.

Barry, A. (1996) 'Lines of Communication and Spaces of Rule', in A. Barry, T. Osborne and N. Rose (eds), *Foucault and Political Reason: Liberalism, Neo-liberalism and Rationalities of Government*, London: University of Chicago Press.

Battles, K. (2002) 'The Dragnet Effect: Depression Era Radio Crime Dramas and Police Communication', Paper presented at the National Communications Association Annual Conference, New Orleans, 23 November.

Berland, J. (2000) 'Cultural Technologies and the "Evolution" of Technological Culture', in A. Herman and T. Swiss (eds), *The World Wide Web and Contemporary Cultural Theory*, London/New York: Routledge.

Carey, J. (1988) 'Technology and Ideology: The Case of the Telegraph', in *Communication as Culture: Essays on Media and Society*. New York: Unwin-Hyman.

Dacy, B.G. (1920) 'Automobile Signals for Danger Spots', *Scientific American*, 6 November: 467–8.

Davis, R. (2002) 'Monitor Keeps Close Eye on Teens' Driving Habits', *USA TODAY*, http://www.dps.state.la.us/tiger/Monitor%20close%20eye.html (May).

Deleuze, G. (1993a) 'What is an Event?' in C.V. Boundas (ed.), *The Deleuze Reader*, New York: Columbia University Press.

—— (1993b) 'What is Multiplicity?' in C.V. Boundas (ed.), *The Deleuze Reader*, New York: Columbia University Press.

'Ding to Beep to Boo-oom' (1936) *Fortune*, November: 36, 50.

Foucault, M. (1977) 'Theatrum Philosophicum', in Donald F. Bouchard (ed.), *Language, Counter-memory, Practice*, Ithaca, NY: Cornell University Press.

—— (1979) *Discipline and Punish: The Birth of the Prison*, New York: Vintage.

—— (1980) 'Truth and Power', in *Power/Knowledge: Selected Interviews and Other Writing*, New York: Pantheon.

—— (1991) 'Governmentality', in G. Burchell, C. Gordon and P. Miller (eds), *Foucault Effect: Studies in Governmentality*, Chicago: University of Chicago Press.

—— (1994) 'Space, Knowledge, and Power', in J. Faubion (ed.), *Power*, New York: New Press.

—— (1997) 'On the Government of Living', in P. Rabinow (ed.), *Ethics, Subjectivity, and Truth*, New York: New Press.

Gleason, S. (1934) 'Auto-stealing Racket Smashed by New Methods', *Popular Science Monthly*, 11–12 August.

Hay, J. (2001) 'Unaided Virtue: The (Neo-)liberalization of the Domestic Sphere', *Television and New Media* 1(1).

—— (2003) 'Unaided Virtue: The (Neo-)liberalization of the Domestic Sphere and the New Architecture of Community', in J. Bratich, J. Packer and C. McCarthy (eds), *Foucault, Cultural Studies, and Governmentality*, Albany, NY: SUNY Press.

Homer, R. (1910) 'Wireless Telegraph Apparatus for Contestant of the Glidden Tour', *Scientific American*, 14 May: 395.

—— (1916) 'An Illuminated Celluloid Hand for Automobile Signaling', *Scientific American*, 8 July: 46.

Latour, B. (1993) *We Have Never Been Modern*, Cambridge, MA: Harvard University Press.

Mattelart, A. (1996) *The Invention of Communication*, Minneapolis, MN: University of Minnesota Press.

Miller, T. (1993) *The Well-tempered Self and Technologies of Truth*, Baltimore: Johns Hopkins University Press.

'The Motor-driven Commercial Vehicle' (1913) *Scientific American*, 27 September: 248.

Packer, J. (2002) 'Mobile Communications and Governing the Mobile: CBs and Truckers', *The Communication Review*, 5: 39–57.

—— (2003) 'Disciplining Mobility: Governing and Safety', in J. Bratich, J. Packer and C. McCarthy (eds), *Foucault, Cultural Studies, and Governmentality*, Albany, NY: SUNY Press.

Ragano, D. (1997) 'Special Report: Are Toyota Automobiles the Communications Medium of the Next Generation?', *Japanese High-Tech News*, http://www.ascii.co.jp/english/news/archive/97/12/12/ (April 2002).

Robins, K. and Webster, F. (1999) 'The Virtual Pacification of Space', in *Times of Technoculture: From the Information Society to Virtual Life*, London/New York: Routledge.

Skerrett, R. (1920) 'Finger Signals for the Motorist', *Scientific American*, 20 March: 305.

Williams, R. (1992) *Television: Technology and Cultural Form*, London/Hanover, NH: Wesleyan University Press and New England University Press.

232

12

SOMETHING SPATIAL
IN THE AIR

In-flight entertainment and the topographies
of modern air travel

Nitin Govil

> There are continuous paths that lead from the local to the global,
> from the circumstantial to the universal, from the contingent to
> the necessary, only so long as the branch lines are paid for.
> (Bruno Latour 1993)

> In 27D I was behind the wing
> watching the landscape roll out
> like credits on the screen.
> (Liz Phair, 'Stratford-on-Guy', from the album Exile
in Guyville, 1993)

How to make time fly

It turns out that films need traveling papers too. In the late 1990s, digital video/versatile disk (DVD) manufacturers and Hollywood studios attempted to restrict the global conduits of media piracy, protect distribution schedules, exhibition windows and international licensing agreements. Working together, the consumer electronics industry and content developers initiated a 'region coding' system, a software encryption process that coded individual DVDs with an electronic watermark recognizable to similarly encoded players targeted for use in particular jurisdictions in six designated regions. Today, most DVDs are issued with this mark of national and regional origin, warping the geometry of conventional geographic projection: Australia is in the same region (number four) as Central and South America; India is in the same region as Eastern Europe and most of Africa (region five). Exempting their international pool of astronauts from this terrestrial logic of region coding, the enterprising folks at NASA bypassed their entertainment supply contracts with Sony and hired a British firm to convert existing portable DVD-players to multi-region platforms for use in space missions. While the everyday media consumer could convert existing players to multi-region capability easily enough,[1] industries interested in pursuing multi-region formats risked incurring the wrath of Hollywood's legal departments, armed to the teeth with cease-and-desist orders.

Major international airlines rely on Hollywood to supply programming for the 30,000 videotapes that each might use in an average month of in-flight entertainment. Preceding home video release, the 'airline exhibition window' found a niche in the logic of staggered international film distribution. Looking ahead, Hollywood was concerned about the possibilities of piracy once these huge stockpiles of video programming were converted to DVD format. However, after offering hand-held DVD players in first-class cabins in 1999, the major world airlines were finding the existing region coding system unwieldy. The dilemma was resolved through a special – and spatial – dispensation. In late 2000, the World Airline Entertainment Association (WAEA), a Chicago-based non-profit organization founded in 1979 to represent over 100 airlines around the world, proposed the creation of a new 'neutral' region in the existing DVD coding system. Under a new 'region eight' category, films released for airline distribution would be cleared for operation only in airline-owned DVD hardware.

Hollywood's role in the creation of this neutral zone seems appropriate to the elasticity of mediatized spaces mobilized by textual travel. 'More an itinerary rather than a bounded site' (Clifford 1997), Hollywood is a complex and ephemeral spatial form: the iconography of the 'HOLLYWOOD' sign erases the geographic spread of Hollywood's international division of labor, invoking a spectral local space that sublimates the thoroughly globalized sphere of media production. If, as director John Ford famously put it, 'Hollywood is a place you can't geographically define … we really don't know where it is' (Miller et al. 2001: 1), then the regional neutrality summoned by Hollywood's alignment with the technologies of in-flight entertainment (IFE) is also a phantom. Abstracted from the geopolitics of locality, but dependent upon their reproduction, blunting at every moment the very corporeal tactility of movement, but embracing its representation in the globalized logic of consumer mobility, the in-flight experience articulates the drama of travel in a space that can hardly be considered 'neutral'. Every act of international travel requires that you declare a national belonging in the ritual of passport presentation; cultural and regional specificities linger in the form of in-flight meal and media offerings, steward outfits and accents.[2] The complex and transitory topographies constituted by new developments in IFE inflect the movement of people and the architectonics of flexible accumulation alike. In-flight entertainment mobilizes an entire industry and 'economy of conventions' (Latour 1993) that bring to bear the impermanent arrangements that we call the *local* and the *global*, those difference-engines that power the spatial imagination of late modernity.

We assume that air is the most available (and inalienable) of resources, that on account of its abundance, as Henri Lefebvre puts it, 'it has neither exchange nor use value, that it is the outcome of no social labor and that no one produces it' (1991: 328). Air*space*, however, is produced through transport policy and technological innovation. Airspace is legally determined through the fictions of national jurisdiction, defined in the accounting of flight accident claims and criminal prosecution of air rage incidents, and invoked by regulatory guidelines on aircraft noise, pollution and waste disposal. The application of industrial policy is by no means wholly instrumental: since the late 1930s, the US Congress has defined airspace as a *public* highway, which denied individual American states the right to tax aircraft as they flew over their territory, but the Paris Convention of 1919 and the Chicago Convention of 1944 gave the nation-state *total* sovereignty over its territorial airspace.[3]

The jurisdictional spaces invoked by aviation policy are as complicated as the airlines' self-imagination in the representation of transit routes and flight pathways. In order to maximize efficiency by decreasing downtime-per-aircraft and optimizing staff scheduling, the airline industry recently overhauled established routing designs. Older airline routes were configured according to a 'line' or 'point-to-point' network, where a single aircraft originated from a base airport, made a number of intermediate stops (to refuel or pick up passengers), and finally arrived at its ultimate destination. As local traffic increased to the degree that certain airports could support flights for travelers to use as connections, the airlines reconceived the airport as a switching center within a coordinated 'hub and spokes' system. Hub and spokes refers to a system wherein routes radiate from a centralized airport (the hub) to a number of 'spoke' airports, vastly increasing the connectivity of cities via networks of exchange defined by the infrastructure of linkage.[4] The entire spatio-temporal economy of airline travel has shifted, as more and more flights are simply connections to other flights. New standards, such as 'minimum connecting times', have changed the way traffic is directed around airports, the way baggage is off-loaded, and the way in-flight service is conducted. There is a reorganization in the spatial imaginary of air travel according to these new transit technologies, with the architecture of travel prioritizing networks and linkages over points of origin and arrival.

The institutionalization of new spatial forms has not, however, erased their hoary antecedents: national governments and state boundaries continue to define the shape of the airline industry. Despite the growing internationalization of the airline industry, accelerated by deregulation in the United States and then Europe in the late 1970s and early 1980s, individual states retain the power to impact on the commercial successes of airlines. Governments provide operational stability, exchange rate policies, competition and anti-trust legislation, set levels of foreign ownership and regulate the labor market in order to provide a stable environment for the airlines that operate within their ambit (Kassim 1997). National differences and boundaries cut across live television reception as an IFE choice, since international carriers encounter different licensing territories as they fly in and out of national airspaces. Similarly, British Airways, Singapore Airlines and Swissair were allowed to buy gaming software from a number of North America-based companies, that had been barred from selling to American carriers because of US Department of Transportation laws which prohibit gambling over American airspace or in any plane flying into or out of the United States. Sometimes, the mobility of IFE actually engages the terrain of cultural and national sovereignty. Sanctioned by the PRC Ministry of Culture, China Southern Airlines prides itself on its large selection of Hollywood films, even as the Chinese government continues to restrict the number of American films allowed terrestrial exhibition in the country. China Southern was also the first Chinese airline to fully comply with the US Customs Service by signing onto the Advance Passenger Information System. This system coordinates the transfer of passenger information (like manifests) between carriers in order to track foreign visitors to the United States, and names in the database can be checked against a number of information systems at US security agencies. The disjunctures between the neutralization of geographic space and the rearticulation of geopolitical difference in IFE service and airline regulation inform the itineraries of connection between spaces and identities that engender the air-traveling public.

One such itinerary of connection and identity formation is the in-flight magazine. Since United and Pan American began to offer their own in-flight travel brochures in the 1930s, the in-flight magazine has become a central feature in airline marketing and brand differentiation. United Airlines' in-flight publication is called *Hemispheres*, and has emblazoned on its spine the words 'Yours to keep', an ironic reference to the utter disposability of the in-flight magazine, which, both literally and as a literary artifact, is located somewhere between the duty-free catalog and the 'motion discomfort' bag. While reading them is a sure sign of in-flight boredom, these magazines are a lucrative trade in the custom publishing business: Swissair, for example, charged $24,000 dollars for a one-page advertisement in its in-flight magazine in 1999 (see Rhodes 1999). These magazines cater to the elite traveler with deep pockets of disposable income and provide valuable customization and branding space for the airline (which is why Virgin Atlantic has six separate in-flight publications and British Airways publishes five magazines). Airline brand differentiation has taken on greater significance as carriers vie for the attention spans of passengers, who, according to industry studies in the late 1990s, engaged in IFE activities for only 15 to 20 per cent of their time on board. Another recent survey notes that 44 per cent of passengers said that the most important feature of airplane travel was a window view (Unsworth 2002). The in-flight magazine coordinates the view outside the window – in travelogues and glossy photographs – with a window into the viewing and entertainment opportunities available inside the cabin.

Recognizing that each passenger lazily scanning the seat-back video is a revenue opportunity, airline IFE often features branding strategies organized around the national. For example, Thai Airways recently screened 15-minute instructional videos teaching tourists how to behave in Thailand, how to address monks, and what to wear in a Buddhist temple. The proliferation of interstitial programming and promotional spots that link the airline to particular, culturally differentiated, types of experience can become overwrought: for example, British Midland's on-screen identity for its new transatlantic routes is represented, oddly enough, by a boy playing with a model taxi and a trout.

British Midland's professed design imperative was to convey 'contemporary Britishness through a series of short scenarios focusing on "relaxing objects" without resorting to overt jingoism or clichéd images of Britain's heritage' ('Observe' 2001). Here, the territorial and associative logic of branding – alongside an act of cultural disassociation in the emptying out of colonial history – results in an surreal abstraction that pushes the limits of interpretation.

Figure 12.1 Hollywood as cover art: a recent in-flight magazine features 'High Gain', a painting by Los Angeles-based artist James David Thomas.

Source: Photo, Nitin Govil.

Similar disarticulations of geographic difference are mobilized by the internationalization of contracted editing labor, employed by the airline industry to curtail national censor regulations. Since most national censor boards restrict themselves to terrestrial reception, editing in-flight films is often left to the discretion of the carrier.[5] The airline industry has its own informal standards for censoring nudity, profanity, depictions of rival airlines, plane crashes and vomiting (deemed problematic for mealtime exhibition). Most main cabin films are edited by outside firms: for example London-based Spafax, which cuts films for Delta, Sabina and Swissair, among others. Films are often left unedited for business class, giving higher-revenue passengers more programming choices and most personal interactive IFE systems currently being used offer original versions. However, there is an insider shorthand that shapes the rationality of in-flight film programming: 'American carriers are regarded as more sensitive to obscenity and violence', European carriers 'are more tolerant of sex than violence, in the Middle East violence is OK but alcohol or sex is not' (Nichols 1995). Meanwhile, the top-ten worldwide in-flight films in 1998 were all from Hollywood studios, with Twentieth Century Fox's *One Fine Day* and Columbia TriStar's *Jerry McGuire* leading the way. Popular Hollywood romantic comedies, like *The Wedding Planner*, can earn $3 million in worldwide airline sales alone. A lot of non-English programming is also acquired from North American media corporations. CBS TeleNoticias, a Miami-based Spanish-language cable channel owned by Telemundo, provides news programming for United Airlines routes between the United States and Latin America (see Levin 1997). Reflecting the programming options of its clients, the World Airline Entertainment Association recently held its annual Technical Committee meeting under the sponsorship of Universal Pictures Non-theatrical and Columbia TriStar International Television.

While most programming produced by these media companies is designed for more conventional exhibition sites, in-flight viewing encourages a desultory spectatorship structured around banality and boredom, inverting the spectacular modes of identification offered by film theory and the commercial industries alike. Similarly, the development of in-flight film exhibition reverses the trajectory of early film history: the shift from a single exhibition site (the projected film at the front of the cabin) towards individuated multi-channel exhibition zones (hand-held or seat-mounted delivery mechanisms for each spectator). Experimentation with in-flight film exhibition began in 1925, when Imperial Airways screened a version of Conan Doyle's *The Lost World* on a converted First World War Handley Page bomber during a short flight near London. A related trial of in-flight television was conducted in 1932 on a Western Air Express Fokker F-10. In-flight screenings remained infrequent novelty acts until four decades later, when an American cinema proprietor, David Flexer, at Inflight Motion Pictures, developed a system for showing films on airlines, partially motivated by his own in-flight boredom. TWA bought Flexer's system, and the first scheduled in-flight film, *By Love Possessed*, starring Lana Turner, had its debut on a Boeing 707 on TWA flight 40 from New York to San Francisco in July 1961, projected onto a home-movie screen by a standard Bell & Howell projector. Inflight Motion Pictures would become the largest IFE firm in the United States domestic industry, and its 16mm system for commercial flights impacted on airport logistics as unionized projectionists changed film reels at terminals before flight attendants took over the task (see Gomery 1992: 141). Pakistan International Airlines was the first non-US carrier to offer regularly scheduled in-flight film service, beginning in 1962. Also in the early 1960s, regulatory pressures on a number of national airline industries curtailed price gouging and fare competition as forms of differentiation, and air carriers resorted to alternative branding strategies that included in-flight service and the so-called 'pink labor' sector of airline hostessing. Innovations would follow at almost the same rate that hostesses' skirt-lengths shortened. In 1971, Trans-Com developed the 8mm film cassette, which allowed stewards to change tapes and to program shorter subject segments. The first in-flight VHS system was marketed by Bell & Howell (Avicom Division) in 1978, and electronic headphones replaced older pneumatic models in the late 1970s (noise-canceling headphones were introduced by Sennheiser in the mid-1990s). Airvision's in-seat video system (using 2.7-inch LCD displays) had its debut on Northwest 747s in 1988, and American Airlines made the first fleet-wide installation of in-seat video in its Boeing 767 first class cabins in 1989.

Delta Airlines premiered live television on a Boeing 767, showing the fourth game of Major League Baseball's 1996 World Series on a single large screen. The transition to individuated exhibition spaces centered around the passenger's seat was made possible by the installation of new high-capacity electrical systems and a number of new media technologies that took advantage of them: Delta's in-seat power outlets installed aboard select aircraft in 1996; Swissair's aircraft-wide Video-on-Demand entertainment system in 1997; Jetblue's heavily promoted use of fleetwide seat-back live (via satellite) in-flight television in 2000. American Airlines and Swissair provided hand-held DVD-players to upper-class customers the same year.

Shifting from the 'gray-flannel' anonymity that characterized in-flight service in the late 1950s, airlines are now committed to new advertising campaigns which are designed to spare passengers from, in the words of one of the industry's chief branding architects, 'the terrible Kafka-like monotony of flying' (Kolm 1995: 204). Caught within the experience of boredom, 'the everyday become manifest as a consequence of having lost its essential – constitutive – trait of being unperceived' (Blanchot 1987), in-flight entertainment mobilizes and directs media consumption while marking and segmenting the passage of time in the air. The repetition of discrete zones throughout the cabin and the themed nature of in-flight programming itself defines and serializes the act of waiting (McCarthy 2001): the in-flight screen 'organizes and narrates the anonymity of suspended time' (Mellencamp 1988). At the same time, the airlines struggle to target the most difficult of exhibition spaces, built around computerized units running in a high vibration, multiple-user environment, where the seat-back doubles as a screen, desk, dining table and occasional diaper-changing platform.

The spatial economy of air/fare

After years of relative price and programming homogeneity, air carriers recently returned to in-flight entertainment as a major marketing strategy, spending the equivalent of billions of US dollars on in-flight communication and entertainment. Designed to combat an annual billion-dollar industry deficit in the early 1990s, IFE emerged as a crucial factor in customer retention, and annual airline expenditure on IFE increased from $400 million in 1992 to $1.75 billion in 1998.

In the US airline business at the end of the decade, economic recession and stalled labor negotiations had afflicted the industry well before four planes were hijacked on 11 September 2001. The tragic events of that day marked the nadir of a downward spiral for the domestic airline industry, which had grown cumbersome and unwieldy after pinning its hopes – and budgets – on business travelers willing to pay almost anything for top-tier airline travel. Bloated with new capital inflows from the lucrative corporate customer demographic, the airlines entered a period of massive expansion in the 1990s. The logic of financier-brokered alliances had proliferated in the post-deregulation era since 1978, providing the 'mix of scale and flexibility needed to generate sufficient revenues for next-generation product development' (Strange and Stopford 1991: 92). However, United States airport directors attending a 2001 conference in Montreal on the fateful day of 11 September found that their expansion plans were stymied by a huge shortfall in passenger travel, even as they frenetically implemented new security guidelines and redesigned baggage claim areas, check-in counters and parking lots immediately after the hijackings.[6] With the collapsing economy and the mercurial rise in travel cancellations,[7] a large number of newly merged air (and media) companies started to fall towards bankruptcy. The increasing prioritization of liquidity by cash-strapped carriers – US airlines lost $10 billion in the year following the hijackings – means that many US carriers now think of IFE systems as discretionary or long-term marketing strategies rather than short-term fixes. Fee-based or 'charge-per-use' has been tried in IFE pricing management, but most airlines still agree that free IFE is the only practical way to highlight the amenities which can differentiate carriers in a meaningful way. In early 2003, however, a number of US carriers tested the idea of selling meals on flights where food service had been cut back after late 2001. America West offered a hot dinner menu for $10 (your choice of chicken kiev or beef tenderloin) to mostly positive passenger reviews, although flight attendants were unhappy about adding yet another retail activity to their repertoire.[8]

Big international carriers have also been hurt by the shifting economies of scale as smaller rivals continue to outperform them. The majors are especially troubled by new budget airlines that offer lower fares and attract short-haul customers with simpler route structures. To compete, many major airlines have established low-cost versions; most international carriers began their lives as localized monopolies that went on to secure international routes through government subvention. However, these initiatives can have embarrassing consequences: for example, Go Airlines was due to break even in its third year of operation (2000), while its parent company, British Airways, saw its stock value plummet. New discount upstarts have homogeneous fleets, fill a high percentage of their seats,[9] have a quick on-the-ground turnaround, avoid formal ticketing procedures, have been aggressive in marketing over the Internet, and usually offer only one class of service. While they cut costs by avoiding hot meals and skimping on IFE, smaller carriers often take the most innovative approach to in-flight media. In building up new fleets, start-ups have the option to buy newer planes which more easily accommodate new technologies; the majors, on the other hand, have to retrofit a substantial percentage of their fleet. Small US domestic carriers, such as JetBlue and Alaska Airlines, were among the first to implement live television reception on their planes, striking deals with the largest satellite broadcaster in the States, DirecTV. This allowed them to air twenty-four channels of live television programming, including four ESPN channels, the Discovery Channel, Animal Planet, the Travel Channel, the Weather Channel and CNNfn. As a smaller carrier with commitment to programming branding from its inception, Virgin Airlines offered new IFE choices in order to compensate for its small fleet and infrequent timetable. Virgin was the first airline to offer seat-back video in the early 1990s and individuated interactive entertainment systems in every class in 1993.

The majors have not been left behind, however. Unable to match the budget airlines in cost-gouging on domestic routes, the majors remain untouched on longer routes. Many larger carriers around the world are flourishing, even in these new economies of scale: Korean Air Lines, Cathay Pacific, Singapore and Thai all reported profits in early 2002, alongside growing tourist inflows into their home countries. On intercontinental routes in particular, the majors are catering once again to the high-end market through an *excessive* differentiation in cabin classes. For example, full-size single bedding is available in British Airways Club World class and Virgin's Upper Class cabin, with Air France planning to join the slumber party. Lufthansa's full-service daily flight between Düsseldorf and Newark, New Jersey, has a sparse forty-eight seats in a specially designed luxury Boeing 737. Cathay Pacific's investment in the redesign of business-class seats seeks to emulate British Airways' lie-flat beds along with providing larger television screens, a cocktail bar and private dressing rooms with full-length mirrors. Taking advantage of their beleaguered competitors across the Atlantic, European airlines, such as Virgin and Lufthansa, have announced plans to deliver web, email and short messaging services (SMS) to passengers by 2003. The most prominent developer of in-flight Internet connectivity is the Seattle-based Tenzing Communications, named after Sherpa

Tenzing who scaled Mount Everest with Edmund Hillary in 1953. The company name cleverly signals an 'innate' capacity to perform well in high altitudes – some colonial pathways are clearly still in service.

For all the talk of recession and budget shortfalls, airline spending on IFE is expected to top US$2 billion in 2002, and reach close to $3 billion by 2005. Of the 11,000 commercial airliners flying in the world as of mid-2002, 42 per cent (some 4,600) had some kind of IFE communications system on board, while 17 per cent (just under 2,000) were equipped with personal television units. The In-flight Management Development Center, an industry consulting group, expects that over half of the world's fleet will be outfitted with IFE systems by 2011, with content licensing revenues for IFE programming producers and distributors estimated at about $130 million per year. *Traveltrade* magazine recently speculated that airline engineers spend more time working on IFE systems than on aircraft maintenance ('That's In-flight' 2000). It is estimated that, by 2003, nearly three-quarters of major airlines will offer in-seat personal video screens in economy class on wide-bodied aircraft, with forecast screen sizes set of 6.5 inches (versus 8.5 to 10.5 inches for first class).

Airline IFE offers a range of services – live entertainment,[10] multiple video and audio channels on demand,[11] games, shopping, connection and gate information, travel booking, gambling, in-flight trivia quizzes (coordinated with crew members walking the aisles giving out prizes). Satellite-based information services such as telephony, the Internet and live television reception, are becoming more commonplace, with automated teller machines and currency exchange in the development pipeline. Communications technology manufacturers and programming content providers are pursuing strategic alliances, spurred on by the possibilities of pushing brand extension across multiple platforms and spaces. Television shows, *Seinfeld*, for example, began in-flight screening on domestic US flights in January 1996 as a result of a syndication deal between United Airlines and Columbia TriStar TV Distribution. Indeed, United auctioned a walk-on role on the show through its frequent-flier program. Yet in-flight syndication is not a significant source of revenue for the television networks, which typically get little up-front cash for their entertainment packages. Instead, the networks are compensated with plane tickets, advertising space in in-flight magazines and a percentage of the ads sold during the programs: even popular shows, such as Paramount's *Frasier*, command only $1,500–2,500 a month in in-flight license fees.

The strategic affiliations between content and technology industries operate alongside re-organization at the level of transit itself, as carriers share institutional resources and market knowledges. Transcontinental flights are now heavily consolidated under route acquisitions such as Singapore Airlines' purchase of 49 per cent of Virgin's transatlantic routes, while code sharing practices subsume transfers between allied airlines under one flight number. The industry's prerogative of a seamless transition between airlines as customers transfer to and fro becomes all the more difficult, since carriers have vastly differing operating budgets for in-flight service. Passengers are sure to notice, for example, as they transfer between a heavy IFE hitter like Singapore Airlines to a smaller carrier like Mexicana, both of which operate under the Star Alliance. While the air travel experience is facilitated by the topography of consumer mobility – the prioritization of an almost transcendent spatial practice that obliterates scalar differences – certain forms of specificity clearly remain. Airlines link the marketing discourse of cosmopolitanism with branding formats that engage the symbolic significance of local cultural 'respect' and differentiation under the protocols of in-flight hospitality. This means that some carriers provide real cream instead of artificial whiteners for Australian coffee drinkers, steamed (not microwaved) hot towels for Japanese passengers, and dedicated tea service for South Asians. After all, food service constitutes the bulk of these cultural diversity initiatives: El Al airlines, for example, offers twenty-two different meal types, including Hindu, Asian vegetarian, Greek Orthodox, and Ethiopian fasting food. Delta Airlines advertises 'ideal performance meals' for international BusinessElite travelers, which include serotonin-laden carbohydrate feasts that put the fliers to sleep (to keep them fresh for post-landing business meetings) and dopamine-charged meals for those who need to stay awake and work during the flight.

In 1946, as part of the new science of in-flight passenger management, Pan American Airways flight attendants were instructed in the basic physiological principle that 'blood cannot be in two places at once'. Suggesting that ornery passengers were calmer after food service because blood was drawn away from tensed muscles and towards the digestive system, new in-flight service manuals demonstrated the relation between the pooling of blood in the body and maintaining sanguine in-flight passenger behavior. It became axiomatic in the annals of in-flight service that food placated the unruly. Since then, the technologies of passenger management have become much more complicated, but airline travel retains, as de Certeau noted of the experience of railroad travel, something of an 'incarcerational and navigational' quality (1984: 113). While the airline passenger is fixed in a restricted space – although airline walls are contoured and colored to suggest the appearance of spaciousness[12] – in-flight media offer the 'organization of passivity' so that 'wasted' time can be channeled towards more useful ends (Lefebvre 1987). For example, there is a new Amnesty International (AI) program that offers passengers the ability to make contributions through their IFE systems by using their credit cards. Defending an initiative linked to new strategies for in-flight shopping and gambling, an AI official claims that 'the beauty of seat-back donations is that people have the opportunity to help while they are looking for something to occupy them at 30,000 feet' ('Flightstore' 2002).

At the same time, IFE technologies that channel commodity consumption into an act of distracted philanthropy, the passenger is integrated into the spatial logic of flight management organized around the locus of the seat itself: part of the new ergonomics of the captive audience. Historically, the airline seat has remained a largely undifferentiated marker for the airlines, but now, seat space, size and integration with IFE systems has become a key issue in airline marketing. Costs have risen accordingly: in the late 1960s and early 1970s, an aircraft could be fitted with film projection and audio channels for less than $50,000; in 1990, air carriers averaged $1,800 invested per seat, $6,000 by 1995; and in 2000, Singapore Airlines spent $18,500 per seat to install its new fiber-optic in-flight entertainment system. Designed to coordinate panel displays, compact disc and DVD-players, these 'integrated cabin management systems' allow the user to 'take charge' of the cabin environment via seat-arm control panels. Now that IFE is 'a convenience supermarket of revenue opportunities', the airline seat has been transformed into what Boeing calls 'a fabric covered electronics rack' (Smith 1996). Wiring the in-flight consumer is, however, no easy logistical task. Accommodating the array of electronic devices designed to bring office and living room to the airline seat requires the building of stronger cabin floors and increased air cooling for the scores of microprocessors and elec-tronics that consume upwards of 100 watts of power per seat. Located at the tactile center of a number of management logics, the newly prioritized place of the passenger is an 'articulated moment in a network of social relations and understandings, constructed on a far larger scale than what we happen to define for that moment as the place itself' (Massey 1994: 154).

The majors are also planning for a 'smart' plasma seat that is wired with sensors that read the passenger's body temperature, height and weight, and is capable of activating built-in air-cushions to mold to the passenger's body. In addition, new monitoring technologies installed in these 'intelligent seats' can warn passengers when they are at risk of deep vein thrombosis (DVT), a condi-tion which can arise by sitting in one position for an extended time, causing blood pooling in the lower extremities and leading to the possible dangerous formation of clots. Qinetiq, a technology research agency operated by the British government, has designed in-seat movement sensors to monitor passenger position within the seat. These inputs are linked to the aircraft's central IFE system and can deliver on-screen prompts for passengers to move their legs when they have been stationary for too long. Qinetiq's seat also provides protection against the numerous recent DVT lawsuits filed by passen-gers against the airlines, and also has possible applications in curtailing air-rage incidents (incidence is up an estimated 400 per cent worldwide since 1995). Centralized terminals placed throughout the cabin allow the crew to monitor passenger movement, locating the 'smart seat' within the surveillance logic of new airline counter-terrorist imperatives.

New monitoring technologies mediate the passenger's bodily space through a matrix of clinical specularity, a feedback loop where one's body information is reflected on the in-flight screen as a surreal subtitle to the not-so-latest Hollywood release. Such medical imaging systems are intimately linked to the history of cinematic technology itself (see Cartwright 1995): they coordinate, as Foucault famously put it, the intersection of gazes which 'form a network and exercise at every moment in space, and at every moment in time, a constant, mobile, differentiated supervision' (1994: 31). Watching, while being watched, the modern air traveler is positioned at the sensuous conjuncture of IFE innovation and airline branding, caught in the specular architectures of commodity consumption. In the most modern of in-flight media technologies, then, the in-flight customers are sold but a single commodity: *themselves*.

Lessons in aerial geography

The haptic nodes of IFE competitive innovation find their *mise-en-abîme* in the reflective ubiquity of the in-flight screen. While screens in serial arrangement proliferate in the main cabin, the US National Transportation Safety Board recently called for video cameras to be installed in the cockpit, insisting that cameras aid post-crash investigation and evidentiary reconstruction. In May 2002, the US Congress and the Transportation Department considered installing video cameras to provide the cockpit with full cabin views in order to keep track of rowdy passengers and to provide visual evidence in case of customer complaints. These developments are part of a post-11 September debate on arming pilots: supported by pilot and flight crew unions, airline surveillance systems coordinate images from as many as ten cameras placed around the main cabin. Long-standing IFE companies with roots in the defense electronics and military avionics industries are repositioning themselves as in-flight security providers as airline media priorities shift post 9/11. United, Delta and JetBlue all use systems with two to four cameras outside the cockpit door and in the rear galley, designed to warn the crew of possible hijack and air rage incidents. Placards placed on cockpit doors advise passengers that they may be under video surveillance, assuaging fears of privacy violation (although the American Civil Liberties Union thinks otherwise). Many US airlines have applied to the Federal Aviation Administration for permission to use surveillance equipment, though the cost of retrofitting an Airbus jet with the new technology can cost US$50,000.

At the same time that in-flight display technologies help coordinate passenger management, the screen still provides more traditional entertainments. For example, an Air New Zealand Boeing 747 was recently equipped with a 'nose-cam' designed to give passengers exterior views of take-off and landing and panoramic views of major landmarks as they fly overhead. The touristic imperatives of exterior video technology are the result of experiments in fire prevention in the 1980s, when the UK Civil Aviation Authority investigated the possibility of installing exterior surveillance cameras to detect fuselage and engine fires in time to avoid disaster. Indeed, panoramic access and landscape cameras have been criticized by air safety officials after a number of incidents in which passengers viewed televised images of their own impending catastrophe. At Melbourne Airport in 2001, for example, when an Emirates Boeing 777 suffered an engine blowout just prior to taking off, terrified passengers saw live images of emergency vehicles approaching the plane. Live television broadcast further enhances these technologies of in-flight simultaneity. As live TV proliferates, airlines lose the ability to censor programming, opening the door for the in-flight viewing of prox-imate airline disaster reportage and rival airline advertising. The carriers are clearly threatened with offering live news broadcasts in-flight. Since the Cold War, protocols of news agency journalism understand international coverage primarily in terms of disaster and conflict stories, although their convention of culturally 'sensitive' news reports is already part of contemporary IFE. As the air carriers remain caught within the competing promises of surveillance and live-ness, the modern aircraft transforms into a network of cameras and screens: in the cockpit and the main cabin, in the seat-back and of the wing. Reflecting one another in a play of entrapment and entertainment, the screen and the seat are carceral technologies that locate the passenger within new logics of 'civil' aviation.

The IFE form that most fully implicates the new spatial dynamics of airline cartography, regulatory convention and industrial self-imagination as a network, is the 'moving' or animated map. These 'sky-map' video displays are an abstract representation of the space of airline travel, illustrating the adjustments of the plane (represented by an oversized icon) over a geographic map punctuated by altitude, temperature, speed and flight time indicators as the map continuously re-centers around the plane itself. Airshow is the leading company providing in-flight moving map technology, and though it was acquired by the military avionics company Rockwell Collins in 2002, its animated map product retains the Airshow name. 'Airshow 100' was the airline industry's first moving map system, marketed to the business aviation sector in 1982 and to the commercial air-transport industry in 1984, with Swissair and SAS as the first commercial customers, followed by Qantas and Air New Zealand. While Airshow provides a fully integrated IFE system, with music, gaming, news and sports programming, it is best known for its signature product, a 'journey management system' installed in over 130 airlines worldwide.

Synchronizing real-time data from the plane's flight-deck avionics, the Airshow map provides passengers with a graphical representation of aircraft location, the usual indicators of flight time, airspeed, temperature and altitude information, and nearby 'points of interest'. The latest model, 'Airshow 400', offers greater customization capability, including the ability to combine customized animated logos (including airline logo and 'no smoking' and 'fasten seat belt' graphics) with localized points of interest, such as the airline's corporate headquarters. Simulating the flow maps of international trade and migration, the path of the plane is indi-cated on the Airshow map by a thick red line that reassuringly confirms that the plane is on route. While the Airshow system can display geographic maps inlaid with geopolitical borders, most airlines avoid the markings of national boundaries on their maps and provide topographical and more general geographic informa-tion. Worried about the associations of danger with certain hot-spots of geopolitical strife, most airlines that use moving map IFE dispense with country names and borders altogether, while others avoid mentioning particular nations.

The affective reassurance of the moving map and the construction of a world cleansed of geopolitical borders is part of the airplane's historical role in modern cartographic technology. In 1916, William Robson, a British military historian, noted that 'there is such an infinite amount of room aloft that there is certainly enough space not only to satisfy the needs of all, but to enable every nation to move in sufficient breathing space' (1916: 175).[13] As an early aerial photography manual suggests, the airplane functioned as a coordinating center for the infinity of airspace, a camera platform to take a series of photographs of natural terrain: scaled, trimmed and mounted in series to create an image of seamless pictorial space (Ives 1920). The potential to map the natural world without invoking the markings of geopolitical strife contributed to post-war confidence in the airplane's symbolic potential as an icon of peaceful internationalism. However, in 1944, the same year that the Brookings Institution claimed that 'hemispheres are what you make them' (Van Zandt 1944), the Chicago Convention deflated the fantasy of assigning names to empty and homogeneous spaces by articulating principles of airspace sovereignty. These principles, called the five 'freedoms of the air', formed the foundation for contemporary international aviation regulation and its recognition of the national sovereign right to air above the state.

In 1944, the Chicago Convention secured territorial and extra-territorial sovereignty firmly within the ambit of the geopolitical boundary, part of a spatial reorganization that initiated the total overhaul of the world geographic map after the Second World War and the decolonization and independence movements that followed. This consolidation – which reinforced the study of geography as crucial template for the propagation of cultural citizenship – was based, therefore, on mid-century regulatory conventions beholden to terrestrially bounded communication systems of surveillance and navigation. While it clearly defined the *lower* limits of airspace as coinciding with the geography of the nation, the Chicago Convention said nothing about elaborating this according to *cuius est solum, eius est usque ad caelum et ad inferos*: an ancient legal proposition that defines property rights as running from the heavens to the center of the earth. Regulatory convention failed to dictate the upper spatial limits to national sovereignty until the space race was fully underway, when strategic and security concerns had ossified into the spatio-temporal blocs that constituted the geographic imaginary of the Cold War. The 1967 'Treaty of Principles Governing the Activities of States in the Exploration and Use of Outer Space, Including the Moon and Other Celestial Bodies' declared in Article II that 'outer space, including the moon and other celestial bodies, is not subject to national appropriation by claim of sovereignty, by means of use or occupation, or by any other means'. Characteristically, the 'Outer Space Treaty' left the lower limit of airspace undefined, but implicitly understood it as the geographic territory of the sovereign state itself (see Elder 1997).

Scanning a map littered simply with city names, air travelers have the impression that they are flying though a pristine geographic space, with mountain ranges, rivers and forests punctuated only by a variety of travel destinations. If all maps are narrative forms, then the in-flight moving map relates the story of a pastoral topography untouched by the vagaries of geopolitical conflict, industrial waste and environmental blight. The continental views of the Airshow map reveal fundamental geologic patterns, providing visual evidence for the 'fit' between, for example, Africa and South America, an essentialized spatial corollary to late twentieth-century globalization (see Lewis and Wigen 1997). The moving map reconciles the 'outside' world of the natural landscape with the 'inside' textures of screened cartography; it transforms, in de Certeau's words, 'the bewitching world by which one was possessed into a text that lies before one's eyes ... the exaltation of a scopic and gnostic drive' (1984: 92). The moving map offers no real interactive interface for the traveler to access,[14] locking the passenger within the static space of the present: the flight information that represents movement, such as altitude and airspeed, is simply displayed against a stationary azure blue sky.

At the same time as it alerts us to the fact of movement (although we should recall that seat monitors are needed to remind us when to get up and move around to avoid deep vein thrombosis), the animated map reinforces the stillness of air travel. The allure of the moving map, 'the non-when of a surface of projection', constitutes an act of forgetting that one is oneself in movement. The animated map makes invisible the very act of movement that makes it possible, 'a fixation that constitutes procedures for forgetting' (de Certeau 1984: 97). Indeed, the comfortable stillness and quiet of flight – hence the popularity of noise-canceling headphones – is jeopardized only when we feel the plane *move*. There are, of course, few things more frightening than movement during flight, and even the slightest turbulence invariably punctures the stillness of the cabin space with audible gasps. Nevertheless, as we land, our flight attendants remind us that our 'luggage may have shifted during the flight', as if *we* have not shifted *at all*.

Not yet beyond territorial airspace, not quite approaching outer space, airplane travel and IFE exalt such virtual enactments of motion. Along the way, the cyberspatial topography of the moving map juxtaposes the political, the geographical and the experiential, sublimating one to the other in a dazzling coordination of a space that is 'homogeneous, yet at the same time broken into fragments' (Lefebvre 1991: 342). Whatever geopolitical, regulatory and industrial conflicts remain, the ubiquity of the in-flight moving map demonstrates that the airlines have truly learned to share the air.

In-flight entertainment articulates the everyday experiences of boredom within these new media forms: the airplane is merely one of the artifacts of the technological sublime (Nye 1994) – the city and the railroad are significant antecedents – that shapes the culture of boredom in contemporary society. However, modern air travel does not simply conform to the common vectors of space-time compression. Air travel coordinates the centrifugal and centripetal movements of the global and the local around media spaces that include the magazine and the map, the seat and seat-back video: movements organized, like 'any spatial story, between the prospective and retrospective mappings of place and the practices that transform them'

(Morris 1998: 57). The complex topography of airline travel, the hybridity of industrial, regulatory and textual practices in the firm and in the cabin, generate nodes of intermediary coherency, a *lingua franca* and inhabited persona for the jet-set: background noise for the screen in our new (un)friendly skies.

Notes

1 See 'The Complete Region-Free Guide' at: http://www.digital-digest.com/dvd/articles/region.html.

2 The speech genre of the in-flight magazine travelogue testifies to this in its routine collapse of locality into authenticity. As one in-flight magazine editor puts it with characteristic aplomb, 'global travelers don't want to read a review of a Paris restaurant by a journalist in Milwaukee' (McKegney 2001).

3 The right of one party to unobstructed airspace above another party's private territory is a significant part of the history of legal property doctrine, which commonly addresses passage over a neighbor's land and possible exemptions from trespass liability based on right-of-way convenience and ease of transport. Based on the rationalized distribution of resources, an attendant 'law of easements ' has been invoked to decide cases concerning radio transmission rights and unobstructed access to sunlight for powering roof-top solar panels (see Gergacz 1982). The advent of airplane technology shifted the legal definition of the boundaries of landed property and the law of easements, and may even do the same for traditional territory-bound notions of intellectual property (see Aoki 1996).

4 The centralization of these cities – and the radiating proliferation of points of contact between them – affirm their status as power centers of the early twenty-first century. These 'world-cities' are 'spatial articulations of the global flows that constitute the world economy' (see Smith and Timberlake 2002).

5 Airlines typically receive monthly lists of available films, which air two to three months following initial release. The production studios often obtain editing clearance from producers and directors, especially as author's rights laws have become more powerful in places like the United States. As airlines become more interested in the early window content market, the traditional practices of airing specially edited films according to carrier specifications will probably undergo some modification. At this point, carrier editing customization (including adding airline logos to a film's opening and closing titles) might be replaced by generic airline master DVDs that would be acceptable to all airlines.

6 In the last few years, modern big city airports have followed the urban design philosophy of the 'aerotropolis', a mixed-use retail, office and business center designed around a central aviation hub that mimics the historical development of modern cities around commercial centers of shipping transport. In such airports as Chicago's O'Hare, Schiphol in Amsterdam, Viracopos in Campinas, Brazil, Incheon, Zhuhai, and Lantau Island near Hong Kong, transport hubs are combined with suburban shopping malls, office buildings with hotels, all with numerous places for sex, food and play. These commercial properties dictate both the changing metric of airport space and the metered rhythms of passenger movement. The once-familiar route of passengers from the parking lot to the plane is being reorganized to accommodate new security initiatives that include baggage screening areas and surveillance-friendly island-style counters that replace the traditional check-in counter line.

7 After 9/11, business travelers concerned with the ubiquitous terror alerts in the US and abroad considered teleconferencing and webcasting rather than flying. Security seminars and self-defense training for concerned business travelers have become the latest airline-related cottage industry. Part *X Files* episode, part National Security

249

Agency briefing, websites for the concerned business traveler offer the latest in travel preparedness. See the National Business Travel Association website at: http://cybercity.nbta.org; for security seminars, see Flightwatch's website at: www.fwamerica.com and at www.corporatetravelsafety.com; for instruction in 'safety strategy courses', see www.appliedpsychology.com

8 The Korean carrier, Asiana, recently spent one month training sixteen flight atten-dants to perform magic tricks, demonstrate cocktail mixing techniques, and lead stretching exercises designed to loosen passengers' aching joints.

9 In mid-2002, Southwest Airlines, one of the most successful US discount carriers, announced that it would start charging 'larger customers' for two seats, prompting the People for the Ethical Treatment of Animals to start a new billboard campaign which implored passengers, 'Don't pay for two seats. Go vegetarian.' How this new campaign lives alongside the vernacular of Southwest's unique boarding protocols – which have acquired the popular moniker of 'a cattle call' – remains to be seen. For more on in-flight body management technologies, see below.

10 IFE kingpin Virgin Airlines experimented with live entertainment shortly after it started up in 1984.

11 Singapore Airlines and Malaysian Airlines both launched audio-video on demand (A/VOD) trials in 1999, experimenting with Matsushita systems that provided passengers with the capability of accessing twenty-five films and over fifty audio CDs at one time, with the capacity to pause, fast-forward or rewind films and music. Until that time, in-flight films were exhibited using an analog master tape for each program on a two-hour loop. Malaysian Airlines' A/VOD system, installed in first and business class cabins, offers twelve video channels, eighteen audio channels, games, information services, a new service updated via satellite, and communication services with email, Internet and live television reception are due to arrive soon.

12 In 2003, B/E Aerospace (a cabin interiors manufacturer) and Color Kinetics (an 'illuminations technology' firm) announced a program that would create a variety of dynamic lighting 'atmospheres' controllable by the passenger in-flight. These effects include: 'sunset ambiance to encourage relaxation and sleep; a sunrise program to awaken and re-energize passengers after an extended flight; and custom effects featuring an airline's signature colors to enhance its brand'. See the Color Kinetics website at: http://oem.colorkinetics.com/casestudies/beaerospace/

13 At the same time, of course, the airplane's deployment as a reconnaissance technology was reorganizing both the spatial and temporal coordinates of the First World War battlefield.

14 When viewed in combination with the audio channel, which provides passengers with select flight-deck chatter, the moving map offers, at least, the partial fantasy of control.

Bibliography

Industry sources

Aerospace Daily
Airfax
Airline Business
Airline Industry Information
Air Transport Intelligence
Air Transport World
Flight International
Tech-FX: An Update on the Emerging Technologies and Technical Issues in IFE
World Airline News

References

(2002) 'Flightstore: Amnesty International Looks to the Skies for Donations', *M2 Presswire*, 13 March: n.p.

(2001) 'Observe In-flight Respite', *Design Week*, 26 April: 8.

(2000) 'That's In-flight Entertainment', *Sydney Morning Herald*, 16 December: 2.

Amin, A. and Nigel, T. (1994) 'Living in the Global', in A. Amin and N. Thrift (eds), *Globalization, Institutions, and Regional Development in Europe*, New York: Oxford University Press: 1–22.

Aoki, K. (1996) '(Intellectual) Property and Sovereignty: Notes toward a Cultural Geography of Authorship', *Stanford Law Review* 48 (May): 1293–355.

Armbruster, W. (2001) 'Aerotropolis: It's Probably Not in Your Dictionary, But You Can Find Examples Around Every Air-cargo Hub', *Journal of Commerce*, 16 July: 10.

Blanchot, M. (1987 [1959]) 'Everyday Speech', trans. S. Hanson, *Yale French Studies*, 73: 12–20.

Cartwright, L. (1995) *Screening the Body: Tracing Medicine's Visual Culture*, Minneapolis: University of Minnesota Press.

De Certeau, M. (1984) *The Practice of Everyday Life*, trans. S. Rendall, Berkeley: University of California Press.

Clifford, J. (1997) 'Traveling Cultures', *Routes: Travel And Translation in the Late Twentieth Century*, Cambridge, MA: Harvard University Press: 17–46.

Elder, B. (1997) 'Free Flight: The Future of Air Transportation Entering the Twenty-first Century', *Journal of Air Law and Commerce*, 62: 871–914.

Foucault, M. (1994) *The Birth of the Clinic: An Archeology of Medical Perception*, trans. A.M. Sheridan Smith, New York: Vintage.

García Canclini, N. (2001) 'Consumption is Good for Thinking', *Consumers and Citizens: Globalization and Multicultural Conflicts*, trans. G. Yúdice, Minneapolis: University of Minnesota Press.

Gergacz, J.W. (1982) 'Legal Aspects of Solar Energy: Statutory Approaches for Access to Sunlight', *Boston College Environmental Affairs Law Review*, 10 (Fall): 1–36.

Gomery, D. (1992) *Shared Pleasures: A History of Movie Presentation in the United States*, Madison: University of Wisconsin Press.

Hanlon, P. (1999) *Global Airlines: Competition in a Transnational Industry*, Oxford: Butterworth Heinemann.

Holloway, S. (1997) *Straight and Level: Practical Airline Economics*, Brookfield, VT: Ashgate.

Ives, H.E. (1920) *Airplane Photography*, Philadelphia: J.B. Lippincott Company.

Kassim, H. (1997) 'Air Transport and Globalization: A Skeptical View', in A. Scott (ed.), *The Limits to Globalization: Cases and Arguments*, New York: Routledge: 202–22.

Kolm, S.L. (1995) *Women's Labor Aloft: A Cultural History of Airline Flight Attendants in the United States, 1930–78*, Ph.D. Dissertation, Brown University.

Latour, B. (1993) *We Have Never Been Modern*, trans. C. Porter, Cambridge, MA: Harvard University Press.

Lefebvre, H. (1987) 'The Everyday and Everydayness', trans. C. Levich, A. Kaplan and K. Ross, *Yale French Studies*, 73: 7–11.

—— (1991) *The Production of Space*, trans. D.N. Smith, Oxford: Blackwell.

Levin, G. (1997) 'Nets Take Airline Flyer to Pump Up Programs', *Variety*, 5–11 May: 221.

Lewis, M.W. and Wigen, K.E. (1997) *The Myth of Continents: A Critique of Metageography*, Berkeley: University of California Press.

Massey, D. (1994) 'A Global Sense of Place', in *Space, Place and Gender*, Minneapolis: University of Minnesota Press: 146–56.

McCarthy, A. (2001) 'Television While You Wait', in *Ambient Television: Visual Culture and Public Space*, Durham, NC: Duke University Press: 195–224.

McCool, A.C. (1995) *In-flight Catering Management*, New York: John Wiley & Sons.

McKegney, M. (2001) 'Airlines' Captive Audience', *Ad Age Global*, 1 February: 33.

Mellencamp, P. (1988) 'Last Seen in the Streets of Modernism', *East-West Film Journal*, 3.1 (December): 45–65.

Miller, T., Govil, N., McMurria, J. and Maxwell, R. (2001) *Global Hollywood*, London: British Film Institute Publishing.

Moore, M. (1999) 'On the Cover', *Hemispheres* (October): 12.

Morris, M. (1998 [1988]) 'At Henry Parkes Motel', in *Too Soon Too Late: History in Popular Culture*, Bloomington: Indiana University Press: 31–63.

Nichols, P.M. (1995) 'Multiplexes in the Sky: Airlines Offer Options for In-flight Entertainment', *Chicago Tribune*, 7 July: 5.

Nye, D.E. (1994) *American Technological Sublime*, Cambridge, MA: MIT Press.

Phair, L. (1993) 'Stratford-on-Guy', *Exile in Guyville*, Matador Records, Inc.

Rhodes, L. (1999) 'Inflight Magazines: Changing How Travelers Read', *Journal of Magazine and New Media Research*, 1.2 (Fall).

Robson, W.A. (1916) *Aircraft in War and Peace*, London: Macmillan and Co.

Smith, C. (1996) 'Executive Travel', *Los Angeles Times*, 25 September: D4.

Smith, D. and Timberlake, M. (2002) 'Hierarchies of Dominance Among World Cities: A Network Approach', in S. Sassen (ed.), *Global Networks, Linked Cities*, New York: Routledge.

Smith, N. (1993) 'Homeless/Global: Scaling Places', in J. Bird, B. Curtis, T. Putnam, G. Robertson and L. Tickner (eds), *Mapping the Futures: Local Cultures, Global Change*, New York: Routledge.

Strange, S. and Stopford, J. (1991) *Rival States, Rival Firms: Competition for World Market Shares*, New York: Cambridge University Press.

Unsworth, R. (2002) 'A Good View Keeps Flyers Happy', *Mail on Sunday*, 4 August: 27.

Van Zandt, J.P. (1944) *The Geography of World Air Transport*, Washington, DC: Brookings Institution.

13

AN ONTOLOGY OF EVERYDAY CONTROL

Space, media flows and 'smart' living in the absolute present

Fiona Allon

> Imagine this: As you walk up to your front door, a smart receiver built in to the lock picks up a special code from your ID badge. It shuts down the security system, unlocks the door and turns up the gas fireplace in the living room. The lighting fixtures notice your ID, too, and on they come – at the brightness they remember from the last time you adjusted them.
>
> (Dolinar 2002)

Alongside the terrain of the physical landscape and the settled localities in which we live is a parallel geography of technologies of transportation, information and communication. This geography, and its successive historical developments, have in turn shaped experiences of both place and displacement, along with corresponding experiences of space and time. Over the last few decades, the contours of this geography have continued to expand, the technologies embodying it defined by an ever increasing intensity, acceleration and velocity. The growth of global information networks, the wide-spread adoption of personal computers and their related networks of everyday communication, along with the pervasive reach of digital technologies in general, have led to further spatial and temporal dislocations and to significant realignments of social life and social space. Images and rhetoric now abound of a world integrated through large-scale media institutions, of a new communications geography defined by media flows and vectors, and of distance 'annihilated' once and for all by high-speed transportation technologies and the instantaneous delivery of information.

'Where do you want to go today?' No other question embodies the connectivity and mobility of the contemporary mediasphere better than this one, asked by Bill Gates, founder and figurehead of Microsoft. Although the answers may be virtually unlimited, one obvious reply is: 'to the smart house', perhaps the most significant component of Gates' vision of interlinked global networks connecting families, homes, businesses and schools. Indeed, Gates' own smart, electronic home – a complex of buildings terraced into a hillside by Lake Washington on the outskirts of Seattle – has been designed so that it can serve as a domestic laboratory for the latest range of smart technologies, from full house automation to broadband infotainment spectacles. As Gates has said, 'the house's entertainment system will be a close enough simulation of how media will work in the near future that I'll be able to get a sense of what it will be like to live with various technologies' (Gates 1996: 247). It will be a technological utopia, he argues, a utopia soon available to us all: 'The installation of silicon microprocessors and memory chips, and the software that makes them useful, will let the house approximate some of the features the information superhighway will bring to millions of houses in a few years' (ibid.).

The guiding principle of the 'home instrumentation' within Gates' smart house is the complete automation and integration of all technological features, from telecommunications and information to security and energy efficiency. Such full automation depends on the interactivity of the various systems within the house so that it becomes a huge network of integrated functions and commands. Gates describes in detail the computerized home-control systems regulating and rationalizing a whole range of domestic functions: the automated thermostat will make the temperature 'toasty on a cold morning', the lighting will match the 'inside brightness to the brightness of the outdoors', the computer will manage the 'minute by minute demand for power at various times of the day'. This technological utopia will not only enable its occupants to be fully immersed in a space that is 'energy efficient and environmentally aware', but one that is also self-regulating and will 'remember everything it learns about your preferences' (Gates 1996: 255–7).

In this vision of customized and embedded computerized systems, able to service individual needs and desires, 'readily available' but not 'confronting', technology is immanent within the very fabric of everyday life. For Gates, a house that 'tracks its occupants', anticipating such needs as musical preferences and tastes, lighting and heating requirements, that 'knows' and remembers what they like, and keeps records of its operations, is simply an initial and desirable step towards the instrumentation of the home and everyday life, indeed all of life. A fully instrumented house, Gates announces, 'presages an instrumented world' (ibid.: 256).

Using the trope of Gates' house, I want to examine the restructuring of social and spatial relations by new information and communications technologies, and the inevitable reconfiguration of senses of inside and outside, presence and absence, and public and private space in contemporary culture. The technological imaginary of the smart house can also help to illuminate the paradoxical ways in which the domestic dwelling is currently being positioned in the electronic mediascape. The contemporary household's use of modern media and communication technologies (and in this respect the smart house presents an exemplary site) demonstrates 'the permeability of the home's boundaries – the constant '"to-and-fro" of bodies, sounds and images across the threshold between private and public domains' (Moores 2000: 102). This is not only evident in the ambiguity between public and private space within the cultural landscape, but also in their reconfiguration as *activities* related to specific *times* and *types* of interaction and engagement frequently carried out in the same place. Thus, I want to focus in part on the production of a particular kind of spatiality – the networked space of the smart house. I want to consider the wider implications of what Gates, for one, is proposing as *the way to live* for the spaces and practices of everyday life, within what is an increasingly technologically mediated existence.

This chapter also looks at the related work patterns and practices organized by post-industrial capitalism (or what Gates calls 'friction-free capitalism'), with its emphasis on the flexibility of labor, decentralization and adaptivity. The networked smart house – a node for the circulation of media and information, as well as a new domain of production and consumption – appears as a significant site in which changes in the social economy of power and control can be observed. It is a site which, while promising greater and greater freedoms (of choice, of mobility, of access, of home-work, of technological empowerment and connectivity), is also a primary site for the further extension of diffuse and intricate mechanisms of control and surveillance.

Gates' house near Seattle presents as an iconic site, a mode of living situated wholly within the space of the flows and eddies of an intense and seemingly unrestrained mobility. Ultimately, for Gates the possibilities of being what he calls 'plugged in at home' work to articulate a domestic space that can be actively engineered, with everyday life managed and controlled as a *perfect system*. But more than this, complex domestic communications systems allow residents to effectively withdraw from their immediate urban environments, to install surveillance technologies to monitor interactions not only within the home ('Kidwatch', for example, a web-based software/hardware package which performs the task suggested by its name), but also between the home and 'outside', and to create well-fortified enclaves of privacy and security whereby the networked house becomes virtually a home fortress.

Such technologies are by no means unique to Microsoft. Indeed smart house technologies are rapidly becoming ubiquitous, with many housing and electronics companies displaying such systems in demonstration homes in new housing estates (George 2000).[1] Smart house systems can also be purchased from a range of computer companies: IBM offers a 'smart home' system, 'Home Director'; Honeywell offers a 'Total Home Management' system; while a number of other, smaller computer and software companies also market systems 'providing total integrated home, security and energy management' (Camphuisen 1999: 23). Equipped with 'smart' networked infrastructures, the houses wired by such systems are increasingly integrated into global spaces of exchange and communication where they can tap into ever-diversifying circuits of media and information. The smart house is also a site that negotiates the need for extension with the need for emplacement, enabling secession from public life at the very same time as networked communications achieve greater levels of integration and interconnection. These processes work simultaneously, with an extension towards global networked infrastructures paralleled by the increased possibility of withdrawal into a 'safe' site of refuge. Media, communication and utility infrastructures which supply and support the continuous connection of the smart house to vectors of exchange, information and energy also produce parallel processes of global engagement and connectivity, as well as withdrawal, secession and securitization (Graham and Marvin 2001: 285). As one smart house enthusiast states:

> The home of the future will be a high-tech, high-touch zone – the hub of your life. You can kiss goodbye the postwar era of the dormitory suburb – where houses stood empty all day while workers toiled away in the factory or the office. Home and work life will be integrated again as they were in the agrarian age.
>
> (Callaghan 1996: 2)

For the more affluent groups of society who can actually afford such complex privatized telecommunications systems, the home becomes both secure sanctuary and networked hub where an array of activities and services such as communication, work, financial transactions and exchange are all possible. Considering that 'electronic amenities', including broadband Internet connections, utility services, energy management applications, home security systems, and high-speed, purpose-built local area networks, constitute some of the fastest growing and expanding industries developing today, these technologies have major social and spatial implications. In North America, for example, 'smart' condominium complexes and common interest developments (CIDs), all provided with highly advanced infrastructure services, and frequently privately administered and governed, are becoming increasingly common features of the urban landscape. Indeed, it is forecast that they will be the predominant form of housing in the twenty-first century (Boyer 1999: 63). Often housing high-income professionals demanding not only broadband communications, but individual control over a whole suite of energy, water, security, interactive banking, home-shopping and voting services, these new urban developments are leading to a 'digital divide' between those who can and can't afford to access information technologies, and also to new patterns of spatial division and exclusion.

The continuous extension of electronic media creates, then, new forms of social interaction and linkage as well as fundamental shifts in the organization of time, space and place. Enabling a range of interactions between the near and the far, frequently in shared time and without dependency on spatial proximity, digital media technologies are not only playing a primary role in reconfiguring the spatial orders of social life, but are also affecting how we directly experience place and territory. While this may not necessarily engender a generalized placelessness (Meyerowitz 1985), it does entail a profound re-conceptualization of notions of space, scale and distance. Media and communication networks effectively constitute a new matrix of spatio-temporal relations which complicates, and overlaps with, existing domains of spatial experience. With the increasing flows of electronic media into the home, the domestic space of the house is being reconstituted as an interactive media node, hub or terminal, connected to myriad networks and circuits of exchange. Global communications networks, and the accelerated flows of media and information products they give rise to, as well as the multiplication of forms and sites of production and consumption, are key vectors affecting the relations between public and private space and indeed the entire spatial organization of urban geographies. With this convergence between domestic architectural space and electronic media, we see the rise of new modes of living organized almost entirely by the reconstitution of 'private space' as 'media space'.

The production of space

The ways in which space is visualized and imagined, and what space is thought to be or do at any particular historical time, are questions that involve the potentials of space as an *imaginary construct*. But spatial imaginings and spatial constructs also have real, material effects and the force to shape material realities. They are effects and forces which extend beyond the phenomenology of individual experience and beyond the closed, discursive domains of metaphor, representation and imagination, to actually constitute and structure not only the physical shape and nature of spaces but the physical experiences associated with them. Spatiality is something that is simultaneously symbolic, material, and representational. As Michel de Certeau has argued, the deployment and use of space 'creates the determining conditions for social life' (de Certeau 1985: 129). Spatial discourses are therefore not simply analytical constructs but forms of knowledge which are productive, producing and shaping material practices directly, as well as the experiential realities linked to them (Foucault 1977 and 1980). As Henri Lefebvre argued, 'space is not a scientific object removed from ideology or politics; it has always been political and strategic' (Lefebvre 1978: 341).

So, from such a perspective, Bill Gates' vision of being-at-home in the Information Age (a vision of both a new way of living and a new world) is also simultaneously a new formulation of, and (by implication) a new configuration of social space. In his initial video account of the networked home of the future and its role in the global information society, Gates' vision was centered, some-what ironically, around a remarkably ordinary, even banal image: that of a modest, blond-brick suburban bungalow, an average suburban home in the year

2004, recently revolutionized by information technology. In the video, an American woman watches a selection of favorite television shows and news updates, which have been automatically selected and saved by her computer and organized as a menu of items on the television screen. In the background her son busies himself with another computer, making on-line connections to various museums and downloading images and text for a school multimedia project. Suffused with the golden hue of domestic harmony, this clip demonstrates Gates' dream of integrated consumption, computing and communications converging around family bliss.

As Walter Benjamin found in his studies of the material cultures of modernity, new technologies invariably imitate precisely the anachronistic forms they were destined to supersede: Gates' 'home of the future' announces, then, its revolutionary break with history by calling on a cultural memory of social harmony and stability, a utopian image of an imaginary past. In this sense, Gates has much in common with a range of late twentieth-century Futurologists, from Alvin Toffler in the 1970s to more recent technocrats, such as Nicholas Negroponte and Kevin Kelly, and their visions of 'electronic cottages' and 'virtual communities' within decentralized democracies (Toffler 1980; Negroponte 1999; Kelly 1995). Promising that the future will be anything *but* like the past, these commentators frequently, and paradoxically, draw upon socially conservative images and the traditional values of a simpler age, images of rural community harmony and close-knit family stability, with which to frame their accounts of the new and the revolutionary. By reviving these forms of communitarian nostalgia alongside their more dynamic visions of technological progress, the Futurologists, proclamations that everything will be new and will change simultaneously involve making sure everything stays the same, indeed that the future also embodies a return to the past.

While on one level this vision of home-centered work, consumption and leisure may seem quite prosaic compared with the futurist rhetoric usually associated with new information and communications technologies, the home has in fact been, for much of the twentieth century, a key site for the demonstration of both the application of new technologies and an illustration of the 'world of tomorrow' (Cockburn and Dilic 1994). In this sense, the forerunners of the smart house are the many scenarios of the 'house of the future' featured throughout the twentieth century in various exhibitions, expositions and world's fairs. Invariably in these displays, the domestic home was one of the most important sites for the display and demonstration of technological innovations, labor-saving devices and gadgetry of all kinds. The various 'home of the future' designs displayed in these fairs and venues all emphasized the ideological harmony between a technological utopia and a housing utopia in which domestic technologies, especially electrical communications technologies in the form of home entertainment machines such as radio, and later, television, were the very source and substance of the comfortable life of the modern era.

One of the first in this long history of 'homes of tomorrow' was the American modernist architect Buckminster Fuller's famous Dymaxion House, built in 1927. One of the most striking features of this futuristic glass and steel house was that it contained a range of home communications technologies, most notably a prototype television set, placed with other entertainment devices such as a radio and phonograph, along with a number of domestic office machines, in what Fuller called the 'get-on-with-life-room' (Spigel 1992: 1). Although Fuller's design appeared at the time as little more than science-fiction fantasy, in 1939 the New York World's Fair took as its motto 'Building the World of Tomorrow', and featured a number of houses which, equipped with electrical appliances and contemporary technologies, demonstrated the imperative to modernize.

It was in the post-war years, however, after the introduction of television, that visions of the 'house of the future' fully wired and connected with state-of-the-art home entertainment machines began to appear. In 1957, the MIT-designed Monsanto House of the Future went on display in Disneyland, in the area called 'Tomorrowland'. The house, which in its design resembled a giant television set, was stuffed with the latest in domestic gadgetry: it had microwave ovens and pictophones, an 'Atoms for Living Kitchen', closed-circuit television in every room, and of course, conventional TV sets (Marling 1994: 6). Similarly, the American Exhibition in Moscow, held in 1959 and scene of the infamous 'kitchen debate' between Richard Nixon and Nikita Khrushchev on the ideological differences represented by kitchen designs, consumer appliances and domestic gadgetry, presented a number of 'ideal home' exhibits. One model home on display contained the RCA Whirlpool 'miracle' kitchen, which was said to be controlled by an 'electronic brain': when a button was pushed, a dishwashing machine automatically raced to the dining table along a hidden track and a robot cleaner polished the floor. In another display, a uniformed guide demonstrated to Khrushchev a display of household robots and a closed-circuit television system designed to monitor activities in every corner of the house (Marling 1994: 276).

It was, however, the popular idea of the home as a 'total entertainment environment' which most occupied the cultural imaginary of the post-war years. Through television and other 'home entertainment machines', the emphasis was on transforming the domestic space of the house into a 'home theater'. Popular media guided consumers on how and where to place the TV set and other technologies, and recommended features such as the electronic regulation of air temperature and quality, termed 'climate control'. The home magazine *American Home*, for example, described the 'home theater' as a space including an electronic cornucopia of technologies such as the television set, radio, phonograph, movie projector, movie screen and loudspeakers. As Lynn Spigel argues, the idea of the home theater promised 'a perfectly controlled environment of mechanized pleasures'. Within the context of domestic media and communication technologies, which were mass-produced and therefore finally affordable to ordinary consumers, 'this new domestic theatricality was hailed as the ultimate communication experience, delivering a dream of spatial transport that had, since the nineteenth century, fascinated the modern imagination' (Spigel 1992: 108–9).

The new media and communication technologies of the current period are surrounded by remarkably similar discourses. This is not surprising given that this genre of American technocratic Futurology has generally approached the home in a paradoxical manner: both a site for the transformative impact of new applications and a symbolic realm of domestication. Within such discourses the home is a space where technology becomes *encultured* and *made safe*, a view resting on and supporting a binary understanding of technology as completely instrumental and the home as a socially neutral, static space, a private, non-technological space into which technology is 'plugged in', or added on, without any disturbance to the fundamental social relations contained and expressed within. Indeed, from this perspective the technology that is seen as 'introduced' into the space of the home is presented as a force that not only maintains and supports these relations but even works to intensify them. The overriding imperative within this rhetoric of the future is one of control, of controlling the potentialities of the future while at the same time ensuring that the future not only remains answerable to the contingencies of the present and existing social relations, but that it also maintains and perpetuates the past and the established social and political order which it represents and supports.

However, if the rhetorical and discursive conventions for talking about and representing new electronic technologies have tended to remain the same, the historical conditions and social formations, along with the actual technologies themselves, have very much changed. Although predictions about the utopian potentials of new communication technologies are still underpinned by notions of social and historical progress and democratic accessibility, the ideal user/worker interpellated by the ideology of the smart house is very different. If the figure of the housebound housewife was most certainly the target for the discourses of 'home modernity' which circulated in the mid years of the twentieth century, then it seems that the double-income professional couple, the 'symbolic analysts', 'knowledge workers' and info-elite are now the figures of smart domesticity in the twenty-first century.

Extension and connectivity

An analysis of Gates' house provides, then, an opportunity to examine the changing meanings, understandings and experiences of space and place within the contemporary experience of technological change and post-industrial economic restructuring. Gates' house is one instance, both concrete and symbolic, of the production of new spatialities along with the potentially new forms of social control that may operate within them. Undoubtedly, new infor-mation and communications technologies *are* transforming the spatial and temporal matrix of society, and reconfiguring the meanings of places and spaces. Such technologies, simultaneously social processes *and* spatial practices, are implicated in the on-going construction and reconstruction of social spaces and social relations, articulating particular spaces (private/public) while also reconfiguring and transgressing the boundaries of others (the imagined space of the nation, the demarcated space of the home).

However, against the overly hyperbolic claims about the 'time-space compression' of the Information Age (Harvey 1989), I want to argue that a more nuanced and detailed spatial logic is actually at work. Rather than a 'loss' or 'annihilation' of space – the premise on which so many accounts of the effects of new technologies are based – I want to suggest that such technologies actually *produce* new spatialities and temporalities. Rather than simply seeing technologies collapsing distances and engendering an all-consuming temporality of the Absolute Present, we also need to consider the reorganization, interplay and coordination of both presences and absences, insides and outsides, spatialities and temporalities, by information and communication technologies. So, against claims that it is impossible to locate oneself in postmodern hyperspace (Jameson 1984), I want to explore the way the smart house is held up as *the* way to inhabit the network society (Castells 1996).

But, how does one actually get to visit Bill Gates' house and have a look around? Perhaps the most appropriate way to visit the house is to accept the promises of the very technologies in question and take the 'virtual tour' provided by the CD-ROM version of Bill Gates' book, *The Road Ahead*. With the CD-ROM loaded into the same computer on which I write, I can be transported to a virtual version of the house and be taken on a guided tour, with a running commentary by a digitally-generated female voice-over. There is, it seems, a certain homology between the CD-ROM technology providing the tour and the object – the world of Gates – which it circumscribes, with both appearing within a technological ensemble promising new dimensions of connectivity and access, and new environments of interactivity. New technologies often give rise to new social spaces and new environments, though such spaces and environments do not exist in opposition to the stable 'places' of human activity, but rather function in a similar manner to the process Marshall McLuhan called the 'extensions of Man' (*sic*) (McLuhan 1964). For McLuhan the reach and extension of electronic media and an electronic information space paralleled, even exceeded, a technological extension and exteriorization of human perception, consciousness and identity, and although his formulations may in themselves not have extended beyond the somewhat banal image of the Global Village, they raise significant points about the contemporary context, defined as it is by ever more dense networks of interfacing and mediation.

Such technologies complicate the relations between the distant and the close, the near and the far, and introduce perspectives which may alternate between the totalizing, static and fixed and the partial, mobile and open-ended. Instead of a binary model of immediate presence or disembodied absence, a third dimension is engaged, an in-between which is neither distant and total-izing nor tactile and close. With computer-mediated communication in particular, the whole idea of structure or textuality as fixed and permanent is to a great extent undermined, especially when information becomes interactive and dialogic, subject to continual change, amendment and variation depending on the conditions of use and reception (Nichols 1996).

Attempting to reverse Le Corbusier's dictum that a house should be a 'machine for living in', Gates' house presents a space which aims to be as *un-machinic* as possible, a place where the boundaries are uncertain, and the machines are cybernetic, attempting to echo the embedded organic compo-nents of the natural world which surrounds them. 'My house is made of wood, glass, concrete, and stone', Gates writes; it is also, he adds, 'made of silicon and software' (Gates 1996: 247). Despite a level of technological intensity unlike any previously applied domestically, smart houses are then less machines for living in than apparatuses for blending the natural and the tech-nological, with the technologies functioning immanently and pragmatically, as simply part of the fabric of daily life. As one architecture firm specializing in smart house systems proposes, 'computers and communications fuse' so that technology becomes 'ubiquitous and transparent' (Week 1997).

In the reception hall of the Gates house, twenty-four high-definition video monitors display images selected from a database containing more than a million digital images of photos, paintings and drawings. As Gates describes it: 'If you're a guest, you'll be able to call up on screens throughout the house almost any image you like' (Gates 1996: 257). The mechanism which enables the personal selection of artwork is an 'electronic pin' worn by guests and occupants of the house. Attached to clothing, the pin sets up a communication channel between the wearer and the house's main computers, allowing a recognition of personalized aesthetic tastes and pref-erences, lighting and heating requirements, and so on. Via the electronic pin the house will know 'who' and 'where' you are, enabling not only the tracking of movement throughout the house, but also the anticipation of needs, wishes and desires, all customized to suit individual preferences, and 'all as unobtrusively as possible'. For example, a zone of light will follow a pin wearer from room to room, appropriate music fading in and out on cue: 'You won't be confronted by the technology, but it will be readily available to you' (ibid.: 252).

This electronic pin, which personalizes your interaction with the computer-ized systems of the house and registers your lifestyle preferences, becomes, in a sense, a prosthetic extension of your self and personality. The pin (in a similar fashion to other personal communication technologies like mobile phones, Walkmans, palm pilots) condenses the desired attributes of the Information Age: customized interactivity and individual freedom, empowerment and choice. But in so doing it also exposes a mutation, a transformation of a mode of power for which we can find a metonym in another, very different kind of pin: the fabled pin produced in the factory analyzed by Adam Smith in *The Wealth of Nations*.

For Smith, a pin produced by a factory organized along the lines of a standardized and rigid specialization of tasks ('one man draws out the wire, another straightens it, a third cuts it'), became an almost iconic object which defined a new age of production and labor. Emblematic of the rational, calculable distribution of working bodies in space and the organization of rational, serialized time (the division of labor), the pin-factory, and the pins it produced, represented a new era of efficiency and production. An industrially made pin – with each worker responsible for only one part of its overall production – symbolized a new conception and organization of bodies and a new way of living and working, trends which would eventually find their logical outcome in the mass production line (Smith, cited in Galbraith 1987: 59).

The nineteenth-century factory was just one site within a whole microphysics of power which was re-distributing bodies, serializing movements, organizing spaces and architectures of enclosure and surveillance (Foucault 1978). But if Smith's pin is metonymic of a particular mode of production, and a particular distribution of bodies in space-time, then Gates' pin is metonymic, it seems, of a very different regime of accumulation, defined by flexibility, by movement, by the unceasing circulation of information within micro- and macro-networks diffused throughout the social fabric, and by personalized interactions with these systems and networks. The stable equilibrium of labor, production and capital signified by the factory has given way to so-called flexible labor markets, increasingly mobile capital, and fragmented, dispersed regimes of production, alongside an endlessly differentiated spectrum of consumption. Within this regime of flexible production and flexible accumulation there are new ways of working (homework) and new ways of living (connectivity) characterized by the dissolution of rigid boundaries, between public and private spaces, for example, but also between markets and economies, and by an emphasis on the productive potential of speed and mobility (of information, finance capital, labor etc) and by decentralization and movement (see Harvey 1989; Castells 1997).

The interior

In 'Paris – Capital of the Nineteenth Century', Walter Benjamin described the emergence of the interior – a private space of intimacy, domesticity and enclosure. According to Benjamin, it was in the nineteenth century that such a space developed in opposition to the public sphere of society and work. Prior to this separation, social and familial life was characterized by an integration of production and consumption, of life and work, within the one place. However, with industrialization, home and work increasingly become separate sites (Benjamin 1983: 166).

Strictly distinguished from the outside realm of production and exchange, the interior began to offer the bourgeois family a compensatory space of privacy in which all the dramas of intimacy could unfold. For the individual whose traces were obliterated in the anonymous crowds and the erratic city life of urban modernity, the interior also provided a compensatory space in which to literally re-inscribe personal identity. Benjamin describes the obsessive efforts of the bourgeois citizen to leave his (sic) trace (spur) on every surface within the home: furniture, for example, was upholstered in soft, plush materials upon which the body could leave its imprint. The interior of the bourgeois dwelling functioned then as a container or 'a kind of casing' in which the private individual was embedded together with all of 'his appurtenances', exactly in the manner of fossils embedded in stone or granite (ibid.: 46). It was from this de-realized space that emerged what Benjamin calls the 'phantasmagorias of the interior' (ibid.: 167).

In Bill Gates' dwelling another, different kind of *phantasmagoria of the interior* is developed. Here, as before, the private citizen assembles the distant in space and time, although this process is aided and abetted by sophisticated communications technologies, media flows and vectors. However, if the interior of the nineteenth century created a private and encased space of enclosure rigidly separated from the outside world, in Gates' interior an intensely private space is fused with an enhanced connectivity to the outside. And if the dwellings Benjamin described were casings in which individuals could leave their imprints in the plush of bourgeois interiors, the smart house registers individual 'traces' in a very different way: all individual interactions and transactions within the networks embedded in and connected to the house can be monitored and tracked and then logged in the databases.

Within these home telematics networks which facilitate home-based consumption (cable and broadband networks, the Internet, interactive TV), home-based working and production (electronic commerce, smart cards, shopping and banking) and even home-based civic participation (electronic voting), there is also the potential to monitor the consumption patterns of households. These home-based media networks bring about the possibility of surveillant systems fully integrated within consumer landscapes. Within such systems, every act of consumption and transaction can be recorded and processed, entailing the accumulation of an unprecedented degree of personalized information – information which represents an invaluable asset for corporate suppliers, data companies, and a host of corporate and commercial interests. Whenever individuals interact with such systems of consumption, they are also themselves leaving tracks and traces of their consumption preferences, habits, financial transactions, and so on (Graham 1999; Bogard 1996). The modern citizen may still seek refuge inside the interior, but with superimposed media and consumption systems, many of which are based in the home, and the increasing sophistication of interactive telematics, the individual's traces are now spatial-ized not only in the plush velvet (or leather, or plastic, or chrome …)

furnishings of the interior, but also beyond in the ethereal networks of cyberspace. In this trajectory, individualized and personalized 'complete' privacy becomes paradoxically synonymous with the total overexposure and publicity of the domestic.

Within this global space of electronic information flows, technology has apparently triumphed over spatial distances, the far is reduced to the near, the elsewhere is both here and everywhere.[2] In these terms, global info-capitalism represents a plenitude of experiences, any of which can be brought 'close to hand', as Martin Heidegger put it, along with a synthetic space-time so that where we are can always already be somewhere else (Heidegger 1996). The elimination of distance in all its forms seems to be what Gates considers the ideal application of the new information technologies. They not only allow public space to be brought under the control and manipulation of private space, but they also allow a domestic space that can become a refuge and sanctuary from the difficulties and confrontations of physical proximity. In overcoming the constraints of distance, the rhetoric of this technological imaginary suggests, we will enter a more connected and engaged mode of human communication and interaction (Mitchell 1996; Rheingold 1995).[3]

The consequences of such a collapse of distance were considered by Heidegger in a number of reflections, not on virtual and digital technologies, but in the very different context of earlier transportation and media technologies: air travel, radio and television. Curious about the contemporary situation in which 'everything is equally far and equally near', Heidegger contemplated the ramifications of a world in which 'distanceless prevails' (Heidegger 1971: 165–6). This erasure of distance seems, then, in the context of Gates' 'friction-free capitalism' to have reached a new degree of intensification: with your network connection, Gates argues, 'you will be able to conduct business, study, explore the world and its cultures, call up any great entertainment, make friends, attend neighborhood markets, and show pictures to distant relatives – without leaving your desk or armchair' (Gates 1996: 4–5).

Yet as Heidegger outlines in another passage (in terms which seem uncannily prescient about the extensions of virtual technologies and the connections through time and space which they enable), near and far do not merely relate to objective spatial lengths which can be simply understood as measurable distances. Heidegger's comments highlight the *always-already lived-in* qualities of space and its dual nature as both physical and imaginary. For him there are always differences and overlaps between the remoteness of things in terms of physical distance and whether they are near in the sense of being 'close' to our thoughts and imagination, and whether they are important and matter to us, what Heidegger terms the 'close-at-hand'. The physically close and short in distance does not in any way correspond therefore with 'nearness', just as in the same way, remoteness does not necessarily relate to that which is, in terms of physical distance, a long way away (Heidegger 1996: 165).

With this in mind, perhaps Gates' project to render everything 'close-at-hand' through technology does not necessarily engender 'nearness'. Similarly, the technological immediacy apparently achieved by what the technocrats proclaim is the overcoming of the 'tyranny of distance' in no way guarantees a sense of intimacy and presence. Conversely, though, a simple renunciation of the facile claims about connectivity and 'presence at a distance' does not consider that what is 'near' may not only include that which is physically close, as in face-to-face communication, but also that which is technologically mediated.

Bringing it all back home

> One of the most powerful seductions of the Net is that it will take us back home ... It will allow us to spend more time with our families and stay closer to our communities. Given the dangers of the world – crime ridden cities, terrorism, suburban alienation and decay – the vision of the home as a safe house connected to the world is compelling.
>
> (Doheny-Farina 1996: 88)

The electronic smart house, then, is not only a space of extension where the coordinates of the domestic realm stretch to incorporate the outer reaches of global culture and bring them into local proximity, but also a *safe* house, a refuge from the intractable problems of the outside world. Within much of the celebratory rhetoric surrounding smart houses, the networked house features as an emblem of millenarian harmony, an essential part of a post-industrial society of revitalized individual freedom and autonomy where, equipped with home interactive telematics, the private individual can herself set the terms of engagement with an external public world while simultaneously maintaining secure boundaries around private space. This dream of complete home-centeredness is in turn seen as central to a notion of a decentralized democracy and a new politics of autonomy and freedom, whereby individuals with unrestricted access to free-flowing information communicate continuously while experiencing new civic responsibilities (Roszak 1994: 147).

One of the key promises made by the application of new technologies is that a heightened sense of privacy and security will accompany this intensified interconnectivity via electronically mediated communication channels between the home and the outside world: 'the Internet will draw us together, if that's what we choose, or let us scatter ourselves into a million mediated communities ... the interactive network will give us choices that can put us in touch with entertainment, information, and each other' (Gates 1996: 314).

Yet this utopian vision of the smart house also betrays a neo-liberal fantasy in which control is returned from the state and corporations to the individual or family based in the home. Nicholas Negroponte seems to advocate exactly such a position with his positive appraisal of the trend for the 'digerati' to move the 'primary locus of activity to rural settings'. Through new communications technologies, he writes, 'the rural returnees enjoy a safer, saner, cleaner, and more private lifestyle, while staying very much connected to learning, work, and art'. In this digital world, which has 'no centre and therefore no periphery', more and more people will be seeking a rural, 'bucolic lifestyle', he argues (Negroponte 1999: 12).

The smart house is central to this rhetoric of techno-communitarianism and an important component of the electronically wired 'Jeffersonian democracy' that many feel will result from increased network connections (Robins 1999). This rhetoric, however, also sits comfortably with neo-liberal economic policies dividing those who use and are dependent upon increasingly down-graded, under-funded public services from those who can afford to maintain privatized telecommunications infrastructures. In such premium network spaces, where residents are able to receive whatever services they can pay for, communications, security and utility infrastructures are frequently privately administered and controlled (Boyer 1996).

Somewhat paradoxically though, communication technologies are invested with the responsibility for social connection, bonding and civic participation at exactly the same time as they increase the possibilities for communities to become fragmented and dispersed. The smart house, a privileged space of privacy and connectedness where the neo-liberal individual can experience new degrees of freedom and autonomy while remaining plugged in and in-touch, is then the latest vehicle in the history of what Raymond Williams called 'mobile privatization' (Williams 1974). Like other institutions of mobile privatization (most notably television, and the world in which it was embedded, along with the car, the analogue suburban home, and the shopping center), the smart house constitutes yet another social space of mobility and a technological liberation from place and geography – a democracy of personal mobility, freedom and autonomy. As Margaret Morse argues, these principles 'guided the creation of systems of transport and social communication which promise liberty in the midst of sociality, privacy amongst community, and an autonomy of protected selfhood nourished by its environment' (Morse 1990: 209).

Thus we have the paradoxical situation of a technological vision of sanctuary that actually means more isolation and hence more (displaced) fear, along with a form of connectedness to the outside world, which is also a defense against it – a way of both reconstituting and neutralizing the public sphere at the same time (Sorkin 1992; Smart 1992; Robbins 1993).[4]

Ontologies of control

The proposed instrumentalization and rationalization of everyday life that the smart house apparently provides is, however, neither new nor unique to the promotion of specific computer technologies; it is a venerable theme in the history of modern technoscience. The 'fantasy of total control, of our will or desire mastering all objects and all circumstances' (Castoriadis, cited in Robins and Cornford 1990: 872) has been a key *technological imperative* guiding the development and implementation of innumerable schemes and programs of modern technological progress. For Kevin Robins and James Cornford, the rationale behind the various proposals for 'electronic homes of the future' is thus quite predictable: 'to subordinate the whole of social life to the principles of efficiency and control' (ibid.: 874). They suggest that information technologies function simply as an extension of long-standing techniques of disciplinary power. The electronic home, they argue, is 'social Taylorism', merely one application of the Taylorist principles of scientific management now colonizing every social sphere from the workplace to the home and everyday life. Extending this particular approach, Kevin Robins and Frank Webster have argued that the Information Revolution represents a 'new regime of social mobilization' which, reconfiguring Fordism–Taylorism, systematically intensifies its technological domination and colonization of a whole way of life (Robins and Webster 1999: 115).

At the same time, although the smart house which participates in the gathering of information for consumer profiles certainly evokes the specter of the all-knowing electronic panopticon, this model of power seems a little at odds with the flexible, decentralized futures painted by various 'silicon positivists', enthusiastic for a life increasingly mediated by computers. From this point of view, the mechanistic and rigid instrumentation of Fordism and Taylorism has been superseded by an altogether more 'natural' form of control: the technologies have become soft and flexible, the planning and discipline of form and space replaced by an emphasis on individual comfort and creative productivity. Indeed the smart house appears, from this perspective, as the perfect cybernetic circuit, a distributed system of flexible and modulating human–machine interfaces, maintained by continuous cycles of circulating information, encoding and decoding, feedback and readjustment.

Gilles Deleuze has argued that the spaces of enclosure that characterized the topography of modern societies – the factory, the prison, the school and the hospital, and certainly the home and family – are in crisis. Strained and in various stages of dissolution, these closed, interior spaces are now being irrevocably reconfigured by socio-technological change. For Deleuze their crisis signaled a shift from the disciplinary mechanisms of an earlier epoch, where the individual was molded, shaped and distributed within and across a vast regime of closed environments, to a more free-floating and flexible mesh of control.

These 'disciplinary societies' are gradually being replaced, he argued, by what he dubbed the 'societies of control' (Deleuze 1988: 3–7).

If the techniques of disciplinary power functioned by organizing the population into distinct, regular spaces of surveillance enforcing continuous conformity to a norm, the new orders of control use the electronic code and password instead to provide, revoke or deny access to systems of information. Within the global networks of computers, apparatuses of control undulate like waves, constantly fluctuating, transmuting fluidly from point to point, and carefully monitoring any interaction within the web of interconnected systems. With this shift discipline is not simply dismantled but rather released, dispersed and rewoven throughout the social fabric: a pervasive form of power linked not to restriction, confinement and enclosure but to multiplication and fluidity, interactivity and access. These modalities, multiple and differential, are the nodal points through which power and control flow in the network society.

So, if Discipline functioned by organizing masses into hierarchical states of equilibrium, Control is precisely about flexible management, self-organization and an incessant mobility between different networks of control and between different times, spaces and registers of experience. Information is precisely the form of control in 'societies that no longer operate by confining people but through continuous control and instant communication' (ibid.: 174). In possession of her electronic PIN or password, her identity configured to the logic of the code, the individual interacts with the system and her presence is registered, her movements are tracked, her details logged in innumerable stacks of information. Within this cybernetic sieve-like system, the boundaries between individuals and the individual's sense of privacy in the home, between institutions and corporations, are indistinct and permeable, constantly crossed by the traffic of information flows, undermining completely the model of the private individual ensconced in an enclosed private space.

Increasingly then, public and private, and their related dispositions of publicity and privacy, seclusion and connectedness, refer less to enclosed and defined spaces, 'spheres', than to *modulations* of engagement (frequently with streams of information both local and global) and to infinitely variable conditions of interaction and control. Thus while panopticism is a strategy of place, an architecture of surveillance which functions by constructing visible locales and by reducing temporal relations to spatial relations, strategies of control utilize instead both modalities of time and the distribution of temporalities (see Bogard 1996: 19). In the public/private workspace of the smart home, the control of time (work-time/private time), rather than spatial separation, becomes the site for the exploitation and ordering of bodies. As Robins and Webster argue, with 'the potential combination of work, leisure and consumption functions in the domestic information terminal ... the previously rigid distinction between production (work time) and reproduction (free time) may be eroded. ... The move is towards work that may be performed at any time (and when the occasion demands, all the time)' (Robins and Webster 1999: 117).

Recast as a significant locus of both production and consumption, the networked house is a strategic arena in the emerging system of control and information capitalism, a site of both economic enterprise, organizational and spatial flexibility and efficient social regulation and management. With the development and implementation of home telematics, the automated house-hold can now join the automated factory as the burgeoning 'homework economy' grows. As Donna Haraway argues, the 'homework economy' not only describes work literally done at home, but a wide-scale restructuring of work patterns including the increase of part-time work, illegal labor, and the large-scale deskilling of many jobs. As a concept it also indicates that the 'factory, home, and market are integrated on a new scale' (Haraway 1985: 86). Within the context of this new regime of production and consumption, the smart house is then not only the potential site for home-based teleworking, but for a range of activities including banking, shopping, commerce and even health care, and status is conferred not just by how much space is at your disposal or, as in Benjamin's time, by how much you physically possess, but by your degree of connectivity (Friedman 1999: 168–9).[5]

However, contemporary media accounts of the proliferation of such tech-nologies generally avoid any discussion of such changes in the social economy of power. For example, one article from an e-business magazine on website-controlled home automation under trial in south Australia, ignores the implications for data collection, social atomization and the monitoring and surveillance of individuals in favor of a simple celebration of opportunity. Instead, under the aegis of enhanced freedom, mobility and connectivity, the automated house is simply a bearer of further improvements for both staying in touch *and* getting away from it all: 'if a light, stove or other electrical appliance is accidentally left turned on while the owner is absent, the owner is notified. ... This is going to give most families a much better start to the holidays, not being two hours down the road and wondering if they turned off the stove' (Camphuisen 1999: 23).

For the family bundled into the car and hurtling down the highway, anxiously wondering if they turned off the stove, the automated smart house will, of course, take care of the problem. As Deleuze puts it,

A control is not a discipline. In making highways, for example, you don't enclose people but instead multiply the means of control. I am not saying that this is the highway's exclusive purpose, but that people can drive infinitely and 'freely' without being confined yet while still being perfectly controlled. This is our future.

(Deleuze 1998: 18)

Networked media infrastructures, such as those supplying smart houses, are configured in highly selective and unequal ways, distributed along, and actually reinforcing, the already existing spatial divisions within the social architecture of places in the urban landscape. These high-tech enclaves and premium network spaces, secured and highly fortified by smart urban design and security technologies, exist in stark contrast to the abandoned landscapes of the excluded. The technologically driven spatial restructuring of the contemporary period provides opportunities for greater connectivity *and* secession for some, but it also simultaneously produces greater social and economic marginalization for many others. These groups are not only frequently denied access to the services of the Information Age but they also may become the objects of surveillance and policing by the very same technologies of freedom which are 'liberating' the lives of the wired-up and connected. As Gumpert and Drucker argue, 'the more we detach from our immediate surroundings, the more we rely on surveillance of that environment', with the result being that 'homes in many urban areas of the world now exist to protect their inhabitants, not to integrate people with their communities' (Gumpert and Drucker 1998: 429). One architectural firm promoting home network technologies seems to confirm this in their claim that 'a smart house is wired, sensuous, but also a security compound' (Week 1997).

In this sense, increasing technological surveillance of public space is paralleled by increased security around the domestic dwelling. Indeed, according to recent research, security is the most appealing aspect of smart house technology for many consumers. In the United States in the late 1990s, 20 per cent of homes had electronic security systems installed (Callaghan 1996). Video surveillance is now a boom industry in most industrialized nations, and more and more applications of smart technology are being channeled into the service of home security.

The smart house – decentralized, individualized and privatized yet also a modulating, open site tied to information flows and networks – provides a key focal point through which to view the increasingly direct role of media and communications technologies in both reconfiguring the boundaries of the home, and in more generally shaping new spatial configurations of social life. Traditional modes of social interaction and urban habitation are profoundly altered by networked infrastructures and media technologies. Yet far from the dissolution of boundaries and the emergence of a domestic space without borders, what we can see is the highly controlled interplay of presence and absence, interiority and exteriority, along with a redefinition of what public and private spaces and activities might actually mean. What is significant then in the context of the smart house is precisely the new manipulations of both time and space: the promise of technologies to enable individual empowerment and connectivity, while simultaneously enhancing surveillance, isolation and control.

Notes

1 The article 'The House of the Future is Here Today' describes a smart house built by British home-builder Laing Homes and a technology company, Cisco, in Watford, north of London: 'it's packed with technology, including video conferencing; TV sets that double as Internet dataports; a kitchen computer that keeps track of what's in the refrigerator; multiple security cameras – even a system for starting the coffeepot from any room in the house ... the house has its own Web site which the home-owner can access from anywhere in the world. Using the site, the owner can control the lights, adjust the temperature, check the security cameras, even turn on the garden sprinkler.'

2 In his essay 'The Overexposed City', Virilio argues that 'Constructed space now occurs within an electronic topology ... Replacing the old distinctions between public and private and "habitation" and "circulation" is an overexposure in which the gap between "near" and "far" ceases to exist.'

3 Mitchell (1996: 10) argues that 'geography is destiny' but communication technologies allow us to finally reclaim and transcend this destiny.

4 See, for example, the essays in Sorkin (1992). Sorkin argues that the new media technologies of 'instant artificial adjacency are rapidly eviscerating the historical politics of propinquity, the very cement of the city' (xi–xv). Similarly, Smart (1992) is concerned that home-centeredness will 'encourage a retreat from public life and public space and serve thereby to increase the sense of insecurity which has become an increasing feature of the "postmodern" urban environment' (530).

5 Friedman (1999: 168–9) cites a recent report which states that in Silicon Valley in 1998 power was measured not by PCs per household but by 'degree of connectivity'. This measurement of power applies to both households and countries, with the crucial question being how extensive is a country's bandwidth.

Bibliography

Benjamin, W. (1969) 'The Work of Art in the Age of Mechanical Reproduction', in H. Arendt (ed.), *Illuminations*, New York: Schocken.

—— (1983) 'Paris – Capital of the Nineteenth Century', in *Charles Baudelaire: A Lyric Poet in the Era of High Capitalism*, trans. H. Zohn, London and New York: Verso.

Bogard, W. (1996) *The Simulation of Surveillance: Hypercontrol in Telematic Societies*, Cambridge: Cambridge University Press.

Boyer, C. (1996) *Cybercities: Visual Perception in the Age of Electronic Communication*, New York: Princeton Architectural Press.

—— (1999) 'Crossing Cybercities: Urban Regions and the Cyberspace Matrix', in R. Beauregard and S. Body-Gendrot (eds), *The Urban Moment: Cosmopolitan Essays on the Late Twentieth Century City*, Thousand Oaks, CA: Sage.

Callaghan, G., (1996) 'The New Cocoon', in *The Weekend Australian*. Section: 'SYTE'.

Camphuisen, A. (1999) *Internet World*, Jan./Feb.

Castells, M. (1996) *The Information Age: Economy, Society and Culture I, the Rise of the Network Society*, Oxford: Blackwell.

Cockburn, C. and Dilic, R.F. (eds) (1994) *Bringing Technology Home: Gender and Technology in a Changing Europe*, Buckingham and New York: Open University Press.

de Certeau, M. (1984) 'Walking in the City', in *The Practice of Everyday Life*, trans. S. Rendell, Berkeley: University of California Press.

—— (1985) 'Spatial Practices', in M. Blonsky (ed.), *On Signs*, Oxford: Blackwell: 123–45.

Deleuze, G. (1988) 'Postscript on the Societies of Control', *October* 59: 3–7.

—— (1995) *Negotiations 1972–1990*, trans. M. Joughin, New York: Columbia University Press.

—— (1998) 'Having an Idea in Cinema', in E. Kaufman and K.J. Heller (eds), *Deleuze and Guattari: New Mappings in Politics, Philosophy and Culture*, Minneapolis: University of Minnesota Press.

Doheny-Farina, S. (1996) *The Wired Neighborhood*, New Haven and London: Yale University Press.

Dolinar, L. (2002) 'The Automated Home'. Online, at: <http://www.future.newsday.com/3/fsmart7.htm> (2 November).

Foucault, M. (1979) *Discipline and Punish: The Birth of the Prison*, Harmondsworth: Penguin.

—— (1980) 'Questions on Geography', in C. Gordon (ed.), *Power/Knowledge: Selected Interviews and Other Writings, 1972–1977*, New York: Pantheon.

—— (1986) 'Of Other Spaces', *Diacritics* 16.1: 22–7.

Friedman, T. (1999) *The Lexus and the Olive Tree*, London: HarperCollins.

Galbraith, J. K. (1987) *A History of Economics*, Harmondsworth: Penguin.

Gates, B. (1996) *The Road Ahead*, Harmondsworth: Penguin.

Graham, S. (1999) 'Geographies of Surveillant Simulation', in M. Crang, P. Crang and J. May (eds), *Virtual Geographies: Bodies, Space and Relations*, London and New York: Routledge: 131–48

Graham, S. and Marvin, S. (2001) *Splintering Urbanism: Networked Infrastructures, Technological Mobilities and the Urban Condition*, London and New York: Routledge.

Gumpert, G. and Drucker, S. (1998), 'The Mediated Home in the Global Village', *Communications Research* 25 (4): 422–38.

Haraway, D. (1985) 'A Manifesto for Cyborgs: Science, Technology and Socialist Feminism in the 1980s', *Socialist Review* 80: 65–107.

Harvey, D. (1989) *The Condition of Postmodernity: An Enquiry into the Origins of Cultural Change*, Oxford: Blackwell.

Heidegger, M. (1971) 'The Thing', in *Poetry, Language, Thought*, New York: Harper & Row.

—— (1996) *Being and Time*, trans. J. Stambaugh, Albany, NY: State University of New York Press.

Kelly, K. (1995) *Out of Control: The New Biology of Machines*, London: Fourth Estate.

Lefebvre, H. (1978) 'Reflections on the Politics of Space', in R. Reet (ed.), *Radical Geography*, London: Methuen.

Marling, K.M. (1994) *As Seen on TV: The Visual Culture of Everyday Life in the 1950s*, Cambridge, MA: Harvard University Press.

McLuhan, M. (1964) *Understanding Media: The Extensions of Man*, New York: McGraw Hill.

Mitchell, W.J. (1996) *City of Bits: Space, Place, and the Infobahn*, Cambridge, MA: MIT Press, 1996.

Moores, S. (2000) *Media and Everyday Life in Modern Society*, Edinburgh: Edinburgh University Press.

Morse, M. (1990) 'An Ontology of Everyday Distraction: The Freeway, the Mall, and Television', in P. Mellencamp (ed.), *Logics of Television: Essays in Cultural Criticism*, Bloomington: Indiana State University Press.

Negroponte, N. (1999) 'Being Rural', *Wired*, 7 June.

Nichols, B. (1996) 'The Work of Culture in the Age of Cybernetic Systems', in T. Druckery (ed.), *Electronic Culture: Technology and Visual Representation*, New York: Aperture.

Rheingold, H. (1995) *The Virtual Community*, London: Minerva.

Robbins, B. (ed.) (1993) *The Phantom Public Sphere*, Minneapolis: University of Minnesota Press.

Robins, K. (1999) 'Foreclosing on the City? The Bad Idea of Virtual Urbanism', in J. Downey and J. McGuigan (eds), *Technocities*, London: Sage: 34–59.

Robins, K. and Cornford, J. (1990) 'Bringing it All Back Home', *Futures*: 870–9.

Robins, K. and Webster. F. (1999) *Times of the Technoculture: From the Information Society to the Virtual Life*, London and New York: Routledge.

Roszak, T. (1994) *The Cult of Information*, Berkeley and Los Angeles: University of California Press.

Smart, B. (1992) *Modern Conditions, Postmodern Controversies*, London and New York: Routledge.

Sorkin, M. (1992) *Variations on a Theme-park: The New American City and the End of Public Space*, New York: Noonday Press.

Spigel, L. (1992) *Make Room for TV: Television and the Family Ideal in Postwar America*, Chicago and London: University of Chicago Press.

Toffler, A. (1980) *The Third Wave*, London: Pan Books.

Virilio, P. (1984) 'The Overexposed City', *Zone* 1/2: 14–31.

Week, D. (1997) Urban Innovations 'Smart House' Demonstration.

Williams, R. (1974) *Television: Technology and Cultural Form*, London: Fontana.

14

'TO EACH THEIR OWN BUBBLE'

Mobile spaces of sound in the city

Michael Bull

In the 1950s, in the United States ... teenagers took their dates
to the drive-in movie in their first car. Without leaving their car,
they passed from the sound bubble of the car radio to the visual
bubble of the cinema. Today, the users of Walkmans and cellular
phones, like Baudelaire's stroller, transport their private sphere
with them. They are in an anonymous crowd, listening to the
music they like; they are absent from their home or office yet in
potential telecommunication with the whole world.

(Flichy 1995: 168)

The media do not simply occupy time and space, they also structure
it and give it meaning.

(Livingstone 2002: 81)

The social spaces of urban habitation are being transformed right in front of our
ears. These transformations have slowly crept up on us over the last thirty years
or so, beginning in the 1960s with the placing of the cassette recorder in automobiles, to the development of the Sony Walkman in 1979, culminating in its
most visible manifestation in the mobile phone. People are now buying mobile
phones faster than they bought television sets in the 1950s. An increasing
number of us demand the intoxicating mixture of noise, proximity and privacy
whilst on the move and have the technologies to successfully achieve these
aims. The use of these largely sound technologies informs us about how we
attempt to 'inhabit' the 'public' spaces of the city.

Yet to understand the use and meanings of these mobile and aural technologies we need to situate them within traditional and 'fixed' media technologies
such as the telephone, gramophone, radio and television. These are the technologies of the twentieth century that have largely transformed the activities
and meanings associated with 'being at home'. The use of these more recent
sound technologies, mobile sound systems, mobile phones and personal stereos
has increasingly confounded and questioned the meaning of public and private
spheres of existence and our shifting and often contradictory relationship to
them. It is interesting to note that today many mobile phone users will find the

use of other mobiles in confined spaces annoying yet will use their own phone with impunity in the same spaces. Are they appealing to some idea of a communal space; the right to be left alone in silence; or merely the relativization of their own sense of being wanted?

Does the street conform to what I want it to be as I walk through it using my personal stereo; does the space of habitation in the automobile appear safe and secure to music; does the voice of the absent other transform the spaces of the street for me into one imbued with proximity and connection, and what becomes of the 'others'? In what sense do these users transform the representational space of communication into a mobile and privatized sphere of communication with absent others or the mediated comfort of the culture industry in the form of voice or music? In this chapter, I address the meanings attached to the sounds of the social as they are enacted on 'the move'.

Sounding out privatized space

First, I wish to briefly discuss what is meant by 'private' space. Most people in the West feel entitled to their own 'private space', whether this is in their room, their home, their restaurant table, a certain space on the street or a space around the automobile on the road. The 'entitlement' to 'private space' is entrenched in Western thought, in principle at least since the Enlightenment. Operationalizing this idea of an individualized 'private space', however, increasingly involves the subject in an array of potential contradictions, both domestically and in 'public'.[1]

Private space has often been associated with property, the ownership of space and place. In the UK, the phrase 'an Englishman's home is his castle' still resonates ideologically, even if the state has largely put paid to it as a viable concept. A geographically identifiable space of bricks and mortar would appear easy to define and defend; yet many of us are wary of the 'prying' eyes of neighbours and erect high fences to protect 'our' space from the gaze of others. Less successful are defences against noise. In the UK, for example, an increasing number of people complain about the noise of neighbours, the noise of aircraft flying overhead, the sound of automobiles entering into our domestic spaces of habitation. The defence against the seepage of noise into one's private space is virtually impossible; sound in its multidimensionality has no respect of space. One resorts to increasing the sound of one's television or sound system, thus increasing the general noise level. Today, noise pollution in British cities is ten times greater than it was a decade ago. In 2002, the UK Noise Association (NSCA 2002) claimed that 32 million people in Britain were exposed to high levels of noise. Noise tests one's notion of the social to its limits.

If the idea of 'private space' is increasingly difficult to maintain even in fixed habitats, then the problem increases whilst we are out on the move. Simmel was perhaps the first sociologist to attempt to explain the significance and desire to maintain a sense of privacy, to create a mobile bubble, whilst on the move. Simmel's concerns were with sensory overload, crowds, strangers and the noisy maelstrom of the city from which citizens retreated. In his analysis, Simmel charted the changing nature of bourgeois civility within the increasingly technologized urban geography of the early twentieth century, addressing the relational nature and problems associated with people continually on the move in the city (Simmel 1997). These concerns took a special form in the twentieth century, namely, the search for aural privacy, made possible by new and mobile media technologies.

A dialectic of noise and privacy in the city

Ever-present sound was not always a requirement for 'retreat' as it tends to be today. In the nineteenth century, middle-class train travellers found the activity of reading sufficient to create their 'private bubble'. These readers were motivated both by the boredom of travel – they were disconnected from the world beyond the window of the speeding train – and by the discomfort experienced by the seating arrangements within the carriages where they were obliged to look at a changing array of passengers opposite them.[2] Yet, historically, the construction of a 'private bubble' of experience often required a level of silence, often institutionalized, as in prohibitions on talking loudly in library reading rooms or, more recently, in cinemas and concert halls. Silence, indeed, has long been thought to be a precondition for thought. Rousseau, as early as the eighteenth century, describes escaping to the countryside to escape the noise of the city in order to be alone with his thoughts (Rousseau 1979). Silence has not, however, been a very successful strategy in the streets, despite a healthy history of noise abatement campaigns (Bijsterveld 2001). With the development of modern road systems and millions of automobiles, this option is now harder to find as millions of us travel to get away from it all, in grid-locked unison (Brandon 2002; Sachs 1992). However, many are not seeking 'silence' but their own, very personalized noise or soundscape.

The dominant view, however, held by many urbanists is that we have fallen silent in the urban street (Sennett 1994). Sennett describes the twentieth-century city as one in which we have become increasingly immersed in our own concerns, passively moving in silence, looking but neither understanding nor recognizing the 'differences' that confront us. The city, according to this view, is increasingly experienced as a 'non-space' (Auge 1995). For others, in contrast, the street has become an aestheticized space (Jenks 1995), in which the street becomes 'spectacle'; a potential visual emporium of delight (Debord 1977; De Certeau 1988). Elsewhere, I have discussed the redundancy of *flânerie* as a contemporary concept, and whilst the notion of 'aestheticization' has potentially great explanatory power in explaining aspects of urban experience, it need not contradict the notion of 'aural solipsism' through which subjects experience the street mimetically, aesthetically making it 'their own' (Bull 2000).

An analysis of the use of mobile sound communication technologies permits me to point to both a continuum within Western urban experience, and a shift that has taken place over the past thirty years. The continuum represents new developments in the search for public privacy and a discounting of the 'public' realm, whilst the transformation lies in urban citizens' increasing ability and desire to make the 'public' spaces of the city conform to their notion of the 'domestic' or the 'intimate', either literally or conceptually. As we increasingly inhabit 'media saturated' spaces of intimacy, so we increasingly desire to make the public spaces passed through mimic our desires, thus, ironically, furthering the absence of meaning attributed to those spaces. We no longer desire quiet, but noise! We demand our own space, but increasingly discount the space of others. Richard Sennett's urban street is now inhabited with people exposing their private lives in public through their mobile phones, largely indifferent to others, whilst some walk past in their aural solipsistic dreams using their personal stereos. Meanwhile, automobile drivers pass by often engrossed in listening to their sophisticated car sound systems or talking on their mobile phones.

Much of our movement through the city is solitary, in-between destinations and meetings. Sole occupancy is often the preferred mode of travel in automobiles throughout Europe and North America (Brodsky 2002; Putnam 2000), whilst personal stereos are by their very nature a largely privatizing technology. Meanwhile, mobile phone users are able to fill the 'empty' urban spaces of the city with their 'own' reassuring noises (Puro 2002). As such, I restrict my discussion here to 'solitary' movement through the city. The use of these technologies binds together the disparate threads of much urban movement for users, both 'filling' the spaces 'in-between' communication or meetings and structuring the spaces thus occupied. The use of sound, music and speech whilst on the move, whether it be in automobiles, through personal stereos or on mobile phones, is usefully understood as representing wider social transformations in everyday life. The intimate nature of an industrialized soundworld in the form of radio sounds (Tacchi 1999; Hendy 2000), recorded music, and television (Livingstone 2002) increasingly represents large parts of a privatized everyday lifeworld of urban citizens. This impacts upon habitual everyday notions of what it might mean to 'inhabit' certain spaces such as the automobile, the street, the shopping arcade (DeNora 2000; McCarthy 2001), or indeed the living room (Livingstone 2002; Silverstone 1994).

In this chapter, I seek to pose a dialectical relationship between media-generated forms of intimacy and the non-spaces of urban culture by arguing that the greater the need for proximity and connection, as expressed through the use of mobile communication technologies, the more alienating the public spaces of daily existence become.[3]

Mediated intimacy/displaced places

From home to street, from private setting to public arena, the media have helped us link these two areas of daily life together in unexpected ways. Whilst there has been much discussion on the nature of space/time compression involved in the use of communications technologies, from the telegraph to the Internet, and on the privatizing potential of television (Harvey 1996; Winston 1998), most empirical research involving the use of these technologies has focused solely upon domestic consumption in fixed locales – in an assumption that media effects and influences stop at the front door! Alternatively, urban geographers often ignore or discount the media as unimportant in discussing the geography of the street.

Some theorists, however, understood that the very meaning of what it is to 'look' or 'hear' is irredeemably media linked. Both Walter Benjamin (1973) and Theodor Adorno (1973) recognized this in their own way, the former focusing on the visual, the latter on the aural. Adorno recognized that sound technologies transform our understanding of proximity, for example, employing the term 'we-ness' in his discussion of sound recordings in the 1930s and 1940s:

> By circling them, by enveloping them as inherent in the musical phenomena – and turning them as listeners into participants, it contributes ideologically to the integration which modern society never tires of achieving in reality. It leaves no room for conceptual reflection between itself and the subject, and so it creates an illusion of immediacy in a totally mediated world, of proximity between strangers, the warmth of those who come to feel a chill of unmitigated struggle of all against all.
>
> (Horkheimer and Adorno 1973: 46)

Increasingly, this sense of 'intimacy' appears to be associated, although not exclusively, with a wide variety of forms of domestic media consumption:

> The fostering of 'we-ness,' dialogical inclusion, and intimate address have remained at the core of broadcasting to this day. ... The early history of broadcast talk consisted largely in the attempt to create a world in which audiences would feel like participants. Today both the programming and reception of most commercial media, in the United States at least, actively cultivate a sense of intimate relations between persona and audience. Media culture is a lush jungle of fictional worlds where 'everyone knows your name,' celebrities and politicians address audiences by first names, and conversational formats proliferate.
>
> (Peters 1999: 215–17)

Claude Lefort has referred to this media phenomenon in similar terms to Adorno, as a 'constant illusion of a between-*us*, an entre-*nous*' in which the media 'provokes an hallucination of nearness which abolishes a sense of distance, strangeness, imperceptibility ... of otherness' (Lefort, quoted in Merck 1998: 109).

Raymond Williams understood this phenomena in terms of 'mobile privatization'. Not the street, but our living rooms, and increasingly our bedrooms, become emporiums of visual and auditory delight. Recently, Sonia Livingstone (2002) has charted the consumption of the media among teenagers within the home. She found that teenagers increasingly liked to consume the media privately, whether television or music: 'The home increasingly becomes the site for individualised media consumption with children spending the majority of their home media use alone in their bedrooms' (Livingstone 2002: 40).

Sole consumption is both pleasurable (especially as compared to consuming with parents) and controllable. Moreover, domestic consumption appears to fuel feelings of omnipotence, as there is no one there to contradict the consumer. Equally, domestic use teaches consumers how to 'fill in' the spaces and times between activities. We increasingly become used to the mediated presence of the media in our own privatized settings.

The desire for company or 'occupancy' whilst moving through the city is thus contextualized through the daily or habitual use of a variety of media. The array of mobile sound media increasingly enables users to successfully maintain a sense of intimacy whilst moving through the city. How, then, do these mobile technologies simulate the intimate spaces of habitation desired by many of our urban users of mobile sound technologies?

Intimate auto-mobility

> Today the highway might well be the site of radio's most captive audiences, its most attentive audience. The car is likely to be your most intensive radio-listening experience, perhaps even your most intensive media experience altogether. Usually radio is a background medium, but in the car it becomes all-pervasive, all consuming ... the car radio envelops you in its own space, providing an infinite soundtrack for the external landscape that scrapes the windshield. The sound of radio fills up the car, encapsulates you in walls made of words.
>
> (Loktev 1993: 203)

When Baudrillard coined the phrase 'to each their own bubble', he was thinking visually. In mobile terms, cities are said to float by as some kind of filmic embodiment (Baudrillard 1989). The daily act of television viewing shifts to the everyday mobile spectatorship of the occupants of automobiles watching the world through the transparent barrier of the windscreen, hermetically sealed off from the duress of the world beyond the screen. The interior of the automobile is likened to a moving living room from which to view the world, a 'phantasmagoria of the interior'. In this way, it is claimed that the visual nature of auto-mobility increases the conceptual distance between the interior (for this read private or domestic space) of the automobile and the world beyond: the public spaces through which we travel (Morse 1998).

Yet sound plays an altogether more 'intimate' role in automobile experience than vision:[4]

> When I get in my car and turn on my radio, I'm at home. I haven't got a journey to make before I get home. I'm already home. I shut my door, turn on my radio and I'm home.
>
> (Jay)

> I can't even start my car without music being on. It's automatic. Straight away, amplifiers turned on. Boom boom!
>
> (Kerry)

> Being inside my car is like, this is my little world, it's my car, it's getting away from work, any hassles I've got … it's an opportunity for me to let my mind focus on all sorts of different things, I might be thinking about work, I might be thinking about relationships, I might be thinking about family. It's because I'm in my own little bubble, in my car that's an environment and I'm in complete control of all the distractions around me.
>
> (Lucy)

Sound technologies make the automobile more 'habitable'. Pleasure and sound increasingly appear to go together as drivers use their car radio and music systems. Recently, Brodsky (2002) found that 'the automobile is currently the most popular and frequent location for listening to music'. Equally, many drivers prefer listening to music in their automobiles whilst alone (Sloboda 1999). Automobiles are potentially one of the most perfectible of acoustic listening chambers. Unlike living rooms where manufacturers cannot control room size, furnishings and numbers of people, it is possible for acoustic designers to create a uniformly pleasant listening environment (Bose 1984). Speakers in the car's front, rear, or in the seats themselves produce an aurally satisfying listening booth:

> I'm in a nice sealed, compact space. … I like my sounds up loud, it's all around you. It's not like walking around the kitchen where the sounds are not quite as I want them.
>
> (Trudy)

The automobile becomes a successful and personalized listening environment that is difficult to replicate in other domestic or public spaces unless one uses a personal stereo. The more sound the more immersive the experience. These feelings are enhanced by sole occupancy, which also permits the driver to have a greater feeling of control and management over his or her environment, mood, thoughts and space beyond the gaze of 'others'. As Trudy comments, 'I can sit back in my car, enjoy the drive, listen to my sounds, not have to talk.' And Lisa:

> I can concentrate on the driving. I do really get quite absorbed in driving. I can listen to the radio or have the music on as a sort of atmosphere provoking thing. Whereas if someone else is in the car I feel I shouldn't have the music on cause you can't hear them and I can't stand that, fighting for noise or quiet. I also find it more relaxing driving on my own because I don't need to worry about them being uncomfortable and feeling that I'm going too fast.

Instead, drivers often prefer to be accompanied by the reassuring voice of the radio:

> There's something about R4 [BBC Radio 4] that's just something about the tone, style and delivery that's very reassuring and comforting. That you know the voices are the same, well they're not always the same but they have the same kind of delivery, that particular style ... it's also the routine.
>
> (Sarah)

The aural space of the automobile becomes a safe and intimate environment inhabited by the mediated presence through 'sound' of consumer culture. The mobile and contingent nature of the journey is experienced precisely as its opposite, whereby the driver controls the journey precisely by controlling the inner environment of the automobile through sound.

Automobiles are also increasingly being used as spaces of interpersonal communication between drivers and 'absent' others.[5] Paradoxically, whilst many drivers prefer to be alone in their automobile, increasing numbers also report using their driving time to communicate directly with others:

> I hold the phone to my ear. ... I often use it to catch up with people that I haven't spoken to for a while. It's a time when I know I'm going to be in the car for a while. I have had journeys that...may have been three hours long and I have spoken to three people during the journey, one for forty-five minutes, another for half an hour, so I may have spent virtually the whole journey talking on the phone.
>
> (Lucy)

Using a mobile phone permits drivers to maintain social contacts during 'road' time. Time and journey are thus transformed into an intimate 'one-to-one' time:

> It's a good way to spend your time, talking and catching up. If I get bored, I'll just put it onto my list – list of numbers. I will just flit through and … say, I haven't spoken to that person for ages … so the people at the beginning or the end of the alphabet do quite well!
>
> (Jane)

If users of mobile phones in the street transform representational space into their own privatized space as they converse with absent others, then this scene is replicated in the everyday use of mobile phones in automobiles. The automobile becomes a mobile, privatized and sophisticated communication machine through which the driver can choose whether to work, socialize or pass the time. As such, the mobile phone adds to the armoury of available aural technologies in the automobile, thus making it a perfect home-from-home.

Intimate streets: the personal stereo

Users of personal stereos also move in their own privatized soundworld. Like automobile drivers, they too can achieve the illusion of omnipotence through proximity and 'connectedness':

> It enables me to sort of bring my own dreamworld. Because I have familiar sounds with my music that I know and sort of cut out people around me. So the music is familiar. There's nothing new happening. I can go into my perfect dreamworld where everything is as I want.
>
> (Magnus)

Personal stereo use reorganizes users' relation to space and place. Sound colonizes the listener, but it is also used to actively re-create and reconfigure the spaces of experience. Through the power of sound the world becomes intimate, known and possessed. This points to the powerfully seductive role of sound, which appears to root users in the world with a force that differs from the other senses (Simmel 1997; Welsch 1997). Sound enables users to manage and orchestrate their spaces of habitation in a manner that conforms to their desires. The sound of the personal stereo is direct, with headphones placed directly in the ears of the user, thereby overlaying the random sounds of the environment passed through with privatized sounds. Personal stereo users construct their own privatized and intimate space of reception:

> It fills the space whilst you're walking. It also changes the atmosphere. If you listen to music you really like and you're feeling depressed it can change the atmosphere around you.
>
> (Catherine)

I think it creates a sense of kind of aura. Even though it's directly in your ears you feel it's all around your head. You're really aware it's just you. Only you can hear it. I'm really aware of my personal space. My own space anyway. I find it quite weird watching things that you normally associate certain sounds with. Like the sounds of walking up and down the stairs or tubes coming in and out, all of those things you hear. Like when you've got a Walkman on you don't hear any of those. You've got your own soundtrack.

(Karin)

Personal stereo users experience the world as a form of 'we-ness' whilst on the move:

I don't necessarily feel that I'm there. Especially if I'm listening to the radio. I feel I'm there, where the radio is, because of the way, that is, he's [the DJ is] talking to me and only me and no one else around me is listening to that. So I feel like, I know I'm really on the train, but I'm not really. ... I like the fact that there's someone still there.

(Mandy)

Yet personal stereo users, in their 'colonization' of space, are equally concerned with solipsistically transcending the urban. If indeed they aestheticize it, they do so by drawing it into themselves, making it conform to their wishes, to be more like themselves. 'Personal space' for users can be defined in terms of a non-spatialized conceptual space. As geographical notions of personal space become harder to substantiate and negotiate in some urban environments, the construction of a privatized conceptual space becomes a common strategy for personal stereo users:

Personal space. I think personal space is gone, in town anyway. Everyone's packed in. I think it's inverted. Because I think your personal space is inside, in the music. You can be in a crowd in town and everybody's crunching up. If you listen to the Walkman, it doesn't really matter that someone's pushing up behind you.

(Paul)

Here, Paul has already discounted geographical notions of private space. For him space is conceptual, existing inside; in the music. By focusing on this conceptual notion of space, the geographical aspect of space ceases to be of primary concern as it is replaced by a privatized, conceptual space 'in the music'.

Personal stereo users are often indifferent to the presence of others: 'When you've got your Walkman on it's like a wall. Decoration. Surroundings. It's not anyone' (Ed). The metaphor here of a 'wall' aptly demonstrates the impenetrability of many users' state, or desired state, in relation to the geographical space of experience. Personal stereo users appear to achieve a subjective sense of public invisibility. The users essentially 'disappear' as interacting subjects withdrawing into various states of the purely subjective.

The space of reception might be described as a form of mobile home. The 'outside' world becomes a function of the desire of the user and is maintained through time through the act of listening. The world is brought into line, but only through a privatized, yet mediated, act of cognition. The users' sense of space is one in which the distinction between private mood or orientation and their surroundings is abolished. The world becomes one with the experience of the personal stereo user.

Intimate sounds of the voice

Mobile phone use is a recent addition to the transformation of public space. Over one billion people now use mobile phones world-wide, with over 70 per cent of the UK population possessing at least one mobile phone. Mobile phones, like other successful consumer technologies, tap into pre-existing, everyday, desires. The desire to be always available; I talk therefore I exist! 'All that separates desolation from elation is a phone call' (Peters 1999: 201).

Mobile phones have quickly become both habitual and necessary for most users, as these comments attest: 'I really don't know how anybody met anyone without mobile phones' (Catherine). 'I just feel lost if I don't have my phone on me' (Sally). Whilst text messaging is also frequently used, nothing quite substitutes for the sound of the voice.[6] The telephone has long been recognized for its intimate qualities (Fischer 1992). The power of intimacy within a spectrum of routinized voices is graphically articulated in the following account of the playwright Arthur Miller, who describes talking to his wife-to-be, Marilyn Monroe, on a landline, of course:

> The motel owner woke me one night to tell me I was wanted on the phone ... her voice [Marilyn Monroe's] was barely audible. ... I kept trying to reassure her, but she seemed to be sinking where I could not reach her, her voice growing fainter. I was losing her ... and suddenly I realized I was out of breath, a dizziness screwing into my head, my knees unlocking, and I felt myself sliding to the floor of the booth, the receiver slipping out of my hands. I came to in what was probably a few seconds, her voice still whispering out of the receiver over my head. ... We would marry and start a new and real life once this picture was done. ... Yes and yes and yes and it was all over, and the healing silence of the desert swept back and covered it all. I left the highway behind me and walked toward the two cottages and the low moon. I had never fainted before. I loved her as though I had loved her all my life; her pain was my pain. My blood seemed to have spoken. The low lunar mountains outside my window, the overarching silence of this

285

terrain of waste and immanence – I felt my happiness like a live glow
in all this dead, unmoving space.

(Miller 1987: 380)

The space between Hollywood, from where Monroe calls, to the Nevada desert,
where Miller receives the call, is transformed by the power of the voice into an
erotic space of aural reception, a privatized soundworld inhabited only by Miller
and Monroe. Whilst this is an 'exceptional' example, it displays the intimate
power of the voice that is re-enacted daily in more routine and mundane
settings. Mobile phone use enables us to enact these intimate voice scenarios in
public and on the move:

> When I am surrounded by people I don't know I can easily connect
> with a familiar voice. ... So speaking on my mobile phone enables me
> to distance myself from an uncomfortable situation and brings me
> closer to a feeling of ease.
>
> (Amy)

For many users, the space of reception becomes re-inscribed and colonized by
the voice of the other. Public speech to an 'absent other' has had to overcome
the inhibitions created by Western cultures that have traditionally put much
stock on the right to have secrets, or to have a personal life beyond the ears and
eyes of others. Yet mobile phone use seems increasingly to deny these preroga-
tives of Western-based cultures. Looked at in another way, we might argue that
the desire to be 'connected' is more important than issues of 'privacy' for many
users, or that notions of a meaningful 'public' have already been so discounted
that it is 'as if' no one else is there to eavesdrop.

Although personal stereo users engage in forms of pleasurable mobile solipsism whilst connected to the mediated messages of the culture industry, mobile
phone users' strategy for being connected is to make a call, or to make sure that
their phone is always switched on so that they are always available to receive a
message. The world might indeed be perceived to be full of pregnant messages!

To speak in public is to transform that space. The relational qualities of the
space become transformed both in the orientation of the user and for others
who are able to 'involuntarily' listen. Users often discount notions of 'listening'
others whilst making phone calls:

> When I'm on the phone it's – I'm concentrating, I'm talking to this
> person I'm talking to and what's going on around me is of secondary ...
> In my own little world. I'm not particularly aware – I work on the
> assumption that these people don't know me, I don't know them, so
> they can only hear one half of the conversation and it's not going to be
> particularly interesting to them anyway.
>
> (Lucy)

Whilst notions of public reserve still occur, they appear to be diminishing. Recent research indicates that the meanings attached to public space amongst many mobile phone users is converging, despite other cultural differences:

> There is virtually no place where Israelis do not use their mobile phone: on public buses and trains, in restaurants, banks, offices, clinics, theatres and classrooms, and of course in the street. Judging by its omnipresence, it seems that there are few limits and restrictions that people abide by. In fact, it is not uncommon for people to use their mobile phone in places where it is prohibited by law, such as in certain parts of hospitals and gas stations.
>
> (Schejter and Cohen 2002: 40)

> Filling public transportation space with chatter, which is virtually nothing but noise to her neighbouring passengers, the phone caller does not seem inclined to restrain her telephone behaviour. Not so long ago, it was normally considered shameful to talk about private business in public. ... These manners seem to have evaporated in this era of perpetual contact.
>
> (Shin Dong Kim 2002: 65)

What we are witnessing today is a profound change in the way many people engage with notions of the public. Mobile phones act to privatize public spaces (Puro 2002) as private discourse fills the street, classroom and every other conceivable public space. In so doing, speakers 'absent' themselves from the spaces they inhabit. In a world where most of us are talking to 'absent others', the street becomes a potentially lonelier place (Harper 2002: 212). Mobile phone use appears to encourage the privatization of public space:

> The use of the mobile phone amplifies the process already under way of ever more frequent exposure of private matters and intimacy in the public sphere. In an interesting counterpoint, though, it also represents the encroachment of intimacy on the territory of extraneousness and of the private on the public.
>
> (Fortunati 2002: 48)

Within this public isolation we are, however, available all of the time, with mothers checking on their children, lovers checking on each other, and employers checking on employees. This 'we-ness' can also be 'fusional' in the efforts to possess and track down one another more effectively. Yet recipients also have the power to disengage, switch off, put us on hold. However, by invoking the perpetual possibility of contact the mobile phone gives the illusion of power to users (De Gournay 2002), in the same way that the home gives the illusion of 'privacy' to its occupants.

Conclusion

> Individual bodies moving through urban space gradually became detached from the space in which they moved, and from the people the space contained. As space became devalued through motion, individuals gradually lost a sense of sharing a fate with others ... individuals create something like ghettos in their own bodily experience.
>
> (Sennett 1994: 324)

> We might conceive a series leading from the man who cannot work without the blare of the radio to the one who kills time and paralyses loneliness by filling his ears with the illusion of 'being with' no matter what.
>
> (Adorno 1991: 78)

In the introduction to this chapter, I asked in what sense do users of mobile phones, personal stereos and sound systems in automobiles transform the representational spaces of the city into a mobile and privatized sphere of communication. These technologies all permit a reorganization of public and private realms of experience where what is traditionally conceived of as 'private' experience is brought out into public realms in the act of individualized listening or talking. These technologies permit users to prioritize their experience in relation to their geographical, social and interpersonal environment, enabling them to exist, in a variety of ways, within their own private sound-world. The site of experience is, therefore, reconstituted variably through the medium of the personal stereo, the automobile and the mobile phone.

The use of these technologies demonstrates a clear auditory reconceptualization of the spaces of habitation embodied in users' strategies of placing themselves 'elsewhere' in urban environments. Users tend to negate public spaces through their prioritization of their own technologically mediated private realm. The use of these technologies enables users to transform the site of their experience into a form of 'sanctuary' (Sennett 1994). Thus users are able to transcend geometrical space through the use of these mobile sound technologies. The nature of this technologized space is often experienced as all-engulfing, enabling the space of habitation to be infused with its own sense of heightened experiential aura. Users habitually exist within forms of accompanied solitude constructed through a manufactured auditory environment, either through mediated music or the voice of the 'other'. The attempted exclusion of all forms of intrusion constitutes a successful strategy for urban and personal management, a re-inscribing of personal space through forms of 'sound' communication. In so doing, users re-claim representational spaces precisely by privatizing them. Representational space has often been perceived for its engulfing or colonizing properties. Lefebvre's original formulation implies this:

Living bodies, the bodies of 'users' – are caught up not only in the toils of parcelized space, but also in the web of what philosophers call 'analogons'; images, signs, symbols. These bodies are transported out of themselves, transferred and emptied out, as it were, via the eyes: every kind of appeal, incitement and seduction is mobilized to tempt them with doubles of themselves in prettified, smiling and happy poses; this campaign to void them succeeds exactly to the degree that the images proposed correspond to the 'needs' that those same images have helped fashion. So it is that a massive influx of information, of messages, runs head into an inverse flow constituted by the evacuation from the innermost body of all life and desire. Even cars may fulfil the functions of analogons, for they are at once extensions of the body and mobile homes, so to speak, fully equipped to receive these wandering bodies.

(Lefebvre 1991: 99)

Lefebvre concentrates on the visual nature of the street here, in which space becomes saturated, thus 'voiding' subjects of the occupancy of their own experience. Yet my analysis of mobile sound media use suggests that consumers actively use these media to re-inscribe the meanings of the spaces they inhabit. Indeed, they use them often to discount them altogether into the spaces of speech, as in mobile phone use, or use sound to blank out or manage their space of habitation, as in personal stereo use. Automobile users often claim that the spaces they habitually travel through hold little interest for them. They 'look' for the purposes of driving, of course, but prefer to be otherwise engaged with the sounds of music or voice.

Auge (1995) has argued that urban dwellers experience time in the continual present, being subject to the prescribed sounds of the shopping mall, airport lounge or the car radio where everything is repeated and everything feels disconnected from place in the non-places of everyday culture. To exist in these public non-places is like being suspended in the continual present. However, this mistakes the shopping mall and the airport for the automobile interior and, of course, even in the shopping mall one can use a personal stereo or mobile phone.

Automobile habitation provides the driver with his or her own regulated soundscape that mediates his or her experience of these non-places and manages the flow of time as he or she wishes. The meaning of these non-places is overlaid by the mediated space of the automobile from which meaning emanates. Drivers can choose the manner in which they attend to these non-places.

The aural space of the automobile becomes a safe and intimate environment. The mobile and contingent nature of the journey is experienced precisely as its opposite, in which the driver controls the journey precisely by controlling the inner environment of the automobile through sound. Much of this is true for personal stereo users who also reconfigure their relationship to the world through sound. They feel empowered and safe – but only for so long as the music plays, whilst mobile phones offer the availability of the voice no matter where.[7]

It would appear that as we become more and more immersed in our mobile media sound bubbles of communication, so then those spaces we habitually pass through in our daily lives increasingly lose significance and progressively turn into the 'non-spaces' of daily lives which we try, through those selfsame technologies, to transcend. The need for proximity either through speech with an absent other or through the mediated sounds of the culture industry masks and furthers the trend of public isolation in the midst of privatized sound bubbles of a reconfigured representational space. In a world of increasing mobility, technology provides a successful and intimate fix for consumers. Yet in the creation of these 'aural solipsistic ghettos' we increasingly appear to enact strategies that deny the recognition of 'difference' encountered in our everyday world (Sennett 1990). The movement through urban space in mediated and privatized 'sonorous envelopes' (Anzieu 1989) may well produce and bolster-up feelings of empowerment. Yet these fragile and often alienating strategies may well be self-defeating in an urban world in which physical proximity and everyday movement are still the a priori grounds upon which much of daily life is founded.

Notes

1   Of course, definitions of private space differ. A culture with no notion of entitlement to space in public would have very little 'road rage', as in India for example. The contradictions involved in defining and maintaining 'private space' whilst driving are described by Adorno: 'And which driver is not tempted, merely by the power of the engine, to wipe out the vermin on the street, pedestrians, children and cyclists?' (Adorno 1974: 40). This, perhaps the first description of 'road rage' (Adorno wrote this in 1942), captures the contradictory nature of the automobile embodied in everyday use whereby the driver is simultaneously all-powerful yet controlled.

2   Schivelbusch charts the popularity of reading habits on trains in the nineteenth century: 'the face to face arrangement that had once institutionalised an existing need for communication now became unbearable because there no longer was a reason for such communication. The seating in the railroad compartment forced travellers into a relationship based no longer on living need but on embarrassment. … As we have seen, the perusal of reading matter is an attempt to replace the conversation that is no longer possible. Fixing one's eyes to a book or newspaper, one is able to avoid the stare of the person sitting across the aisle. The embarrassing nature of this silent situation remains largely unconscious' (Schivelbusch 1986: 74–5).

3   This is not to imply that all spaces become 'emptied' of meaning. Parts of the city, such as Covent Garden in London, also become arenas of spectacles with an array of performance artists performing before a mobile public. I am more concerned to articulate the meaning of the mundane and everyday nature of much urban experience.

4   The following interview extracts are drawn from a series of qualitative interviews of Walkman users (1995–1998), automobile users (1999–2001) and mobile phone users (2001–2002) carried out in London, Cambridge and Brighton by the author.

5   Despite the widespread use of mobile phones in automobiles there has been almost no study undertaken on the subject. Recent work on mobile phone use fails to mention automobiles (Katz and Aakhus 2002), despite the fact that increasing numbers of drivers report using the phone whilst driving. The Transport Research Laboratory Report, undertaken for Tesco Insurance Company in 2002, found that use in the UK varied according to the age of the driver: 34 per cent of all people say

that they make calls from cars – 52 per cent aged between 25 and 34 years, and 16 per cent aged between 55 and 64 years (*Guardian*, 22 March 2002, p. 11).

6   Whilst I discuss the role that sound plays in notions of proximity in mobile phone use, I do not discount its other functions such as text messaging. Many users prefer to text precisely because there is no sound and therefore it is more 'private'. Texting can be done beyond the surveillance of others at work or in the back of the classroom.

7   To be sure, the use of mobile sound technologies has also impacted upon how women perceive and experience the public spaces of the city. Female Walkman users, for example, often feel empowered, both by being 'accompanied' by the friendly sounds of music and by developing strategies of non-reciprocal gazing through the use of the Walkman (see Bull 2000, especially chapter 6). Equally, women have embraced the mobile phone on a par with men, often using it as a security device, despite the apparent dangers of using these technologies in public. More women are now driving than ever before, and this is not necessarily connected to extensions of the traditional domestic role occupied by women (Brandon 2002).

Bibliography

Adorno, T. (1974) *Minima Moralia: Reflections on a Damaged Life*, London: New Left Books.

—— (1976) *Introduction to the Sociology of Music*, New York: Continuum Press.

—— (1991) *The Culture Industry: Selected Essays on Mass Culture*, London: Routledge.

Anzieu, D. (1989) *The Skin Ego*, New Haven: Yale University Press.

Arato, A. and Gebhardt, E. (eds) (1992) *The Essential Frankfurt School Reader*, New York: Continuum Press.

Auge, M. (1995) *Non-places: Introduction to Anthropology of Supermodernity*, London: Verso.

Baudrillard, J. (1989) *America*, London: Verso.

—— (1993) *Symbolic Exchange and Death*, London: Sage.

Bauman, Z. (1993) *Postmodern Ethics*, Oxford: Blackwell.

Bijsterveld, K. (2001) 'The Diabolical Symphony of the Mechanical Age', *Social Studies of Science* 31 (1): 37–70.

Bose, A. (1984) 'Hifi for GM Cars', lecture to EECS Seminar, 19 March, published as 2 audiocassettes. MIT Archives, MC 261.

Brandon, R. (2002) *Automobile: How the Car Changed Life*, Basingstoke: Macmillan Press.

Brodsky, W. (2002) 'The Effects of Music Tempo on Simulated Driving Performance and Vehicular Control', in *Transportational Research Part F*, Oxford: Pergamon Press: 219–41.

Brown, B., Green, N. and Harper, R. (eds) (2002) *Wireless World: Social and Interactional Aspects of the Mobile Age*, London: Springer.

Bull, M. (2000) *Sounding Out the City: Personal Stereos and the Management of Everyday Life*, Oxford: Berg.

—— (2001) 'Soundscapes of the Car: A Critical Ethnography of Automobile Habitation', in D. Miller (ed.), *Car Cultures*, Oxford: Berg.

Debord, G. (1977) *Society of the Spectacle*, Detroit: Black and Red.

DeNora, T. (2000) *Music and Everyday Life*, Cambridge: Cambridge University Press.

Flichy, P. (1995) *Dynamics of Modern Communication: The Shaping and Impact of New Communication Technologies*, London: Sage.

Fortunati, L. (2002) 'Italy: Stereotypes, True and False', in J. Katz and M. Aakhus (eds), *Perpetual Contact: Mobile Communication, Private Talk, Public Performance*, Cambridge: Cambridge University Press.

Frisby, D. and Featherstone, M. (eds) (1997) *Simmel on Culture*, London: Sage.

Harper, R. (2002) 'The Mobile Interface: Old Technologies and New Arguments', in B. Brown, N. Green and R. Harper (eds), *Wireless World: Social and Interactional Aspects of the Mobile Age*, London: Springer.

Harvey, D. (1996) *Justice, Nature and the Geography of Difference*, Oxford: Blackwell.

Hendy, D. (2000) *Radio and the Global Age*, Cambridge: Polity Press.

Horkheimer, M. and Adorno, T. (1973) *The Dialectic of Enlightenment*, Harmondsworth: Penguin.

Jarviluoma, H. (ed.) (1994) *Soundscapes: Essays on Vroom and Moo*, Tampere: Tampere University Press.

Jenks, C. (ed.) (1995) *Visual Culture*, London: Routledge.

Katz, J. (1999) *Connections: Social and Cultural Studies of the Telephone in American Life*, London: Transactional Publishers.

Katz, J. and Aakhus, M. (eds) (2002) *Perpetual Contact: Mobile Communication, Private Talk, Public Performance*, Cambridge: Cambridge University Press.

Kay, K. (1997) *Asphalt Nation: How the Automobile Took Over America and How We Can Take it Back*, Berkeley: University of California Press.

Kim, Shin Dong (2002) 'Korea: Personal Meanings', in J. Katz and M. Aakhus (eds), *Perpetual Contact: Mobile Communication, Private Talk, Public Performance*, Cambridge: Cambridge University Press.

Lefebvre, H. (1991) *The Production of Space*, Oxford: Blackwell.

Livingstone, S. (2002) *Young People and the Media*, London: Sage.

Loktev, J. (1993) 'Static Motion, Or the Confessions of a Compulsive Radio Driver', *Semiotexte*, vol. VI (1).

McCarthy, A. (2001) *Ambient Television*, Durham, NC: Duke University Press.

Merck, M. (1998) *After Diana*, London: Verso.

Miller, A. (1987) *Timebends: A Life*, London: Methuen.

Miller, D. (ed.) (2001) *Car Cultures*, Oxford: Berg.

Morse, M. (1998) *Virtualities: Television, Media Art, and Cyberculture*, Bloomington: Indiana State University Press.

National Society for Clean Air (2002) *National Noise Survey 2002*. Online at: http://nsca.org.uk

Peters, J. (1999) *Speaking into the Air: A History of the Idea of Communication*, Chicago: Chicago University Press.

Puro, J.P. (2002) 'Finland: A Mobile Culture', in J. Katz and M. Aakhus (eds), *Perpetual Contact: Mobile Communication, Private Talk, Public Performance*, Cambridge: Cambridge University Press.

Putnam, R. (2000) *Bowling Alone: The Collapse and Revival of American Community*, New York: Simon and Schuster.

Rousseau, J.-J.(1979) *Reveries of a Solitary Walker*, New York: Penguin.

Sachs, W. (1992) *For Love of the Automobile: Looking Back into the History of our Desires*, Berkeley: University of California Press.

Schejter, A. and Cohen, A. (2002) 'Israel: Chutzpah and Chatter in the Holy Land', in J. Katz and M. Aakhus (eds), *Perpetual Contact: Mobile Communication, Private Talk, Public Performance*, Cambridge: Cambridge University Press.

Schivelbusch, W. (1986) *The Railway Journey: The Industrialization of Time and Space in the 19th Century*, Berkeley: University of California Press.

Sennett, R. (1990) *The Conscience of the Eye*, London: Faber and Faber.

—— (1994) *Flesh and Stone: The Body and the City in Western Civilization*, New York: Norton.

Silverstone, R. (1994) *Television and Everyday Life*, London: Routledge.

Simmel, G. (1997) 'The Metropolis and Mental Life', in D. Frisby and M. Featherstone (eds), *Simmel on Culture*, London: Sage.

Sloboda, J.A. (1999) 'Everyday Use of Music Listening: A Preliminary Study', in Suk Won Yi (ed.) *Mind, Music and Science*, Seoul: Western Music Institute: 354–69.

Stockfeld, O. (1994) 'Cars, Buildings, Soundscapes', in H. Jarviluoma (ed.), *Soundscapes: Essays on Vroom and Moo*, Tampere: Tampere University Press.

Urry, J. (1999) 'Automobility, Car Culture and Weightless Travel' (draft), Lancaster University Online at: http:/www.lancaster.ac.uk/soc030ju.html

—— (2000) *Sociology Beyond Societies: Mobilities for the Twenty First Century*, London: Routledge.

Welsch, W. (1997) *Undoing Aesthetics*, London: Routledge.

Winston, B. (1998) *Media Technology and Society, a History: From the Telegraph to the Internet*, London: Routledge.

INDEX

294

HM 1206 .M433 2004

MediaSpace

DATE DUE